Facing Catastrophe

To Geory —

Hope you will
find this interesting!
Thanks for all your
support.

— Carl

FACING CATASTROPHE

Food, Politics, and the Ecological Crisis

CARL BOGGS

Foreword by Peter McLaren

political animal
PRESS
TORONTO · CHICAGO

Political Animal Press
Toronto • Chicago
www.politicalanimalpress.com

Distributed by the University of Toronto Press
https://utpdistribution.com/

Cataloguing data available from Library and Archives Canada

ISBN 978-1895131-47-5 (paperback)
ISBN 978-1895131-48-2 (ebook)

Typeset in Adobe Caslon, designed by Carol Twombly and Brandon Grotesque, designed by Hannes von Döhren.

Printed and bound in Canada

Contents

Foreword

In this, one of the darkest hours of our national life, Carl Boggs has produced another galvanic new work. *Facing Catastrophe: Politics, Food and the Ecological Crisis* is a bedrock mandate to take immediate action in confronting the ecological disaster that is currently upon us. Such a crisis has most recently been exacerbated by the savage countermeasures to popular democracy installed by the Trump administration and by neoliberal governments around the world that are either shifting towards fascism or have gone full-throttle authoritarian populist. The Trump administration has yet to hold a reckoning over its own relationship with authoritarianism, since it is deeply immersed in tabloid culture and stacked with sycophants (such as the fawning Mike Pence) all too willing to deliver the necessary panegyrics in support of its *de facto* emperor whose lack of humility is unexampled except in the case of, say, Alexander the Great or Julius Cesar. Given the rightist tendencies gaining prominence in all parts of the world, it should come as little surprise that countries around the world have allowed the concentration of carbon dioxide in Earth's atmosphere to reach a record high, including a surge in concentrations of two other greenhouse gases, methane and nitrous oxide. The Trump administration, a ghoulishly cultic and gangrenous Gemeinschaft given over to ethno-nationalism, extractive neoliberalism, white supremacy, a tailored condescension towards self-preening liberal elites, and a sedulous avoidance of even addressing the current ecological crisis is emblematic of the obstacles confronting a concerted challenge to the Great Acceleration. Any such system that is able to camouflage its high tech forms of gangsterism and outlawry, and that affords a leader the ability to rule by means of the chilling intimacy of tweets and the scorching tirades and fascist vitriol of a dime-store tyrant aimed at political rivals with a high ecological IQ all but guarantees that future generations will be born into a losing struggle for democracy and a sustainable biosphere. We are so close to the Tipping Point that it won't be long before we will be unable to seize the opportunity to imagine a worse scenario, because, in effect, the worst-case scenario will already be upon us. Is this so surprising in a culture driven by the retaliatory political bloodlust and gut wind of a bourgeoisie and its business propagandists attempting to rescue a capitalism in serious crisis, in which the vaunted doyen of popular will—the authoritarian leader—preaches freedom yet shutters dissent, advocates liberty yet flaunts constitutional governance, provokes protests then reframes them as riots, promises peace and security yet makes violent and visceral declarations against the "deep state" during chest-beating campaign rallies that include threats to shut down the mass media and silence any and all critics of the regime, enjoins the popular majorities to be good citizens by participating lockstep in a zero-sum partisanship that amounts to little more than a sobered endorsement of the ruling regime while at the same time paints a picture of the nation state using false narratives completely unmoored from reality (such as Trump being God's "chosen one")? Such an inerrant fostering of collective self-delusion and willful blindness through a focus on grand conspiracies designed to bumfuzzle the public is completely on-brand for Donald Trump and his unclubbable clutch of White House zealots, and rests upon long-standing denials that historical agency is a product *of* the people rather than an inert force that acts *upon* people and that we are creators of history and not simply its creatures. United States Attorney General William Barr and chief immigration advisor Stephen Miller are two characters that you could easily imagine would have enjoyed working for CIA Director Allan Dulles and Sidney Gottlieb, "the Josef Mengele of the United States," who headed MK-ULTRA, back in the 1950s.

In such times as these, God has fallen into the wrong hands, as it were. Christofascism is providing a dark spiritual ballast for the tilt-a-whirl politics of lies, chaos and conspiracies that marks the current fact-free White House administration and reflects Trump's knockabout street level swagger and his choice of who sits on his Evangelical Advisory Board and his decision to roll back nearly a hundred environmental rules and propose to cut the budget of the Environmental Protection Agency by 31%.

While the genealogy of populism is complex, its most reactionary neoliberal variants rely on exploiting tensions between rural and urban areas and the frustration among the increasingly displaced and marginalized industrial working class and rural populations facing the globalization of agricultural production and the messy politics of capitalist agribusiness. In order to remove regulatory fetters from extractive capital and advance its agenda of commodification of rural lands and natural resources under the banner of resource nationalism, this has resulted in attacks by the Trump regime on environmental protections and activists and a post-truth assault on environmental data and science in general, not to mention a legitimation of the increasing militarism linked to resource wars that dramatically threatens world peace. Reactionary populists backed by fossil capitalism have been effective in consolidating the power of the executive branch in order to punish their opponents and in using all forms of propaganda to conflate natural resources with social identities by demonizing "politically correct" environmental activists whom they claim are putting the ideals of globalization (i.e., the Paris Accords and the United Nations and European Union) before American interests. This has made immiserated constituencies increasingly vulnerable to the nativism, isolationism, nationalism and white supremacy propagated by the administration as they become more and more convinced that democratic norms and institutions overpopulated by government elites as well as progressive environmental groups are protecting the country's internal enemies—immigrants, refugees, the LGTBQ community, feminists, multiculturalists and intellectuals—who supposedly responsible for the demise of America. The partnership between Big Tech and Big Oil has made fossil capitalism one of the greatest threats to the survival of the planet. As Boggs notes, most of all free water goes to farming where it takes 2400 gallons of water to produce a single pound of beef, and 685 gallons for one gallon of milk, whereas only a few gallons of water is needed for grains and vegetables. We are already ensepulchured in a post-apocalyptic mindset when it comes to the current environmental crisis, we are already thinking in terms of the failure of our efforts to redress this crisis and this defeatism is buried beneath many sincere attempts at mounting strategies and tactics of resistance. The dead-man-walking attitude has sucked the soul out of much of the environmental movement.

That massive urban oil field known as Los Angeles, where rust-splotched pumpjacks known as "nodding donkeys" or "stripper wells" dominate drill sites kitty corner to inner city schools and children's parks make possible an impressive cornucopia of asthma-inducing toxic fumes—

capable of destroying even the most resilient brain and lung tissue of those condemned to live in the poorest areas of the city—available on a 24 hour basis.

As a scholar and activist living in Los Angeles, who shares a unique personal history of ecological politics and a history of involvement with the German and European as well as American Greens, Carl Boggs has been at the forefront of ecological politics for over half a century, long before the Cold War had thawed and socialism emerged from ideological hibernation. A storied activist who helped to organize the first Earth Day designed to draw attention to the destruction of the natural habitat, and who established a working relationship with the most important ecological thinkers of the twentieth century—Barry Commoner, Murray Bookchin, Rudolf Bahro—Boggs is well positioned within the contemporary Weltgeist to arbitrate the current threat of ecological disaster and to prosecute what is at stake politically and existentially in the moment-by-moment unfolding of this precipitous historical juncture known as the Anthropocene. It is a juncture marked by forms of governance that support the realization of particular wider social projects and values—in this case neoliberalism and political liberalism—and animated by a practiced inattention to the history of US race and class relations and a motivated amnesia with regard to the lives lost or destroyed by past imperialist ventures and a grave failure to recognize the worth of others, including non-human animals. It is a juncture that is saturated in despair and that has fallen prey to what Sartre called the liberty of indifference and is in dire need of a wide-ranging analysis by a multidisciplinary scholar and critical sociologist with a granular grasp of world history, political science, critical theory, cultural politics, environmental science and social movements and who has written impressively on a wide range of topics that include but are not limited to imperialism, militarism, contemporary cinema and Gramscian Marxism. Clearly, few are as well positioned as Carl Boggs to craft what amounts to a left manifesto for forging a sustainable future at a time when the struggle for a democratic socialism has become more fierce and fraught with danger. The challenge of developing a politics of liberation sits squarely within Boggs' wheelhouse and he does not fail to deliver.

Boggs' passionate injunction in *Facing Catastrophe: Politics, Food and the Ecological Crisis* is guided by the lodestar of universal social justice (which includes an amalgam of civil rights, economic and environmental rights and animal rights). On a more personal level, this work constitutes a *cri de coeur* from a writer and activist clearly outraged by the steady erosion of human decency in a beleaguered world that has become more and more enveloped in fear and repression, more prone to the machinations of the national security state, and more vulnerable to capitalist immiseration and to converging economic, political, military, and environmental problems.

In our adiaphoric universe held together by separation and stitched together by the cold intimacy of post-digital togetherness (the more we are connected, the more we feel isolated), where we remain the victims of indoctrination into the psycho-cultural apologia of the American Dream with its racialized version of what Freud calls "the narcissism of minor differences", we continue to spawn a technological and algorithmic culture supported by the calculation-driven logic of the capitalist market dominated by a dehumanizing fetishism of exchange value and the commodity form. Empathy, solidarity and a concern for the well-being of others is on life support. The historical legacy of an eco-destructive capitalism cannot be gainsaid, despite the rhetorical fancy-dancing of the right and the rising social-democratic demands from more progressive constituencies (that unfortunately still fit comfortably within the dominant American entrepreneurial narrative).

And this harsh reality is in no way tempered by the realization that the fossil fuel industry lobbyists, corporate oligarchs and financial behemoths have a powerful stranglehold on government policy and are able to re-direct its moral grammar according to the imperatives of the market—not to mention pulling the bureaucratic levers of state-sanctioned violence. When our imperishable understanding that democracy and capitalism are mutually constitutive eventually breaks apart, thanks to the work of Carl Boggs and others like him, we are less likely to be assuaged by the false consolation that capitalism, with all its faults, is still the best of all possible worlds. The legacy of Voltaire's Dr. Pangloss—that we live in the best of all possible worlds—must be challenged by each generation in ways that require a steadfast commitment to the belief that all that is, is not for the best, and that a collapsing ecosystem is not a situation that we can dismiss simply because we could imagine a worse scenario. The idea that people make history by reading the word and the world alongside each other undergirds the public pedagogy that animates *Facing Catastrophe*. Critical pedagogy is not something that is solely associated with teachers and schools—I am thinking here of the "Teachers Groups" at the Tvind alternative high school in Jutland, Denmark who decades ago helped to create the first multi-megawatt wind turbine that was 54 meters tall with a 54 meter wingspan. Critical pedagogy is something that should animate the entire public domain, in which educators, public servants and cultural workers offer critical analyses of the most pressing challenges to our democracy, including those that have direct consequences to our environment and food supplies. This aspect of public pedagogy is clearly evident throughout *Facing Catastrophe*. That there is an alternative to nuclear power and fossil fuels is a message that can—and must—animate our educational curricula from public school to university but the pushback against climate science by the current Trump administration constitutes a serious obstacle in furthering this objective. But reclaiming climate science is only the beginning. True, we need to wean U.S. society away from its addiction on fossil fuels but not at the expense of supporting a system designed to perpetuate the same capitalist social relations that drive the fossil fuel industry. Boggs' largely ecumenical approach argues that any critical ecology must de facto support a "deep ecology" approach that undermines the economic principles that support capitalism, that is directed towards overcoming capital's abstractive logic of domination and that displays a willingness to transition to a new social order that we have historically called democratic socialism. Over time, Marxism has been enriched by infusing elements from Kant and Hegel, hermeneutics and Freudian theory, as evidenced in the work of Lukacs, Marcuse, Fromm, Adorno and Horkheimer, especially as this pertains to the notion of the dialectic, the structure of thought and the structure of reality. Boggs rightly points to the work of critical theory and ecosocialism as axiomatic in analyzing and understanding the ways in which the ruling elite is gaslighting the public and steering society towards barbarism. And in creating the necessary features of the political revolution that needs to follow. Boggs is clearly in agreement with Marcuse that character structure is related to the destruction of nature, thus the very instinctual structure of individuals must be reshaped in order to avoid future genocides and ecocides. As Che Guevara put it, a socialist society needs a culture of socialism to support it.

Against the sweet, business-as-usual mediocrity of our collective governance that commits us to nothing except valorizing our lives as consumers, Boggs combines pragmatic approaches and shareable ideals that can help us contour the politics of our daily lives outside the social universe of value augmentation and thus equip ourselves and our constituencies with the critical knowledge and optimism of the will to engage social movements in a fight for all of our lives. Boggs dialectical maneuvers in this regard are refreshing and innovative and renders this work both sophisticated and accessible to non-academic audiences. One of the most relevant political takeaways from this work is that relying on the state to curb carbon emissions won't work with our present political system; it will instead require a fundamental restructuring of the entire system of American governance so that it is able to serve the needs of the popular majorities. We owe a great deal of gratitude to Boggs' important revivification and deepening of ecological rationality, and we must do our best to ensure that it not be compromised—especially by the aerosol intellectualism that pockmarked academia's postmodern transgression into identity politics and that foments helplessness in the face of neoliberal assaults on political life—if our attempt to bring about the creation of new life-affirming modes of production and consumption—new relations between humans and the natural habitat that lead to human flourishing within a larger democratization of ownership and restoration of nature—are to come into fruition. Another masterwork by Carl Boggs. Another opportunity to take stock of the current existential threats to life on this planet. Yet another day when, as Boggs warns, the possible outcomes of our investigations, our warnings, and our actions are increasingly narrowed by the diminishing windows of opportunity ahead.

Peter McLaren
Distinguished Professor in
Critical Studies, Chapman
University (USA) and
Chair Professor, Northeast
Normal University (China)

Preface

The familiar and overused vocabulary of "crisis" has been endowed with so many applications and meanings – most famously Karl Marx's theory of capitalist crisis – that it has nowadays lost much of its power to convince, much less shock. If indeed "crisis" is perpetual, then what can be so urgent, so menacing – and where do we look for "solutions"? Does anybody need to pay much attention? Could the worsening global crisis or time-honored "crisis of democracy" or familiar economic crisis instill fear among mass populations largely immersed in their own, more immediate problems? Even threat of nuclear catastrophe, once a source of mass psychological dread in the United States and Europe, seems to have dissipated. At present we face an entirely different sort of crisis – the steady descent toward ecological collapse that threatens planetary life as we have known it. That crisis could eventually be more catastrophic than any of the others – yet as of this writing the political response in the U.S. and elsewhere has fallen woefully short of the challenge.

The central motif of this book is that the modern ecological crisis, now visible in many symptoms across the world landscape, reveals more clearly with each passing moment the utterly destructive character of globalized corporate power. Revisiting the famous Marxist injunction "socialism or barbarism", it is clear to see how the ecological crisis threatens the natural habitat more severely than even most environmentalists seem prepared to recognize. This seemingly new challenge (one actually a century or more in the making) has inspired, or more accurately forced, new ways of viewing not only economic development but political action, cultural behavior, natural relations, and perhaps most crucially social change.

This book assumes the inevitably difficult and protracted journey toward ecological sanity demands a fundamentally new outlook, including a radical *politics* bold enough to move beyond a record of historical failures, whether in the case of liberalism, social democracy, or Communism. In the absence of such a departure, the planet is condemned to unspeakable disaster, the result of which might be described as ecological suicide. My earlier book *Ecology and Revolution* might be viewed as a precursor to this volume, motivated by the same mood of urgency, the same ecological sensibilities, the same emphasis on radical politics though more ambitious in scope. Here far greater attention is devoted to problems of agriculture and food that I argue ought to be situated at the very center of the crisis.

The pursuit of a distinctly *ecological politics* places emphasis on the constituent elements of both ecology and politics. An ecological outlook suggests a transformed relationship between humans and nature, society and the natural habitat, that extends moral status to nonhuman beings and communities. It lays out a path toward sustainable development, counter to the globalized corporate growth-machine and its delusions of unlimited, exploitable planetary resources. That outlook involves multiple and overlapping forms of domination across state governance, mode of production, global relations, and the class structures. Against the exercise of unrestrained power, ecological values are intrinsically anti-authoritarian, subversive of the exploitative and repressive features of capitalist rationalization long critically analyzed within the traditions of both Karl Marx and Max Weber.

My view of politics here is motivated by a desperately needed *revitalization of politics*, starting with the industrialized societies. Some variant of ecological politics has surfaced in many countries, but then only briefly or sporadically as in the case of the early-1980s European Green parties. My focus is on a distinctly *transformative* politics that surpasses the work of particular groups, organizations, movements, even parties. "Politics" from this viewpoint refers to key requisites of fundamental change: a well-defined alternative ideology, dynamic organization and leadership, resources for mass mobilization, effective strategy, orientation toward winning governmental power. Unfortunately, the legacy of major oppositional forces to date – anarchist, socialist, Communist, Green – provides little cause for optimism, in the U.S. or elsewhere. Erstwhile anti-capitalist parties have, in one country after another, suffered the fate of deradicalization following years of electoralism and reformism.

Given this reality, it seems appropriate to refer to a pervasive "crisis of politics" that happens to coincide with the ecological crisis. Until the first predicament is resolved, the second one will forever remain in limbo, unsolvable. One problem today is that so many environmentalists fix their gaze solely on the (obviously crucial) threat of climate change. But the modern challenge goes well beyond the fossil economy and carbon footprint, however significant that has been. Worth noting here is that some of the seminal theorists of ecological crisis (Rachel Carson, Barry Commoner, Murray Bookchin, Rudolf Bahro, et al.) scarcely addressed the problem of global warming, which did not enter public discourse until the 1990s. Further, while planetary warming has surely increased over the past century or so – mainly from accelerated carbon emissions – precise calculations regarding the *impact, scope,* and *timing* of such change vary wildly. Long-range computer modelling by its very nature varies significantly, so that the supposed "consensus" among thousands of international scientists can be rather misleading.

One problem with such modelling is the number of variables that must be taken into account, some of which (e.g., the role of agriculture and food production) have so far been largely downplayed if not ignored. There are wide-ranging differences, even among scientists affiliated with the IPCC (Intergovernmental Panel on Climate Change), although media coverage, such as it is, obscures real disagreements over data, modelling, and estimates of long-term carbon impact. Many reputable scientists believe planetary adaptability to carbon emissions and global warming could be greater than generally believed. My approach broadly accepts the worsening climate-change scenarios but remains open to wide variations in possible outcomes. One important variable is the availability – and competition for – vital natural resources: water, arable land, timber, scarce metals and minerals as well as fossil fuels. Other factors include the role of transnational corporate power, population growth, declining health of forests and oceans, and rampant urbanization. Yet another (often overlooked) factor is the mounting threat posed by agribusiness and the capitalist food system to ecological sustainability.

The global food complex is ruled by corporate oligopolies, a McDonaldized fast-food empire, and powerful meat and dairy interests. This behemoth alone devours massive resources (including fossil fuels, water, and land), degrades forests and oceans, is responsible for obesity and related health problems across the planet, produces untold air and water pollution, and maintains some of the most repressive workplaces. No exit from the ecological crisis is thinkable without engaging the moral and environmental consequences of the looming nightmare.

A central thesis of the following chapters is that a *political* rupture with the status quo, with its existing class and power relations, will be needed to stave off the crisis. There can be no routine, painless "greening" of a neoliberal world order rooted in the incessant accumulation of wealth, power, and geopolitical advantage, and protected by the largest military apparatus in history. Environmental reforms along lines of green technology, cap-and-trade carbon programs, pollution controls, recycling projects, electric vehicles – all quite laudable as far as they go –will be futile without a full departure from the corporate-growth machine. So long as the most all-encompassing power structure the world has ever known remains intact, its chieftains will do anything to block future transition to a post-capitalist, ecologically sustainable society.

Ecological politics has long been central to my intellectual concerns, political outlook, and movement activism. I helped to organize the first Earth Day in 1970 and later participated in both European and American Green parties, having been active in the "left-Green" tendency of an ecological project that remains hopeful but unfinished. During the 1960s and 1970s (and later) my experience gave rise to personal relationships with arguably the most important ecological thinkers of the twentieth century: Barry Commoner, Murray Bookchin, Rudolf Bahro. Commoner was a colleague at Washington University in St. Louis throughout the 1970s. I was temporarily involved with *Environment* magazine, founded by Commoner, and my girlfriend in St. Louis, Michele Prichard, worked at Commoner's research center before becoming national secretary of the Citizen's Party that sponsored Commoner's improbable run for the White House in 1980. It might be said his candidacy was managed out of the apartment I shared with Michele in Santa Monica. Despite some political differences, my relationship with the scholar-activist called "the Paul Revere of the Environmental Movement" went on for many years after Commoner moved to New York City, and he remained a source of personal inspiration and ecological awareness that I have valued to this day.

As for Bookchin, I was attracted to his writings that offered a more radical version of ecology from the time I first read his *Post-Scarcity Anarchism* in 1969. I did not meet Bookchin, however, until 1981, when as professor of sociology at UCLA I organized a conference titled "Marxism and Anarchism" and invited Bookchin to be keynote speaker. Spending several days with him, I was overwhelmed by his combination of intellectual power, political commitment, and passionate activism – a charismatic figure whose work still appeals to many progressives in the U.S. and around the world. I invited him back to Los Angeles several years later, at which time he lectured around the area, visited my classes, and was interviewed for my KPFK radio program. Bookchin's ecological imprint on American society is probably unmatched, not only by virtue of his prolific writings but his community-based activism, his legacy at the Institute for Social Ecology in Vermont, and his leftward influence on Green politics. His profound contributions, unfortunately ignored by Marxists, should be vital to the future development of any ecological radicalism.

Paradoxically, my interaction with both Commoner and Bookchin came at a time when those two giants of modern environmental theory grew more hostile to each other – in part owing to their sometimes fierce political disagreements, as Commoner preferred a strategy of electoralism and reformism while Bookchin gravitated toward an outlook of cultural revolution aligned with the counterculture and new left. Commoner opted for the Citizens Party, Bookchin for the more radical Greens. Bahro, a co-founder and architect of the West German Greens, was instrumental during the early 1980s in merging the most progressive elements of socialism and ecology; his book *From Red to Green* is still an important contribution to European leftist thought. My involvement with the Greens in both Europe and the U.S. brought me in contact with Bahro and some of his activist friends in 1983, the year I promoted Bahro's speaking tour of California. Despite his intellectual stature, Bahro had no relationship with either Commoner or Bookchin: my interaction with all three of these ecological giants was therefore particular to each, yet their combined influence on my intellectual and political maturation would be enormous – an influence visible throughout this book.

A fourth, more recent influence on my ecological journey was the seminal organization *Earthsave*, launched in the late 1980s at the time John

Robbins' classic book and documentary *Diet for a New America* gained enormous popularity. The group, relatively small but far-reaching in its influence, was the first to integrate four dynamic sets of issues within a common outlook: the environment, health/medicine, animal rights, corporate power – all linked organically to the growing challenges of food and agriculture. What might be called "vegetarian politics" first gained wide attention with the appearance of Robbins' initial work, followed by other important books *The Food Revolution* and *Healthy at 100,* which happened to coincide with the pivotal writings of John McDougall and Colin Campbell. It was Campbell's epic 2006 work, *The China Study* – largest and most impressive comparative study of food and health ever conducted – that came to occupy a special place in my own development and the outlook pervading this book.

As each ecological thinker mentioned here has known, without the smallest doubt, the grave threat now facing humanity demands vast material resources, institutional leverage, and political energies that have yet to be effectively mobilized. The world remains a great distance from reversal of a crisis that has no precedent in modern history, yet counter-forces adequate to the task appear nowhere on the horizon. My argument here is that we face a *political* crisis just as daunting as the *ecological* crisis; anti-system change is urgently needed, and time is running short. The very immediacy of this challenge is exacerbated by the complex, multifaceted, global character of a power structure that appears more solidified with each passing year, yet beset with contradictions sharpened by an unyielding planetary ecosphere. That power structure, moreover, can hardly be described as "democratic", especially in the U.S., given its unsurpassed concentration of corporate, state, and military interests that drastically curtail popular access and radical opposition. No ecological politics, no popular insurgency can hope to transform this system from within its sprawling institutional and ideological networks of domination. There can be no seamless "greening" of such a corporate-state apparatus, no liberal-reformist "solution". The ultimate question is: how long can this destructive, unsustainable system perpetuate itself before it collapses – or is overthrown?

Writing this book has been a lengthy, demanding, at times unsettling work motivated by the goal of a vibrant, democratic, sustainable ecological society – otherwise known by the label "ecosocialism". My hope is that the critical perspective developed in the following chapters will have something of an impact as we go forward into an uncertain and perilous future. Toward this end I would like to thank the editors at Political Animal Press, Lewis Slawsky and Alex Wall, for their generous encouragement and help through different phases of the work. This effort never would have come to fruition had it not been for the enduring love and support of my wife Laurie Nalepa.

Carl Boggs
Los Angeles, California
May 2020

This book is dedicated to the memory of my
dear friend and colleague, Tom Pollard.

Introduction

As the global ecological crisis deepens by the day, effective political response – whether by international organizations, social movements, political parties, or national governments – appears at best weak and scattered. The present challenge is so grave that only a radical, transformative strategy has any chance of success, yet that strategy remains painfully elusive. Counterforces, such as they are, have gained little momentum at a time when planetary catastrophe seems more probable than generally acknowledged.

The new challenge facing humanity like the darkest specter – sometimes referred to as the "Great Acceleration", alternatively as the "Great Disruption", the "Anthropocene", or just the familiar "Tipping Point" – has yet to generate any correspondingly urgent political mobilization aligned with new modes of production and consumption, new relations between humans and the natural habitat. Powerful ruling interests across the globe now appear ready to drive the planet headlong toward ecological suicide. As of the completion of this book (Spring 2020), it might be credibly argued that modern environmental movements have made little ground since their inception in the late 1960s – a generalization sadly most relevant to the American experience. That happens to be the point of view advanced by the widely-accessed Jeff Gibbs documentary, *Planet of the Humans,* which appeared in April 2020 just as this text was going through its final stages.

To be sure, the crisis – unparalleled in depth and scope – is hardly confined to the ecological sphere: it is simultaneously economic, political, cultural, and above all global in its interlocking dynamics. Aside from climate change, the world confronts mounting poverty, shrinking natural resources, crumbling public infrastructures, civic violence, mass migrations,

1

and perpetual warfare. What underlies this predicament, as Barry Commoner stressed many decades ago, is a collapsing *ecosystem*, the health and sustainability of which underpins all other human systems, starting with an economy transformed by corporate globalization since the 1950s.[1] Capitalism, nationally and globally, corrodes the logic of an ecological rationality – the very rationality needed to arrest the descent into barbarism.

With historical conditions now ever more dire, the political *modus operandi* across the globe remains trapped in outmoded beliefs, tired formulas, and familiar myths: free markets, technological fixes, reformist bromides, electoral solutions – in other words, continued business-as-usual. We hear predictable voices of denial and obscurantism from those fearing threats to a precarious corporate, government, and military status quo. At the same time, for reasons more fully elaborated in later chapters, an entire generation of progressive and environmental movements – overwhelmingly immersed in liberal reformism if not identity politics – has never been able to escape the political impasse.

In the midst of record economic growth and material abundance, the planet we inhabit suffers from a more blighted side of modernity: widening social miseries, resource shortages, food crisis, urban deterioration, sharpening geopolitical conflict – not to mention the stubborn threat of nuclear war. With anti-system opposition too weak to make a dent in the vast fortress of economic and governmental power, the title of Helen Caldicott's book *Sleepwalking to Armageddon* seems tragically appropriate as we survey the 2020 world landscape.[2] At a time of ecological challenges previously unknown, nations allocate increasing resources to the military and law enforcement, wars, surveillance, technological growth, and corporate subsidies. Nowhere are these self-destructive impulses more visible than in the United States, currently the world's largest polluter and second (behind China) in total carbon footprint. The U.S. spends more than one trillion dollars yearly on its sprawling warfare system and national security-state, not counting funds for endless wars in the Middle East and elsewhere.

A major source of political impasse is the great concentration of corporate, state, and military power across the industrialized world, legitimated by sophisticated communications and media empires that disseminate propaganda, often disguised as news and entertainment. A kindred problem is the erosion of political traditions that historically associated with oppositional tendencies – liberalism, anarchism, socialism, Communism – going back to World War I if not earlier.

Aside from the ecological challenge, intensifying social inequalities of global capitalism are fully unsustainable and getting worse. A remarkably small nucleus of corporate elites manages a sprawling world system, its industrial development, commerce, banking, trade, communications worth hundreds of trillions of dollars. Elites with that much control over material, technological, and human resources obviously exercise similar control over politics and culture, not to mention armed force. This unprecedented assemblage of wealth and power shows no signs of ebbing, despite wishful thinking among many progressives and leftists always on the lookout for "divisions" in the power structure. Oxfam International has reported that the leading 62 billionaires, many of them technology moguls based in the U.S., hold as much wealth as half the world population. What C. Wright Mills anticipated in the mid-1950s, writing in his classic *The Power Elite,* has come to pass many times over.[3] Those interests share the same overriding agendas and outlooks.

According to Peter Phillips in his volume *Giants,* there are just 389 global elites who work as "key managers of concentrated capital, the facilitators of capital growth, and the system's protectors .... They generally know of each other, hold significant personal wealth, share similar educational and lifestyle backgrounds, and retain common global interests. Nearly all serve on the boards of directors of major capital investment firms or other major corporations or banks."[4] These ruling interests exercise control over a world economic system presently worth about $255 trillion, with the U.S. and Europe holding at least two-thirds of that total. Against such incomprehensible levels of wealth, 80 percent of the global population lives on less than ten dollars per day.[5] Meanwhile, no more than 100 companies have been the source of more than 70 percent of total greenhouse emissions since 1988.[6]

At the top of this international pyramid are 17 financial behemoths – Bank of America, JP Morgan Chase, Citigroup, Goldman Sachs, Wells Fargo included – that drive the world economy. As Phillips notes, "It is these firms that set the priorities for monetary investments in businesses, industry, and governments ... Where the investments occur is less important than a continuous return that supports growth in the overall market.

Therefore, investments in war, tobacco, fossil fuels, farmland, pesticides ... are all just investments requiring adequate returns."[7] The underlying dynamics here clearly favor economic agendas over any form of ecological priorities.

Throughout the twentieth century, to be sure, radical opposition appeared from time to time: early socialism, council communism, 1930s Spanish revolution, Western Communist parties, new left, new social movements among others. In recent decades ecological sensibilities did surface, within the sixties counterculture, modern environmentalism, feminism, and strains of community activism. Yet none of these ever gained a share of governmental power, or even wielded much influence over that power. One noteworthy exception was the 1980s European Greens, with origins in West Germany, which set out to merge local activism with mainstream electoral politics rooted in mass support and dedicated to a new (ecological) path forward. Yet the Greens, like Socialists and Communists of an earlier period, suffered from a process of deradicalization starting in the late 1980s. The predictable result was accommodation to domestic and global forms of corporate power. At the time of this writing (Spring 2020) progressive and environmental groups remain scattered across the terrain, but few identify with anything resembling ecological radicalism, and fewer yet have built mass support for distinctly *political* objectives. Many are hobbled by an identity politics that obscures class-based struggles, ignores the problem of U.S. militarism and imperialism, seems oblivious to the threat of nuclear war, and views the ecological crisis as something of a peripheral concern.

Entering the third decade of the twenty-first century, the planet humans have inhabited for so many thousands of years now seems on the verge of a Tipping Point – an historical juncture where reversal of the ecological crisis might soon be impossible. Inevitably, the future is filled with a variety of dystopic images and frightening symptoms. While the Earth has endured seven of the hottest years in recorded history over the past decade, the chieftains of world capitalism – driven as always by endless material growth – remain seemingly impervious to probable catastrophe ahead. The global corporate juggernaut spews more carbon emissions into the atmosphere month after month, year after year, as the saturation level (now approaching 450 parts per million) matches what Intergovernmental

Panel on Climate Change (IPCC) scientists warn is close to the point of no return. Since the mid-1990s this system has unleashed more carbon into an overly stressed ecosphere than the total for all preceding history, and that trajectory is sadly nowhere being disrupted much less overturned.

We live on a planet where the dire effects of global warming – even for less than worst-case scenarios – intersect with multiple threats linked to ecological decline, starting with such resource challenges as land, water, and soil; food availability is sure to be at the core of such challenges. As noted, greenhouse emissions currently stream into the atmosphere at higher rates than ever: since the end of World War II the carbon footprint has increased by 85 percent, with no indications of overall slowing. Economic growth proceeds with religious fervor, worldwide use of fossil fuels actually having increased by roughly three percent in 2018.

With no significant change of course – even with adoption of modest reforms and new technologies – the future hardly elicits much optimism. That is so even if targets set by the Paris Accords were to be met *immediately*, because existing amounts of greenhouse pollution will be felt decades ahead given significant lag time. As David Wallace-Wells observes in his book *The Uninhabitable Earth*, the growth regime "threatens to make parts of the planet more or less unlivable for humans by the end of the century. That is the course we are speeding so blithely along – to more than four degrees Celsius of warming by the year 2100."[8] That means vast regions of the world would be overcome by unbearable heat, desertification, ocean contamination, and resulting drastic food shortages. In fact, those horrendous outcomes would be experienced well before the end of the century.

If, as the IPCC contends, the Tipping Point is an elevated two degrees of warming, then spikes of three or four degrees warming (conceivable with the present global trajectory) can only spell unmitigated disaster. Wallace-Wells comments: "At three degrees, southern Europe would be in permanent drought, and the average drought in Central America would last nineteen months longer and in the Caribbean 21 months longer. In northern Africa, the figure is 60 months longer – five years. The areas burned each year by wildfires would double in the Mediterranean and sextuple or more in the United States."[9] At a four-degree rise, naturally, matters would deteriorate to the point of full-scale catastrophe: the food crisis alone would render the planet largely unlivable. Should temperatures increase further, humans in most parts of the world would not be able to move around freely without perishing.

Assuming "normal" developmental patterns, the outcomes mentioned above could take effect in perhaps a few decades. The urgent question here is: at what point do the debilitating symptoms of climate change (and ecological crisis in general) become too extreme, too overwhelming, too disruptive to ignore? When will humans be *forced* to thoroughly reconsider the same developmental path that nations have followed for many decades? If little or nothing is done at a cooperative *international* level, can humanity hope to avoid a descent toward oblivion? Here Wallace-Wells aptly concludes: "Between that [dystopic] scenario and the world we live in now lies only the open question of human response."[10] And that, in turn, clearly poses the imperative of political action.

There will be no forestalling ecological collapse until radical change occurs in three decisive spheres of modern life: the economy, politics, culture. At present fossil fuels (oil, gas, coal) continue to drive the global economy, huge cities depend on exhaustive (often wasteful) use of natural resources, transportation revolves around private cars and trucks, and wars continue to be fought over valuable resources and terrain. While capitalism has long depended on vast exploitation of fossil fuels to achieve highest possible levels of economic development, a new era of "fossil capital" gained momentum with World War II, often referred to as the "Great Acceleration". Ian Angus, in *Facing the Anthropocene*, writes: "Given capitalism's inherent need not to just grow, but to grow faster, it's possible something like the Great Acceleration would have occurred even if the Depression and war didn't happen, but that is just speculation. In the real world, capitalism's worst depression and most destructive war set the stage for the economic and social changes that have pushed the Earth System into a new and dangerous epoch."[11]

At the same time, economic growth is pursued as something of a religion in both advanced and developing nations while population increases worldwide by 75 to 80 million people yearly. Grave challenges are ritually sidestepped, deflected, stonewalled, or finessed by means of reform palliatives while escalating crisis gives rise to diverse manifestations of anti-politics.

Corporate globalization generates new zones of power, where democratic access and political accountability are widely deflected or blocked. Western political systems are governed primarily through mechanisms of oligarchical power and authoritarian governance. In this context, ecological priorities call into question the capitalist logic of growth, consumerism, and profit-maximization celebrated across a media that reduces politics to a protracted cycle of spectacles, scandals, smear-mongering, and conspiracy theories.

This state of affairs seems especially visible in the U.S., where media culture has systematically corrupted public discourse. One recent case in point is the Democrats' hysterical response to Donald Trump's 2017 ascent to the White House – an event never supposed to have occurred. One of Trump's first moves was to withdraw the U.S. from the 2015 Paris Accords – a move Democrats might have been expected to denounce as part of their "resistance". Yet nothing of the sort happened: life-and-death environmental concerns were overridden by a steady diet of false claims that Russians had manipulated the 2016 presidential election, that Trump was effectively serving "Kremlin interests". Convenient to "explain" how the entitled Hillary Clinton lost to a bombastic real-estate tycoon, a flow of groundless conspiracies played across the corporate media, virtually nonstop, for nearly three years. Amidst all the political *Sturm und Drang*, the media sound and fury, pressing issues were simply pushed aside. Left fringes of the party did ultimately raise prospects of a Green New Deal, but even that was obscured by the continuous media propaganda barrage.[12]

While greenhouse emissions were pushing the Earth toward a two-degree (Celsius) threshold, little consideration was given to changing the economic system responsible for the global threat. We have seen, instead, standard business practices mixed with endless rhetoric about sustainable energy combined with reforms that would fall short of disturbing routine corporate practices. A "greening" of capitalism is apparently the chosen path for many environmentalists in the U.S., Europe, and Asia. To be sure, a vigorous Green New Deal could be a dynamic point of departure, but we still face the thorny question of whether it will be transformative enough to set in motion an historic shift away from perpetual growth, expanded consumption, and profit-maximization. If carbon emissions continue to climb through 2030 and beyond – and there is no indication otherwise – it could be too late to reverse the downward planetary slide; the Tipping-Point will have been reached, then surpassed.

Our understanding of the crisis begins with capitalist development in the West after World War II, though destructive trends had surfaced in preceding decades, during the earliest phases of capitalist industrialization. For Karl Marx, the historic expansion of productive forces under capitalism was driven by endless capital accumulation, concentrated economic and state power, and spread of this system to every region of the globe. Capitalism signified continuous industrial, scientific, and technological growth on a foundation of market relations and class exploitation. For Max Weber, on the other hand, the guiding motif was capitalist rationalization – industrial growth made possible by a mixture of efficiency and control through advancing bureaucracy and technology. Social conflict was endemic to the system, but its sharp contradictions would be regulated and contained by expansion of a rational-legal order marked by concentration of power, oligarchical structures, and institutionalization of class conflict. Weber, aligned with the so-called "elite theorists" (Robert Michels, Vilfredo Pareto, Gaetano Mosca) anticipated widening governmental power leading to some form of corporate-state capitalism. Later theorists Mills and Herbert Marcuse would combine elements of Marx and Weber in their critical analysis of modern American capitalism.

The crucial point here is that later phases of capitalist rationalization permeate every realm of social, economic, and political life within industrialized nations. Since the global crisis is largely a product of modern capitalism, systemic contradictions necessarily figure as part of both theoretical exploration and political response. There is currently no way of knowing just how and where those contradictions will first explosively surface, although the crisis does already offer insights. We do know, meanwhile, that historical experience reveals a legacy of failed political traditions, as noted above.

Yet another problem here is that modernity – for our purposes, capitalist rationalization – calls into question elements of Enlightenment ideology wedded to endless material growth and human domination of nature. Familiar ideals of individualism, freedom, and social progress end up submerged under broadening domination embedded in corporate-state power. As Theodor Adorno and Max Horkheimer have argued, modernity tends to evolve into a system of "total administration" as ruling elites look to "steer society toward barbarism."[13] The power structure employs heightened efficiency and control to subdue not only labor but local communities and the natural habitat: ecological destruction winds up the logical outgrowth of capitalist rationalization.

For Adorno and Horkheimer, and later theorists such as Herbert Marcuse, modernity contains within its own trajectory a logic of extreme domination: widespread institutional controls, oligarchical rule, social hierarchy, exploitation of nature. Those subjected to this regimen become alienated from the workplace, from their fellow humans, from their surrounding environment. The capitalist growth machine – ever more corporatized, technologized, and globalized – has been able to expand with few constraints, ethically, politically, or ecologically. Andreas Malm points out in *Fossil Capital* that "pouring crap into the environment is a fundamental feature of capitalism and it is not going to stop so long as capitalism survives."[14]

Among concepts invoked to measure developmental quality of life among societies, none requires more critical deconstruction than the term "economic growth", a formulaic standard of liberal-capitalist economics. Ecological imperatives of a limits-to-growth regimen are generally seen as invitations to backwardness and poverty, or at least a worsening of living standards for already affluent countries – more unbearable yet for developing countries reliant on the same resources (including fossil fuels) that for many decades underpinned industrialization in the West and Asia. It would be rank hypocrisy (and stupidity) to insist that nations like Brazil, Mexico, Indonesia, South Korea, and Egypt, for example, do what the U.S., Germany, and Japan never considered doing: sharply curtail their economic growth. What appeal could such a developmental agenda have in a world of crushing poverty and fragile infrastructures?

Critical reflection, however, transfers the growth modality into a different zone of understanding. Since it is the advanced industrial societies that have the most destructive impact on the natural habitat, and contribute most to climate change, the reduced-growth modality must extend primarily to those societies, starting with North America and the EU. How is growth to be measured and judged? Viewed in post-capitalist terms, the criteria must look entirely different than what is taken for granted by mainstream economists and politicians.

If we start with the U.S., dramatic reductions in resource utilization and Gross Domestic Product (GDP) can be easily imagined for a scenario where living standards can be maintained, even elevated. A list of possible growth cutbacks would indeed be a lengthy one: diminish military spending by two-thirds while dismantling bases abroad, socialize medicine and other wasteful private sectors, massive shift toward public (and green) transportation systems, fuller adoption of sustainable technologies, elimination of the superfluous insurance, advertising, and marketing sectors, an agricultural and food industry transition from McDonaldization and the meat complex toward plant-based diets, local farms, and agroecology. Altogether these (and other) epic initiatives could reduce GDP by *half* without making a dent in overall everyday affluence – at the same time cutting the carbon footprint by roughly the same amount. This very formula could be implemented across the globe, within societies at varying levels of development and military strength. It is difficult to see how the ecological crisis might be reversed in the absence of such a deep economic conversion.

Deepening global crisis might be expected to force growth-reduction measures and policies in coming years, both saving natural resources and stabilizing the climate system – yet we foresee just the opposite: full-speed ahead. Looking toward 2050 – not that far away – leading economies are projected to expand dramatically, their ruling elites seemingly oblivious to mounting threats ahead. China is predicted to easily dwarf all other economies, with a GDP at $50 trillion, followed by the U.S. at $34 trillion, India at $28 trillion, and such nations as Japan, Indonesia, Brazil, Germany, and Mexico reaching more than six trillion GDP.[15]

These projections mean a possible *doubling* of international wealth in just another decade. Two systems (China and India) will account for $78 trillion GDP, their combined populations rising to more than three trillion people. The top three nations will accumulate more wealth (and utilize more resources) than the rest of the world combined. Can extreme and lopsided development of this sort be conceivably sustainable? Would natural resources be available for such growth? What about the fate of agriculture, land, water, and food supply? How much more devastating will be the carbon footprint of just the three most wealthy nations? Can such combined economic and population growth – seemingly bereft of constraints – do anything but accelerate the descent into planetary barbarism?

As growth spirals out of control and natural resources become ever more precarious – and here we have mentioned only the few leading countries – what is likely to be the contours of geopolitical conflict? What about the prospect of several new failed states, or semi-failed states, in a period of sharpening resource warfare in the Middle East, north Africa, and beyond? In fact, these questions appear to contain their own answers. Just as fossil-fuel consumption is predicted to rise steadily by 2030 and beyond, so too is military spending and everything (border clashes, covert operations, international surveillance, armed preparations) that invariably accompanies it.

Within the next decade, annual U.S. military spending will spiral to well over one trillion dollars, followed by China ($736 billion), India ($213 billion), Russia ($140 billion), and Saudi Arabia ($98 billion).[16] The world will indeed be armed to the teeth, constantly on the verge of military conflict including nuclear war. The U.S. will surely retain its hundreds of military bases scattered across the globe, including it risky nuclear deployments. War zones will break out virtually anywhere that resources are abundant – and where other conflicts surface. More frighteningly, geopolitical conflict is bound to encourage further proliferation (and maneuvering) of nuclear weapons on a world scale.[17]

While the corporate-state apparatus continues to assault the global habitat, it simultaneously works to undermine democratic politics – with varying degrees of success. Capitalist rationalization narrows the public sphere, corrodes public discourse, and stifles political opposition – a state of affairs consistent with Marcuse's familiar notion of "one dimensionality". In the U.S. such one-dimensionality is reinforced by postwar growth of the largest warfare state in history, a pervasive security-intelligence apparatus, and slavishly compliant media. American society has seen the further rise of interconnected corporate interests in the form of agribusiness, the meat complex, Big Pharma, petrochemicals, the medical system, and Wall Street. None of those interests has ever shown much concern for environmental problems.

Reputed beacon on democratic politics, the U.S. is now best described as an oligarchical system run by a power elite comprised of Fortune 500 corporations, banking interests, the military-industrial complex, technology giants, and global communications firms – all connected in different ways to an expanding authoritarian state. The outlines of this behemoth were drawn by Mills in his classic *The Power Elite* several decades ago. Nowadays conventional references to "democracy", "free markets", and individual self-interest have been essentially hollowed out, turned into propaganda messaging. Across the decades power at the summits has grown more, not less, tightly integrated as well as concentrated, owing in great measure to U.S. imperial expansion.

Mills saw what few mainstream or even critical social scientists managed to see at the time – the postwar growth of a military-industrial complex that came to occupy the center of American domestic and international power.[18] His analysis holds even more weight today than it did in the 1950s, at the height of the Cold War. Yet most environmentalists and other progressives tend to minimize if not overlook this enormous threat to human survival. To start, militaries of the world combined presently consume trillions of dollars in natural resources yearly, the U.S. alone contributing roughly one trillion of that total. This obscene level of waste and destruction is expected to at least *double* by 2030. Meanwhile, the sum total of all that preparation for war (and warfare itself) accounts for nearly three percent of worldwide carbon emissions, especially as military production and operations rely heavily on fossil fuels. Armed-forces buildups further heighten geopolitical tensions and risks of war, including nuclear war, while threatening to turn local resource conflicts into outright warfare.

The expanded military capabilities of increasing numbers of countries also feeds authoritarian tendencies: massive institutional expansion, surveillance and intelligence operations, covert actions, and military presence in outer space, all accompanied by a rise in xenophobic attitudes. Here again the U.S., the only truly international military power, is primarily responsible for this historical tendency. Victor Wallis, writing in *Red-Green Revolution*, observes: "War not only brings death and destruction to targeted zones, it also has dramatic effects on the society whose government initiates it. It swallows up a huge share of that society's resources, preempts any capacity within that society to plan for economic/ecological conversion, creates a permanent pretext for political repression and fosters a self-perpetuating culture of violence …".[19]

Despite often-heated electoral competition, the major parties in the U.S. (Democrats and Republicans) are beholden to the same economic interests while supporting identical military and imperial objectives. Although Republicans are more likely to downplay or ignore environmental problems while Democrats usually promise reforms, differences shrink when it comes to actual policy; neither party is prepared to confront the growth machine or military-security apparatus. "Bipartisanship" remains the guiding outlook around issues related to corporate power, economic growth, and foreign policy. Corporate-state power is anchored in a sprawling network of media outlets, think tanks, big lobbies, and academic institutions.

It should be hardly surprising, therefore, that in the midst of life-threatening crisis the system remains nearly paralyzed, useless as a vehicle of genuine change. Only at the fringes of American politics do we fine a sense of ecological urgency. As for such leading corporations as Monsanto, Pfizer, McDonalds, Cargill, Google, Amazon, and Bank of America, the prevailing mood is business-as-usual, though sometimes with a nod to environmental concerns. Here Noam Chomsky, writing in *Who Rules the World?*, comments: "It is hard to capture the fact that humans are facing the most important question in their history – whether organized human life will survive in anything like the form we know – and are answering it by accelerating the race to disaster. The same goes for the other huge threat to human survival, the danger of nuclear destruction, which has been looming over our heads for seventy years and is now increasing."[20]

In place of political and media attention lavished on looming ecological disaster – perhaps other threats such as nuclear war – the American establishment has been obsessed with mendacious nonstop coverage of a non-event lasting three years: Russian intervention in the 2016 presidential election that brought novice Donald Trump to the White House. This outright hoax conveniently served to deflect attention from deeper problems in the economy and foreign policy while "explaining" Hillary Clinton's unacceptable loss. Moreover, it championed an image of democratic politics lifted directly from civic textbooks – an open, participatory system of free markets, personal freedoms, and competitive elections. The reality is precisely the opposite: a two-party duopoly dominated by Wall Street, corporate power, and warfare/security state. This order is shaped by an ever-narrowing public sphere that has nothing to do with Russia or any other foreign state. As for the U.S. media, it too is owned and controlled by giant corporations the managers of which typically speak in one voice on issues that matter.[21]

In reality the American political system is designed to stifle opposi-tional forces, and generally does so quite effectively. While the problem of climate change is frequently depicted as an "existential crisis", there is no politics adequate to the historical moment. It is true that some state gov-ernments have taken up green agendas, but the U.S. Congress has stead-fastly failed to pass relevant legislation. With significant global warming ahead (temperatures sure to move past the targeted two degrees Celsius), the natural habitat will encounter more destructive challenges that could result in millions of deaths – while governance in the U.S. and elsewhere, with few exceptions, remains trapped in a matrix of normalcy. Other issues (taxes, guns, immigration) routinely take precedence. The most severe of all crises ever is commonly met with a mood of fatalism, even denial, the threat ahead seemingly to big, too remote, too distant. Writing in *The Uninhab-itable Earth,* David Wallace-Wells comments: "If the planet is warming at a terrifying pace and on a horrifying scale, it should transparently concern us more, rather than less, that the warming is beyond our control, possibly even our comprehension."[22] He then adds: "Today political nihilism radi-ates almost everywhere … ."[23]

The present crisis extends far beyond anything expected by Marx or even later Marxists, who were largely fixated on class conflict rooted in economic contradictions ultimately leading to systemic collapse. Environ-mental decline pervades every sphere of capitalist development in ways never imagined by earlier Marxists, including even "Western" Marxists and Frankfurt School theorists who looked to address a broader range of social and cultural factors within their critical framework. Commoner's thesis that the ecosystem underpins and stabilizes all other human systems is surely worth reaffirming here. Within advanced capitalism ecological problems can no longer be so obtusely overlooked: with unsustainable eco-nomic growth, systemic breakdown is unavoidable, whatever the level of class struggle – the main questions being when, under what circumstances, and what humans choose to do about it. Our political response to that breakdown will, sooner or later, determine the very fate of planetary life.

To be decisive, such response will have to be emphatically *radical,* integral to anti-system opposition capable of overturning corporate-state power, on a global scale. As of 2020, unfortunately, no counterforce with significant mass support has been able to challenge such massive power. The modern crisis obviously encompasses more than ecology, but that dimension – thoroughly interwoven as it is with other realms – figures to be most lethal for ruling elites in coming decades. The capitalist order has become so dysfunctional, so irrational that one hardly knows where to begin in looking for weakest links in the system. Presently hundreds of large cities and mega-cities are cauldrons of environmental disaster, most over-crowded, riddled with poverty, disease, addictions, violence, and mal-nutrition, overcome by resource shortages and failing public infrastructures. From Mexico City to Jakarta, from Seoul to Sao Paulo, from Mumbai to Cairo the dystopic nightmares cannot be missed.

With no vigorous or durable oppositional forces in sight, the challenge has reached a point where even the modest Paris goals (avoiding a two-de-gree Celsius temperature rise by 2030) have little chance of success. Matters could of course worsen dramatically, especially in the (probable) absence of far-reaching political solutions. The existing global patterns of produc-tion and consumption, firmly established in the West, seem more taken for granted than ever. When it comes to the ubiquitous food complex, moreover, little has changed: heavy reliance on dysfunctional meat-based agriculture and fast-food industry, centered in the industrialized societies, persists without interruption. The deepening relationship between food and ecology, agriculture and the global crisis, is far too often ignored right across the ideological spectrum.[24]

In the U.S. and other industrialized countries, meat and dairy con-sumption has long been standard fare, cherished for its supposed nutritional value – high in protein, a source of health and vitality. It has also become something of an addiction for Americans and Europeans, a product often consumed to extremes, beyond ordinary dietary needs. Such addiction is illuminated by the fact that meat of all types is profoundly unhealthful, environmentally destructive, and wasteful in terms of the vast resources it demands. It is well known that, as societies become more affluent, ani-mal-foods intake rapidly increases, associated with notions of health and progress. Modern agribusiness and the McDonalds system are built on this very excessive mode of consumption, always maintained by huge marketing and advertising operations.[25]

By 2018 meat consumption in the U.S. had reached historic levels of 220 pounds yearly per capita, ranking it first in the world. Fossil fuels used in the raising, processing, shipping, marketing, and selling of meat and dairy products are responsible for perhaps the largest of all carbon footprints that, given widespread habituation to animal foods, is routinely overlooked. That footprint could reach more than 30 percent of the total, though calculations vary greatly. Beyond that, the animal-foods complex requires staggering amounts of water, cropland, soil, and forests, meanwhile accounting for some of the worst air and water pollution ever.

The damage caused by meat and dairy interests has been long overlooked within the political and media establishment. These interests have taken the lead in blocking corporate regulations and environmental reforms. Even modest proposals for a shift to plant-based diets are met with a flow of angry myths, lies, and distortions uncritically repeated across the political and media establishments. Food propaganda is all the more effective given the addictive character of meat consumption in so many societies, long associated with ethnic and religious traditions, celebrations, special occasions, and everyday family life.

As global corporate power extends its reach across the planet, capitalist domination shows few signs of weakening, its longevity bolstered by continued economic and technological growth. What Marx said about nineteenth-century capitalism can now be extended to the entire global terrain: "The bourgeoisie cannot exist without constantly revolutionizing the instruments of production, and thereby the whole relations of society."[26] From the U.S. to Russia and China, from Europe to Brazil and Mexico, from Japan to North Africa, economic growth remains a guiding priority, while obligatory hostility to even modest limits-to-growth scenarios is universally embraced.

It is through the ceaseless pursuit of power and wealth that world capitalism embellishes its dominion over the natural habitat, where everything (including many billions of animals) is turned into commodities. Such "development" amplifies the primary contradiction between a growth-obsessed economy and ecological sustainability. By virtue of their very pursuits, ruling elites proceed as if such contradictions can be safely ignored. As Commoner and others have argued, a destructive economic order eventually negates the conditions of its own reproduction – a dynamic that understandably could never have been addressed by either Marx or Weber. So long as the growth mania holds sway, reformist "solutions" – market incentives, alternative technologies, green consumerism, policy initiatives – will never be enough, whether carried out by liberals, conservatives, social democrats, traditional socialists, or Communists.

The unfortunate truth is that the world has already passed the limits of growth-driven development, sometimes referred to as the Earth's carrying capacity, even while corporate and state managers still cannot envision a developmental model at odds with waste, inequality, destruction, warfare, and resource-depletion. For short-sighted capitalists, obsessed with immediate profitable returns, there is no possibility of a dynamic, functioning, sustainable future, much less a political strategy for getting there. Paul Gilding, writing in *The Great Disruption,* notes that "we've been borrowing from the future, and the debt has fallen due."[27] During the twentieth century, world economic growth expanded more than 20 times – coinciding with an era of perpetual wars, escalating civic violence, increased social misery, massive forced migration, and badly deteriorating natural habitat. Still, the growth machine continues as if Enlightenment rationality were being fully realized with every advance of twenty-first century modernity.

Riddled with such dysfunction and conflict, the global order relies on a mixture of force and ideology to sustain its hegemony. Since World War II it has been the U.S. – along with some European and other partners – that serves as international enforcer, using the United Nations, World Bank, International Monetary Fund, and World Trade Organization to neutralize (or, if needed, destroy) potential anti-system forces, whether movements or governments. More than that, Washington has been able to depend on its powerful military, intelligence, and surveillance capabilities in cases where armed intervention seemed necessary. The result has been several bloody wars for regime change, but more frequently some combination of covert action, sabotage, NGO subversion, proxy wars, and imperial propaganda to keep a sprawling world order intact. Needless to say, complex forms of ideological control are generally preferred as they are less costly and produce far less blowback.

For the U.S. and other industrialized societies, ideological modes of domination are the more reliable sources of legitimation, whether in the form of nationalism, cultural norms, liberal-capitalist fictions, or sim-

ple technological rationality. It is this latter phenomenon that now most
shapes the landscape, especially where it intersects with corporate power,
the military, education, the media/entertainment complex, and medical/
pharmaceutical interests. Indeed technological rationality, so integral to the
larger process of capitalist rationalization, has probably done more to reinforce human domination of the natural habitat, consistent with Marcuse's
view of technology as both structure and *ideology*.[28] While conceding the
obviously great achievements of modern technology, it is still worth under-
scoring the role technology plays in perpetuating both capitalist hegemony
and the ecological crisis.

At present capitalist rationalization is most visible in the power wielded
by such technology giants as Google, Microsoft, Facebook, Apple, and
Amazon. So pervasive (and invasive) as to be nearly invisible, this unique
oligopoly helps shape popular consciousness in the realms of governance,
work relations, culture, education, food choices, and more. It helps define
mass attitudes supportive of U.S. foreign policy and decisions by Washington to militarily intervene around the globe. Technological domination has
been, in Weber's formulation, "the most fateful force in our modern life"
– though, writing in the early twentieth century, Weber paid little attention
to the ecological consequences of modern technology.

The global crisis, more fearsome than anything before it, requires
nothing short of an epic struggle to revitalize politics in a period when
oppositional forces appear especially weak in the West. While some might
believe a radical breakthrough is imminent, the reality points to something
less optimistic: mass publics in the industrialized societies have not been
drawn to leftist movements and parties, while "populism" seems to have
been captured by the right, veering toward reaction, ultra-nationalism, and
authoritarianism. Such a milieu is hardly friendly to ecological radicalism.

A newly-revitalized politics – radical, ecological, democratic – will
have to burst through the old parameters of liberalism and socialism, both
much too aligned with Enlightenment myths of economic and technological progress. Any ecological politics will be forced to move beyond the
limits, moreover, of environmental reformism characteristic of major green
organizations and movements in the U.S. and Europe. Those constraints
are a product of lobbies, legislative timidity, green consumerism, a single-issue focus, and strictly local initiatives. Ecological theorists going back to

the early 1960s recognized that new challenges demanded new modes of thought and action. All earlier traditions had taken for granted the imperative of full-scale industrialization as mechanism of social progress. Worth mentioning here is that Soviet rule, and Communist systems in general, were likewise dedicated to rapid industrialization – and were likewise beset with the very environmental horrors that came from *capitalist* modernization. The deep contradictions of global capitalism identified by Marx and Engels (capital vs. labor, private accumulation vs. social needs, etc.) are now joined by an even more explosive contradiction – the deepening rift between economic growth and ecological sustainability, with planetary survival increasingly at risk.

Simply put, unfettered corporate globalization is destroying the natural habitat, with no effective counterforces in sight. A narrow obsession with economics, fatal to so much leftist thinking during the twentieth century has become even more intellectually and politically debilitating in the present milieu. While full-scale industrialization across the planet is the central dynamic, other variables enter the picture, starting with a global food complex that deserves far more attention than it has received anywhere along the ideological spectrum.

For reasons of denial, ignorance, or simple bias, progressives and leftists have rarely been moved by the great ecological harm done by the animal-foods industry, including massive carbon footprint. Meat-based diets – major source of obesity and chronic illnesses – utilize many times the natural resources (above all land and water) of plant-based foods. The meat and dairy sectors consume staggering amounts of fresh water, chemicals, cropland, and fertile soil, contaminating air and water, destroying huge expanses of oceans and forests, accounting for more greenhouse emissions than all vehicles in the world. It would be a mistake to overlook the McDonaldized fast-food system, among the most rationalized of capitalist sectors, given its dark legacy: health nightmares, workplace repression, environmental miseries.[29]

When it comes to specifically meat and dairy consumption, matters worsen as these foods gain wider popularity with each advancing phase of economic development. Meat has long been associated with modernity and higher living, a sign of health and vigor. Lucrative government subsidies reduce the otherwise burdensome cost of meat, while ubiquitous advertising and marketing stoke meat options among mass consumers mostly unaware of nutritional disasters that await. The McDonaldized system is trumpeted worldwide as a pinnacle of technological advance, yet that façade barely conceals ecological ruin, health dangers, workplace tyranny, and unspeakable animal suffering.[30]

That food issues have been so widely ignored is a fact of astounding importance. In a world of unlimited access to research and information, the particularly dark side of capitalist rationalization should hardly be a matter of secrecy, yet the topic rarely enters thought processes of most environmentalists and progressives. If denialism around climate change is pervasive, so too is the reluctance to face questions related to agriculture and the looming food crisis. Books and documentaries on the topic are produced overwhelmingly *outside* progressive circles; the issue is generally considered extraneous, a matter of personal choice – nobody's business. Meanwhile, a question is worth asking: how might a viable ecological politics make headway where a major source of unsustainability – the global food complex – remains obscure, beyond serious discussion. The very theories, organizations, and movements that proclaim abiding reverence for "nature", the "natural habitat", and "environmental sustainability" all too often seem oblivious to forces warring against the very object of their veneration.

This predicament reveals the extent to which modern environmentalism continues to be remains saturated with such provincial outlooks as anthropocentrism and speciesism. Indeed, few leading environmental theorists or activists even *mention* that dimension of ecological crisis. Ideological myopia runs deep, all the more so when it comes to such ostensibly *personal* behavior as food consumption. Marxist ecologists have been notably indifferent to this problem, as if issues related to production and class exhaust most everything. A similar indifference, willful or not, afflicts the work of others along the ecological trail: Commoner, Bookchin, Joel Kovel, George Sessions, Bill McKibben, Al Gore, Naomi Klein, James Hansen, Robert Jay Lifton. Some have even gone so far as to debunk anyone linking ecological crisis to problems of agriculture and food.

Well into the twenty-first century, there can be no excuse for such narrow provincialism and willful ignorance. In the documentary *Cowspiracy*, environmentalist Howard Liman puts the matter sharply: "You can't be an environmentalist and eat animal products, period. Kid yourself if you want.

If you want to feed your [meat] addiction, so be it. But don't call yourself an environmentalist." Rhetorical overreach? Moral condescension? Not so, if we take seriously the indefensible burden imposed on the planetary habitat by unsustainably high levels of meat and dairy consumption – levels increasing year by year. While precise estimates of carbon emissions from the global meat complex differ, some believe the amount could reach 40 percent or higher.[31]

A revival of politics adequate to the mortal threat will depend on the human capacity to investigate, analyze, and solve the dynamics of ecological unsustainability, and food crises surely rank at the top of any reasonable list. A preoccupation with fossil fuels, or "fossil capital", does not come close to exhausting our field of environmental concerns – though, sadly, most groups and organizations proceeds as if this were the case. More crucially, the ecological challenge will require fundamentally new ways of viewing economic development and political governance, not to mention cultural traditions, if the struggle for planetary survival is to be won. Angus writes: "In the Anthropocene, the common ruin of all, the destruction of civilization, is a very real possibility. That's why we need a movement with a clear vision, an ecosocialist program that can bridge the gap between the spontaneous anger of millions of people and the beginning of an ecosocialist transformation."[32]

Setting in motion an alternative course to business-as-usual is the most imposing task now facing humanity – and that challenge will only intensify moving forward. In Michael Lowy's words, from his book *Ecosocialism:* "The struggle against the commodification of the world and the defense of the environment, resistance to the dictatorship of multinationals, and the battle for ecology are intimately linked in the reflection and praxis of the world movement against capitalist/liberal globalization."[33] Unfortunately, the "world movement" referred to by Lowy has yet to achieve much-needed political expression.

The human species continues to struggle mightily with troubled and failed legacies from the past, along with accumulated environmental horrors inherited from earlier decades and centuries. Andreas Malm writes in *Fossil Capital:* "For every year global warming continues and temperatures soar higher, living conditions on earth will be determined more intensely by the emissions of yore, so that the grip of yesteryear on today intensifies..."[34]

As the ominous Tipping Point appears more imminent than commonly believed, as the Great Acceleration reaches its upper limits, the famous Paradigm Shift envisioned decades ago by Deep Ecologists and others is now more than ever a moral imperative, a life-and-death challenge.

1

Food and the Global Challenge

The intensifying global ecological crisis has brought the world – above all its most economically developed countries – to a point of no return. Existing political, economic, and cultural patterns, all dedicated to endless material growth, can no longer be sustained. The planet faces a specter of mounting environmental horrors, resource depletion, geopolitical conflict, food shortages, and social breakdown at a time of population growth, reckless urbanization, and accelerated climate change. As world population expands from 7.7 billion people to perhaps nine billion by 2030 – with resulting pressures on public infrastructures, water sources, cropland, forests, and oceans – conditions are sure to reach and then pass the fearsome Tipping Point.

In reality we have already entered an era of living precariously, on the edge – a predicament well beyond the threat of global warming as such. While rampant economic growth lies at the heart of the problem, several trends converge to produce what has been dubbed "The Great Acceleration", "Great Disruption", or "Anthropocene": continued economic and population expansion, urban deterioration, resource shortages, land shrinkage, loss of biodiversity. A crucial, usually overlooked, dimension of this historical juncture is *food* production and consumption – in particular the irrational reliance on meat and dairy sources that typically accompany rising levels of material abundance. Poverty, hunger, resource pressures, pollution, global warming, crowded cities, health disasters, loss of biodiversity – all these are closely interwoven with the sprawling global food complex.

As we rapidly approach the point of no return, beyond which reversal of the crisis is no longer possible, reformist or incremental solutions of the sort preferred by ruling elites (liberal or conservative), as well as most environmental groups, become obsolete; radical measures are desperately needed, and indeed are the only viable response One problem with reformism (extending to such international treaties as the 2015 Paris Accords) is that within its fixed parameters the corrosive developmental patterns of advanced capitalism are not (and *cannot*) be even minimally disturbed.

As the global crisis widens and the human predicament worsens, solutions appear increasingly remote, beyond the reach of effective political intervention. Any perspective apart from the fragile but apparently stable present seems irrational, utopian. Alternative models of public life lack concreteness, although such models can be found here and there as theoretical schemes. In his provocative book *Half-Earth*, Edward O. Wilson articulates a profound sense of this futility, writing: "May I now humbly ask, just where do we think we are going – really?"[35]

Now in the third decade of the twenty-first century, neoliberal capitalism expands full speed ahead with few apparent impediments or challenges. Reforms – adoption of green technologies, more sustainable consumer choices, infrastructure refinements, product recycling – have done little to dent the vast fortress of corporate globalization. On the contrary, the path to ecological disaster has scarcely been interrupted: unlimited growth, at odds with any reasonable economic, moral, or ecological constraints, will sooner rather than later give rise to a non-livable planet, whatever the impact of climate change. Further, imminent food crises will be more decisive to this eventuality than is generally believed.

Agribusiness and the Food Complex

Writing in his classic *The Modern Crisis* several decades ago, Murray Bookchin warned: "We may well be approaching a critical juncture in our development that confronts us with an historic choice: whether we will follow an alternative path that yields a humane rational, and ecological way of life, or a path which will yield the degradation of our species if not its outright extinction."[36] Today, with the ecological crisis developing more or less unchecked, Bookchin's historical imperative takes on new urgency. To speak of an "ecological way of life", as Bookchin does throughout his work, suggests the importance of far-ranging changes in every realm of human existence, perhaps none more than in the production and consumption of food, that necessary yet most fragile of all human activities.

One problem here is the enormous global increase in animal-foods consumption. People in the industrialized societies (especially the U.S., Europe, now China) consume more animal products per capita than at any time in modern history, with disastrous consequences for the environment, natural resources, human health, and of course the billions of animals caught in the barbaric assembly lines. By 2018 Americans were eating a record 220 pounds of beef, pork, and poultry per capita yearly, relying on cheap, readily transportable, often subsidized products.[37] These patterns, steadily on the upswing since World War II, are driven by aggressive marketing, advertising, and lobbying campaigns that seamlessly mesh with long-ingrained everyday habits. They are encouraged by a rash of fashionable diet schemes celebrating the virtues of animal proteins while warning about the supposed horrors of "carbs" (carbohydrates). Such deepening protein obsession corresponds to the postwar rise of a McDonaldized fast-food economy.

For the U.S., intake of meat and dairy foods has grown from 167 pounds per capita in 1960 to the previously mentioned 220 pounds per capita in 2018. The domestic market for beef, pork, poultry, and other meats is expected to reach a staggering $7.3 trillion by 2025, despite recent modest shifts toward plant-based diets. Meanwhile, in the face of all the harsh environmental consequences, American exports of beef and other animal goods to dozens of countries are steadily increasing.

Global consumption of meat and dairy foods is expected to *double* over the next two decades, a function of heightened economic growth, rising population, and widening access to such products – assuming systemic contradictions do not undercut such unsustainable patterns. According to the U.N. Food and Agriculture Organization (FAO), the worldwide per capita intake of meat alone is projected to be roughly 45 kilograms in 2030, compared to 24 kilograms in 1966, paralleled by elevated dairy consumption (from 74 kilograms in 1966 to 90 kilograms in 2030).[38] As might be expected, China, with its 1.4 billion population and continuing economic growth, is at the forefront of this historic dynamic, having already taken the lead in poultry consumption. Industrialized nations currently represent about 20 percent of the world population while consuming 40 percent of all animal products, a total that should increase as China, Brazil, and a few other large countries enter the ranks of the most highly affluent societies. For China alone, per-capita intake of meat products has expanded roughly *three times* since the late 1960s.

The ongoing rise in worldwide meat and dairy consumption has been described as something of a "food revolution" marked by cheaper and more accessible diets comprised of beef, poultry, pork, cheese, and other animal foods. It could be just as easily characterized as the onset of a global "food crisis" likely to bring sharply reduced croplands, more deforestation, ocean depletion, global warming, and (sooner than generally believed) alarming food *shortages* in many parts of the world. Increasing livestock populations across the planet mean accelerated pressure on land, soil, water, public infrastructures, and the atmosphere – an egregiously unsustainable scenario. It further augurs heightened soil, food, water, and atmospheric pollution, along with proliferation of animal wastes, methane gases, toxic emissions, and fossil-fuel driven carbon footprint.

The very idea of a "food revolution" is illusory, a verbal embellishment designed to conceal impending horrors. In *Full Planet, Empty Plates*, Lester Brown writes: "The world is in transition from an era of food abundance to one of scarcity. Over the last decade (first decade of the new century) world grain reserves have fallen by one-third. World food prices have more than doubled, triggering a worldwide land rush and ushering in a new geopolitics of food. Food is the new oil. Land is the new gold."[39] The worsening "geopolitics of food", moreover, is deeply interwoven with both cause and effect of climate change. What Brown describes here is sure to worsen, leaving widening sectors of the world population vulnerable to extreme food shortages, hunger, famine, and disease. Meat-based diets, heavily dependent on shrinking natural resources and environmentally destructive, are bound to hasten disaster.

As more countries reach advanced industrialization, their expanding populations shifting toward animal products, cropland inevitably diminishes. This problem is aggravated by the growth of massive urban centers with their vast residential and commercial encroachments, roads, highways, parking lots, shopping malls, and entertainment complexes. Shrinking fertile land occurs at a time when food production must steadily increase to feed more people eating higher on the food chain. As more societies follow this trajectory, planetary integrity becomes ever more precarious.

The American food complex, like other sectors of the economy, has undergone the most extreme capitalist rationalization – from factory farms to processing, transport, financing, marketing, and retail operations. It represents a classic example of oligopolistic power, above all in the meat industry. The rise of large-scale agribusiness, organically linked to the McDonaldized fast-food economy, is shaped by corporate agendas and technological rationality, maintained by well-funded political lobbies, government subsidies, price supports, and nonstop media advertising. A few giant food conglomerates have taken over the landscape. Economies of scale, consolidation of power, bureaucratic and technical controls, government and media supports, Wall Street financing – these dynamic elements of modern corporate agriculture are especially visible in the meat sector. As Holt-Gimenez puts it: "The concentration of capital in the agribusiness and agri-foods sector has given rise to multibillion oligopolies that control credit, farm inputs, services, processing, distribution, and retail."[40]

Just a handful of transnational corporations – Tyson Foods, Cargill, Archer-Daniels Midland, Wal-Mart, Monsanto, McDonalds – exercise control over the sprawling food terrain, reaping untold profits while having preponderant influence over American food choices. In 2017 the four largest food enterprises marketed 82 percent of all beef products, 85 percent of soybeans (mainly for animal feed), and 63 percent of pork. Linkages between corporations and the federal government (including the all-important Department of Agriculture, USDA) have been so tight as to guarantee a more or less free reign to the food cartels. Federal and state regulations have been weak to non-existent; democratic controls largely invisible. This results in what Christopher Leonard, in his book *The Meat Racket,* calls "The Food Dictatorship."[41]

The multifaceted American agribusiness system and its network of farmers, processors, and retailers – reinforced by its capacity to colonize federal agencies like the Packers and Stockyards Administration (PSA) – is largely hidden from public view, its nefarious work effectively off-limits to the media. The oligarchy that dominates the meat complex is virtually impregnable and unaccountable, a state of affairs supported equally by Democrats and Republicans. Corporate elites set the rules for production, pricing, processing, and sales; there is nothing resembling a free market. Fossil fuels, drugs, antibiotics, and chemicals are used with abandon, with scant regard for consequences. The meat industry remains among the most profitable in the U.S. (and the world), made possible by its vast underpaid and super-exploited work force comprised mainly of immigrants.

At the top of this pyramid can be found five leading meat corporations: Tyson, Cargill, JBS Swift, National Beef Company, Archer Daniels Midland (ADM). Tyson alone constitutes its own self-contained empire of farm operations, feed mills, slaughterhouses, trucking centers, maintenance shops, and sewage plants. Such "vertical integration" permits huge companies like Tyson to rationalize their operations in the service of control, efficiency, and profit maximization.[42] Tyson produces millions of pounds of beef and poultry daily through its assembly-line processes, while maintaining vertical integration. Millions of cows, pigs, and chickens are assembled, kept under brutal conditions, and killed. Tyson managers exercise nearly total control over the whole process, facilitated by a centralized computer network and command room.

Thanks to such vertical integration, Tyson – and kindred corporations – can solidify their oligopolistic status, thus undermining competition. For several decades Tyson management has been refining this business model, in the process taking over no fewer than 33 smaller firms. Its own lobbies, working through the American Meat Institute, National Chicken Council, and National Pork Producers among others, work nonstop to strengthen this "business model". In 2001, Tyson acquired IBP, Inc., the largest beef packer and number two pork processor in the U.S.

Tyson is now the second largest marketer of chicken, beef, and pork products, in control of major brands such as Jimmy Dean, Hillshire Farm, Sara Lee, Ball Park, and State Fair. It processes a wide variety of animal-based and prepared goods at 123 food plants in the U.S. and abroad, including 54 chicken facilities, 13 beef facilities, and six pork facilities, slaughtering and packaging 42.5 million chickens, 171,000 cattle and 348,000 pigs weekly. In supplies McDonalds, Taco Bell, KFC, Wendy's, Wal-Mart, Kroger, and IGA among others. In 2018 it employed 113,00 workers. In 2015 it secured profits of $1.2 billion from revenues exceeding $41.3 billion. Meanwhile, Tyson has been charged with several corporate violations: smuggling undocumented workers, price manipulations, air and water pollution, undisclosed use of antibiotics, animal mistreatment.[43]

As of 2018, Tyson's economic and cultural imprint on American society, for all its harm, continued to expand – much like such meat juggernauts as Cargill, ADM, ConAgra, and JBS USA (all mainstays of a national oligopoly). Seemingly above traditional anti-trust laws and Congressional oversight, this oligopoly has been able to consolidate its hold over important areas of the food economy. Referring to existing trends, Leonard writes: "Driven in part by government subsidies to big farms, the business of American food production became more consolidated than at any point in history."[44] He adds that, while the poultry industry is controlled by Tyson and a few subsidiaries, the crucial grain trade is dominated by only a few corporate giants, led by ADM and Cargill. Cattle and pork operations, moreover, were being increasingly colonized by the sprawling Tyson network. As for the vital biotechnology sector, Monsanto has effectively taken over important seed operations through its patent on genetically modified crops and kindred investments.

Cargill, a 150- year-old company involved in beef and poultry foods along with grain marketing, has 150,000 employees at food operations in 70 countries. It is a world leader in trading corn, wheat, and soybeans, mainly for animal feed; its feedlot business by 2018 now the third largest. Cargill slaughters 13 million hogs yearly, or 36,000 each day, while functioning as a transmission belt for the fast-food industry, supplying 22 percent of the domestic market. Dedicated to an aggressive globalization model, the corporation has a reputation for skirting government regulations while supporting policies (and practices) that favor high levels of meat and dairy consumption. Cargill has also been deeply involved in commodity food speculation, earning record profits (nearly three billion dollars in 2017) while fighting to retain a low-wage labor force largely devoid of union protection and employee benefits. Like Tyson, ADM (Archer Daniels Midland), and a few others, Cargill benefits from the great advantages of vertical integration.[45] ADM, founded in 1902, had revenues of $63 billion and profits of $1.3 billion in 2016 from 270 plants and four crop procurement facilities employing 32,300 worldwide. Like other predominately food corporations, ADM has moved to diversify its operations during the past few decades, moving into beverage, storage, industrial, and financial sectors, as well as bio-enhanced products. In the years 2009 to 2011 *Fortune* magazine depicted ADM as a "model business", in fact the best of all food companies.

And like other profit-driven corporations, ADM lobbied Congress and state governments for generous subsidies amounting (all together) to tens of billions since the mid-1990s.

These behemoths share horrendous records in their treatment of workers, communities, the environment, and animals. Frequent "product incidents", low wages, stingy benefits, brutal working conditions, air and water pollution, price fixing, animal abuse – all these contribute a long and tortured legacy. To this must be added their huge contribution to fossil-fuel emissions and global warming that will be further explored in the next chapter. Most animal-food complexes are located in the Midwest (across Iowa, Kansas, Texas, Colorado, Nebraska) where low-wage immigrant labor works the crowded, dirty, cruel assembly lines for "processing" cattle, pigs, chickens, and sheep. In such regions the American meat industry has dramatically expanded since World War II, when mass production was being carried out by a deskilled and exploited workforce, deployed well beyond public view. Here we have what Eric Schlosser describes as the "hardest view of the world."[46] In this bleakest of settings, capitalist modernity has come to integrate the most advanced conditions of technological rationality with the darkest features of food dictatorship.

For all these horrors, what should amount to a widely condemned public scandal – akin to Upton Sinclair's expose in *The Jungle* – is met with massive government supports (tax reductions, subsidies, deregulation, legal breaks) and political disinterest or outright coverup. One reason for this despicable state of affairs is the far-reaching influence of food (especially meat) lobbies working at both federal and state levels. It is these lobbies that bolster a system promoting cheap and accessible meat consumption, weak anti-trust laws, readily available grains for animal feed, and maximum corporate dominion over workers and livestock. Such lobbies spend billions of corporate dollars that, combined with tax monies, buy off legislators and colonize such federal agencies as the USDA and PSA. Any semblance of opposition to the meat oligopoly is generally silenced or crushed. Organizations like the National Cattlemen's Beef Association (NCBA), Poultry Growers' Association, and Meat Institute regularly block legislative measures or reforms that might lend advantage to plant foods over animal products. Real public discussion over such issues, in legislatures, the media, or presidential debates, rarely occurs.

While meat and dairy profits have soared since the 1990s, the system contributes more than one trillion dollars yearly to the U.S. economy. To ensure that beef, chicken, and pork remain plentiful and cheap, the federal government doled out roughly $300 billion in agricultural subsidies from 1995 to the present. Material support for plant-based foods has always been grudging, minimal. Justified originally to help struggling farmers, agribusiness subsidies are now best viewed as another form of corporate welfare: It is Tyson, Cargill, ADM, and ConAgra that have been aided most.[47]

Like Big Pharma and kindred interests, the meat lobby utilizes quasi-populist arguments to legitimate its operations, Leonard writing: "To shape the debate, meat company lobbyists use an increasingly common tactic in the Washington influence industry. They stoke a 'grassroots' movement of ordinary people (farmers, consumers, rural folk) who contacted lawmakers to voice complaints, and make suggestions that perfectly mirror the interests of big business." He adds that, in the meat industry "there is no more effective group to enlist for such an effort than famers themselves."[48] Tyson and the others want the fewest possible restraints, a laissez-faire approach promoted by the NCBA and similar lobbies.

The U.S. meat and dairy complexes spend lavishly to ensure high-level consumption of their products, relying on favorable scientific and academic research, leverage over government agencies, interest-group campaigns, Congressional and state legislation – not to mention support from the corporate media and internet. Leaving aside recent slight decreases in beef and pork intake, these efforts have achieved overwhelmingly positive results: overall intake of animal foods remains on the upswing. In 2014 the meat industry spent $108 million on political campaigns, another $6.9 million to lobby the federal government, and a staggering $4.5 billion on TV and radio advertising, according to the Center for Responsive Politics.[49] One major target is the USDA, officially charged with regulating meat and dairy interests but actually a *promoter* of those very interests through its respected dietary guidelines and other initiatives. In 2016 funds earmarked for lobbies totaled $6.5 million for dairy, $3 million for livestock, and $2 million for poultry and eggs.[50]

A leading meat lobby is the aforementioned NCBA, which donates to political causes, advertises, and uses public relations to "increase profit opportunities for cattle and beef producers by enhancing the business cli-

mate and building consumer demand." The NCBA is indispensable to the
Meat Promotion Coalition, which includes ranchers, dairy facilities, food
service entities, meat packers, processors, and retailers. The Coalition has
long fiercely opposed-environmental, health, and animal rights groups that
work against the power of meat and dairy interests. The NCBA itself sponsors a beef "check-off" program, going back to the 1980s, which allows the
USDA to funnel millions of dollars to the organization for its influential
lobbying activities.[51]

The meat and dairy industry earmarks hundreds of millions of dollars
to win Congressional opposition to even most tepid reforms. In summer
2011, Congress was able to block anti-trust legislation, a move supported by
both Democrats and Republicans at a time when the USDA, the PSA, and
other regulatory agencies had been effectively stripped of their power.[52] In
fact the U.S. meat lobby had long been a bipartisan operation, Democrats
at times even more than Republicans viewed as a party of agribusiness. The
lobby and such corporate affiliates as Monsanto and Wal-Mart gave some
of their biggest contributions to the Democrats Bill and Hillary Clinton.[53]

The Clintons were especially close to Tyson Foods, as well as one of its
corporate allies in the meat business, Wal-Mart, where Hillary served on
the Board of Directors. The Clintons' attitude was basically one of maximum corporate freedom: let the agribusiness and meat juggernauts monitor and regulate themselves. It was the Clintons, moreover, who helped
usher in the age of vertical integration during the 1990s as the food giants
(not only Tyson but Cargill, ConAgra, and Smithfield Foods) decimated
smaller businesses and built domination over the lucrative meat and dairy
markets. Hillary's 2016 Democratic primary campaign against Bernie
Sanders famously ignored the agribusiness horrors in Iowa, the state where
the presidential campaign started – hardly surprising, as she had long been
cozy with the meat industry and its lobbyists.[54]

The American food empire is nowadays so integrated and powerful
that Leonard's characterization of it as a "food dictatorship" seems hardly
exaggerated. It is a veritable corporate-state fortress, perhaps the most
visible legacy of capitalist rationalization marked by oligopolistic power,
bureaucratic controls, and technological innovation. Familiar meat industry
claims that the system is governed by "free markets" are nothing short of
laughable. Democratic accountability within the system is likewise a fic-

tion, as the industry has managed to colonize large sectors of both federal and state governments.

Meat and The Ecological Crisis

In the third decade of the twenty-first century, climate change has emerged as perhaps the most threatening of all global challenges, throwing into question the very prospect of human survival as we have experienced it across many centuries. This is one facet of the ecological crisis, which intersects with virtually every other problem that humanity now faces. While ecological decline has been visible for many decades, the crisis sharpened after the 1940s when a new era – alternatively known as the "Great Acceleration", "Great Disruption", or "Anthropocene" – emerged. Climate change is a product of historical conditions shaped by rampant economic growth, reckless urbanization, population surges, agribusiness horrors, and the ravages of fossil capitalism. The agribusiness and meat dimension is all-too-often overlooked in the developmental matrix.

Here we take for granted that global-warming estimates are based on well-established scientific evidence – that is, its general contours are no longer a matter worthy of debate. The U.N. sponsored International Panel on Climate Change (IPCC) has since the late 1980s issued five, well-documented reports, compiled from the research of thousands of scientists around the world, warning of environmental disaster as planetary warming proceeds steadily, year after year.[55] The IPCC warns that the current global economic trajectory will result in a non-livable planet in a matter of a few decades – a dystopic specter recognized by hundreds of independent environmentalists from Bill McKibben to James Hansen and Jane Goodall. Many believe the IPCC reports are actually too conservative, too lacking a sense of urgency. The more severe consequences of the global crisis – melting ice, severe weather episodes, resource shortages, food problems, etc. – could in fact be felt sooner than generally anticipated. Rapid and sustained capitalist growth throughout the postwar years, altering every part of the planet, is surely a central factor in this calculus; yet there are others: population growth, militarism and warfare, urban chaos, the global meat complex.

According to the reported scientific consensus, eight major signs of global warming are presently visible, each arguably worsening by the year: (1) diminishing arctic sea ice; (2) rapidly melting glaciers; (3) rising air temperatures over oceans; (4) elevating global sea levels; (5) increasing general humidity; (6) rising atmospheric temperatures; (7) warming oceans; and (8) declining snow covers.[56] Ocean heat has increased dramatically over just the past two decades, causing shrinkage in sea-ice areas by 5.4 percent and weakening ecosystems both within and near the oceans. Historical records show that sea levels have been steadily rising at rates of 0.1 inches per year since 1900, accelerating in the past two decades and threatening some coastal areas, public infrastructures, and fragile ecosystems. Rising planetary heat exacerbates these tendencies, the surface temperature of Earth having increased by nearly two degrees Fahrenheit during the past century. According to the National Aeronautical and Space Administration (NASA), the seven warmest years have been recorded since 2010, with 2016 the hottest, 2017 the third hottest, and 2018 the fourth hottest.[57] Such a lethal trajectory cannot be sustained for long, especially given that far more devastating consequences are sure to arrive in coming decades.

Global warming stems from the large-scale release of greenhouse emissions – mostly carbon dioxide (CO_2) methane (CH_4), and nitrous oxide (N_2O). Carbon amounts to roughly 70 percent of those harmful gases, having risen by 40 percent since the onset of the industrial revolution. Methane comprises nearly 25 percent of the total, having increased 150 percent the past few decades mainly owing to emissions from animal-foods production, its warming effects many times (some scientists say up to 30 times) greater than those of CO_2. The conventional view is that carbon is the predominant if not sole culprit, evident from a screening of Al Gore's documentaries *An Inconvenient Truth* and *Truth to Power*, though recent attention has also focused on the more potent methane that is largely associated with meat production. In *Comfortably Unaware*, Richard Oppenlander writes, referring in part to methane emissions: "While it's important to be aware of ... CO_2 emissions from cars and industry, the single most devastating factor that affects global warming and our environment is caused by what you eat."[58]

Greenhouse emissions work by trapping heat at alarming rates, and are the result of fossil-fuel use (coal, gas, oil) for energy, along with methane pollution from environmental release and livestock operations involving vast animal waste and effluence. Looking at absolute numbers, these warming sources steadily increase even while alternative (green) energy options represent a (slightly) larger percentage of ever-expanding world economic activity. (In the end *rates* of emission increase matter far less than total planetary numbers.) In 2015, the leading national source of greenhouse gases was China, with 22.7 percent of the total, followed by the U.S. (15.6%), European Union (8.7%) India, (5.7%), Russia (5.4%), and Japan (2.9 %).[59] With continued global economic growth, rapid population increase, widening auto use, and elevated animal-food consumption, those numbers can only worsen over time.[60]

Unless such trends are reversed quickly and radically, the planet is almost certainly headed for ecological catastrophe. While estimates naturally vary, the global food system could presently account for 30 percent of all greenhouse gases, with livestock being among the worst sources. To livestock can be added meat and dairy processing, transportation, and the entire McDonaldized fast-food sector. Smaller assessments of the meat complex to climate change (around 20 percent) calculated by the Worldwatch Institute, Meridian Institute, and some environmentalists, could turn out to be rather conservative.[61] Whatever the specific numbers, the growing threat to global sustainability has been routinely ignored by governments, the media, most scientists, and academics in relevant fields of study. Worldwide meat consumption has increased fivefold over the past five decades – rising nearly automatically with economic development – yet there is oddly little sense of concern in the public sphere.

According to IPCC reports, planetary air temperatures could rise nearly one degree Celsius by 2030, two degrees by 2065 and as much as seven degrees by 2090 – a horrifying scenario, to be sure. Food production (again, especially meat and dairy) contributes abundantly to this trend. Further, this same warming pattern – leading to rising sea levels along with cycles of droughts, floods, and harsh weather episodes – means that broad food availability will become ever more unpredictable and chaotic. As of 2020, weather anomalies around the globe had already exerted a disruptive influence.

The IPCC states that greenhouse emissions had increased more than 30 percent from 1990 to 2012 (from the 2013 report). This dramatic rise took place during a period of sustained economic and population growth, along with hugely elevated meat consumption, bringing new pressures to water resources, soil fertility, and cropland space. Meanwhile, an expanding meat complex was destroying forests in Brazil, Indonesia, Central America, and elsewhere, reducing an indispensable source of carbon absorption and oxygen release. Clearing forests (mostly for animal foods) accounts for more CO_2 than every truck, train, and bus in the world. Further, livestock and other animal systems involve using chemical fertilizers and pesticides which are responsible for at least two percent of all greenhouse emissions. Livestock alone contribute massively to global warming, not just from their encroachment on cropland and need for resources but from their waste and methane production. Highly industrialized nations (North America, Europe, Russia) followed closely by China, Brazil, and Argentina contribute most to this part of the carbon footprint.

Rising global population reinforces the escalating consumption of meat and dairy foods. Worldwide demand for meat alone is expected to increase by 50 percent by 2030, as more societies reach industrialized status where eating higher on the food chain is associated with better health. Of course, more animals necessitates larger feed operations (or CAFOs), along with more industrialized agriculture and processing systems that devour more land and water while adding to the carbon footprint.[62] In most countries, including the U.S., government efforts to regulate the meat complex for environmental purposes have been modest at best.

As increasing food production stimulates global warming, ecological deterioration in turn reverberates to materially weaken global food quality and availability. Here the ecological crisis enters an unfolding dialectic: the meat complex and the natural habitat dialectically impact each other on a steadily downward spiral, resulting in greater food scarcity, hunger, malnutrition, poverty, and social turmoil. Planetary warming, dramatic weather shifts, and more extreme climate episodes lie at the core of this Great Acceleration. Severe events – huge storms, floods, droughts, heat waves, etc. – have already hit many areas of the world: Australia, Russia, the Mideast, Amazon River Basin, several African countries, the U.S. Midwest, Mexico, and parts of China are among the worst cases. These can lead to widespread cropland destruct ion, soil erosion, extensive crop spoilage, economic ruin

of farmers, significant loss of life. With surface global temperatures sure to
rise across the twenty-first century, these trends will only sharply intensify.

As we have seen, the recent years have been among the hottest ever
recorded, weather patterns frequently oscillating from severe drought to
unseasonal flooding. The Houston flooding of summer 2017 was one of
the worst ever for a major city. After 2000, Australia struggled through
a decade of horrendous drought culminating in the record-breaking heat
wave of 2009 and followed by heavy rain and flooding across the country,
with great harm to farmers and the food economy in general. According
to respected climate scientists, extreme weather episodes will be a major
problem for Australia in coming decades; vast wildfires of 2019-20 have
been some of the worst in human history. The same could be said for Russia, where unusually high temperatures have triggered hundreds of wildfires
and decimated much of the country's wheat crop in recent years. Large sections of the U.S. – Midwest, Southwest, South, California – have endured
lengthy drought periods that, if persistent, could severely damage some of
the most important agricultural regions in the world.

Aside from climate-related episodes, the impact of the global ecological downturn on food systems extends to shrinking cropland, water
depletion, air, water, and soil pollution, rising sea levels, ocean acidification,
and accelerated deforestation. With larger populations to feed, expanding
cities, and elevated meat and dairy consumption, worldwide demand for
food of every sort is certain to skyrocket precisely when the global food
infrastructure faces new pressures and harsher limits. The crisis has already
laid waste to corn, soybean, rice, wheat and other crops in many parts of
the world – crops that in the U.S. and other big meat-consuming nations
are routinely turned into animal feed at rates exceeding 50 percent of the
yield.[63]

The IPCC and FAO expect rising challenges to a vulnerable food
system in coming decades, worsening over time, although global patterns
of production and consumption are even now unsustainable. The idea that
climate change might somehow have a positive impact on agricultural efficiency has been widely debunked, in part owing to what is known about the
meat complex. Recently for example, a scientific group published a 10-year
study of four large commodity crops – rice, soybeans, corn, wheat – under
global-warming conditions: heightened temperatures, more drought and

heat waves, rising carbon levels in the atmosphere.[64] They found that wheat and corn output declined by 5.5 percent and 3.8 percent, respectively – probably conservative findings relative to what can be anticipated going forward. Other research indicates that just a one-degree Celsius rise in average global temperature will significantly reduce corn yields across much of the world.[65]

When such projections are understood in worldwide terms – against the backdrop of rising population and elevated meat consumption – it is easy to see that agriculture in its present form will struggle to continue to feed the world, especially as the enormous stresses of climate change intensify. Here the Worldwatch Institute concludes: "The bottom line is that it is becoming much more difficult for the world's farmers to keep up with the world's rapidly growing demand for grain.... We are entering a time of chronic food scarcity, one that is leading to intense competition for control of land and water resources – in short, a new geopolitics of food."[66]

As that scenario unfolds, we can expect a cycle of socio-economic impacts – the uprooting and disbanding of entire communities or even regions, violent territorial clashes, mass migration, competition over land everywhere, and sharpening resource wars. It should be increasingly difficult to ignore the probability that a confluence of economic growth, ecological crisis, mounting food demand, and social turbulence will generate worldwide conditions for a descent into barbarism – a probability not so far into the future as commonly imagined. Already in 2007 and 2008 food shortages led to drastic increases in the cost of many basic products, forcing hundreds of millions of people into food scarcity, severe malnutrition, disease threats, and poverty. This resulted in food-related riots in more than 40 countries.

The natural habitat, less adaptable and resilient as time passes, is now fully out of balance with the voracious demands of agriculture and the food economy. Normalcy has been supplanted by flux, unpredictability, resource insecurity, and turmoil. Most crops and livestock are vulnerable as the Earth continues to heat, a condition exacerbated by depleted forests, oceans, problematic water sources, and melting ice. Brown warns: "The world has never faced such a predictably massive threat to food production as that posed by the melting mountains of glaciers of Asia."[67]

As indicators of climate change worsen, the consequences for agriculture and general food infrastructure will similarly mount – felt beyond the realm of food production as such. Millions of poor people worldwide depend on farming as livelihood, meaning that disruptions in the food complex will harm those with fewest resources. It follows that any far-reaching shocks to the global food supply will have disastrous effects, exacerbating already high levels of poverty, hunger, malnutrition, and displacement, especially in the poorest countries. Throughout the history of capitalism, populations subject to its domain have been accustomed to cycles of boom and decline, with economic downturns normally short-lived; crises were temporary. Moving into the new conjuncture of forces, however, the situation changes dramatically. Writes David Wallace-Wells, in *Uninhabitable Earth*: "We have gotten used to setbacks on our erratic march along the arc of economic history, but we know them as setbacks and expect elastic recoveries. What climate change has in store is not that kind of thing – not a Great Recession or a Great Depression but, in economic terms, a Great Dying."[68] That is a stark description of what will happen when we have moved past the Tipping Point.

The problem is that, over time, ecosystems have evolved in rough synchronicity with natural resources, climate patterns, and human needs, a dynamic now being threatened. By 2018 it had become evident that global warming posed a greater threat to food production than anyone imagined; even small increases in global mean temperatures can be disastrous. According to NASA, measurements rose nearly one degree Celsius from the 1950s to 2017, the second hottest year since 1880.[69] As temperatures climb – possibly reaching a few degrees higher by 2050 – the consequences for agriculture will then be cataclysmic, a prospect usually downplayed even by the IPCC as well as other environmental sources.

Also downplayed is the undeniable impact of population increases across the globe – a crucial element in the ecological crisis. Here Brown comments, in *World on the Edge*: "Population growth is as old as agriculture itself. But the world is now adding close to 80 million people per year. Even worse, the overwhelming majority of these people are being added in countries where cropland is scarce, soils are eroding, and irrigation wells are going dry. Even as we are multiplying in number, some three billion of us are trying to move up the food chain, consuming more grain-intensive livestock products. As incomes rise, actual grain consumption per person climbs from less than 400 pounds, as in India today, to roughly 1,600 pounds, as in the United States, where diets tend to be heavy with meat and dairy products."[70]

The historic 2015 Paris Climate Conference has, for the first time in more than two decades of UN gatherings, set universal standards and more-or-less binding agreements, the goal being to keep warming trends below two degrees Celsius into the foreseeable future by reducing the overall carbon footprint. Of the 190 countries meeting in Paris, 174 had signed the agreement by late 2018. The U.S. withdrew in 2017 after President Trump denounced the plan as a fetter on U.S. (and world) economic growth. Despite Paris having been widely celebrated as a "turning point" in the fight against climate change, the obligation of national parties turned out to be just loose and flexible enough to permit average temperatures to rise by two or even three degrees Celsius over the next few decades. That scenario, according to most environmental scientists, would spell further catastrophe for global food production, among other disastrous consequences.[71]

Many scientists and environmentalists have concluded that, even with some reduction of carbon emissions, the world can expect substantial and widespread increases historically unprecedented extreme events, not to mention severe agricultural crises. Indeed, these scenarios are already visible. As worldwide temperatures rise, the far greater likelihood of extremely wet weather – like that encountered with Hurricane Harvey in 2017 – could lead to massive flooding episodes. Some parts of the world will encounter dangerously wet conditions as other parts face increased heat and droughts. In fact, between 70 and 90 percent of the planet is already beginning to experience one extreme or the other, neither of which is good for agriculture. As global warming continues along its deadly path, matters worsen to varying degrees: scattered regions of North America, Europe, Asia, and Australia can expect to see record temperatures combined with prospects for an increase in devasting weather episodes. Areas where food production has for decades or centuries been adequate to feed large populations could now enter into precipitous decline, no longer agriculturally sustainable.[72]

A rise of average global temperatures by at least two degrees Celsius – the probable outcome whatever the fate of the Paris accords – will be especially calamitous for biological diversity. Scientist Rachel Warren and associates, reporting in the journal *Science*, found that 18 percent of insects,

16 percent of plants, and eight percent of vertebrates will lose more than half their geographical range once the temperature reaches two degrees higher than before the industrial revolution.[73] Worse, should temperatures warm by three degrees Celsius (a conceivable scenario by 2050, or sooner), then 49 percent of insects, 44 percent of plants, and 26 percent of vertebrates would lose more than half their geographical range. The very survival of these species would be placed at extreme risk. What this portends for world ecosystems – including food systems – is beyond frightening.

The Paris climate pact, like similar international efforts going back to the U.N.-sponsored global summit at Rio in 1992, falls short in terms of goals, mechanisms, and logistics. Its elevated aspirations and claims are advanced, unfortunately, in a world bound to contradict those aspirations and claims. In the end, the agreement is neither universal nor binding enough to reduce greenhouse emissions at levels required to meet stated goals. More problematic yet, there is little in the accord that takes into account fatal obstacles to ecological rationality: transnational corporate interests, geopolitical conflict, and media systems wedded to perpetual economic growth, fossil-fuel exploitation, growing consumer demand, and unsustainable food complexes. What little the Paris documents have to say about the dysfunctions of the animal-based food economy is hardly inspiring.

For Paris to be an historical "turning point", there would have to be better recognition that inherited models of economic development are obsolete, needing to be jettisoned in favor of ecologically sustainable alternatives. Yet there is no such recognition. As Steffen Böhm observes: "The simple truth is that the Paris agreement is blind to the fundamental, structured problems that prevent us from decarbonizing our economies to the radical extent needed."[74] What Böhm presumably has in mind is a full break with fossil-fuel capitalism, a system that has powered industrialism for more than two centuries. The Paris signatories appear to believe that a combination of green technologies and enlightened market mechanisms will serve to at least slow the downward spiral of climate change. But preponderant evidence suggests that capitalism in any guise – with its growth-driven, profit-oriented, nature-destroying logic – is incompatible with transition to an ecologically-sustainable society. Put differently, huge transnational corporations worth trillions of dollars in revenue – and more trillions of dollars invested in fossil fuels – can hardly be expected to relinquish their hold over the world economy.

This stubborn fact of life is nowhere more visible than in a food sector dominated by agribusiness, meat, and dairy interests, including a McDonaldized fast-food complex that shows no signs of weakening even as more nations develop and move up the food chain – a trajectory barely acknowledged by the Paris organizers. At the same time, we face the limits of a strictly carbon discourse of the sort that defines the Paris accords. Recommendations there and elsewhere often dwell on carbon reductions through raising fuel-economy standards, capping emissions from power plants, and expanding green energy sources for cars and appliances. The problem here resides in what is being ignored: the growth-economy itself, shrinkage of natural resources, and devastating consequences of how societies produce and consume food.

At this point we encounter the food dilemma: as climate change sharpens, the worldwide intake of animal products expands steadily and alarmingly, with no end in sight. Highest consumption levels are now most visible in North America, Europe, China, and a few other industrialized countries, but in coming decades several other nations will enter that special club: Brazil, Argentina, Mexico, Indonesia, South Korea among them. As societies become more economically developed, large-scale shifts toward meat and dairy consumption are eminently predictable, costly as that is. While energy systems, the transport sector, industry, and buildings are the usual fixation of governments, businesses, and environmental groups looking to reduce carbon emissions, the equally significant role of food production is typically downplayed or ignored.

A 2006 FAO report titled "Livestock's Long Shadow" calculated that the massive livestock sector is responsible for more greenhouse emissions than the entire global transport footprint – that is, roughly 20 percent of the total. That amount was expected to rise with the steady growth of population, economies, and meat consumption. It follows that the increased carbon footprint of animal foods would more than negate efforts to reduce gases from electricity, transportation, and kindred sectors.[75]

In 2008, IPCC Chair Dr. Rajendra Pachauri called for a worldwide decrease in meat consumption to fight global warming, though levels of decrease were never specified. (fn) At the same time, James Hansen, prominent scientific advocate of urgent measures to reverse the crisis, told an interviewer that "... if you eat further down on the food chain, rather than animals, which have produced many greenhouse gases and used much energy in the process of growing that meat, you can make a bigger contribution in that way than just about anything. So that, in terms of individual action, is perhaps the best thing you can do."[76]

Responding to the 2006 FAO conclusions and other (relatively few) reports on the meat economy, two researchers from the World Bank – Robert Goodland and Jeff Anhang – argued the FAO numbers were rather conservative, that in fact animal products (notably livestock) might contribute as much as *half* of all greenhouse emissions.[77] One crucial point, according to the authors, was that the FAO drastically under-reported the number of food animals worldwide and their impact in terms of methane pollution. Thus, FAO arrived at its 20 percent level on a very low total of 21.7 billion animals, whereas even in 2002 rough estimates were closer to 50 million, taking into account all the cattle, sheep, goats, horses, pigs, and poultry raised for meat. (By 2018 that figure reached an estimated 70 billion.) Moreover, the FAO overlooked the especially potent effects of methane, nearly 40 percent of which comes from livestock activity: the methane impact, Goodland and Anhang conclude, rises to at least 22 percent of total carbon emissions.[78]

From all indications, moreover, the global methane imprint has expanded dramatically the past two decades as meat and dairy consumption – combined with a surging livestock population – has steadily increased, with little sign of leveling off presently visible. This rise in methane levels alone (a factor often significantly downplayed) could seriously impede reaching even modest targets for reducing carbon footprint set at Paris.

Goodland and Anhang argue that the FAO report – along with similar commentary on the animal-foods carbon footprint – downplays key factors related to livestock: widespread clearing of land, expansion of grain harvests to feed animals, deforestation, profligate water use, polluted rivers, lakes, and oceans. There are also carbon and other emissions from wasteful processing, transporting, and consumption of meat and dairy products.[79] Even if, as an army of critics maintain, the Goodland/Anhang finding that the global meat complex produces 51 percent of greenhouse emissions is vastly exaggerated (amounting instead to somewhere between 20 and 30 percent), the situation is nonetheless alarming: with population growth, rising meat consumption, and increasing livestock in a world of finite resources, the crisis is destined to spiral out of control.

Projections based on computer-modelling vary somewhat when it comes to atmospheric warming, but even slight increases (say, two degrees Celsius) can be disastrous for global agriculture. The combined effects of warming, economic and population growth, resource shrinkage, declining arable land, water shortages, and animal-based agriculture will be especially catastrophic, ensuring perpetual and severe food crisis. Estimates indicate that by 2040, if not sooner, the planet will require *double* the food output to feed a much-larger population. Should the world experience increasing droughts – and that is already happening – the basic grain yield could shrink by as much as 20 percent. Many parts of the world can be expected to suffer extreme drought: China, Russia, India, the Middle East, North Africa, Mexico, even the United States. The capacity of existing main grain exporters will be largely nullified, meaning high levels of poverty and starvation for regions experiencing a deficit.

Should the world population reach nine billion or more by 2050, which seems probable, strains placed on global food production will be unbearable. That will be more emphatically the case should more nations move up the food chain, as expected. Grain availability will become a severe, likely unsolvable, challenge. In *Full Planet, Empty Plates,* Brown writes: "On the supply side of the food equation, we face several challenges, including stabilizing climate, raising water productivity, and conserving soil…. It will take a hug cut in carbon emissions, some 80 percent within a decade, to give us a chance of avoiding the worst consequences of climate change. This means a wholesale restructuring of the world energy economy."[80] It would also presumably mean vast changes to world agriculture, including a drastic shift from animal-based to plant-based systems of production.

If the globe does not see a sharp reduction in meat and dairy consumption during the next decade or so, the global food deficit will inevitably result in economic, social, and probably political chaos. Yet there are few efforts to reverse this downward spiral – virtually nothing in terms of social policy for any of the leading industrialized societies. This is scarcely a matter of "denialism", as in resistance to warnings about the threat of climate change; looming catastrophe seems almost more self-inflicted. Here David

Wallace-Wells laments: "A state of half-ignorance and half-indifference is a much more pervasive climate sickness than true denial or true fatalism."[81]

The global crisis poses the greatest threat to the food supply, especially in poorer areas of the world. According to a 2018 FAO report, the number of chronically hungry people had reached 815,000 – a total sure to increase unless prevailing developmental trends are quickly reversed.[82] An estimated 20 million people, mostly children, die yearly from hunger and its effects. While more than enough grain is harvested today to feed the world population, over 70 percent of U.S. grain and nearly 40 percent worldwide is fed to animals for meat production.[83] More alarming yet, a majority of the global population (several billion) will live in regions facing severe water shortages by 2030, if not sooner. For the corporate system to continuously expand its wasteful and destructive meat regime under present conditions is sheer insanity.

The Plague of Speciesism

It would be short-sighted to explore the ecological (and food) crisis without addressing the problem of speciesism – the ideology underlying the human exploitation of animals. It is an outlook deeply rooted in a range of political, religious, philosophical, and cultural traditions, so taken for granted in most societies that debate on the topic remains firmly taboo. Future efforts to reduce human consumption of meat face the challenge of overturning speciesism, one of the most deeply entrenched human beliefs.

The first tenet of speciesism is that it extends moral permission to humans to objectify, commodify, exploit, and do great harm other beings, with impunity. That animals might possess intricate and worthwhile lives – or experience pain and suffering – is invariably dismissed as a topic of discussion. Writes Jeffrey Moussaieff Masson in *When Elephants Weep*: "Humans often behave if something like us is more worthy of respect than something not like us. Racism can partly be described, if not explained, in this way. Men treat other men better than they treat women, based in part on their views that women are not like them. Many of these so-called differences are disguises for whatever a dominant power can impose. The basic idea seems to be that if something does not feel pain in the way a human feels pain, it is permissible to hurt it."[84]

We do, in fact, have abundant evidence that non-human beings can suffer egregiously in many ways from the actions of human beings, from deprivation to isolation, injury, torture, and of course, destruction. Humans have forever hunted, attacked, experimented upon, incarcerated, and eaten other sentient beings as a matter of routine, horrors carried out without much thought or guilt. Time-honored flimsy justifications for such practices, however, can no longer be taken seriously, even as the practices continue as if technologically or psychologically predetermined. Jane Goodall has shown that chimpanzees differ genetically from *Homo Sapiens* by less than one percent, possessing speech abilities, a social existence, and some intellectual acumen.[85] Masson has arrived at precisely the same conclusion for elephants that, like most animals, also have the potential to connect emotionally and socially with humans.

Peter Singer, in his classic *Animal Liberation*, argued several decades ago that other sentient beings ought to receive equal consideration of interests when it comes to matters of pain and suffering. Drawing from the utilitarianism of Jeremy Bentham, Singer wrote that "we need to consider our attitudes from the point of view of those who suffer by them, and by the practices that follow from them", adding that "practices that were previously regarded as natural and inevitable come to be seen as the result of an unjustifiable prejudice."[86] Such an imperative, even today, seems more removed from the human experience than it ought to be, after decades of powerful supportive argumentation.

When it comes to meat and the great harm it does not only to the environment but to human health and billions of animals each year, personal habits remain so firmly ingrained as to appear fixed, unchangeable. Facing the difficulty of change, Singer asks: "Habits not only of diet but also of thought and language must be challenged and altered. Habits of thought lead us to brush aside descriptions of cruelty to animals as emotional... (or) a problem so trivial in comparison to the problems of human beings that no sensible person could give it time and attention."[87] This know-nothing mentality, it should be emphasized, exists across the ideological spectrum. For most humans on the planet it would seem the problem of a meat-centered diet is remote, out of sight, too daunting to even comprehend. If animals matter at all, such concerns end up deflected, emptied of moral (or ecological) relevance. Here Singer comments: "If animals are no longer quite outside the moral sphere, they are still in a special section near the outer rim. Their interests are allowed to count only when they do not clash with human interests. If there is a clash – even a clash between the life of a non-human animal and the gastronomic preference of a human being – the interests of the nonhuman are disregarded."[88]

One common psychological maneuver in the history of speciesism is the belief that nonhumans live a "savage" existence, meaning they are unworthy of moral consideration. Humans prefer to see themselves as unique, infinitely superior to others, Singer noting: "While we overlook our own savagery, we exaggerate that of other animals." He adds: "Humans kill other animals for sport, to satisfy their curiosity, to beautify their bodies, and to please their palates. Human beings also kill members of their own species for greed or power. Moreover, humans are not content with mere killing. Throughout history, they have shown a tendency to torment and torture both their fellow humans and their fellow animals before putting them to death. No other animal shows much interest in doing this."[89]

Singer's point is that the very sentience of animals deserves moral consideration. While this critical outlook is dismissed through sheer habit and ignorance, it is similarly opposed by such vested interests as agribusiness, multinational corporations, the McDonalds food sector, the medical complex, and Big Pharma. These interests spend billions of dollars to keep both the meat complex and exploitation of animals proceeding at full speed.

After Singer, Tom Regan in *The Case for Animal Rights*, argues for animal priorities on grounds that nonhumans are to be viewed as subjects of a conscious (and social) existence. The same animals that are routinely objectified, exploited, and killed have their own life-experiences and needs, a phenomenon understood by pet owners but rarely extended to other animals possessing the same degree of subjectivity. Insofar as that is true, then human beings clearly have no ethical justification for annihilating that subjectivity as they mindlessly do, often just for sport. If this is true – and Regan emphasizes the superiority of a rights perspective over Singer's utilitarianism – then, no matter what the prevailing norms, vegetarianism must be considered an imperative of daily life. Writes Regan: "Since this [meat] industry routinely violates the rights of these animals ... it is wrong to purchase its products. That is why, on the rights view, vegetarianism is morally obligatory, and why, on that view, we should not be satisfied with anything less than the total dissolution of commercial animal agriculture as we know it, whether modern factory farms or otherwise."[90]

Here Masson's observation seems especially salient: "It is clear that animals form lasting relationships, are frightened of being hunted, have a horror of dismemberment, wish they were back in the safety of their den, despair for their mates, look out for and protect their children whom they love."[91] In his pathbreaking book *The Inner Life of Animals,* Peter Wohlleben explores the wide range of emotions and experiences shared by humans and other animals: intelligence, communications, fear, loss, empathy, grief, desire, and obviously pain and suffering. He writes: "... if researchers know so much about the intelligence of pigs, why isn't the image of the smart pig publicized more? I suspect it has to do with eating pork. If people knew what kind of an animal they had on their plate, many would completely lose their appetite. We already know this from primates: could any of us eat an ape?"[92]

Against this backdrop, as the vast majority of people on Earth non-chalantly consume huge quantities of meat, we see parallels with the wide-spread denial of global warming. The ruling interests particularly want to cling to an undisturbed business-as-usual which, after all, is essential to their drive toward accumulated wealth and power. After describing climate change as something of a "hoax" perpetuated by China, Donald Trump was taken to task by environmentalists as a backward denier – before he withdrew the U.S from the Paris accords. Within months, however, Trump's move was scarcely noticed in a setting where the mentality of denialism remains persuasive across the vast range of human practices detrimental to the natural habitat and, within it, most forms of nonhuman life.

What is true for climate-change delusions extends more egregiously into the arena of meat production and consumption – just one area, after all, of extreme cruelty toward animals. The phenomenon of denial in this case, however, more commonly takes the form of silence as opposed to political outbursts against "mass hysteria" or well-funded "research" to debunk global warming. It turns out that both modes of psychological escape are thoroughly intertwined. In fact, meat consumption and the acceleration of global warming move apace, fully in tandem. Environmentalists justifiably disturbed by the refusal to accept ecological reality generally fail to extend their outrage to the problem of speciesism, the meat nightmare, and destructive agricultural practices. It might not be too farfetched, however, to suggest that the ecological threat can be reversed only when the plague of speciesism is finally overcome.

Speciesism lies at the center of a long-held ethos of domination that humans exert over the natural habitat – an ethos shared by liberals, conservatives, socialists, and others content with the status quo. It is simultaneously embedded in a culture of hunting, eating, medical research, and otherwise conducting warfare against non-human nature. It is logically connected to the process of capitalist rationalization, with its fetishism of science, technology, and commodification of everything. In that way, among others, speciesism helps frame the modern crisis, intersecting as it does with other modes of domination. It is impossible to speak of the "domination of nature", from whatever vantage-point, without referring to the barbaric legacy of speciesism. The fact that this legacy has been so fully accepted and legitimated across centuries lends no convincing rationale to its perpetuation, any more than it would for racism, ethnocentrism, or ultra-nationalism.

If humans have enslaved, exploited, tortured, and killed animals throughout history, routinely and wantonly, the bulk of these activities have been carried out within modern economic systems, replete with sophisticated technology. In recent times, of course, that order has been mostly capitalist where development involves perpetual domination and violence, where the social and natural worlds are fully open for exploitation. In this context John Sanbonmatsu appropriately refers to speciesism as a "mode of production."[93] As such, it is embedded in forms of institutionalized violence far more pervasive today than at any point in history.

If, as Sanbonmatsu argues, speciesism is a mode of production, "… it is not a fixed ideology or an unchanging essence but rather a complex, dynamic, expansive system that is materially and ideologically implicated in capitalism as such."[94] With deadly efficiency, it intersects with the spread of technological rationality, whether in factory farming, slaughterhouses, the fast food system, gun culture, or military warfare. Speciesism allows for the mass killing of nonhumans to be justified and routinized, mostly out of ordinary sight. It is normalized and sometimes celebrated within media culture, advertising, lobbying, scientific research, and academic work, typically without provoking outrage. Whether in the context of capitalism or other power structures, speciesism helps legitimate a natural hierarchy cutting across class, racial, gender, cultural, national, and other sources of conflict. Perhaps most of all, it habituates populations to extreme cruelty and violence.

Human savagery directed at animals – indeed at the entire natural habitat – is facilitated not only by stubborn denial of everyday horrors but by narratives of "progress" inherited from Enlightenment rationality. Here both speciesism and the larger crisis are endemic to modernity, capitalist or otherwise. This same motif permeates the classic *Dialectic of Enlightenment*, written several decades ago by Theodor Adorno and Max Horkheimer, who write: "In this world divested of illusion in which men, following the loss of reflection, have again become the cleverest of animals and are busy enslaving the rest of the universe (assuming always that they do not tear themselves to pieces), respect for animals is regarded as no longer sentimental but as a betrayal of progress."[95]

Adorno and Horkheimer argue that "... enlightenment is as totalitarian as any system", the basis of both psychological alienation and generalized social domination that seamlessly extends to the natural habitat."[96] The much-discussed "domination of nature" that finds its way into some environmental thinking is therefore part of the general Enlightenment project that, in the name of freedom and abundance, generates ever-more rationalized systems of violence and control. Thus: "The paradoxical nature of faith ultimately degenerates into a swindle and become the myth of the twentieth century; and its irrationality turns into an instrument of rational administration by the wholly enlightened as they steer society toward barbarism."[97] The authors could not be more explicit in their denunciation of speciesism as a manifestation of modern barbarism, reflected in human efforts to colonize every sphere of the planet.

The disastrous effects of the meat complex for the global environment, including natural resources, forests, and oceans – not to mention human health – has been abundantly evident for many decades, revealed by a series of IPCC documents, extensive scholarship, even media reports. Colin Campbell's epic work, *The China Study*, the largest comparative analysis of food and diet ever undertaken, shows conclusively the deleterious effects of meat and dairy consumption on humans relative to plant-based diets.[98] Less evident is the unfathomable harm done to animals caught up on the corporate meat machine, first documented by Upton Sinclair in *The Jungle* more than a century ago and more recently by John Robbins and others.[99] Little critical thinking is required to see the deep interconnectedness of these issues and their direct relation to the global ecological crisis.

When it comes to speciesism and its obvious underpinning of the crisis, however, critical thinking easily and conveniently vanishes across the political spectrum. Historically, leftist political opposition – socialism, anarchism, Communism – was expected to challenge the ruling interests in pursuit of radical change. With the modern crisis fueled by global corporate power, however, such opposition has been compromised and weakened: when it comes to speciesism leftists have been rather silent, their denialism often more fervent than that of the right.

The sad truth is that the political left, with few exceptions, has always viewed human violence toward animals with indifference or outright approval.[100] Such violence is experienced as distant and trivial in a world burdened with more serious (human) problems – though such crude and self-serving dualism (inherited in part from Marxism) is nowadays clearly more difficult to sustain. European leftist politics has especially viewed animal concerns as a big distraction, vegetarianism a practice associated with extremists and eccentrics.[101] Others, within and outside Marxism, have framed any discussion of speciesism as a primitive attack on science, technology, and modernity – that is, on the Enlightenment. In the end, the leftist consensus has been that animals can (and should) be useful for whatever purposes humans deem profitable or enjoyable.

This paucity of critical thinking, while disturbing, further amounts to an ideological obstacle in facing the ecological crisis. Refusal to consider the vast consequences of the corporate meat complex is one of the great political tragedies of the modern period. What is at once a theoretical failure is simultaneously a measure of moral obtuseness and *political* futility. For leftist politics today it seems that rational, universal ideals have strict limits, compromised by an uncritical dogmatism of the sort usually associated with rightwing ideology. Moreover, where leftist thinking has been defined as "scientific" – true for parts of the Marxist tradition – this conceptual (and ethical) deficit only worsens.

In this vein, Sanbonmatsu observes that, "Like other scientific thinkers of his time ... Marx did not try to come to terms with the consciousness of other beings. For him, nature – including other animals – was indistinguishable from 'mans's body' – hence a resource for humans to develop and control as a means to their own self-flourishing."[102] Here both Marx and Engels held to a view of natural relations that revolved around a harsh dualism bifurcating human and animal existence consistent with traditional anthropocentrism. Humans were in many ways cut off from nature, above their surrounding ecology – living a qualitatively different existence than nonhuman animals. On this crucial point the Marxist tradition fits squarely within dominant strains of Western thought, both religious and philosophical. "But while such a dualism was relatively uncontroversial a century and a half ago," notes Sanbonmatsu, "it is no longer scientifically credible today. After nearly five centuries of portraying other animals as little more than automata ... modern science is at least confirming what most ordinary human beings have known for millennia – namely, that other animals feel and think and experience the world."[103]

This emphatically one-dimensional view of "nature" in Marx and Engels should be enough to dispel fanciful notions of an "ecological Marxism" that some hope will revitalize contemporary leftist politics. There is nothing in their work – or that of more recent Marxists – to even remotely suggest valuation of nonhuman nature, or of animal life. In *Natural Relations*, Ted Benton shows that a profound dualism opposing human and nonhuman species permeates Marx's own work from start to finish.[104] Elsewhere, Benton writes: "Marx's attribution to animals of a fixed and standardized mode of activity in relation to nature and its apparent failure to recognize in any significant way the social life of nonhuman animals are both at work (in his writings)".[105] In other words, we encounter in the Marxist tradition a harsh variant of speciesism that unfortunately persists throughout leftist politics to this day. This is no simple theoretical flaw or oversight but is endemic to the theoretical structure. Without confronting (and transcending) such ideological myopia, any hope of reversing the ecological crisis will be short-circuited.

What the struggle against speciesism anticipates is a complex, multifaceted, dialectical view of natural relations based on a continuum from human to nonhuman species already implicit in Darwinian biology. That suggests that modernity as such requires further deconstruction insofar as the interwoven problems of anthropocentrism, speciesism, and instrumental rationality amount to formidable barriers to any future ecological politics. Benton adds: "If we recognize the continuities between humans and other species in our social and psychological as well as organic needs, then the ethical case for transformation of those relations is clear: liberation of nonhuman animals as well as full human emancipation require it ... It is evil to continue to treat them merely as instruments or resources to be exploited for specifically human purposes."[106]

2

The Road to Disaster

As we enter the third decade of the twenty-first century, the world faces mounting scarcity – accelerated depletion of natural resources that will confront humanity with a choice between radical change and business-as-usual. The existing corporate-state model of continuous and expanded growth is doomed to fail, probably sooner than we might want to contemplate. That system, now centered in North America and Europe but spreading across Asia and Latin America, will bring increasing harm to the global natural habitat, while its elites scurry for new markets, profits, and natural resources with few material, ethical, or environmental constraints. In its increasingly unsustainable mode of production and consumption, neoliberal corporate globalization is headed for ruin and collapse, its multiple contradictions increasingly visible for all to see. Unfortunately, effective political opposition to the power structure that exercises control over this system remains marginal at present.

This dystopic picture of seemingly imminent ecological collapse can be situated partly within the threat of global warming, one result of what has been called "fossil capital".[107] Elevated carbon emissions come from increasing reliance on coal, natural gas, and oil as energy sources for industry, commerce, extraction, transportation, and agriculture. But that is hardly the full story: if the planet is approaching its natural limits, close to the famous "tipping point", the problem nowadays is a matter of shrinking natural resources in a broader context of population growth, urbanization, geopolitical conflict, and unsustainable modes of food consumption, as well as climate change. Indeed, these factors are deeply and organically interconnected, all the more so as the ecological crisis worsens. The mounting threat to vital resources – to cropland, topsoil, water, forests, oceans – cannot be understood strictly as a function of global warming insofar as that is simultaneously cause and effect of the crisis.

The extreme global pressures on natural resources is such that national governments, as well as international organizations, lack the power to effectively intervene. As the planet adds on average roughly 85 billion people yearly – while economic development is associated with vastly elevated meat and dairy consumption – the path to disaster is now hastened by intensifying competition for waning resources, above all food and water. Under these circumstances, human survival will depend on new political departures embedded in radically alternative forms of economic and cultural life. An ecological politics will be needed to reverse the crisis and lead the planet toward full sustainability.

A World of Shrinking Resources

As public fixation on the threat of global warming understandably widens, attention to other facets of the modern crisis is all too often left out of the equation. Nowhere is this void more obvious than in the threat of natural-resource depletion – perhaps most glaring when it comes to the problem of food. Today, in nation after nation, population increase accompanies heightened levels of resource-intensive, wasteful, and destructive consumption of animal products.

By 2030 the planet will face the insurmountable challenge of feeding nine billion people, a total expected to reach as many as ten billion by 2050. Within the coming decade an estimated five billion people will be eating high on the food chain – approximating the advanced industrial pattern of today – with its accelerated pressure on cropland, water, forests, oceans, and other precious resources. As population inexorably expands yearly, and while dozens of congested world cities far exceed their infrastructural limits, the food supply cannot possibly match elevated demands. Severe food shortages have already impacted nearly a billion people, with no sign that matters will improve. Asian countries (China, South Korea, Vietnam, Thailand, Indonesia) figure to be especially impacted in coming years, as these countries experience vast increases in meat and dairy consumption.

Global population has increased by more than 60 percent since the 1980s, while growth in food production has not exceeded 20 percent. Improvements in agricultural productivity have reached limits at a time when available cropland, fertile soil, and water resources are shrinking, exacerbated by climate change. At present, the livestock system and its sprawling infrastructure take up more than 30 percent of usable global land – and that expanse, though even now unsustainable, increases substantially year by year. (Urbanization also devours more arable land, a problem addressed in the next section.) Given such a trajectory, in Lester Brown's words, "… the number of people trapped by hydrological poverty and hunger will almost certainly grow, threatening food security, economic progress, and political stability."[108] In this context our very positive understanding of "economic progress" is sure to be thrown into serious doubt.

The international data on food consumption is hardly reassuring. According to FAO research, world per capital overall meat intake stood at 24.2 kilograms in 1965, then skyrocketed to 34.6 kilos in 1995 and 41.3 kilos in 2015 – a roughly 70 percent increase over that time span. By 2030 that level is projected to reach 45.3 kilos per capita. More alarmingly, those numbers are far higher for the industrialized nations: from 61.5 in 1965 to 86.2 in 1995 and then to 95.7 in 2015, that is, easily more than *double* the world average and (in 2015) more than *triple* that of developing nations selected for the report. For industrialized countries (including several new entries), the per-capita consumption for 2030 is expected to reach about 100 kilos.[109] Although global averages for beef have leveled off since 1965 – from 10 kilos to an expected 10.6 kilos in 2030, the numbers for poultry (1.2 kilos in 1965 to 10.5 kilos in 2015) and pork (9.1 kilos to 15.3 kilos) have risen dramatically.[110]

The increase in overall global dairy consumption has been sustained across the same period, but at smaller rates: from 74 kilos per capita in 1965 to 83 kilos in 2015, projected to reach 90 kilos by 2030.[111] In 2015, dairy intake in the leading industrial societies quadrupled that of the less developed nations. By 2030, of course, the ranks of the former will have proliferated significantly, aggravating the challenge to planetary food supplies as well as general ecological sustainability. According to FAO data, worldwide dairy intake has grown by an average of four percent yearly for the past several decades – slightly behind meat at roughly six percent. The 2030 projections for both will fall short of those increases, but overall global consumption if expected rates hold will be catastrophic for both resource utilization and global warming.

Given this picture, it is presently difficult to imagine how ecological sustainability can be reached any time in the near future. By 2017, more than 70 billion farm animals were being raised and processed at any given time for sprawling meat and dairy complexes. Fully one-third of all arable land was given over to livestock – a reality bound to worsen as the animal-foods industry expands. Nearly 50 percent of the world's grain goes to livestock at a time of mounting food insecurity for many poorer societies. In countries with the most meat- and dairy-intensive diets, water diverted to livestock and the feed required can increase to more than 70 percent. The U.S. has long occupied the very apex of this food pyramid: the average American, in 2015, consumed 1,140 pounds of grain each year, four-fifths indirectly through meat, milk, and eggs consumption – four times that of India. The U.S. intake of meat alone – 210 pounds yearly per capita – contributes hugely to the crisis, yet that is the very model of "prosperity" embraced by most developing nations.[112]

The consequences of such dietary patterns – generally overlooked or downplayed by environmentalists, including those of the left – are multiple, even leaving aside their impact on climate change. Among these, water (used intensively across the animal-foods complex) stands out as the most far-reaching, and urgent. By 2017 the planet was maintaining, or trying to maintain, nearly one billion acres of land irrigated by water, and those levels would only increase.

Multiple challenges – from population to food, land, natural resources, global warming, human health, and animal welfare, intersect with the deepening crisis. From this standpoint, it is a mistake to focus on global warming alone, as is nowadays common. At present many urban centers across the world, and many nations, face severe water shortages. One problem here is that, with high levels of meat production combined with sporadic rain patterns, many regions must rely on underground water sources as aquifers are being depleted, wells run dry, and water tables recede. Stressed regions can be found in China, India, and Mexico, as well as in developing countries in the Middle East and Africa. These areas must deal with population pressures along with shifting food preferences toward meat and dairy. Confronting water shortages and expanded food requirements, these areas are forced to borrow extensively from the future – already untenable where conditions are becoming drier.

Rapid urbanization, moreover, refocuses this challenge in the struggle among rival sectors for shrinking natural resources. As Brown writes in *Full Planet, Empty Plates:* "In the competition for water between farmers on the one hand and cities and industry on the other, the economics do not favor agriculture."[113] This is bound to lead to catastrophe for food supplies in a world already faced with warmer temperatures, droughts, erratic rainfall, and rising aridity. Brown adds: "We live in a world where more than half the people live in countries with food bubbles based on over-pumping. The question for each of these countries is not whether its bubble will burst, but when."[114]

In such nations as Syria, Israel, Afghanistan, Pakistan, Yemen, Saudi Arabia, and Ethiopia this predicament is reaching the tipping point. Aquifers and wells are severely over-pumped, yet prospects for refilling such crucial water sources deteriorate yearly, undermining agriculture. As this occurs, governments turn increasingly to imports of grain and other foodstuffs – a "solution" that itself cannot be much longer tolerable. This is especially true for a country like Mexico, a very dry, populous region with 120 million people, with a vast meat complex where water demands mean pumping already exhausted aquifers and wells. Mexico City, a sprawling urban center of 25 million people, provides a case study in contemporary food and water challenges.

At present more than one billion people live in areas that already face severe water shortages – a number destined to rise as per-capita water availability declines. It is worth considering that 70 percent of the world's fresh water is now used for agriculture, compared to 20 percent for industry and ten percent for residential demands. Counted among those agricultural needs is no less than *half* of all water going to livestock and grain harvests for animal feed. How long can this state of affairs persist before economic collapse and social upheaval begin to pervade the global landscape?

The stubborn reality here is that animal-based food production requires up to 75 trillion gallons of water yearly, rendering it the main source of water scarcity – more than personal waste, more than recurrent droughts, more than global warming, more than water pollution (itself overwhelmingly caused by animal wastes). To produce simply one pound of beef requires 2500 gallons of water. The numbers for one gallon of milk are 1000 gallons of water, with one pound of cheese consuming 900 gallons and one pound of eggs nearly 500 gallons.[115] The corporate meat complex proceeds as if water remains the inexhaustible natural resource it has been for millennia, but of course that is a sad delusion. Alternative paths do exist, as reflected in some remarkable statistics: the average meat-consuming American requires about 4200 gallons of scarce water daily, compared with just 300 gallons for the typical vegan.[116] How such evidence can be so consistently ignored or dismissed raises urgent questions more fully explored in later chapters.

With rising economic and population growth, warming of the atmosphere, and drying up of fresh-water sources, global demand figures to outstrip global supply in 2030 by at least 40 percent. Water shortages will hit such regions as the Middle East, North Africa, and Asia hardest, just where rise in population is expected to be highest. Thus, half of India will face dire water problems, with China, Ethiopia, Egypt, Pakistan, and Iran not far behind. Large cities will especially face water crises, impacting not only direct usage but food production. In 2019, 14 of the world's largest 20 cities were already facing unprecedented water shortages, with no sign of any turnaround. Atmospheric warming is destined to only worsen matters.

Beyond water, the issue of disappearing global cropland is probably the most crucial for food production, though the two (water and cropland) are closely interwoven. If world population is increased by 85 million yearly and urbanization advances more rapidly than ever – and if climate change moves along a harmful trajectory – then the planet indeed faces a perilous downward slide. For many centuries, humans have benefited from readily available cropland, needed to feed comparatively small populations, but that situation has come to a resounding end. As megacities encroach on surrounding land, we encounter a mixture of conditions: environmental deterioration, rising aridity, increased livestock populations, greater diversion of grains to feed animals, proliferation of toxic wastes, soil depletion from overuse – all at a time when tens of millions more people yearly are making new demands on food supplies. To say this developmental model is both destructive and unsustainable is an extreme understatement. The reality is that more food will have to be produced on a rapidly shrinking agricultural base. So long as all of these factors converge, the world faces mounting

shortages, malnutrition, starvation, and, ultimately, social and psychological chaos. Writes Michael Klare: "But no matter how much corporate or
government officials might wish to deny it, there are not nearly enough
nonrenewable resources on the planet to perpetually satisfy the growing
needs of a ballooning world population; what's more, existing modes of
production are casing unacceptable damage to the global environment."[117]

At present the world is losing at least one quarter of its available
cropland resulting from a disastrous combination of factors mentioned
above. Neither technological nor "market" solutions will be of much help,
especially given expanding population. Livestock grazing is perhaps the
leading factor, and the global totals of cows, sheep, pigs, and other food
animals (roughly 70 billion in 2018) is projected to increase well into the
future. Historically all societies have moved upward on the food chain as
they industrialized, as they became more affluent. As cropland decreases,
there is dangerous erosion and contamination of soil that is not likely to
be replenished any time soon.[118] By 2019 nearly three billion people were
moving up the food chain, consuming grains at levels higher than ever:
worldwide grain intake per capita has increased from about 400 pounds to
1600 pounds since the 1950s.[119] The only way such catastrophic trends can
be reversed is through a radical shift from meat-centered dietary patterns.

Owing to the consequences of global warming, water shortages, and
sprawling livestock populations, desertification emerges as a severe problem for many countries – India, Pakistan, Mexico, Ethiopia, Nigeria, even
the U.S. among them. Topsoil is being lost or degraded. Aridity sets in.
Animals strip land of its vegetation. As a result, dust storms are likely to
occur more often, further complicating efforts toward agricultural productivity and food availability.[120] One obvious remedy for this downward spiral
would be plentiful water, yet, as we have seen, its availability too becomes
more problematic.

If water shortages and shrinking cropland plague the future, then the
problem of deforestation is not far behind. Four overriding trends – economic growth, population pressures, heightened meat consumption, climate change – converge to build a perfect storm of ecological devastation,
with no effective counterforce in sight. As rising demand for food continues
across future decades, with livestock occupying more land, not only fertile
cropland but other badly needed resources (savannas, grasslands, temper-

ate forests, rainforests) are sure to be drastically reduced. Already by 2018 roughly 30 percent of tropical forests across Latin America and elsewhere had been cleared for commercial farming, mainly for livestock and grains to feed animals. In Central America alone, just since 1990, more than half of all irreplaceable rainforests have been systematically burned down for cattle grazing. Aside from space for animal-based agriculture, deforestation is linked to urbanization, dams, logging, and soy production.[121]

If the present trajectory holds – and resistance is virtually nonexistent – then all planetary rainforests could be partly or significantly denuded by 2030. This would be a major tragedy, as the forests help ameliorate climate change while protecting biodiversity. As the *Guardian Weekly* warned, deforestation nowadays signifies the most "rapid route to destruction".[122] Brazil, Central America, and Indonesia have been the countries most severely impacted so far. In many cases large corporations have crushed local resistance (often from indigenous groups) to ongoing deforestation. Most crops and animal products developed from within the cleared zones – soybeans, corn, beef, pork, dairy products, palm oil – are marketed as export goods in the global economy, demand coming largely from industrialized nations. For corporations like Cargill, Con Agra, McDonalds, and Monsanto, the diminished rainforest areas represent nothing so much as exciting new frontiers of investment and profits.

In 2018 the world's rainforests comprised only two percent of the entire planetary landmass but contained some 50 percent of all plants and animals – but that number is now rapidly dwindling. Thousands of species disappear each year.[123] The giant corporations exploiting these regions seem to have no interest in preserving an irreplaceable natural habitat. For this and other reasons the epic battle to protect global forests is simultaneously a fight on behalf of endangered animal and plant species, survival of indigenous peoples, human rights, and economic justice, not to mention ecological sanity.[124] Should corporate predators have their way, this fight will be doomed.

Among the worst consequences of the modern crisis is loss of biodiversity – a result of what might best be described as the human war against nature that began with the industrial revolution. The effects of this perpetual war lead to what has been called the "sixth mass extinction", a transformation with increasingly dire repercussions. The escalating destruction of biological species – mammals, birds, reptiles, plants, insects, etc. – comes with habitat ruination, planetary heating, and intensified capitalist rationalization. At least 50 percent of all animal species has been lost since the 1970s, a factor in worsening ecological imbalance.

We have seen in the discussion of global warming that methane produced by livestock adds to the crisis alongside carbon dioxide. Animal-based agriculture generates several types of emissions – methane, nitrous oxide, animal waste, soil contamination with toxic runoffs, air and water pollution, oceanic destruction, chemicals, petroleum-based fertilizers, antibiotics fed to animals. Human-produced debris, trash, and garbage, moreover, has grown so immense that finding places to destroy or dispose of it has become extremely problematic. By 2018 more than 70 percent of all fishing areas were heavily polluted, with vast oceanic "dead zones" proliferating across the planet.[125]

It has been reported that cows, chickens, pigs, turkeys, and other food animals produce a staggering five million pounds of excrement every *minute* – 130 times more than the entire U.S. population.[126] The waste includes methane, antibiotics, pesticides, hormones, and various chemicals. The meat complex emerges as the main culprit, going beyond carbon emissions to an unmanageable set of problems. Richard Oppenlander writes: "Whether discussing land, water, or the air we breathe, our food choices heavily affect the level of pollution and ecological sustainability. The more you choose to eat animal products, the more you contribute to worldwide pollution."[127] It is frightening to imagine just how this will worsen by 2030.

What the *Guardian* has described as a "rapid route to destruction" seems especially resonant to oceanic deterioration. Oceans are, along with forests and soil, the lifeblood of the planet, but all are now in rapid decline. They are the source of roughly half of the oxygen that humans breathe. Like forests, they absorb vast amounts of carbon and other greenhouse emissions. Oceans further help regulate overall climate patterns. Presently every ocean on the planet is under extreme duress owing to waste dumps, toxic runoffs, over-fishing, and the effects of global warming. In September 2016, a report by 80 scientists from 12 nations found that oceans had absorbed 90 percent of "enhanced heating" from climate change since the 1970s.[128] This gives rise to terrible chain of results: oceans become more acidic, sea levels rise, pollution spreads, and "dead zones" (as in the Gulf of Mexico) widen. As oceanic ecosystems deteriorate, this intersects with declining forest habitats to deliver a two-pronged blow to planetary livability and environmental balance. Among many effects, food sources derived from oceans are expected to dwindle rapidly. A dialectic is stealthily at work here too: as global warming destroys the oceans, they simultaneously exacerbate global warming.

Entering the third decade of the twenty-first century, the deepening gulf between food production and ecological sustainability becomes more difficult to ignore, even in the face of corporate lobbies, advertisers, and their political agents. Looking ahead more than 20 years ago, Lester Brown could write: "For the first time in history, the environmental collision between expanding human demand for food and some of the Earth's natural limits will be felt around the world."[129] From the vantage point of 2020, this warning is best seen as a profound understatement.

As we have seen, several factors converge to heighten this crisis – global warming, rising population, skyrocketing energy demands, depleted natural resources, shrinking cropland, and mounting wastes, combined with hundreds of millions of people moving up the food chain. Elevated meat and dairy consumption will only hasten this process, harming food productivity and accessibility. The very fact that animal-foods intake is expected to rise by roughly four to five percent yearly – in a period of sharply reduced land, soil, water, forest, and ocean resources – should be alarming enough. This pattern of consumption, appearing as a mark of development and prosperity, ultimately ensures just the opposite: a world of poverty, hunger, shortages, and decay.

By 2030 there will be no fewer than five billion people living at the top, or close to the top, of the food chain. No countervailing forces currently resist this trajectory. The energy needed to keep up with this historic shift will be astronomical. Food productivity, having steadily increased across the centuries before more recently dropping off, will enter a phase of precipitous downturn. As noted, in 2017 Americans were eating over 200 kilos of animal foods per capita – a level numerous other countries were approaching: Australia, Britain, Israel, Argentina, Brazil, and Canada to name some. Poorer nations like India, Pakistan, Mexico, and Ethiopia were at levels (10 to 50 kilos per capita) distantly removed from the U.S. and other industrialized societies.[130]

A pressing question turns on what happens when those lower on the food chain move up dramatically and in large numbers. Answers to that question will become tragically visible by 2030, if not sooner. The "collision" referred to by Brown will, at long last, be impossible to dismiss. What will the vast expansion of meat-centered diets bequeath? Fertile soil? Fresh water? How much of grain harvests will directly – and indirectly – go to animals? How much energy – fossil fuels and beyond – will be required to keep the corporate meat complex thriving? What will be the tipping point? Answers to such queries will have much to say about the future of human (and animal) survival.

The spread of neoliberal globalization has led to the reproduction of a model of economic development – and indeed social life – that is perpetually wasteful and destructive. The 2015 Paris Accords, trumpeted as an epic move to curb global warming, turns out to be essentially cosmetic, a modest reformism dependent on technological innovation to reverse the downward trajectory. In fact, long-established patterns of resource consumption are destined to move full speed ahead, Paris or no Paris, green technology or no green technology. It follows that the U.S. withdrawal from the agreement, rejectionist on its face, ends up being little more than symbolic.

Scanning the world political terrain, one can see that (as of 2020) anti-system forces are difficult to locate across the globe – few movements, no parties, no governments, no international organizations fitting that description. All important global actors fully endorse the credo of unlimited economic growth as an end in itself, and that includes most of what nowadays passes for "left opposition". Development proceeds as if the planet had in its finite domain essentially limitless resources, driven by pursuit of more commodities, more profits, more wealth, more power. Alternative models of doing business are ridiculed, sometimes identified with Soviet Communism. Corporate power almost invisibly dominates the social, ecological, and moral terrain, reproduced through wealth generation, institutional rationality, and sense of ideological purpose.

This aggressive order carries with it a deep obsession with fossil fuels, mass consumerism, agribusiness, and (for the U.S.) a military culture. Further, limitless economic growth not only fuels high levels of mass consumerism but heightened consumption of animal foods. The much-feared tipping point – especially for natural resources – cannot be too far into the future. Meanwhile, as liberals and progressives continue to be mired in multiculturalism and identity politics, the ruling interests are perfectly happy to further consolidate their boundless wealth and power.

World Cities: A Dystopic Picture

The ceaseless growth of major urban centers across the globe inevitably raises the question of resource utilization and ecological balance, as well as questions of the relationship between city and rural life, the impact of cities on arable land and food sources, the rise of concentrated centers of power, the erosion of democratic politics. In his classic but under-appreciated text *The Rise of Urbanization and Decline of Citizenship*, Murray Bookchin writes: "Urbanization is not only a social and cultural fact of historic proportions; it is a tremendous ecological fact as well." At a time when the overwhelming majority of people in North American and Western Europe regard themselves as city dwellers, we are obliged, if only for ecological reasons, to explore modern urbanization. We must explore not only its impact on the natural environment … but more significantly these days, the changes urbanization has produced in our sensibility toward society and toward the natural world."[131]

For Bookchin, inspired by a social-ecological perspective, modern urbanization can be understood in its present incarnation as something of a cancerous phenomenon that poses a deadly threat to the city and countryside alike. It gives rise to a "dehumanizing of city life, a destruction of community, and a denaturing of agrarian life."[132] Bookchin adds: "Today, it would seem that the city has finally achieved complete dominance over the countryside. Indeed, with the extension of suburbs into nearby open land on an unprecedented scale, the city seems to be literally engulfing the agrarian and natural worlds, absorbing adjacent towns and villages into sprawling metropolitan entities – a form of cannibalism that could easily serve for our very definition of urbanization."[133] What Bookchin argued three decades ago has come to pass many times over as imperious world cities (their populations at or surpassing ten million) have multiplied across the globe.

One might conclude, following Bookchin, that such urban centers have been at war against the natural habitat, responsible for an egregiously wasteful and destructive use of resources. They are teeming bastions of poverty, congestion, crime, and disease, not to mention general alienation and powerlessness. One might contrast this reality with what cities embodied historically, at least in something resembling their Athenian ideal – something of an ethical, social, and political community based on rough harmony with nature, with the countryside. These traditional (and smaller) cities possessed a semblance of cohesion essentially lacking in the present-day metropolis, whether Tokyo or Mexico City, New York or Moscow, Sao Paolo or Shanghai.

As the world city in all its oversized material, social, and environmental development has come to dominate the global terrain, it transforms everything before it. Bookchin writes: "Urban environments are highly synthetic rather than natural. Dwellings tend to be concentrated rather than dispersed. Personal life is not open to the considerable public scrutiny we find in small towns or rooted in the strong kinship systems we find in the country. Urban culture is produced, packaged, and marketed as a segment of the city dweller's leisure time, not infused into the totality of daily life and hallowed by tradition as it is in the agrarian world."[134] While contemporary urban centers are in crucial ways economically, institutionally, and technologically integrated – concentrated in their power and influence – in broad social terms they are fragmented, dispersed, and chaotic, scarcely locales of personal self-activity and collective empowerment. Thus: "Like the modern market, which has invaded every sphere of personal life ... urbanization has swept before it all the civic as well as agrarian institutions that provided even a modicum of autonomy to the individual."[135]

More accurately, it is *corporate* domination – not the abstract functioning of "markets" – that nowadays so fully transforms urban life, from one setting to another Here we face a virulent form of corporate-state power that wages ongoing warfare against the natural habitat, both as it progressively engulfs the rural landscape and as it fosters unsustainable development. Thriving centers of material production and personal consumption, world cities exemplify dysfunction – economically, socially, ecologically.

World cities presently dominant human existence. Since 1950 global urban populations has expanded many times, from less than one billion people to roughly five billion in 2018. That number could increase by another billion by 2030, at which point two thirds of the global population will reside in huge cities. Megacities (with ten million people or more) totaled 30 in 2018 – a number that should reach 41 by 2030. As of 2020 the largest cities were Tokyo (38 million), Delhi (26 million), Shanghai (24 million), Sao Paulo (21 million), Mumbai (21 million), Mexico City (21 million), and Beijing (20.4 million).[136]

As complex webs of human activity the cities devour roughly three-quarters of all energy resources – 82 percent of natural gas, 76 percent of coal, 63 percent of oil, and 72 percent of all renewables. With their frenzied industrial growth and material consumption, they naturally have a voracious demand for resources of all types: water, fossil fuels, metals, wood, petrochemicals, technology. As we have seen, moreover, food supplies constitute the most urgent of needs, all the more so as affluent populations eat more animal products. In this context, urban energy demands are likely to double existing levels by 2030, if not sooner, creating "unmanageable food shortages".[137] World cities are densely populated, forced to import food supplied and processed from farms, plants, transportation systems, and retail outlets. Supply chains can be lengthy, requiring immense human labor power, technology, and natural resources. Virtually by definition, sprawling urban complexes are heavily dependent on food networks outside city boundaries.

These cities have already exceeded the limits of sustainability, severely taxing their environs. Infrastructures needed to support the constant human activity are already excessively burdened, especially in less developed societies. Beneath the glitter and wealth of great urban centers catering to international trade, businesses, cultural life, entertainment, and tourism lie zones of poverty, blight, and violence. Problems of infrastructural frailty – water availability, sanitation, public health, education, security, transportation – have worsened, veering out of control in many countries. Among problems at the top of the list will be food and health.

At present overcrowding, inadequate housing, and erratic public services are typical of such world cities as Mumbai, Djakarta, Bangkok, Mexico City, and Cairo. With 70 million new urban residents each year, mostly in developing nations, high-density sprawl could be matched by spiraling homelessness, resulting in further marginality for hundreds of millions of city dwellers. With overcrowding and homelessness come poverty, crime, disease, and urban deterioration. Resource depletion can only exacerbate these dystopic trends.[138] Here again the overriding challenges of economic growth, urbanization, population pressures, resource depletion, and global warming evolve as deeply interconnected.

The steady expansion of urban space across the planet brings a dramatic increase in automobile traffic and thus more fossil-fuel emissions even where energy use is ameliorated by efficient mass transit systems and wider adoption of electric cars. One reason is the simple explosion of private auto ownership, especially where previously there was little, as in China and India. The world is moving rapidly toward nearly universal car ownership for individuals and families. That could mean an increase to nearly two billion cars in 2030, from a total of 1.2 billion in 2018 – a near doubling of machines that not only produce more carbon emissions but take up more land for roads, freeways, parking lots, garages, and other sites of a fossil-fuel driven infrastructure. China alone is expected to have 600 million autos on the road by 2030. Even where those autos are mainly electric or hybrid, the entire network of production and consumption (including factories, transport, offices, roads, and other facilities) will remain heavily fossil-fuel intensive. In the meantime, we have seen a deepening automobile culture, from Los Angeles to Beijing, that will be difficult to overturn.

In coming years the great urban reckoning will be most sharply felt in the realm of food consumption – all the more so if, as expected, the tendency of people to eat higher on the food chain with rising urbanization and affluence continues. It could hardly be otherwise: widening urban space inevitably encroaches on valuable (irreplaceable) cropland, itself rendered more problematic from the effects of climate change (especially drought), deforestation, soil erosion, and water shortages. Reduced cropland comes at precisely a time when increasing meat intake requires *more* land for both livestock cultivation and grain harvests turned over to animal feed. More generally, a labyrinthine food system charged with growing, processing, storing, transporting, and selling vital goods for millions of urban dwellers has already run up against material, social, and ecological limits.

Urbanization further aggravates the global food crisis. Brown writes: "The world is now living from one year to the next, hoping always to produce enough to cover the growth in demand. Farmers everywhere are making an all-out effort to keep pace with the accelerated growth in demand, but they are having difficulty doing so."[139] In terms of grain alone, massive pressures from diverse sources – urbanization, population growth, meat consumption, climate change – are generating intolerable shortages, and these can only worsen over time. Yet for corporations and governments it is simply business-as-usual, driven as always by the religion of endless economic growth.

In *Full Planet, Empty Plates,* Brown writes: "In every society where incomes have risen, the appetite for meat, milk, eggs, and seafood has generated enormous growth in animal protein consumption. Today some three billion people [mostly urban dwellers] are moving up the food chain."[140] At present the leading meat consumers are China and the U.S., followed by such developing nations as Mexico, Brazil, India, and Argentina – a combined population of nearly two billion. With development especially advanced in densely populated Asia, moreover, several nations with megacities are following the Chinese pattern: Thailand, Vietnam, the Philippines, South Korea among them. Here Brown concludes, ominously: "As food supplies have tightened, a new geopolitics of food has emerged – a world in which the global competition for land and water is intensifying and each country is fending for itself. We cannot claim that we are unaware of the trends that are undermining our food supply and thus our civilization." [141]

The world now faces probably the most severe and explosive of all contradictions – that between food resources and food demands. For reasons discussed above, this contradiction sharpens with each passing year. Its debilitating consequences are already being felt in rising levels of food shortages, malnutrition, famine, and health problems on a distressingly large scale in such countries as Pakistan, India, China, and Ethiopia. Worth emphasizing here is that nothing is fixed or inescapable about modern urban trajectories; these are human-built zones of economic, social, and technological transformation. Going further: megacities as well as their smaller incarnations cannot be understood apart from the process of neoliberal globalization dominated by a merger of corporate and state power.

As of 2020 cities represented 80 percent of planetary economic output and 70 percent of total energy consumption. By 2030 cities will house upward of 60 percent of the world's population, meaning several billion people will face worsening of those conditions mentioned above. Writing in *Can a City be Sustainable?*, Gary Gardner comments: "… if developing countries achieve a level of affluence similar to that of modern wealthy countries, scholars estimate that global material use will grow to three to five times its current level. Herein lies a conundrum: the train that urbanites ride is now too heavy for the rails beneath. Additional passengers – or additional baggage for additional passengers – could buckle the tracks and derail the cars."[142]

The operative word here is "will" rather than "could": given present trajectories, such an outcome – severely depleted resources – is unavoidable. Water alone figures to be an explosive trigger of ecological disaster. Solutions, moreover, will not come easy. They reside neither in comfortable market nor technological remedies but rather in alternative paths of development. And the concerns cannot be restricted to a focus on climate change but will have to extend to problems of the sort explored in this book, including reversal of the deepening (and fatal) imbalance between economic development and the natural habitat.

Global urbanization is tightly connected to two developments destined to worsen climate change: worldwide mobility with growing affluence and intensified heat-trapping of large cities owing to massively concentrated human activity. As to the first of these, mobility is associated in great measure with enormous spikes in the tourism industry, with its increased travel demands, entertainment, and communications, much of which is scarcely ameliorated by green sources of energy. Global use of planes, trains, buses, trucks, and cars is now at an all-time high, while tourism itself amounts to roughly eight percent of total greenhouse gases. Regarding the heat impact as such, many large cities (especially those exceeding ten million population) already measure four to six degrees Fahrenheit higher than surrounding areas. Metropolitan Los Angeles, among other cities, is estimated to be on a path toward a six-degree Fahrenheit temperature rise over the next few decades.[143]

This challenge is exacerbated by a political reality in which a more concentrated power structure becomes increasingly detached from the problems of mass society. As Bookchin has argued, urbanization has been marked historically by declining levels of democratic participation and citizenship. Global elites operate within their own insular bubble. Thus: "Like the modern market, which has invaded every sphere of personal life

... urbanization has swept before it all the civic as well as agrarian institutions that provided even a modicum of autonomy to the individual."[144]
Bookchin adds: "Politically and economically, power was to concentrate
and centralize into fewer hands, linked together by an endless number of
bureaus, bureaucrats, and shared interests that were to prepare the way for
the technobureaucratic nation-state so characteristic of our time."[145]

Facing Demographic Limits

Entering the third decade of the twenty-first century, the world is rapidly approaching its natural limits, where the dreaded tipping-point will
soon be reached and then passed. At the heart of this unprecedented conjuncture of forces is what Lester Brown refers to as a "demographic train
wreck", characterized by severe imbalance between available resources and
heightened demand for those resources.[146] The collision between rampant
economic growth and ecological sustainability revolves more centrally
around questions of food production and consumption. Insofar as global
food production per capita has essentially peaked – after many decades of
steady expansion – while population surges at 85 million people yearly, we
are faced with a lethal predicament that is only bound to worsen.

Despite enormous opposition from all points on the ideological
spectrum, the mounting impact of population growth must be urgently
addressed: the planet is expected to number between nine and ten million inhabitants by 2050 – far beyond the 7.7 billion in 2019. Could the
undeniably burdensome demands of such an enlarged human footprint on
the Earth's carrying capacity somehow *not* be crucial to future ecological
calculations? Chris Hedges has stated what ought to be starkly obvious:
"All the measures to thwart the degradation and destruction of our ecosystem will be useless if we do not cut population growth."[147] The problem
is not strictly ecological. As Brown notes: "If world population growth
does not slow dramatically, the number of people trapped in hydrological
poverty and hunger will almost certainly grow, threatening food security,
economic progress, and political stability."[148] After all, population levels are
an ironclad multiplier of total amounts of material consumption, energy
utilization, and general resource demands.

Confronting massive population increase will be strategically central to all challenges ahead: global warming, shrinking cropland, water shortages, declining forests, ocean pollution, health crises, food availability. Any future transition to an ecological model of development, to a post-carbon society, will require determined limits to both industrial and population growth – limits fiercely resisted not only by the ruling interests but sectors of the environmental and progressive movements. Issues related to population are typically ignored or downplayed in American public discourse and receive little attention in the most densely populated countries. Moreover, those few liberal environmentalists who insist on linking ecological crisis and population growth are ritually attacked as misanthropic, irrational "Malthusians", even racists, fearful of teeming Third World masses.

World population growth has tripled since 1950, surging from 2.5 billion people to six billion in 2000 and then 7.5 billion in 2020. This surge has been met with heightened urbanization, rising prosperity, massive increases in energy utilization, and greater intake of meat and dairy products. Meanwhile, natural resources and public infrastructures are strained well beyond capacity. U.N. reports show that the highest growth rates are in many of the poorest nations – regions where environmental sustainability is already most difficult to achieve. In Africa, total population is expected to rise threefold by 2050, reaching nearly 3.5 billion people on a continent that even now cannot feed its inhabitants. While European populations have stabilized with advancing development, there will be some increases across the continent, as well as the U.S. (expected to reach 370 million people by 2030).

The predicament in many parts of Africa – Ethiopia, Egypt, Nigeria among other nations – has grown especially threatening. Nigeria, for example, will become the third most populous country in the world by 2050, if not sooner, with over 400 million people and counting. With far more people to feed, arable land is becoming scarce while grasslands in the north are being degraded and water sources are diminishing. How can sufficient food, nutrition, and health be guaranteed under such conditions? The livestock sector is encroaching on larger zones of arable land with each passing day. Vital crops – corn, beans, potatoes, wheat – are increasingly at risk. The consequences will be many, and devastating: malnutrition, famine, poverty, severe health problems, joblessness, environmental horrors. Could other devastating effects (ethnic conflict, civil war, migrations) be far behind?

The neoliberal corporate globalization celebrated in Europe and North America – one promising endless abundance and freedom – lies at the heart of the crisis. It is this model, sadly, that is being emulated by such developing nations as Mexico, India, Pakistan, Indonesia, Brazil, and Argentina. Yet this very combination of boundless economic and population growth is ultimately fatal. Here the Ehrlichs write: "Rich nations have developed an economic system that increasingly depends on consuming humanity's stored inheritance, but which provides very unequal access to it, a system that has encouraged humanity to reach an astounding level of over-population. It is a temporary game. It should be obvious that an economic system based on consuming our limited capital is inherently self-destructive, but our short-term vision blinds us to the results of our actions."[149]

This predicament, however, is rarely "obvious" to left-wing critics long troubled by population concerns. A recent case in point is Chris Williams writing in *Ecology and Socialism,* where he attacks Brown and the Ehrlichs as "resource-depletion doomsayers" whose claims regarding the "population explosion" serve to reinforce the prevailing (liberal-capitalist) ideology. Any deference to the population-growth myth of finite earthly resources belongs to the "ideological armory of capitalism", deflecting attention from the real origins of ecological crisis – namely, destructive consequences of the world capitalist economy.[150] Williams' arguments relies on three familiar claims: the "doomsayers" are Malthusian, they fail to recognize that world population has a slowing "growth rate", and most crucially, they ignore the dynamic of "social relations" (class factors) that shape how natural resources are used and distributed.

The first point – Malthusian ideological bias – is both distressingly predictable and totally irrelevant. Williams follows the formulaic path of saddling overpopulation theorists with Malthusian "class prejudice", a conceptual ploy seemingly buttressed by the (well-established) conclusion that Malthus' own predictions of geometric population increase have been falsified. Since Malthus was known to exhibit a profound contempt for the poor masses, this was clearly behind his obsession with population control in a world that, in the late eighteenth century, had fewer than one billion people. Williams cites several passages from Marx whose scathing criticism of Malthus for ignoring the impact of capitalism are well known – indeed Marx was perfectly correct in his attacks.

The problem here is that Malthus' outmoded views have nothing to do with the contemporary ecological crisis, which bears little relation to Malthusian ideas or the world he inhabited. Whether population expansion today is geometrical or simply incremental is irrelevant on a planet that presently cannot sustain a level of seven billion humans, much less a projected total of nine or ten billion in coming decades. Planetary catastrophe could scarcely be imagined two centuries ago. The era of Malthus (and indeed Marx) has so little in common with the existing predicament that we are best advised to simply forget about those remote debates. Why critics persist in such archaic discourse is puzzling. Further, none of the targeted critics (Lester Brown, Paul and Anne Ehrlich, et. al.) claim any intellectual lineage with Malthus or rely heavily on his work – nor, importantly, do they exhibit the extreme class bias attributed to Malthus. The Malthusian bogeyman is an ideological detour that should finally be laid to rest.

Williams and other progressives argue that population growth distracts from more pressing issues of corporate power, class interests, and spreading poverty. He refers to the logic of a "falling rate of population increase": although world population continues to rise, its *rate* actually peaked in the 1960s and continues to grow slightly as humans age, societies become more affluent, and fertility rates decline. Economic development in particular functions to limit family size, as it has done in Europe, North America, and Japan, Williams noting: "This reduction in growth rate undermines the presumption that human population has reached the earth's carrying capacity."[151] He states that, according to demographic projections, by 2030 the planet will comfortably be able to feed at least eight billion people. Leaving aside the failure to look at longer-term developments – along with a fixation on food shortages – this conclusion resonates little in a world already overcome by the effects of climate change, diminished water supplies, soil erosion, deforestation, ocean depletion, and overall vanishing arable land. It further overlooks the extent to which many countries, with hundreds of millions of people, are moving rapidly up the food chain. Even with little or no population *growth*, ecological crisis is destined to worsen.

Reliance of the "falling rate of population increase", moreover, to show the earth's capacity is not threatened is likewise irrelevant, since what ultimately matters is the *absolute* number of humans on the planet and their consumption levels, relative to the general resource base and environmental resiliency. Further, a decline in growth *rate* is to be expected given larger population totals with each passing year; what matter most are the actual numbers and their consumption patterns within given ecosystems. At present levels even small increments of population growth will be hugely consequential – though at levels of 85 million additional humans each year those increments are hardly "small". Focus on lower fertility rates in Europe seems likewise meaningless, as Europe has less than ten percent of the world population. Given its present trajectory, global population could reach well over nine billion people by 2050. How could it be rationally argued that such population levels would not exert unsustainable pressures on natural resources, already fragile urban infrastructures, social life, and political stability? Diatribes against "Malthusianism" are scarcely helpful in this context.

Population growth in India is especially illustrative of the way natural habitats are being stretched beyond tolerable limits. According to 2011 census data, the Indian population had expanded to 1.2 billion – an increase of 180 million in just a single decade. By 2017 that had reached nearly 1.4 billion. Reports indicate that the number could *double* over the next 50 years, despite a reduction of growth *rate* to 17.6 percent relative to the previous decade. The population of just two Indian states already exceeds that of the entire U.S., while demands for water, arable land, and other resources heighten year by year. While poverty escalates and compromised ecological systems deteriorate, economic "development" in India is slated to benefit a tiny stratum of the wealthy and powerful. At the same time, with nearly 30 percent of the population illiterate, the Congress government was allocating less money to education, thus undermining prospects for curbing population growth, which tends to fall the more educated the population.

The impact of absolute numbers should not be confused with questions of population *density*, with which Williams and others seem needlessly distracted. Density is one factor among many, but in itself is hardly central to environmental sustainability. Dense populations, common to many advanced urban areas, can be more or less in sync with their natural surroundings. The more pressing issue concerns the distribution of inhabitants relative to ecosystem carrying capacity. The moment when overpopulation is reached is that of ecological imbalance – that is, when resources are depleted faster than they can be renewed. While certain highly populated urban centers might appear sustainable when viewed in isolation, they usually achieve this by importing (or exploiting) resources (oil, water, wood, food, etc.) and labor from elsewhere. Much depends, therefore, on how specific populations utilize resources in the ecological context. Trends toward unsustainability – largely the result of excessively high levels of consumption in the wealthiest nations – cannot be attributed to density as such, nor do Brown and the Ehrlichs make such a claim.

At odds with their supposed Malthusian contempt for the poor masses, Brown and the Ehrlichs lay primary blame for the ecological crisis on the wealthiest countries of Europe and North America. In one article the Ehrlichs go to extremes to point out that Holland can effortlessly support a population of 1000 persons per square mile because it can import massive amounts of oil, fresh water, foodstuffs, and other critical resources. The nation is far from self-sustaining.[152] As previously noted, a very small concentration of richest populations accounts for more than two-thirds of environmental destruction, mainly owing to its privileged levels of consumption. The unfairly criticized Ehrlichs are abundantly clear on this point: "The key to understanding overpopulation is not population density but the numbers of people in an area relative to its resources and capacity of the environment to sustain human activities; that is, to the area's carrying capacity."[153]

While most nations can be viewed as overpopulated to some degree, it is the affluent North that remains the worst offender, the Ehrlichs noting that "almost all the rich nations are overpopulated because they are rapidly drawing down stocks of resources around the world."[154] (This generalization is made without reference to elevated rates of meat and dairy consumption.) Such passages scarcely reveal the ideological temperament of Malthusian racism toward lesser-developed nations or cultures. Quite the opposite: the Ehrlichs emphasize a basic logic of demographics – namely, that the most affluent societies manage to accumulate their own wealth by importing resources from outside their own borders and by exploiting vast labor and material needs in order to develop their prosperous, but otherwise unsustainable, economies.

Adhering to the "shibboleth of absolute overpopulation", Williams calls attention to the destructive consequences of world capitalism, of a neoliberal system that creates social inequality, poverty, lopsided resource distribution, and ecological ruin. The problem is not too many people but rather "… historically how many human beings the earth can support depends primarily on the level of productivity of the existing population and the social relations within which they are embedded."[155] The reason food and other resource problems have surfaced in recent years has everything to do with the specific character of *social relations* and little to do with resource availability as such.

Williams' argument is consistent with a Marxist outlook and has a certain plausibility: as I have argued throughout this book, untrammeled corporate power is a decisive factor in the worsening global crisis. The question arises, however, as to precisely how much difference a transformed system allowing for more egalitarian resource allocation (and better public services) would make given the general constellation of forces at work – climate change, shrinking arable land, and water shortages not to mention population pressures. Even the most radical measures, beneficial as they might be, are unlikely to save planetary life from its downward trajectory. Williams' approach takes for granted boundless resources into an indefinite future, despite obvious limitations mentioned above.

No doubt a radical shift in class and power relations would help alleviate the crisis and delay its worst consequences, but not so much that population levels would be marginal to the broader ecological calculus. There is little to suggest, however, that fundamental changes in global "social relations" (a dramatic shift toward ecosocialism?) are on the near horizon: existing patterns of growth, production, and consumption, however attenuated by reforms, will surely be with us for decades. Anti-system groups, movements, and parties remain fragmented and weak, scarcely visible as agencies of new (ecological) models of development. Here leftist critics of overpopulation discourse seem trapped in a form of ideological denial, convinced the crisis will be overcome once (a politically remote) new developmental path is adopted for the entire planet. That is an especially debilitating form of utopianism.

The limits of a conventional leftist outlook run deeper yet: prospective egalitarian alternatives to the world capitalist system, while attentive to ecological priorities, can be expected to follow an Enlightenment trajectory that identifies human progress with endless industrial and technological rationalization. Capitalist modernization, with its deep contradictions and dysfunctions, would be supplanted by a more progressive modernity rooted in roughly the same high levels of production, consumption, and resource exploitation. That at least has been the path chosen historically by the different socialist, social-democratic, and Communist traditions. Neither Williams nor other Marxists lay out a distinctly ecological model geared to the limits of growth and recognition that the natural habitat imposes strict constraints on economic development. Nor do they consider the problem of food in terms of meat consumption that devours unsustainable resources as more societies move upward on the food chain.

One question here is whether Enlightenment rationality, long embedded in the domination of nature, might be compatible with an ecological politics in a world where so many developing nations are striving (many successfully) to reach the affluence of wealthier nations. In the absence of curbs on both economic and population growth – North and South – the Enlightenment scenario (whether driven by "liberal" or "socialist" agendas) will eventually lead to ecological disaster, as the natural habitat is sacrificed to the seductive appeals of material prosperity.

When it comes to population, leftist critics typically arrive at static, ahistorical views of time and process: existing conditions are seen as immune to worsening trends even with the addition of two or three (perhaps several) billion people exerting new pressures on the planet's carrying capacity. Some, like Williams, take comfort in the fallacy of a "falling rate of growth" or in prospects for an imminent transformation of "social relations", but neither of these tropes currently has much relevance. On a crowded planet, people everywhere will need – and surely demand – a wide variety of public goods and services: housing, transportation, health care, education, food, security. The mounting collision between expanding population and shrinking resources means that governments are destined to fail this test, ensuring social turmoil and political instability.

The problem of worldwide food resources relative to demand – largely ignored by the left – figures to accelerate onset of the tipping-point. The world now loses about one percent of its arable land each year, and that trend could worsen given the effects of climate change and urban sprawl.

Per capital cropland for grains, vegetables, and fruits diminishes yearly, especially in countries like Russia, China, and India (40 percent of world population). World grain production rose steadily from 1950 to 1990 but has stalled since with no sign of greater yields on the horizon. Meanwhile, a larger percentage of grains (currently 40 percent will go to animal feed as populations move up the food chain.

Downplaying of the ecological crisis in relation to populations pressures by Williams and others is most evident on water issues. Bill McKibben has observed that "We're every day less oasis and more the desert. The world hasn't ended, but the world as we know it has – even if we don't quite know it yet."[156] Of all the natural resources, water is most indispensable for all human activity. Global warming could accelerate harsh weather events, drought, soil erosion, and diminished aquifers across the planet. Hundreds of lakes, rivers, and streams are drying or have become polluted at a time of dramatic rise in human demand.[157] Between 1950 and 2010, as world population grew from 2.5 billion to seven billion, global renewable water supplies declined per person by an astonishing 63 percent, and this will probably worsen by 2030. China is already in the midst of a severe water crisis. Around the world more than one billion people lack safe drinking water, guaranteed to exacerbate health problems. And of course, water shortages will severely harm agricultural output and food availability in a period of intensifying worldwide demand.

The rising threat of water shortages forces a more critical assessment of meat and dairy production that requires several times more water than plant-based foods. Most progressives avoid this issue, perhaps fearful of calling into question long-established dietary (personal) habits shared by the vast majority of people in the industrialized societies. When it comes to animal products, American environmentalists of all political views move into denial, a stunning lapse in a world where animal farming is uniquely harmful in terms of human health, animal cruelty, pollution, resource depletion, and global warming. As noted, the meat complex utilizes one-third of the worldwide grain harvest, and that figures to worsen as countries like China, India, Brazil, and Mexico become more affluent. Old ecosystems including rainforests are being destroyed to clear vast regions for livestock grazing and crops to feed animals. Meanwhile, the meat complex utilizes enormous fossil-fuel resources in the form of fertilizers, pesticides, transportation, processing, and food delivery.

As industrializing nations rely more on animal farming, grain stores available to humans will gradually decline, bringing the planet ever closer to food catastrophe. Americans now consume four times the grain per capita than inhabitants of India and other poorer countries, but only about one-tenth of that total is eaten directly; the rest goes to livestock and poultry.[158] Many nations – including those with huge populations – scramble to find diminishing grain resources in support of escalating meat consumption, but how long such desperate maneuvers can stave off food crises at a time of shrinking per capita outputs is problematic. In 2017 the U.S. was contributing nearly half of all international grain exports, but that cannot be sustained with population growth and skyrocketing meat and dairy intake.

On a planet where more than a billion people are drastically underfed, at least two billion – accustomed to rich, costly, unhealthy, carbon-intensive diets – are wastefully *overfed*, with all the attendant health and environmental problems discussed more fully in chapter three. As food prices inevitably rise, moreover, the relatively wealthy will have plenty to eat while hundreds of millions of poor will be condemned to severe malnutrition, even famine, as in the case of several African nations. No wistful projections of a more rational world system can delay or short-circuit this impending disaster. Familiar reassurances by elites (sadly echoed by many leftists) that limitless economic and population growth is perfectly manageable, even desirable, take on an increasingly dystopic character.

The glib contention of Williams and others that food output has always seamlessly matched population growth, though far from the truth, has obviously less relevance to *future* projections. The urgent question today is whether global food availability can satisfy the needs of nine or ten billion hungry people in a period of accentuated climate change, rampant economic development, shrinking arable land, severe water shortages, and tens of million people yearly moving up the food chain. This dire predicament would have to be confronted even if Robert Malthus had never written a single word.

Environmentalists critical of population growth like Brown and the Ehrlichs have been wrongly pilloried as neo-Malthusian ideologues, as cruel enemies of the global poor. The issue of an overburdened natural habitat cannot be isolated from tens of millions of new inhabitants making ever-larger demands on the ecosystem each year. This means absolute population numbers relative to available resources, not rate of increase or density patterns. Sustainability demands that resource use be replenishable, minimally harmful to the environment, and sufficient to meet basic human needs everywhere. Beyond that, it ought to support a comfortable quality of life taking into account a world of finite, often threatened, resources.

Population management will therefore have to be a central priority for any future ecological politics if, as mentioned above, all other initiatives are not to be largely wasted. Brown is often attacked for his supposed extremism on this issue, yet his proposals are quite moderate: universal education, improved family planning, widespread access to birth control, greater female access to jobs and careers. He argues that the planet, given high consumption rates of affluent nations, could effectively support no more than 2.5 billion people – nearly five billion more than presently inhabit the Earth. David and Marcia Pimental offer a more pessimistic figure of two billion people.[159] Of course significant reductions in world population would take decades under the best conditions, and even those would be meaningless unless accompanied by a major shift in production and consumption patterns.

Lacking an epic transformation of class relations, power structures, and ecological priorities, the planet is headed toward deepening crisis with no apparent exit. That is a guaranteed outcome so long as the most powerful countries follow business-as-usual even as their leaders proclaim the need for environmental renewal. In any event, the transition to a more rational, sustainable world system will depend on the human will and capacity to impose significant limits to both economic and population growth.

The Specter of Resource Wars

In an era of intensifying ecological crisis, nations of the world are inescapably thrown into a geopolitical cauldron of sharpening conflict over land and resources. In the absence of a drastic change in trajectory, the road ahead is most likely paved with conflict, violence, militarization, and warfare. The problem of food availability figures to be at the center of national rivalries, Brown writing: "As land and water become scarce, as the Earth's temperature rises, and as world food security deteriorates, a dangerous geo-politics of food scarcity is emerging".[160]

At present no alteration of course is on the horizon, despite global ini-tiatives in Paris and other international gatherings. World capitalism is the domain of multinational corporations and huge banks, all dedicated to the incessant accumulation of wealth and power; public, ethical, and ecological values have little if any register in such a world. Put differently, the ruling interests have no abiding interest in confronting the crisis, especially where substantial reforms might curb their wealth and power. As certain resources begin to shrink, moreover, the geopolitical terrain is destined to witness sharpening conflict over that wealth and power which, in some cases, will assume a military character.

Well into the twenty-first century, economic conflict, trade wars, and resource competition have been met with rising conservatism and nation-alism across the planet. While powerful (and less-powerful) nations are driven by their own material interests, the very likelihood of internation-ally binding agreements seems increasingly remote, almost utopian. With a worldwide fossil-fuel complex worth many trillions of dollars, it is no wonder that few nations or corporations seem prepared to break their reliance on oil, gas, and coal in a setting where alternative technologies cannot begin to serve as substitutes. Many countries depend heavily on fossil-fuel exports, including the U.S., Russia, Iran, Mexico, and Venezuela. Fossil-fuel-based investment, research, and development remains fully on the agenda, whatever the aspirations toward a "green" model.

The seductive lures of growth and prosperity ritually override ecolog-ical priorities, urgent as those priorities might be. All corporate interests – banking, agribusiness, energy, fast food, the military – share in the growth mania. Nowhere is this more embraced than in the U.S., a beacon of mod-ern capitalism empowered through global supremacy, with an ideology of national exceptionalism and heavy reliance on military force to secure geopolitical objectives.

Resource wars, fueled by a mixture of economic, political, military, and geopolitical interests, figure to be part of the global scene well into the future – a specter often ignored by those obsessed with climate change. Civic violence, local insurgencies, economic conflict, terrorism, and international strife will be the predictable outcome of resource competition, with the U.S. typically at the center. Michael Klare refers to a "New Geography of Conflict" that is destined to shape the global terrain across future decades. He writes: "Whereas international conflict was until recently governed by political and ideological considerations, the wars of the future will largely be fought over the possession and control of vital economic goods – especially resources needed for the functioning of modern industrial societies." The reasons involve "the priority accorded to economic considerations by national leaders, the ever-growing demand for a wide range of basic commodities, looming shortages of certain key materials, social and political instability in areas harboring major reserves of vital commodities, and the proliferation of disputes over ownership of important sources of supply."[161]

Geopolitical conflict will likely intensify over crucial resources like oil, water, scarce minerals, and timber, mostly centered in the Middle East, Asia, and parts of Africa. Klare sees Africa as primacy zone of conflict: "All the preconditions for recurring violence can be found here – large concentrations of vital materials, numerous territorial disputes in areas harboring valuable deposits, widespread political instability and factionalism, the presence of private armies and mercenaries, and a history of collaboration between foreign resource firms and local warlords."[162] In 2018 several powers – European, North American, Asian – had moved to secure a presence in Africa, along with several transnational corporations. Targeted areas include Ghana, Zimbabwe, the Sudan, Ethiopia, and Congo. Conflict over vital resources could be domestic as well as international, involving global interests, local groups, government forces, warlords, and perhaps even terrorist groups.

Klare argues that behind the "shift in policy is the belief that the defining parameters of power and influence" have changed since the Cold War ended. While in the past national power was thought to reside in mighty arsenals and the maintenance of alliances, it is now more associated with economic dynamism and the cultivation of technological innovation, Klare adding that national security depends on fuller engagement with the global economy.[163] Klare emphasizes the role of corporate globalization here, but his suggestion that older competition between states and alliances is obsolete must be questioned – witness the present strife involving the U.S., Russia, China, and Iran, along with aggressive moves to revitalize NATO in the European context. What we have today is a tight *merger* of economic, political, and military strategies.

What seems inescapable in any discussion of resource wars, however, is the convergence of major trends identified elsewhere in this book. Thus, Klare observes that "the growing demand for resources is driven ... by the dramatic increase in human numbers" – again, by 85 million people each year. He continues: "... of equal importance is the spread of industrialization to more and more areas of the globe and the steady worldwide increase in personal wealth, producing an insatiable appetite for energy, private automobiles, building materials, household appliances, and other resource-intensive commodities."[164] Among the latter, of course, would be *food*, especially that derived from the animal-foods complex.

The rising demand for energy and consumer goods, including meat, will be most sharply obvious in Asia and the Pacific Rim, where growth rates (in China, India, Japan, South Korea, and Thailand) have been notably brisk – a trend sure to escalate in coming years and probably decades. As of 2020, China is poised to become the leading industrial power in the world. Klare writes: "As global consumption rises and environmental conditions deteriorate, the total available supply of many key materials will diminish and the price of whatever remains will rise." One problem here is that poorer societies will fall drastically behind. Regarding water, not only crucial to agriculture but an irreplaceable good for every human activity, "conflict may arise between states over the distribution of the limited resources available."[165] And those resources, as we have seen, will be further stretched as nations develop economically and move up the food chain.

Fossil fuels, water, arable land, timber, valuable minerals – these figure to be at the center of future geopolitical conflict, centrally involving major nation-states that are biggest consumers of natural resources. It has been argued that U.S. wars in the Middle East, starting with Iraq in the early 1990s, have launched a new era of resource wars over oil, what Antonia Juhasz describes as the "Bush Agenda" but a project that clearly extends to American imperialism as a general phenomenon.[166] This "agenda" blends economic, political, and military strategies, usually cloaked in high-sounding ideals: fighting weapons of mass destruction, defeating terrorism, democracy promotion, human rights, "humanitarian intervention". While broader global objectives drive U.S. foreign policy, these professed goals serve as ideological cover for more naked economic and military designs.

Juhasz argues that, "to date, the Iraq war represents the fullest and most relentless application of the Bush Agenda", geared to "an ever-expanding American empire driven forward by the growing powers of the nation's largest multinational corporations and unrivaled military."[167] As oil is critical to economic growth and corporate globalization, war against Iraq could be viewed as a predatory maneuver to secure one of the largest fossil-fuel reserves in the world, whatever the loss of life and material costs (several trillion dollars). Moreover, Iraq could be viewed as something of a template for subsequent resource wars.

American corporate and military interests are undoubtedly motivated by heightened access to large oil and gas deposits, even as the U.S. moved after 2010 to achieve what is considered energy "independence", thanks to shale processing and fracking to secure domestic natural gas supplies. The Bush elites enjoyed a special relationship with such powerful interests. Combined profits of the leading fossil-fuel enterprises have surged to hundreds of billions yearly. Such giants as Lockheed-Martin, Raytheon, ExxonMobil, Chevron, and Northrop-Grumman have been central to both the warfare state and economic globalization. Further, according to U.S. national security strategy, aggressive moves in the Middle East, North Africa, and Central Asia are meant to preempt efforts by such nations as Russia and China to establish their own sphere of operations in those regions.[168] And those regions, it turns out, are among the most resource-rich in the world.

According to Juhasz, the Bush Agenda is driven mainly by oil interests, demonstrated by the influential role of such corporations as Bechtel, Chevron, ExxonMobil, and Haliburton in the Iraq war and subsequent occupation that gave rise to political disaster and military blowback, its reverberations still felt across the region.[169] This was supposed to be a template for U.S. intervention elsewhere, but Washington was forced to rethink crucial aspects of its geopolitical strategy. We know the U.S. has been intervening around the globe for many decades, though not always in search of resources. Even in the case of Iraq other priorities entered the picture – for example, defense of Israeli interests in the Middle East. After 2010, moreover, when U.S. control of Iraq began to crumble, the oil gambit emphasized by Juhasz and others seemed far less relevant – all the more so as widespread shale processing and fracking gave the U.S. heightened energy independence.

By 2016 relations between the U.S. and Russia had begun to deteriorate, in part owing to geostrategic conflicts over Ukraine and other parts of the former Soviet Union that have impacted the rest of Europe including the NATO alliance. Those conflicts have intensified over enormous supplies of natural gas that the EU has long received from Russia – more than 50 percent of the total by 2018 estimates. As the U.S. becomes more independent as a fossil-fuel producer, it has sought to market larger and larger flows of natural gas – a supposedly "cleaner" type of carbon – to EU nations. The Russian firm Gazprom has built a 765-mile gas pipeline to Germany, a project that Denmark (surely with American backing) has tried to block. Mounting tensions in the region are all the more fearsome when the rivals happen to be nuclear superpowers and the Washington power structure is in the grips of a massive anti-Moscow frenzy.

It might be that future resource wars will lead to an expansion of economic-military strategy into other arenas – water, land, timber, minerals, etc. Perhaps water, so crucial to agriculture and food production, will become the "new oil", as some observers have predicted. Here a purely military approach will not always be the preferred option, which hardly rules out wars for other purposes. In fact, the familiar instruments of corporate globalization (World Trade Organization, World Bank, International Monetary Fund, specific trade agreements) can work efficiently to ensure the capacity of leading national powers (the G-8) to achieve substantial resource leverage.

In the all-important realm of food, these international organizations have systematically favored the powerful and wealthy nations. For example, WTO rules have long permitted nations to subsidize agricultural producers and exporters, deny smaller governments the ability to establish price supports and market protections, and offer subsidized inputs (fertilizer, seeds, tools, etc.) to farmers. One result is that many smaller farmers are undercut by cheaper subsidized products and forced off their land, while control over food supply is concentrated in the hands of those able to sell crops and goods on the world market, including huge agribusiness interests. Here it goes without saying that WTO rules are never the outcome of democratic processes. This variant of resource wars is devastating to local communities, farmers, labor, and smaller business enterprises – not to mention food production in general.

Eric Holt-Gimenez, writing in *A Foodie's Guide to Capitalism*, refers to this economic form of warfare to "the corporate food regime".[170] He points out that the IMF and World Bank often work in tandem to "force countries of the South to open up their economies to international markets by removing controls on international finance capital, privatizing state-held industries and services, and deregulating labor markets." One result of such policies is to make smaller nations increasingly dependent on food from the U.S. and other leading producers, with often disastrous ramifications.[171] As this process moves forward, corporate agriculture destroys land and soil, undermines biodiversity, exploits precious water, generates carbon emissions on a large scale, and forces millions of farmers, peasants, and workers into poverty.[172]

Meanwhile, the food behemoths are making record profits, facilitated by the economic benefits of globalization. Writes Holt-Gimenez: "Virtually all the world's food systems are tied into today's regime, controlled by a far-flung agri-food industrial complex, made up of huge monopolies like Monsanto, Syngenta, ADM, Cargill", and others including Wal-Mart and Amazon. Together, these corporations are powerful enough to dominate the governments and multilateral organizations that make and enforce the regime's rules for trade, labor, property, and technology."[173] By perpetuating corporate domination of the global food system, a variant of resource wars is advanced, in which case military intervention could end up superfluous.

When it comes to food, as we have seen, water becomes the most precious of resources – one that, moreover, is uniquely threatened by the ecological crisis. Moving well into the twenty-first century, conflict over critical (and endangered) water supplies is destined to escalate, notably in the Middle East, Africa, and many regions of Asia. Conflict, possibly leading to war, figures to be especially acute over water sources shared by two or more countries.[174] The problem of resource shortages throughout Africa has sharpened since the 1990s, as water availability and arable land are becoming increasingly problematic. Several nations have entered into conflict over available resources, especially those related to food production: Libya, Egypt, Ethiopia, Somalia, Sudan, Algeria among others. This state of affairs has already fed into the spread of local militias, terrorist groups, and civil unrest.

Recognizing the heightened global demand for water, Klare writes: "As populations grow, societies need more water for both daily human use and for food production ... To complicate matters, global population growth is heavily concentrated in in those areas of the world – North Africa, the Middle East, South Asia – where the supply of water is already proving inadequate for many human needs. Rapid urbanization in these areas and the expanding use of water in industrial processes are also contributing to an increase in demand."[175] This is to say nothing about the potential impact of climate change with its warming trend, increasing drought episodes, and extreme weather events. Conflict over shrinking water availability is sure to intensify. Klare adds: "... in regions where water is scarce, states view combat over vital sources of supply as a legitimate function of national security."[176]

As of 2019 the global supply of fresh water was becoming more problematic relative to global demand: less than three percent of the world's total water is usable fresh water, much of it located in glaciers and underground aquifers now being over-exploited. Roughly 70 percent of this water is being appropriated by humans for agriculture, nearly half of which is used to nourish the meat complex – and that figure will naturally rise as meat consumption expands. Economic growth, population increase, rising meat intake, and climate change are converging to generate an unprecedented surge in water demand, but adequate new sources are unlikely to be discovered. It follows that competition – among local communities, economic interests, and rival nations – will be fierce in coming decades.

As Klare predicts, water struggles can be expected both between and within states, though "it is interstate conflict over shared water sources that is of greatest concern. The major shared systems of the Middle East and Southwest Asia – the Nile, the Jordan, the Tigris-Euphrates, and the Indus – have been the sites of conflict throughout human history ... and that conflict persists today. The inescapable logic is that growing scarcity combined with rising populations will produce an increasingly unstable environment."[177] The problem is compounded by the fact that population growth in these regions has some of the highest rates in the world. Further, it is possible that mounting conflict over scarce resources will intersect with longstanding ethnic, regional, and political rivalries.   Egypt, Israel, Ethiopia, Pakistan, India, and China could be sites of future violent conflicts over water. The involvement of the U.S. and European states in these struggles, as well as transnational corporations and international organizations, can hardly be discounted.

The tight connection between water and food is exacerbated as shortages of the former – needed for every phase of food production – become more severe. Competition around food resources itself escalates as more nations lose the capacity to feed their own expanding populations, with potentially grave social and political consequences. Imported grains and other foodstuffs can extend only so far. Klare writes in the post-drought milieu of 2012: "Because so many nations depend on grain imports from the U.S. to supplement their own harvests, and because intense drought and floods are damaging crops elsewhere as well, food supplies ae expected to shrink and prices rise across the planet."[178] It turns out that both corn and soybeans, crucial to providing livestock feed, are among the most vulnerable to heat and drought. And that could mean a significant rise in food prices worldwide.

As of 2020, the world capitalist economy was destroying the planetary habitat – and its natural resources – at an intensifying rate. Everyone talks about "greening" but no one talks about limits to growth, much less restructuring the food system. In this context all nations will be forced to adapt to a new reality of shrinking resources, especially those related to agriculture and food production. Such adaptation is far less likely to produce a global ethos of commonality and cooperation than one of geopolitical rivalry and resource wars. The idea of a worldwide Green New Deal (a global ecological Keynesianism) figures to be short-circuited by rising national competition endemic to resource wars. Meanwhile, as Klare notes: "… only by raising crop yields while reducing inputs of water, oil, fertilizers, pesticides, and other materials can the world hope to avoid a series of devastating famines."[179] That means the search for fertile farmland, declining with each passing year, can only intensify across the globe. China and India figure to be at the center of this worsening geopolitical drama.

We are now beginning to see the larger political reverberations of this particular crisis. Food shortages and rising prices have historically been met with social protests and upheavals, a recipe for domestic or even global chaos. Writing in *World on the Edge*, Brown notes: "One more recent reason for government breakdowns is the inability to provide food security, not necessarily because the government is less competent but because obtaining food is becoming more difficult."[180] One likely result is the proliferation of failed states – those with declining institutional capacities, weakened public infrastructures, and loss of political legitimacy. Resource struggles are hardly the only factor here, but they can still be decisive. The Middle East and North Africa presently comprise the largest number of failed states, including Yemen, Somalia, Iraq, and Libya – all in some way harmed, directly or indirectly, by U.S. military intervention. Other states can be said to be on the verge of crisis: Pakistan, Saudi Arabia, South Africa, Nigeria, Kenya. Not only food and water problems, but military conflict and population flows contribute to the phenomenon of failed states. Ecological crisis will undoubtedly become simultaneously cause and effect of this problem.

Libya has come to exemplify the chaos, violence, and instability of a failed state, conditions set in motion by the ill-fate U.S./NATO military attacks of 2011. At present (2020) Libya has no coherent governing apparatus, no legal or political integrity, no civil peace in a setting where many rival armed forces, militias, and gangs compete over terrain and resources. The enormous trove of resources in Libya, especially its oil reserves, ensure intervention of rival forces from such countries as the U.S., France, Turkey, Egypt, and Qatar. The weapons flow is unceasing. Comments U.N. Special Envoy Ghassan Salame: "More than ever, Libyans are now fighting the wars of other countries that appear content to fight to the last Libyan and to see the country entirely destroyed in order to settle their own scores."[181] At the core of this fighting is access to oil, the parties clearly oblivious to the pressures of global warming.

To the extent resource problems intensify, political consequences will extend beyond the spread of failed states. Popular insurgencies, migrations, civil wars, and interstate warfare – not to mention terrorism – could be on the near horizon. Political violence, in some cases aggravated by superpower intervention, could be the wave of the future, independent of what global warming might bring. Countries on the edge in terms of extreme resource challenges – Pakistan, India, China, Ethiopia, Mexico – could be among the first trapped within this dystopic scenario.

Aside from such resources as land, water, and timber, conflict over scarce ("rare") minerals is expected to soar owing to the importance of such substances in military hardware, computers, autos, batteries, and smart phones. One problem here is that China has a virtual monopoly over both production and processing of such minerals, including lithium, terbium, yttrium, and 15 others. This deficit turns out to be especially critical for the U.S., as, for example, each F-35 fighter demands 970 pounds of these metals. In fact, China presently supplies roughly 80 percent of these minerals to the U.S. and its ever-insatiable Pentagon. (The U.S. now has just one mine where scarce minerals can be accessed, the Chinese dozens. What happens in the event geopolitical conflict between China and the U.S. begins to worsen – a specter that appears more probable than not?

As contradictions within the global economy sharpen, the number of countries impacted will rise. According to some reports, such nations as China and India will have increased their industrial output fivefold, while no fewer than 19 or the top economies by GDP will be those currently identified as "emerging". China and India would be the largest third largest economies, with the U.S. second and Japan fourth, followed by Germany, the U.K., Brazil, Mexico, France, and Canada, with Russia ranked fifteenth. Other rapidly developing countries would include Turkey, Indonesia, Thailand, and Egypt.[182]

The question at this juncture is what such overheated economic growth, in so many nations, would mean for intensification of global resource wars. What will be the ecological impact of energy, water, food, and other resource pressures in such a transformed world? Would the U.S., Europe, and Japan (perhaps also China) willingly give up their privileged status within an increasingly competitive world system? Would the leading powers be able to continue pursuit of elevated living standards characterized by expanding levels of consumption? Could all these nations, possibly joined by others, manage to accommodate populations moving steadily up the food chain?

As throughout the postwar years, much revolves around the trajectory of American economic and military power – likely to be at the center of resource wars for years, perhaps decades to come. The picture allows little room for optimism. An economic system that continues to devour vast energy, water, and other natural resources is protected by the largest military apparatus ever built, ruled by a power structure in control of a trillion-dollar yearly budget, a sprawling national security-state, an empire of bases, supreme nuclear complex, and foreign policy dedicated to international primacy. That power structure is governed by an insular elite, largely unaccountable to any democratic process. It wages perpetual warfare that is backed, indeed celebrated, by a subservient warfare state and compliant media.[183]

The American war machine is firmly embedded in the social and political life of the country. Not only does the Pentagon extend its activities to more than 100 nations, it devours untold natural resources from energy to water, food, timber, and scarce minerals. At present more than 50 percent of all disposable federal revenues go to the military, a total augmented by $54 billion by President Trump. This does not count money (several trillion dollars) spent waging foreign wars at any given point in time. The Pentagon undergirds the U.S. violent and costly agenda for world military domination – an agenda that fuels the ecological crisis through its waste of resources, impact on war zones, and contribution to air, water, and atmospheric pollution. Its support of proxy wars and lucrative weapons sales to dozens of countries only worsens matters.

Among worst features of the U.S. warfare state is its massive carbon footprint – reportedly two to three percent of the world total of greenhouse emissions.[184] Bases, equipment, weapons, vehicles planes, ships – all this consumes huge quantities of fossil fuels that, despite widening introduction of alternative energy sources, is bound to steadily increase. The American military-industrial labyrinth exists within its own bubble, responsive mainly to its own militaristic and bureaucratic logic. Shielded from political and media scrutiny, Pentagon elites follow their own rules, norms, and objectives. Thus, not only is the military carbon footprint beyond the call for corrective reforms, that footprint is scarcely *acknowledged* within the public sphere. While the Pentagon is responsible for more pollution, chemical emissions, and toxic wastes than the entire chemical and petrochemical sectors combined, it is fully shielded from criticism.[185] Meanwhile, the Paris accords designed to fight climate change have nothing to say about the glaring military impact on global emissions.

In view of this imperial reality, it would be illogical to think that Washington might do anything but wage resource wars with great vigor. The overriding global imperatives – military superiority, nuclear domination, economic growth, corporate globalization – remain fully embraced by an elite driven by the ethos of national exceptionalism. The Trump presidency, moreover, upholds an especially fierce sense of ideological nationalism. Throughout its postwar history the U.S. has intervened across the planet economically and militarily, has carried out covert operations for regime change, deployed armed forces close to identified "enemies" (Russia, China, Iran), routinely violated international law and treaties, and supported outlaw states (Israel, Pakistan, India) in their dangerous pursuit of nuclear weapons. It has overridden global treaties to protect the environment and, as noted, pulled out of the Paris Accords as well as the several-member Iran nuclear agreement. For Washington, it appears that no deviation from imperial politics is currently on the horizon.

Entering the third decade of the twenty-first century, U.S. power stands opposed to any binding decisions that might help reverse the ecological crisis. Those decisions would include international resolve to better manage natural resources, limit greenhouse emissions, control population growth, demilitarize interstate relations, and initiate a shift away from animal-based food production. This would mean an emphatically *progressive* form of globalization, at odds with American embrace of national exceptionalism and world military supremacy. The familiar illusion of an American politics grounded in democracy, human rights, and peace clashes with the reality of a power structure rooted in corporate domination, militarism, and perpetual warfare. Unfortunately, unless we see a fundamental change in class and power relations – and soon – the superpower will remain the greatest threat to ecological sustainability as the planet hurtles ever-faster toward disaster. Until that happens, we face the most dangerous phase of capitalism and imperialism the world has ever known.[186]

3

The McDonalized Society

The modern food system would seem to be a great triumph of capitalist rationalization and its advanced technological regimen, bringing more and better products to billions of people around the world. Meat and dairy foods, vegetables, fruits, grains - all these are now more plentiful and available to larger populations than at any time in history. Food would appear to be the ultimate achievement of Enlightenment progress through science, technology, and industrial productivity. As the planet yields record amounts for food entering the third decade of the twenty-first century, prospects for feeding more than seven billion people – perhaps even ten billion – might be considered optimum.

This apparent triumph turns out to be a great mirage – the idea of a bountiful modernity barely conceals a world hurtling towards chaos and collapse, mired in deepening contradictions rooted in ecological decline. Heightened material output is illusory at a time when one billion people feast on expensive, harmful animal products while several billion others face diminishing food availability and scarce resources. In *The End of Food*, Paul Roberts writes: "On nearly every level, we are reaching the end of what may one day be called the 'golden age of food' ...".[187] The entire wobbly system now rests on an economic model supported by cultural norms that are increasingly irrational, in need of radical change if planetary survival is to be guaranteed.

The modern crisis extends well beyond challenges posed by economic growth or the capitalist food system as such, to include the corporate system of meat production, consumption, and marketing. This problem has been largely ignored at a time when the public sphere is understandably

94

fixated on the threat of climate change. In 2017 Americans alone were consuming 270 pounds each of animal products yearly – an increase from 167 pounds in 1980, 198 pounds in 1990, and 215 pounds in 2000.[188] This pattern will intensify across future decades while the worldwide intake is expected to *double* by 2030 as more countries develop and enter the "affluent" zone. By 2020 the U.S. market for animal products will reach an anticipated $7.3 trillion, bolstered by an army of corporate managers, lobbyists, government agencies, academics, marketers, and advertisers all doing everything possible to ensure high levels of consumption. Not surprisingly, on this front – the imperative of sharply reducing meat and dairy consumption – we see precious little movement away from lethally untenable global food trends. Here Paul Gilding notes in *The Great Disruption*, "We've been borrowing from the future, and the debt has fallen due."[189]

Food and Capitalism

One cannot possibly talk about food issues in American society – or the world – without taking into account capitalist development across the past century or more. That system, built on mass production of commodities and maximum profits, has fueled capitalist rationalization marked by continued technological innovation, along with a fast-food regimen that has flourished in the U.S. and a few other industrialized nations.

Food is best understood as something of a special commodity – its need and consumption universal, necessary for human survival. In *A Foodie's Guide to Capitalism*, Eric Holt-Gimenez writes, "… under the capitalist mode of production food is a commodity, just like any other. It doesn't matter if the food is fresh organic arugula or a Big Mac, teff from the highlands of Ethiopia, or Cheez Whiz from Walmart. It doesn't matter whether you need it or not, whether it is good or bad for you, whether it is locally produced or traveled from afar, or whether it was corralled, caged, free range, or led a happy life. If enough people *want* it, and have the money to buy it, someone will turn it into a commodity and sell it."[190] Yet, as noted, food is anything but an ordinary commodity. Holt-Gimenez adds: "Because food is indispensable to human labor, and since human labor is a part of the values of all commodities, the value of food permeates the entire economic system."[191]

Commodity production leads to mass markets and economies of scale, whether in agriculture (agribusiness), huge food corporations like Cargill and Con Agra, or vast retail operations such as McDonald's and kindred fast-food conglomerates. Market power expands with large-scale transnational enterprises. As elsewhere, resources – technology, labor, energy, etc. – become far less expensive with growing economies of scale. Technology contributes to remarkable advances in labor productivity and thus food output. Further, as Holt-Gimenez points out, this system of "mass food" does not have to "pay for any of the social and environmental harms caused by the industrial model of food production such as pollution, greenhouse gas emissions, food contamination, antibiotic resistant bacteria, diet-related disease, poverty, dispossession, and displacement."[192]

In the case of the American food system, we have witnessed a massive shift over the past century from agriculture based primarily on small farms to a network of giant corporations. In 1900, 40 percent of the population lived on farms, declining to barely two percent by 2000. This change has been accompanied by other developments – for example, in Marion Nestle's words, "from a society that cooked at home to one that buys nearly half its meals prepared and consumed elsewhere, and from a diet based on 'whole' foods grown locally to one based largely on foods that have been processed in some way and transported long distances."[193] Meanwhile, thanks to an intense focus on advertising and sale, American society faces a rather unique problem – food overabundance. Nestle points out that "many of the nutritional problems of Americans – not least of the obesity – can be traced to the food industry's imperative to encourage people to *eat more* in order to generate sales and increase income in a highly-competitive marketplace."[194]

The global corporate system has come to dominate the terrain of food production and consumption, including the growth of the massive animal-foods complex, which amounts to a form of warfare against billions of sentient beings tortured and killed daily to satisfy consumer preferences. The worldwide food system as presently constituted not only does great harm to land, forests, oceans, air, atmosphere, and biodiversity, but also, perhaps above all, to animals. Capitalist rationalization, with its fixation on technology, hierarchical organization, and economies of scale reproduces daily (and routinely) the savagery of corporate food production. It is a per-petual assault not only on labor and the environment but on huge animal populations forced through this enormous apparatus of violence and cru-elty. To speak of the domination of nature, while correct, is too general and abstract as to properly characterize the system kept in place here, Jonathan Safran Foer writing in *Eating Animals*: "We have waged war ... against all of the animals we eat."[195] An industrial machine built on routinized murder surely goes beyond familiar references to ecological devastation found in so much of the literature.

For many decades the livestock population continued to expand, by 2018 having reached a global total of some 70 billion – its harmful impact on ecosystems, the atmosphere, and commodified animals intensifying year by year. Central to this barbaric process has been the sprawling cattle com-plex established to produce and market beef goods to more consumers in more countries. In his pathbreaking book *Beyond Beef*, Jeremy Rifkin traces the evolution of beef products across more than two centuries, showing how the development of cattle systems has been tightly linked to capitalism and earlier forms of colonialism.[196] In the U.S., the epic nineteenth-century westward push across frontiers was associated with cattle, male culture, beef consumption, and capitalist modernization. Cattle was always a deeply embedded economic and cultural part of the "West".[197]

The rise of what Rifkin calls the "industrialization of beef" refers to a deep connection between stockyards, slaughterhouses, banking networks, transportation systems, and food- retailing operations. Urban centers such as Chicago, St. Louis, and Kansas City became vast sites of beef processing that, by the late nineteenth century, became linked to ideals of affluence and progress. As meat was the prime food choice, it was readily associated with health, strength, and (for men) virility. The meat industry grew especially concentrated and profitable by the time of World War I, the corporation Swift and Armor joining the ranks of Big Capital. The system was becom-ing more integrated, bringing together massive livestock enclosures, meat packing, food processing, finance, rail networks, warehouses, and public utilities.

At the start of the twentieth century, the expanding beef complex – fueled by generous government subsidies – would colonize virtually every realm of American life. The complex became increasingly rationalized, fully dependent on technology, bureaucratic order, assembly lines, and mass production. As in other areas, emphasis was placed on speed, efficiency, and predictability, in much of the same way Ford's auto industry gave rise to the ultimate productivity regimen in Detroit. Yet this regimen would have is dark side, as Upton Sinclair documented in his 1906 book *The Jungle*. Meatpacking revealed both the horrors for animals and Dickensian conditions for workers, a complex riddled with violence, coercion, exploitation, and corruption.[198]

Writing in the 1990s, Rifkin had argued that little has changed in the sphere of beef production since the days of Sinclair. Working conditions remain horrendous with poverty wages, few benefits, high rates of disease, and little if any union leverage for a largely migrant labor force. Regulations, including health and safety standards, are lax and poorly enforced. Corporations augment their power by means of structural expansion, technological innovation, product diversification, and (in many cases) globalization. Several massive business conglomerates have entered the picture, including IBP, ConAgra, Excel, Cargill, Walmart, McDonalds, and Monsanto. Scattered functions of the beef economy are typically assembled and integrated, from grain processing to feeding arrangements, water storage, use of drugs and chemicals, transportation, marketing, and retail operations. As this process unfolds, engulfing more of the landscape, land and resources utilized by this sprawling complex will sooner or later become unsustainable, especially where (as in the U.S.) demand for beef and related products continues to rise. At present livestock occupy nearly one-third of the available planetary land mass. As the cattle system expands, limits to resource depletion will inevitably be reached. One reason meat demand increases stems from its association with privilege, affluence, and health – all celebrated within a powerful advertising system. The industrial-agricultural conversion of grains into meat products brings with it urgent resource challenges related to arable land, water, soil, and forests of the sort more fully discussed in chapter two. Population growth alone will not allow this unsupportable trajectory for long, Rifkin writing: "A new neo-Malthusian threat looms before us, more frightening and sinister than anything else that has come before."[199] Written in 1994, these words now appear scarcely hyperbolic, describing instead what can only be identified as the ever-sharpening global food crisis.

This rapid industrialization of food – or "foodopoly" – is accompanied by rising levels of corporate power visible in agribusiness, fast-foods, chemical firms, banking, and marketing operations. The system is increasingly oligopolistic, fueled by globalization, mergers, buy-outs, and market take-overs – all naturally to the detriment of consumers, workers, the environment, and indeed democratic accountability. There is nothing resembling a "free market" across this concentrated state-corporate apparatus. Within such a matrix of power, most governments (global, national, local) end up so powerless they cannot exert much political leverage. Meanwhile, as advanced industrial societies witness larger numbers of people addicted to meat, those societies can simultaneously be viewed as "addicted" to both economic growth and animal products, the two dynamics moving in tandem. Both developmental patterns have indeed taken on the dimensions of sacred culture, one reflection of what has alternatively been called the "Anthropocene", tipping point", or the "Great Disruption".

As of 2018, the industrialized societies were consuming many trillions of dollars yearly in animal products. Super corporate profits in this sector are made possible from relatively cheap (fossil-fuel) energy, a steady flow of new and improved goods, widespread use of chemicals and drugs, and of course nonstop advertising. Convenience and affordability are indispensable, whether at local stores, supermarkets, sports venues, or fast-food outlets. The industrialized food system has evolved into a sprawling global complex seemingly impervious to change, able to resist most reform initiatives. It constitutes a vast power structure into itself, managed by aggressive capitalists with an increasing hold over the corporate media and popular culture. The industrial system appears fixed, routinized, highly profitable, Roberts writing: "The inertia of the modern meat economy is really just a variant of the enormous momentum that is now driving the large food system on its perilous trajectory."[200] As noted, the food economy has taken on strongly oligopolistic features, meaning a sector dominated by a few corporate giants: Nestle, PepsiCo, Cargill, Archer Daniels Midland (ADM) JBS, Tyson Foods, Kraft-Heinz, Walmart, Coca Cola. Of these, Cargill, ADM, JBS, and Tyson operate primarily within the meat industry, with yearly revenues well into the tens of billions, their work forces in the tens of thousands.

Nestle remains one of the largest and most diversified of these corporate behemoths, with annual revenue (2017) of $92 billion and a labor force of 323,000.[201] Its products – 43 percent sold in the U.S. – include processed foods, milk products, water, powdered beverages, pet foods, and pharmaceuticals. Nestle's international expansion began in the early 1990s, extending to Europe, Asia, and Africa. It has merged with or purchased outright several food companies – Libby's, Stouffer's Pellegrino, Gerber, Dryers among others. In 2018, Nestle and Starbucks reached a $7.15 billion distribution arrangement. The company has come under strong criticism for its health, safety, and environmental violations going back several decades, along with highly questionable standards of its many products such as bottled water.

Among the largest international food conglomerates, Cargill had revenues of $155 billion in 2017 and a worldwide labor force of nearly 150,000. It ranks 15th on the Fortune 500 list, slightly ahead of AT&T, specializing in such areas as meat-processing, grains, oils, processed foods, and several agricultural commodities. Cargill operates in 66 countries and supplies 25 percent of all American grain exports. With six domestic meat-processing facilities, it furnishes 22 percent of meats to the U.S. market. It recently built a rather fancy Protein Group Headquarters, a cultural gesture to the elevated status that protein-laden foods (meat and dairy) have achieved in American society. In recent years Cargill was targeted with numerous EPA lawsuits over air pollution and other environmental violations, along with protests over food contamination and poor working conditions.[202]

With 270 plants and 420 crop procurement centers worldwide, ADM had revenues of $62 billion in 2016 with a workforce of 32,000. A diversified conglomerate, it built an empire on global grain elevators, storage facilities, transportation networks, and ethanol production. Its general carbon imprint is said to be among the largest, and the company has faced many federal lawsuits for extreme levels of air and water pollution. JBS is similarly diversified with 2017 revenue of $50 billion and more than 78,000 employees in the U.S. and Latin America. In 2007, JBS Swift became the largest beef processor in the world, before acquiring Smithfield in 2008. It also carries out waste management, commodity trading, cleaning products, and biodiesel fuels. It has a long record of health violations and product recalls at its American meat-processing plants.[203]

While not strictly or even mainly a meat business, Walmart merits dubious attention as the largest grocery retailer in the U.S., with overall reserves (2017) reaching \$500 billion – and the largest conglomerate in the world with a labor force of 2.3 million at nearly 12,000 stores in 28 countries.[204] By 2005, Walmart had taken over 20 percent of the American grocery retail market, more recently having refined its operations to include an ordering service called "Walmart To Go". With an additional 700 local markets in the U.S., Walmart now effectively competes with Kroger, Target, K-Mart, and Whole Foods. Fiercely anti-union, the management has faced a torrent of protests and lawsuits in recent decades, mostly related to harsh working conditions, gender and racial bias, and privacy violations.

Among many sectors of the world economy, the modern food complex occupies a special place within capitalist rationalization – a process driven by refined technology, globalization, organizational power, oligopolistic markets, and a vast low-wage labor force. As usual, the food system intersects with other areas – transportation, technology, energy, pharmaceuticals, chemicals, commodities, trading, banking. It now constitutes the exemplary form of corporate power, wealth, and capital accumulation.

The Fast-Food Debacle

Any reference to "McDonaldization" must extend to a fast-food economy that nowadays commodifies far more than food products. Here we have an advanced form of capitalist rationalization – high tech, globalized, routinized, pervasive – increasingly visible in fast foods but also in office supplies, coffee houses, auto servicing, retail businesses, and even higher education. While McDonalds itself as an iconic system of fast-food restaurants is the best-known brand of this genre, many others include KFC, Taco Bell, Burger King, Carl's Jr., Domino's, Subway, Papa John's – all corporate chains reaping huge profits from mostly animal-based foods, with an impact felt across the U.S. and the world.

Fast foods gained popularity after World War II and have been expanding ever since, bringing new habits, consumerism, technology, labor relations, and cultural patterns along with health problems. Their business model and operating procedures have become universalized, spreading from restaurants to gas stations, convenience stores, retail outlets, airports, stadiums, universities, and high schools, shaping food choices across the landscape. With top-down organization, routinized production, a low-wage deskilled labor force, and standardized consumer items, the McDonaldized sector aspires to the most elaborate form of capitalist rationalization. It brings meat and dairy products at affordable prices to an apparently unlimited consuming public.

Capitalist rationalization in this sector, as in others, favors maximum corporate power and profit-making based on elevated productivity, uniformity, managerial controls, and branding appeal. Corporate giants like McDonalds and KFC have enough freedom and flexibility to prevail against counterforces such as governments and unions. In an era of hyper-commodification, these chains celebrate an image of a capitalist paradise. Until recently, moreover, the sector operated as if mounting concerns about health and the environment were hardly worth addressing. Eric Schlosser comments in *Fast Food Nation* that business culture – in its exploitation of communities, workers, consumers, and animals – harkens back to an era of social Darwinism.[205]

From the 1950s to the present, McDonalds has typified what we now mean by "fast-food nation". It is the world's largest restaurant chain with 37,000 outlets in 120 countries, a yearly (2017) revenue of $23 billion, and 1.9 million employees. Known primarily for its hamburgers, McDonalds also sells a variety of convenience food products to 69 million customers daily. The chain has further come to symbolize globalization, shaping economic life, food choices, and health issues across the world. Thanks to McDonalds and kindred chains, "fast food" is identified with the wonders of modernity, affluence, and mobility. The corporation does business freely in China and Russia (where it has more than 500 outlets).

The huge McDonalds workforce is comprised mainly of low-wage, deskilled labor adaptable to high-tech assembly lines where jobs are generally interchangeable. Since the late 1990s, management has stressed automation, hoping to replace human workers with electronic kiosks and other robotic mechanisms. Research has shown that McDonalds workers have been paid on average well below subsistence wages. Many employees must rely on some type of public assistance. In recent years McDonalds workers have filed numerous complaints over health and safety violations with the Occupational Safety and Health Administration (OSHA) – usually with limited results. The mega-corporation's dismal health, labor, and environmental records were brought to public attention during the famous London McLibel trial, subject of a later documentary titled *McLibel*. Similar criticisms were brought forward by Schlosser in *Fast Food Nation*, and later by Morgan Spurlock in his 2004 documentary *SuperSize Me*, which dramatized the severe hazards of eating Big Macs and related products. The fast-food transnational managed to endure these and other assaults while even thriving and expanding, thanks to its huge advertising and marketing capabilities.[206]

In his classic *The McDonaldization of Society*, George Ritzer brilliantly lays out the contours of a special mode of capitalist rationalization that drives the fast-food industry. The familiar Weberian theory of rationalization informs this system quite well, but Ritzer takes the approach further in his penchant critique of the McDonalds empire. Writes Ritzer: "Weber described how the modern Western world managed to become increasingly rational – that is dominated by efficiency, predictability, calculability, and non-human technologies to control people … McDonaldization is an amplification of an extension of Weber's Theory of Rationalization. For Weber, the model of rationalization was the bureaucracy; for me, the fast-food restaurant is the paradigm of McDonaldization."[207] Ritzer adds, in the tracks of Weber, that this process turns out to be one of the major influences across world history.

Such a thriving fast-food system, Ritzer argues, is the ultimate expression of modernity, highly profitable in a society of maximum physical mobility, where people have easy access to cars and public transportation, where workers and consumers "prefer to be on the move".[208] Modernity is shaped by "the increasing influence of the mass media, (which) contributes to the success of fast-food restaurants. Without saturation advertising and the ubiquitous influence of television and other mass media, fast-food restaurants would not have succeeded as well as they have". Another component of modernity – technology – remains a driving force behind capitalist rationalization. Thus: "… technological change has probably played the greatest role in the success of McDonaldized systems. Initially, technologies such as bureaucracies, scientific management, the assembly line, and the product of that production system, the automobile, all contributed to the birth of the fast-food society. Over the years, innumerable technological developments have both spurred and been spurred by McDonaldization ... Many technological marvels of the future will either arise from the expanded needs of a McDonaldization society or help create new areas to be McDonaldized."[209]

Ritzer's expectations regarding the appeal of McDonalds – including the rapid pace of market globalization – could not have been more prescient. In various ways McDonaldization recycles central features of classical Fordism: mass production, standardized production and work, markets for mass-produced goods, low-wage labor force. Nowadays, as Ritzer observes, "homogenous products dominate a McDonaldized world. The Big Mac, the Egg McMuffin, and Chicken McNuggets are identified from one time or place to another." Further, "Technologies such as Burger King's conveyer system, as well as the french fry and soft drink machines throughout the fast-food industry, are as rigid as many of the technologies in Henry Ford's assembly line system."[210] Within this paradigm, work routines are standardized, jobs are extensively linked, labor is functionally homogenous, and both "The demands and the actions of the customers are homogenized by the needs of the fast-food restaurant."[211] McDonalds represents not simply a fast-food system but, more pervasively, a fast-food *culture* extending beyond the historical features, providing the benefits of Weberian rationality – efficiency, predictability, calculability, and control.[212]

McDonaldization is driven by capitalist rationalization most emphatically in the realm of managerial *control* through mechanisms of bureaucracy and technology, inspired by the first manifestations of "Fordism" and "Taylorism" that arose within assembly-line production at Detroit auto factories and elsewhere. It gave rise to a specific type of "mass worker", deskilled and interchangeable, easily subject to routinized methods of domination. Often labeled "scientific management", the system demanded a homogenous, alienated, subordinated workforce. Fordism was designed to control labor by means of repetitive technology and then ultimately to *replace* labor through refined technology such as computers, robots, and (nowadays) artificial intelligence – schemes vigorously pushed by McDonalds and kindred chains.

This routinization and subordination of labor would reduce the labor process to a repressive apparatus of laws, rules, procedures, even mathematical formulas that would be reflective of Weber's famous "iron cage".

As Ritzer notes: "Once human skills were codified, the organization no longer needed skilled workers."[213] Human creativity and individual autonomy were properties deemed entirely antithetical to this tyrannical process. Programmed and rationalized functions have extended to all phases of McDonaldization, which in effect raises Fordism to new heights within an economic sector that employs (in the U.S.) nearly one-third of the labor force. That system creates "McJobs" that result in a "high level of resentment, job dissatisfaction, alienation, absenteeism, and turnover."[214]

The fast-food industry is meant to reproduce an impersonal and anonymous setting not only for management and employees but for customers. As Ritzer points out: "The fast-food restaurant also dehumanizes consumers. By eating on a sort of assembly line, diners are reduced to automatically rushing thru a meal with a little gratification derived from the dining experience or from the food itself. The best that can be said is that the meal can be efficient and is over quickly. Some customers (ironically) might even feel as if they are being fed like livestock."[215] McDonalds depends on uniformity and predictability, its corporate patterns following a programmed, scripted, orchestrated process similar to that of other rigid bureaucracies. And of course, the food products are assembled, processed, and served along these same lines. As for the quality of these products, the fast-food system routinely delivers harmful doses of fat, sugar, salt, and meat to tens of millions of unwitting customers daily.

Eric Schlosser refers to McDonaldization as the "great food commodity machine" – a paradigm of both eating and everyday life that thrives on efficiency and affordability but conceals a world of unspeakable harm, suffering, and destruction.[216] This supposed beacon of modernity works against the best interests of workers, consumers, the environment, and perhaps most of all to the billions of animals ritually terrorized through the vast, globalized conveyer belt of torture and killing. Its assembly lines engulf both people and animals, leaving in its wake pollution, waste, carbon emissions, irrational use of agricultural products, and untold damage to human health.

The global reach of McDonaldization is presently such that it figures to be increasingly difficult to undermine, much less abolish, as a major source of food consumption. The ultimate goal of both Fordism and McDonaldization has been to technologize and robotize the workforce, to substitute obedient machines for potentially restive workers. Ritzer pessimistically concludes that " ... the future will bring with it an increasing number of non-human technologies with a greater ability to control people and processes."[217] Humans are already trapped in the workings of high-tech surveillance networks in the U.S. and other industrialized societies, a phenomenon fully consistent with McDonaldization. This is especially worrisome when considering the prospects for reversing the ecological crisis.

Technology, Food, Culture

If McDonaldization is one of the most developed forms of capitalist rationalization, its consequences transcend the fast-food system, permeating most of social life. In Ritzer's words: "... McDonaldization affects not only the restaurant business but also education, work, health care, travel, leisure, dieting, politics, the family, and virtually every other aspect of society. McDonaldization has shown every sign of being an inexorable process, sweeping thru seemingly impervious institutions and regions of the world."[218] Here modern technology has steadily evolved into a set of cultural norms embedded in the matrix of modern power structures. And food itself has been technologized beyond the McDonalds context, to agribusiness, the energy sector, chemicals, medicine, and advertising.

The continuous refinement of capitalist rationalization involves a complex process especially adaptable to the fast-food industry: a fixed system of rules and regulations, division of labor, simplification of functions and tasks, and subordination of humans to bureaucratic and technological processes from which escape seems difficult if not hopeless. A Weberian "iron cage" of rationality tightens to erode individual and social autonomy. Further, as rationalization develops across the public (even private) landscape, "society would eventually become nothing more than a seamless web of rationalized structures" that would stifle human creativity and initiative.[219] Human activity becomes routinized, thus relatively predictable and manageable. As Marcuse argues, this development would have vast historical consequences not only for workplace freedoms but, more broadly, for critical thought and political opposition.

The tendency of advanced capitalism to generate deep contradictions was fully recognized by both Marx and Weber, the latter referring to the industrial order as a "heartless machine". Those contradictions, reflected in mounting class conflict, were destined to intensify over time – as indeed they have in most capitalist societies since the nineteenth century. Yet working-class upheavals directed against the power structure itself have rarely made significant headway: across the twentieth century the owners and managers of capitalism have been able to fight off counterforces and stabilize their hegemonic position. One dynamic behind this epic achievement has been rationalization of the economy and, by extension, important spheres of public life. Nowhere has this phenomenon been more fully realized than in the U.S. and Europe – those parts of the world, ironically, that Marx believed would be epicenters of proletarian revolution.

Capitalist rationalization, in turn, has been fueled by the twin dynamics of bureaucratic organization and technological innovation. Weber, later Marxists like Antonio Gramsci, and theorists of the Frankfort School saw in this process a sharpening of authoritarian trends. Where Marx viewed commodity fetishism as endemic to capitalism, Weber looked to instrumental rationality as central to elite control and mass consent, anticipating what some in the Frankfurt school would describe as the "totally administered society". However understood, capitalist rationalization brought new layers of domination that would undercut prospects for individual autonomy, free markets, and democracy.

It was capitalist rationalization, moreover, that would keep crisis-tendencies in check, staving off the collapse that Marx and later Marxists had predicted. Here technology as such would take on special meaning – an ensemble of forms and techniques that would end up fully embedded in the class and power relations of modern state-capitalism. Technology would be crucial to systemic continuity and stability, a feature not only of production but of culture and politics. Whether approached from a Marxist or Weberian standpoint, to imagine the expansion of technology apart from history and social relations would be illusory. With few exceptions, technology has widely served the advance of capitalist development, giving impetus to familiar benefits of calculation, routine, prediction, and control.

Capitalist rationalization intersects with, and helps transform, every realm of society. In this sense, technology is clearly far from being neutral.

In the food sector, as we have seen, technological innovation is largely carried out within the framework of McDonaldization. In the case of automobiles, technological innovation has promoted spatial mobility, travel, entertainment, and diverse forms of consumerism – all naturally requiring huge energy consumption. For corporations and banks, we have hyper-computerized modes of doing business and communicating on a world scale, tied to corporate power and wealth accumulation. Sophisticated robots and artificial intelligence nowadays help drive both productivity and social control, including surveillance. As for the military, the role of great technological advances should be obvious, from nuclear weapons to missiles, robots, drones, self-driving vehicles, and digitalized information gathering. Technological rationality helps reproduce efficiency and domination across the entire state-capitalist landscape.

At this point we could extend the focus from sector to sector, beginning with a technocratic, bureaucratic, commodified medical system heavily reliant for its treatments on drugs, surgery, and myriad expensive techniques – often to the detriment of alternative paths such as nutrition, preventive care, and holistic remedies. In fact, professional medicine in the U.S. and elsewhere has done little to combat the scourge of chronic diseases, from heart conditions to cancer, diabetes, or various other harms caused by fast-food and meat-centered diets. We know that the emphasis on prescription drugs to "treat" or "remedy" such chronic problems usually fails to solve them, deflecting attention from underlying causes. As for innovative medical techniques – knee-replacement, heart surgery, artificial limbs, hormone therapy, etc., – these can improve quality of life for millions of people, but the general level of health continues to seriously decline in societies where technocratic methods prevail.[220]

Technological rationality marks a convergence of multiple and overlapping phenomena: computer technology, communications, mass advertising, surveillance – all linked to corporate, government, and military power, not to mention globalization. It serves both ideological legitimization and structured domination, beyond Taylorism or Fordism and even McDonaldization that mainly originated at the workplace. Technology as ideology extends across the public landscape, shaping and reshaping education, culture, labor relations, consumerism, daily life – surely the most effective form of ideological hegemony in advanced capitalism. The corporate media, its scope and efficiency heightened by continuous technological refinements, exerts deepening influence on mass consciousness, reinforced not only by media culture but corporate and government surveillance.

Viewed against the backdrop of global crisis, capitalist rationalization actually worsens conditions that are destroying the natural habitat. As technology enhances corporate productivity and efficiency, it thereby contributes to the growth mania, consumerism, resource exploitation, and multiple types of pollution. It also fuels the routinized processing of fast foods – among the most harmful legacies of technological rationality.

Herbert Marcuse, among the most profound critics of capitalist rationalization, theorized modern technology as a crucial arena of domination, with deep roots in the Enlightenment. He took Weberian analysis to new levels, technological rationality morphing into a type of *political* rationality, or ideological hegemony.[221] While technology as such benefits the larger society in many ways, in other ways it clearly benefits the ruling interests. It further enables the integration of prevailing economic, political, and cultural forces at the summits of power. Writes Marcuse: "Today domination perpetrates and extends itself not only thru technology, but *as* technology, and the latter provides the great legitimization of the expanding political power, which absorbs all spheres of culture."[222]

Within one-dimensional society, which for Marcuse represents the fullest expression of capitalist rationalization, the "iron cage" becomes institutionalized and works against both critical thought and political opposition. To the degree it impedes social change, political struggles to reverse the ecological crisis will have to face the stifling effects of technological rationality. Thus "Technical progress, extended to the whole system of domination and coordination creates forms of life (and of power) which appear to reconcile the forces opposing the system and to defeat or refute all protest in the name of the historical prospects of freedom from toil and domination. Contemporary society seems to be capable of containing social change – qualitative change which would establish essentially different institutions, a new direction of the productive process, new modes of human existence. This containment of social change is perhaps the most singular achievement of the advanced industrial society …".[223] Of course, this was the very meaning of Taylorism and Fordism historically, and is currently what mostly underpins McDonaldization.

Technological rationality helps perpetuate the entire matrix of domination, Marcuse writing: "By virtue of the way it has organized its technological base, contemporary industrial society tends to be totalitarian. For totalitarian is not only a terroristic political coordination of society, but also a non-terroristic economic coordination which operates thru the manipulation of needs by vested interests. It thus precludes the emergence of an effective opposition against the whole."[224] Such hegemony equates to "one dimensional" thought confined to the parameters of technological discourse, "systematically promoted by makers of politics and their purveyors of mass information. Their universe of discourse is populated by self-validating hypotheses which, incessantly and monopolistically repeated, become hypnotic definitions or dictations".[225] Though *One-Dimensional Man* appeared in 1964, the broad trajectory of American politics would seem to confirm Marcuse's earlier view: in neither the U.S. nor any other advanced capitalist society have anti-system forces made significant headway.

For Marcuse, enlightened "instruments of progress" have been organized into repressive technological and administrative systems where individual and social autonomy has been subverted, a view consistent with Ritzer's later analysis of McDonaldization – both with roots in Weberian sociology. This is a universe not only of institutional domination but of ideological controls visible in mass marketing, advertising, and outright state or media propaganda. Surface images of progress would provide a façade behind which manifestations of irrationality (domination, alienation, violence, war) tend to thrive. The very ramifications of modern food production and consumption – McDonaldization, agribusiness, animal horrors, health afflictions – would effectively validate this motif year in and year out. In this as in other cases, illusions of progress would encounter the actuality of barbarism.

The twenty-first century has seen the rise of corporate oligopolies like nothing before in history. The dramatic rise of high-tech giants – Microsoft, Apple, Facebook, Google, Amazon, Twitter, etc. – is a development of vast historical significance, merging computer systems, technical planning, data collection, and mapping operations within an overarching economic matrix. In this context capitalist rationalization would seem to have reached its zenith, its reach far beyond anything imagined during earlier phases of computer technology or indeed McDonaldization. In contrast to

Taylorism and Fordism, which championed principles of hierarchy, control, discipline, and division of labor at the workplace, a maturing Silicon Valley culture views its own, more advanced, variant of technological rationality as entirely different, more liberating – a domain of freedom, democracy, and creativity resonant with Enlightenment ideology. Contemporary high-tech chieftains see their work as emphatically liberating, purposeful, even spiritual.

The new technology behemoths are in the process of remolding every sphere of life in advanced capitalist societies, yet to say that their progressive claims are vastly exaggerated would be an understatement. The Silicon Valley template turns out to have more in common with McDonaldization than its propagandists will admit. The first reality is that, with the Internet, social media, and other sectors of the new technology, we are dealing with a globalized oligopoly able to dominate the worldwide flow of markets, communications, knowledge, and decision making. Beneath all the libertarian pretenses we see just the opposite: concentrated power, social manipulation, conformism, homogenization of political thought. This would have more in common with Marcuse's one dimensionality than with the open society claims of Jeff Bezos (Amazon) and Mark Zuckerberg (Facebook).

The new technology bears little resemblance to its countercultural origins as a beacon of human emancipation, a global network of cooperation and spiritual values. Nowadays, in contrast, we see a powerful merger of corporate, technological, military, and academic interests that have colonized the public landscape, with the same "totalitarian" consequences spelled out by Marcuse and earlier theorists of the Frankfurt School.[226] There is no happy tribe or commune ready to appropriate technology for truly liberating ends. The vast "cathedrals of knowledge" – corporatized, instrumentalized, and commodified – turn easily in the directions of networked power presided over by the gatekeepers of knowledge, data, and opinion.

Referring to the grandiose ambitions of such tech giants as Microsoft and Google, Franklin Foer refers to the "hegemonic egos of its leaders."[227] Knowledge, defined as the unending search for information – amounts to something of a theological belief while also setting up mechanisms enabling super profits. The "cathedrals of knowledge", however dispersed and conflicted they might be, function in a way to dominate both time and space, eroding ideological and cultural diversity along the way. Driven by a strong moralizing elitism, the Silicon Valley oligopoly blocks genuine multiculturalism in favor of an ideologically murky identity politics.

The administered society so anticipated by Marcuse enters the picture here: after all, the new technology is here to stay, now a relentless juggernaut that no contemporary force can easily resist – or transcend. At this juncture both knowledge and power are historically interwoven. Foer cites Peter Diamandis as observing: "Anybody who is going to be resisting this progress forward is going to be resisting evolution. And fundamentally they will die out."[228] Thus, if Google can painstaking map the entire world and utilize information toward any set of interests, where can a counter to such super-intelligence be located? Any effort, it would seem, will be checkmated before it gains the slightest momentum. This has profoundly negative implications for critical thought and political opposition, and that would surely include efforts to reverse the global crisis.

Google, with a yearly revenue surpassing that of 70 countries, has the technological capacity to accumulate, process, store, and utilize information with few limits or regulations. That includes information about every single individual who enters the system, a function that in effect overrides privacy. Corporations follow their own rules and procedures, some fully hidden from view. Surveillance activities at Google largely proceed in the absence of effective oversight or monitoring – a frightening specter when linkages between the tech sector and such federal agencies as the NSA, FBI, DEA are taken into account. The familiar goal of the NSA, as the film *Citizen Four* dramatized, is to secretly "collect it all" for whatever purposes the intelligence managers decide.[229] Again, this marriage of advanced technology with the intelligence apparatus tightens where there is no political accountability or even media transparency. Never has a corporate stratum enjoyed more power over the public terrain by means of its control of knowledge and communication.

This phenomenon has become more authoritarian than anything imagined by Marcuse and Ritzer: beneath the vaunted "hacker culture", new-age spiritualism, and visions of libertarianism, we find the most rationalized order ever, a tribute to heightened manifestations of capitalist modernization. Hierarchy, secrecy, rules, control – these are the basic features of a corporate-state system where technology rules and so much public discourse is routinized. The fabled liberalism of Silicon Valley must be viewed in this historical context, just as familiar celebrations of multiculturalism can be debunked in a world that tolerates little *ideological* diversity. What Marcuse theorized several decades ago has been confirmed many times over: technological rationality functions to ensure conformity, ritualized thinking, and data worship, all the while reducing ideological pluralism and political conflict. Not only Google, but Apple, Twitter, Facebook and Microsoft are hyper-rationalized business operations geared to profit maximization; libertarian ideals exist for cosmetic appearance.

In this universe of mechanical images and data manipulation, ecological values – indeed ethical concerns in general – end up remote, detached, bothersome. The process of gathering and using information is thoroughly routinized and standardized – hardly different from the McDonaldized culture despite a more enlightened façade. Insofar as technological rationality works to abolish conflict in favor of order and routine, it actually depoliticizes. Describing the governing ethos of Silicon Valley, Foer writes: "If algorithms can replicate the process of creativity, then there's little reason to nurture human creativity."[230] Indeed human virtue (volition?) is automatically embedded in hyper-rational patterns of information gathering and processing. Google, like Apple, Microsoft, Facebook, and Amazon, has managed to build its data empire into global networks of power, wealth, and status. These are what might be called the "gatekeepers" of knowledge and culture, armed with plenty of certitude and hubris. Observes Foer: "Silicon Valley routinely trashes cultural and economic gatekeepers – while its own companies are the most imposing gatekeepers in human history."[231]

The technology behemoths embrace idealism, righteous causes, at times even utopian visions while orchestrating information flows for most of the planet. Theirs is the world of networks, systems, algorithms, databases, and mapping, at odds with the two-way-flow of information and democratization of knowledge that Silicon Valley loves to celebrate, its power hidden, and operations shrouded in the mystery of dark technology. Google, with its enormous wealth, unprecedented global reach, and massive search engines, is nowadays considered much too powerful to regulate. Extensive coordination among many of the tech giants, Wall Street, government agencies, and academia threatens freedom, democracy, and privacy in the form of a heightened surveillance order. That order amasses data on all persons, uses that data for myriad purposes, saturates public life with cameras, pinpoints GPS coordinates, stores data across entire societies, and frequently targets questionable or deviant opinions. Here technological rationality reaches new levels, a force behind the rise of "surveillance capitalism" – a system increasingly in conflict with labor, consumers, democracy, and indeed the natural habitat.[232]

The undeniable fruits of modern technology – providing wider access to information, smoothing communication flows, facilitating human transactions, driving economic output – hardly overrides the one-dimensional character of technological rationality. Like earlier phases of economic rationalization, this more technologized order fights ethical, political, and ecological constraints; "externals" matter peripherally, if at all.

Within those parameters, the great promises of Enlightenment ideology have been reduced to empty illusions. Whatever the ruling ideology, the fate of the natural habitat has ranged from neglect to devastation. As the leading capitalist power, the U.S. should bear culpability for more of these consequences than any other nation. Others, including China, Europe, and Russia, may not be far behind, whether measured according to greenhouse emissions or a variety of other environmental indicators. The many fictions of capitalist modernity – free markets, economic progress, globalization, technological panaceas, democracy – offer psychological comfort but, unfortunately, no viable solutions to the ecological crises.

Driven by capitalist rationalization, the war against nature – against land, forests, oceans, the atmosphere, all living creatures – escalates daily, with few constraints. Obsessed with the endless accumulation of wealth and power, and driven toward maximum consumption of natural resources, the rulers of this decaying order have shown little interest in altering the path to disaster.

The Global Meat Addiction

In American society, as throughout the industrialized world, we see a food system dominated by animal-based agriculture, huge meat-processing industries, fast-food outlets, and huge marketing operations that saturate the media and popular culture. Grocery stores, convenience stops, restaurants, and public gathering places offer primarily meat, dairy, and sugar options. Global food-industry profits now extend to hundreds of billions of dollars. By far the most popular food choices – those celebrated for every occasion, across national and cultural divides – turn out to be those most harmful not only to the environment and to animals but to human health, where the toll far exceeds any previous reckoning.

This problem is so deeply entrenched that any future exit from clearly unsustainable patterns of collective behavior currently seems difficult to imagine; levers and agencies of change appear nowhere in view. One glaring problem is that so much is organized around the meat complex – vested economic interests, political lobbying, social policies, media advertising, even academic research. Consumer behavior and everyday lifestyles have evolved to reinforce this hegemonic system. Not surprisingly, while animal-based foods are championed throughout the corporate, medical, media, and academic sectors, the undeniably superior virtues of plant-based foods are generally denigrated or at least minimized. Efforts to show a relationship between dietary habits and health outcomes are usually met with myths, distortions, and outright lies, though often cloaked in scientific discourse.

Modern food choices, as with the entire realm of consumption, are embedded within a framework of ingrained habits, addictions, and lifestyles fitting capitalist priorities – reinforced by perhaps the most successful propaganda apparatus in history. Influence accumulates within a sprawling complex of vested interests, including the food, medical, drug, agricultural, and insurance industries, John Robbins writing: "These are industries profiting from keeping you ignorant, confused, and misinformed, buying and consuming products that lead to unnecessary suffering and death …".[233]

As this system expands, the health of the planet deteriorates while the health of human populations worsens, the result of accelerated economic growth, widening use of toxic chemicals, and the McDonaldization of food patterns. In the case of the U.S., its health-care system is the most resource-utilizing in the world, in 2008 amounting to nearly 20 percent of domestic output. Increasingly high rates of death from cancer and other chronic diseases (more than one million yearly) – associated with high levels of obesity – speak volumes about the dysfunctional, poorly accessible, and iatrogenic (counter-productive) features of American medicine. The U.S. spends nearly three trillion dollars yearly on medicine, yet its health

outcomes have generally not ranked very high compared to other industrialized nations, in great measure owing to heavy meat and dairy consumption along with absence of universal health care. The familiar notion that
such outcomes can be altered through more spending, more expertise, more
technology, more pills, more special diets – amounts to one of the grand
illusions of the present era.

In the U.S., chronic diseases have become more or less endemic to
patterns of food consumption – cancer being one condition that persists in
large numbers despite recurrent media promises of new "cures" and breakthrough "remedies". Prevailing modalities reflect the power of big business
to shape health agendas, a problem associated with the harm done by distorted science, faith in technology, and failure of medical intervention to
curb probably the worst plague of modern society. The cancer toll exceeds
500,000 deaths yearly even after hundreds of billions of dollars are spent on
research, technical development, and treatment. For early critics like Ralph
Moss (in *The Cancer Industry*) and later investigators like Devra Davis, John
Robbins, John McDougall, T. Colin Campbell and Samuel Epstein, the
major hospitals, clinics, institutes, and agencies set up to fight cancer have
generally done more to serve corporate interests than to improve general
health conditions.[234]

After working many years at the American Cancer Society (ACS),
Davis wrote *The Secret History of the War on Cancer*, an insider's critique of
an industry she argues has done more to block than to advance efforts at
understanding the real causes of cancer.[235] Following Moss, she paid close
attention to the role of corporate influence – dishonest advertising, expensive lobbying, business takeover of government agencies, scientific distortions, political scheming – which dwells on symptoms, technical solutions,
and surgery or drugs to the exclusion of preventive, holistic, nutritional
remedies. The ACS, riddled with big-business interests, spends less than
ten percent of its budget on independent studies, perhaps worried its long-
standing bias might be compromised by the "wrong" findings. At centers
like Sloane Kettering and ACS, cancer is typically seen as an invading agent
rather than an *internal* process of health deterioration, resulting from diet,
lifestyles, and other contextual factors.[236] The disease is often conceded by
medical experts to be the "price of modern life", though usually amenable
to drug therapy.[237]

For American society, at least, no important center dedicated to fighting cancer – the ACS, Sloan Kettering, the National Cancer Institute (NCI), major universities – devotes much attention to social and environmental causes of disease formation, or to lifestyle factors including nutrition. Such factors are generally treated as peripheral to the "scientific" interpretive framework. There is little focus on the fast-food diet, or meat in general, shown by dozens of reputable studies to be strongly implicated in most types of cancer.[238] In 1997, the American Institute for Cancer Research (AICR), joined by the World Cancer Research fund, issued a report on the basis of 4,500 studies for the World Health Organization (WHO) concluding that up to 70 percent of all cancers stem from lifestyle-related causes – above all consumption of meat and dairy products. These findings were supported by Campbell's seminal book, *The China Study* (2006) based on exhaustive comparative analysis of dietary patterns, but the American medical-scientific establishment carried on as if the study never appeared.[239] Other independent research (that is, not funded by vested interests) has arrived at much the same conclusions.[240]

As Robbins comments in his exploration of cancer and diet in *The Food Revolution* (2001), the price paid by the American public for corporate and academic distortion of cancer research – visible, for example, in the stonewalling of critical studies – can be calculated in the millions of deaths for the U.S. alone.[241] Scientific research has for decades shown an undeniable linkage between meat or dairy intake and cancer, yet the vast majority of Americans, thanks to media advertising, remain ignorant and therefore disempowered on matters related to their own health.

Campbell's *The China Study* illustrates this connection more systematically than any previous work – a project based on data gathered in China and elsewhere, reinforced by extensive clinical research. Campbell found that nutritional factors play a role in explaining different cancer rates across geographical, class, ethnic, and gender differences. High intake of animal proteins and fats both activates and accelerates bodily processes that can lead to cancer.[242] Obstacles to this line of thinking are erected by corporate interests (food, agribusiness, medical, pharmaceutical) that obscure or distort independent findings like those of Campbell. In his book Campbell calls attention to the watershed 1980s congressional McGovern Report that warned about the hazards of meat consumption, but was roundly dismissed by government, medical, and media establishments, with public debate largely squelched. The report's dietary goals – less meat, more plant-based foods – were harshly attacked by the National Academy of Sciences, an entity dominated by meat and dairy interests that had long extolled the virtues of damaging high-protein, high-fat diets.[243]

The prestigious American Council on Science and Health (ACSH), promoted as a consumer interest group yet dependent on meat and dairy producers for nearly 80 percent of its funding, follows the same bankrupt premises. The ACSH strongly favors meat and dairy foods, denouncing critics as conspiracy theorists and quacks. At the AICR, moreover, nutritional issues receive little focus within an organization supposedly dedicated to uncovering sources of cancer, as that research emphasis conflicts with mainstream drug, medical, and food interests. Scientific efforts to broaden or diversify work in the field are routinely met with intimidation, personal smears, and lies of the sort Moss and Davis exposed after spending years within the cancer industry.[244] The very idea of cancer prevention was always ridiculed at the AICR, as well as at the ACSH and ACS. Notes Campbell: "In the world of nutrition and health, scientists are not free to pursue their research wherever it leads. Coming to the 'wrong conclusion', even though first-rate science, can damage your career."[245] Following Moss, Campbell refers to this corruption of medical research as the "science of industry". The American food, medical, and drug corporations remain today among the most powerful and profitable in the world, and they stand to lose most from any fundamental shift in public approaches to cancer.

This array of corporations, lobbies, marketing operations, and public-relations firms – along with government agencies they colonize – monitor and influence the bulk of health-related research in the U.S. They deeply influence university work, including grants, conferences, journals, workshops, and medical school curricula. Rarely at these sites is linkage of lifestyle and cancer taken seriously, since overriding emphasis is placed on drug research and treatment. The Federal Nutrition Board itself welcomes to its circle representatives of such firms as Burger King, Dannon, Taco Bell, Coca Cola, Nestle, Pfizer and Roche – all fiercely resistant to alternative directions in medicine. Recommendations typically go no further than their moneyed obsessions will allow.[246] As for the all-important National Institutes of Health (NIH) with its 27 institutes and centers, nowhere does its far-reaching work encompass social, nutritional, or environmental dimensions of health, and little funding for independent research is generally available.

Today the vast majority of scientists, doctors, and healthcare practitioners remain aligned with a medical-industrial complex in which "private" and "public", business and government sectors converge within a system of concentrated power. The role of Big Pharma in this bureaucratic process is difficult to exaggerate. After frustrating decades of working in biomedical research, Campbell writes: "I have come to the conclusion that when it comes to health, government is not for the people. It is for the food industry and the pharmaceutical industry at the expense of the people."[247] As mounting evidence reveals the limits of ideological rigidity in mainstream approaches, the system continues recklessly along the same technocratic, iatrogenic, authoritarian path. Meanwhile, the wealthiest nation in the world – with by far the most costly medical system – remains afflicted with the highest cancer rates, matched by worsening levels of diabetes, arthritis, and heart disease, symptomatic of a society marked by deteriorating medical, social, and personal health.

Capitalist modernity is shaped by the most sophisticated forms of technological rationality – a component of both structural domination and ideological hegemony that in the U.S. strongly impacts the practice of medicine. Here economic rationalization unfolds alongside what might be called the medicalization of American society, a development that requires, and celebrates, the ubiquitous power of its esteemed technical apparatus.[248]

While trumpeting individualism (often expressed in the form of consumerism), liberal ideology embraces a technocratic instrumentalism that works against human subjectivity. In a society where personal alienation and social misery are so widespread, who can be astonished to find an endless list of "disorders" requiring (physical and mental) treatment by chemical miracles in the form of mind-altering (or mind-numbing) drugs? Alienation gives rise to a variety of psychological coping mechanisms such as addictive behaviors related to shopping, food, gambling, the Internet, alcohol, tobacco, pharmaceuticals, and street drugs. This impulse toward escape stems from anxiety, stress, depression, and physical ailments. All too often "medication" and "addiction" end up as twin expressions of the same rationalized, administered order.[249] Such patterns occur at highest rates for *legal* substances including fast foods, sugar, alcohol, tobacco, and drugs such as opioids and anti-depressants. Those forms of habituation have become so common, so thoroughly embedded in the culture, as to be routinely over-looked as addictive.

This motif extends to food habits, above all the meat, dairy, and McDonaldized diets. Since these products (especially when consumed in large amounts) are so harmful to human health, and since the evidence is hardly secret, it might be worth asking why hundreds of millions of people regularly do such harm to themselves. True enough, negative consequences are typically obscured within a society that normalizes meat habituation. A complex psychology enters daily eating patterns shaped by tradition, ethnicity, convenience, and special celebrations, not to mention the pres-sures of social conformity; habits are constantly being reinforced from many sources. As noted, moreover, modern capitalism is rife with lobbies, advertising, and government subsidies helping to perpetuate already deeply ingrained habits. The plain and unfortunate truth is that, for American society and other industrialized societies, the vast majority of people some-how manage to go along with a litany of myths, lies, and distortions about food, especially meat and dairy products.

Told ritually that meat is the optimum food choice, people see little connection between eating routines and seemingly distant ramifications for health, the environment, and the animals they consume. Such psycholog-ical detachment is reinforced by media narratives about the great benefits of meat and dairy consumption. Beef in particular has long been associated with affluence, strength, health, and (for men) virility. These myths can be difficult to challenge when so few counter-narratives are visible. When severe health problems arise, as they inevitably do, people rarely give much thought to altering their food choices, instead searching for easy-to take pills, magical diets, even surgery.

The worsening American meat addiction has given rise to severe health problems, beginning with an obesity rate more than 40 percent and rising. In *Fast Food Genocide* (2017), Joel Fuhrman concludes that "fast food is sui-cide", arguing that "addiction to fast food is likely to be the most far-reach-ing and destructive influence on our population today."[250] Fast foods, as is well known, contain not only fatty meats but sugar, oils, additives, chemi-cals, and antibiotics, yet they appeal to consumers because of convenience and standardized fare. As of 2019 only four percent of Americans say they never consume fast foods.

Despite mounting health debacles, Americans remain more addicted to harmful foods than ever, kept ignorant by a cycle of myths and lies that animal products are the best (or only) source of protein, that large amounts of protein are needed for optimum health, that "carbs" (vaguely described) are somehow dangerous, that animal fats and proteins have nothing to do with obesity, that chronic diseases are unrelated to diet, that "processed" foods are more harmful than fast foods, that beef and similar meat products reflect a "good life" beyond anything possible from plant-based foods. The tightening linkage between meat and modernity, meat and status, in itself poses deep psychological obstacles to change. We are told that eating at the very top of the food chain is to be pursued and valued. While there is little impetus to rethink harmful practices, the extreme unsustainability of meat-centered diets seems to have grown more visible in the midst of ecological decline, so too have the health ramifications In his book *Beyond Beef*, Jeremy Rifkin writes: "Living atop the protein ladder has turned out to be very precarious. The affluent populations of the northern hemisphere are dying by the millions from grain-fed beef and other grain-fed meat."[251]

Americans now consume among the heaviest meat and fast food based diets in the world. While mainstream discourse focuses on genetic factors, excessive "carbs", and "processed" foods, the steady post-World War II rise in obesity can be traced more accurately to radical changes in nutritional habits, above all the increased consumption of meat and dairy products.

Foods rich in saturated fats – basic to the McDonaldized regimen – are the main contributors to obesity, again having little to do with genes or carbs. Compared to the Big Mac (with its 67 percent fat content) and milk shake (64 percent), plant foods (vegetables, legumes, grains, fruits) contain negligible if any saturated fats. Americans presently consume on average a staggering 36 percent of calories from fats, with no decline in sight. As Campbell shows in *The China Study*, most Chinese derive less than 10 percent of calories from saturated fats and thus experience far less obesity and by extension, fewer chronic diseases.[252] The afflictions of modernity and affluence, Campbell notes, are traced to meat-based diets, leading to a population that is "sick, overweight, and confused."[253]

If obesity derives largely from harmful eating habits, logic dictates that remedies lie in dietary and lifestyle alternatives. Such logic does not register within a medicalized society, however, where such options are either dismissed or routed into prescription drugs consistent with an historical preference for quick and painless remedies. While here and there temporarily beneficial, the overall record of expensive medical shortcuts has been less than stellar. The same can be said regarding highly touted special dietary plans. The Food and Drug Administration (FDA) has approved a litany of drugs to fight obesity, but none delivers permanent reversal of the condition and all have serious adverse reactions. These drugs, including widely consumed Didrex, Bontril, Xesical, and Meridia, have been placed on the "do not use" list by Sidney Wolfe and associates in their *Best Pills, Worst Pills* (2006). The authors write: Sibutramine (Meridia) is another in the long list of diet drugs that have never been shown they can be taken safely for a long enough period of time to reduce the morbidity and mortality associated with obesity."[254]

In their overall assessment of anti-obesity drugs, Wolfe and associates comment: "No diet drug ... has ever been shown to confer a health benefit in terms of reducing the serious complications associated with long-term obesity."[255] Weight reduction pills, moreover, tend to raise blood pressure while aggravating heart problems, thyroid conditions, and glaucoma. They also commonly give rise to extreme addictions. Further, the extent of weight loss from prescription meds is usually minuscule compared to the effects of a placebo. Many decades of experience with diet pills reveals harm far exceeds any benefits, yet tens of millions of Americans fill prescriptions each year, as the obesity "epidemic" worsens. Wolfe and associates conclude: "Prevention is the best treatment for obesity. Our advice about losing weight and diet pills has been the same for 20 years: eat less, exercise more. This approach to losing weight is slow but effective. The only one who profits from it is you. That's why it isn't sold."[256] Meanwhile, aggressive marketing conducted by Big Pharma has sharply intensified: advertisements for weight-loss drugs saturate TV, radio outlets, newspapers, magazines and the Internet.

Drugs most often prescribed for obesity – statins – have been hugely profitable for Big Pharma, with such blockbusters as Crestor reaching yearly sales of over five billion dollars. Statins such as Crestor, Lipitor, and Zocor have long been best-sellers, despite often tepid results; the number of regular statin users totals approximately 70 million (in 2018). Both the American Heart Association and American College of Cardiology, closely aligned with the drug industry, pushed this regimen despite such adverse reactions as hemorrhaging, strokes, elevated blood sugar, muscle weakening, and loss of vital nutrients.[257] Hospitals, clinics, doctors, and pharmacists are now more aggressive in touting weight-loss medications, presumably on the faulty notion that diet has little to do with obesity. The idea that excessive weight might be related to harmful behaviors, lifestyle choices, or social factors is soundly rejected.

The biomedical model fashionable in the U.S. relies heavily on disease theory, which detaches people from the larger social-psychological context. Human capacity to make key choices, to alter their life circumstances, to shape their health outcomes, is negated. If obesity is a disease, hovering over impotent and defenseless victims for a lifetime, the only hope is medical intervention to manage a problem that will never vanish. Diet pills end up the main option for those looking to "control" (not fully overcome) their obesity. It follows that if people are either invaded by some disease agent or have inherited genes for obesity – that is, are subjugated to external forces beyond their control – they become powerless, their human subjectivity eviscerated.

That individuals might alter their dietary and other lifestyle patterns – overcoming addictions without diet pills or surgery – works against the disease model. Yet if ordinary human behavior such as gambling, shopping, and sex is addictive and therefore changeable, it is hard to see why such change could not extend to eating. Food is, of course, essential to life, so it can be easily overlooked in any discussion of addictive behavior. The question here concerns not food as such but rather excessive amounts of *harmful* food, where habit and dependency (unrelated to pathogens or genes) contribute to weight problems and chronic diseases. One complication is that health-destroying food choices are not only legal but widely approved and vigorously advertised within the dominant culture at a time when myriad weight-reduction programs fuel a multi-billion-dollar industry.

As obesity in the U.S. (and much of the advanced industrial world) worsens, businesses reap huge profits from the health miseries of tens of millions of people, Big Pharma in the lead. In *The World is Fat* (2010), Barry Popkin writes: "Today, the drug industry dominates public expenditures and activity related to most health problems. This is as true for obesity as it is for other conditions."[258] . Reliance on pill therapy allows users to embrace illusions of betterment while retaining familiar dietary habits and lifestyles – fully the preference of established medicine and media culture. [259]

Along with drug-oriented "solutions", we find an endless parade of diet programs marketed through books, videos, workshops, seminars, and conferences. These schemes do not usually reject drug therapy, but they do raise questions about efficacy of the medical model. The very notion that obesity can be reversed by altering food habits implies the *possibility* of change through self-transformation, as in the famous Atkins program and its various offshoots. Many diet fads operate from the assumption that obesity can be remedied by adopting a low-carbohydrate diet – in effect turning to the very meat, dairy, and fast foods primarily responsible for obesity in the first place.

While extensive research points to a diet rich in plant foods as the overwhelmingly best option to fight obesity, such "low-carb" champions as Robert Atkins and John Mansfield argue that people should consume animal fats and proteins with few limits.[260] Atkins and Mansfield claim that obesity rates have increased at the very time Americans have become obsessed with jettisoning high-fat diets, many turning to low-fat vegetarian or vegan alternatives – but evidence for such a shift is lacking. On the contrary, per capita intake of saturated fats in the U.S has steadily risen as the McDonalds regimen is still popular, increasing by 13 pounds per capita since the early 1970s.[261] Despite overwrought warnings about "carbs" (forgetting the different *types* of carbs), moreover, it is difficult to ignore a stark reality: vegetarians rarely have weight problems, while regular consumers of fast foods and other animal products are far more likely to suffer from obesity. Claims that the real problem is too many low-fat diets runs up against the formidable McDonalds system. Sadly, Atkins, Mansfield, and many others have clung tenaciously to their diet schemes at a time when chronic diseases stemming from the standard American diet have reached new levels.[262]

The Atkins scheme offers a quick fix by means of a high-protein, high-fat, low-carbohydrate diet, telling people that "eating rich foods can be your path to weight-loss". Its great appeal – Atkins' books have long been best-sellers – is that people can feel comfortable eating whatever they want.

Robbins comments: "This is the classic profile of a fad diet scam. Promise people they can eat whatever they want, tell them this is a new and amazing revolution, promise them that it won't take any effort, tell them the result will be nearly instantaneous, and make sure they think that everybody else is doing it. Who could resist such hype?"[263]

The continued popularity of low-carb diets, which fail to distinguish between simple refined carbohydrates and healthy complex types, reflects one of the most impressive propaganda triumphs ever, the deadly work of corporate food lobbies, phony science, and media advertising. The mythology of Atkins and kindred diets revolves around a process known as ketosis, whereby the body metabolizes muscle tissue instead of fat, allowing short-term weight loss. Ketosis itself results in significant health problems: muscle breakdown, dehydration, kidney problems, mental disorders, increased risk of heart disease. As Robbins observes in his detailed critique of the Atkins fraud, familiar claims that this diet helps reverse heart disease have never been confirmed by a single research finding. In fact, the Atkins diet produces exactly the opposite results.[264] In the long term, any weight loss comes from reduced caloric intake, not from the rich, fatty foods that are recommended.

In *The China Study*, Campbell points out that "there is a mountain of scientific evidence [including his own] to show that the healthiest diet you can possibly consume is a *high-carbohydrate* diet. It has been demonstrated to combat heart disease, reverse diabetes, prevent a multitude of chronic diseases, and indeed, it has been conclusively shown to produce significant weight loss."[265] The carbohydrates in question are not those in refined foods but rather in fruits, vegetables, and grains. The actual problem here is that Americans generally eat vast amounts of simple, refined carbohydrates but little in the way of more healthful carbohydrates. Further, more harmful carbs are usually combined with a high intake of meat, dairy, and fast foods – the "diseases of affluence". As this is written (early 2020), the U.S. is more awash in unhealthy foods than at any time in its history, the problem destined to worsen in coming years. While the rapacious diet industry earns $50 billion revenue annually, fast-food consumption is predicted to reach record levels by 2020 as the system pervades American life, bolstered by corporate interests and abetted by government, academia, and the media.

At this juncture, despite all the appearances of social and technological progress, American medicine has turned ever more iatrogenic, beyond what Ivan Illich described in his aforementioned classic *Medical Nemesis*. More recently, Gary Null describes the phenomenon of "death by medicine", whereby the medical profession, hospitals, technical devices, and drug therapies must be counted as one of the leading causes of mortality in the U.S.[266] Adverse reactions to legal medications rank at the top of the list. With doctors writing more than three billion prescriptions yearly, Americans consume more than half the world total of medicinal drugs. According to the Nutrition Institute of America, conventional medicine accounts for an estimated 700,000 fatal episodes yearly, the largest number resulting from harmful drug experiences: abuse, overdoses, accidents, adverse reactions, addictions. Anti-depressants are now the most widely prescribed of all medications.[267] Opioids such as codeine, morphine, fentanyl, and oxycodone, usually offered for pain relief, have high abuse potential, including severe addictions, lowered blood pressure, dizziness, and comas – as of 2019 accounting for as much as 50,000 deaths yearly.[268] These drugs, along with such illegal substances as heroin, currently lie at the center of what is probably the greatest drug-abuse crisis in American history.

Yet another iatrogenic problem, in the U.S. and globally, stems from the precipitous overuse of antibiotics, now rapidly exhausting their potency to counter bacterial and other infections. As pathogens spread more rapidly across the globe, infections from various diseases and injuries become more severe, often fatal. As new classes of antibiotics lose their medicinal power, their overuse for both humans and animals (in food production) has taken the world into a dangerously post-antibiotic era when bacterial forms erect massive resistance to even the most potent medications, straining already depleted public-health systems. This increasing menace is the fully predictable outcome of an irrational antibiotic's regime spanning several decades.

Three decades ago, Illich wrote prophetically about the perils of "disabling professions" ruled by technocratic experts and corporate managers, driven by power, money, and arrogant claims to a specialized knowledge that in the end legitimates a dysfunctional and unstainable medical complex.[269] Today that complex, alongside agribusiness, the food industry, and Big Pharma, is a profoundly authoritarian, commodified, and in many ways a destructive sector of American life. A self-proclaimed repository of modernity, wisdom, and healing, the American healthcare industry continues to resist every progressive alternative while reinforcing patterns of domination across the entire society.

The Healthiest Food Regimen

Worth including in a book on food, ecology, and politics is a further, more systematic reflection on how evidence-based research supports a drastic, widespread shift away from meat and dairy products toward plant-based alternatives. Never-ending corporate propaganda has obscured and mystified this fundamental reality by subsidizing hundreds of biased studies, funding lobbies for agribusiness and fast-food interests, and shaping national (U.S.) guidelines that stress the "health benefits" of meat and dairy consumption in the face of contradictory, independent research. Dozens of harmful diet programs trumpet the value of protein and fat-laden animal products over those fearsome "carbs" that happen to be mainly derived from plant-based foods. The American public is understandably left confused, overwhelmed by a nonstop barrage of distorted, misleading messaging from the giant meat oligopoly and corporate media.

We are routinely told that the great health (indeed other) benefits of a vegetarian (or vegan) diet have never been empirically demonstrated, that "evidence" is largely anecdotal, inconclusive. In fact, there are hundreds, perhaps thousands of studies that clearly demonstrate the superiority of plant-based foods. Unfortunately, a vast stratum of "experts" – academics, doctors, dieticians, medical-school professionals, diet-fad authors, pharmaceutical lobbyists – maintain, against all credible research and experience, that animal foods are not only advantageous but *necessary* for optimum health. While outright fictions are routinely propagated by those bought and controlled by the corporate food complex, tens of millions of Americans suffer from obesity and resulting chronic diseases (cancer, heart conditions, diabetes, etc.) associated with the standard modern diet. As people are targeted by seductive propaganda, they are unable to make sensible basic food choices. In his classic *The Food Revolution,* John Robbins writes: "It's a shame that we allow people and industries to keep us bewildered and alienated from our own personal power."[270]

A diet heavy in animal products – meat or dairy proteins, saturated fats, cholesterol – is one most likely to bring on chronic disease and death. Even a cursory glance around the world reveals an undeniable fact: countries with the highest per capita intake of animal foods also have the greatest incidence of cancers, heart disease, diabetes, and other chronic afflictions. The evidence behind this is hardly "anecdotal", though plenty of that is available. Worsening health problems endured by Americans since World War II have coincided with rapid growth of the McDonalds fast-food economy –a correlation in no way accidental. Irrefutable evidence from legions of studies from around the world can be overlooked but never erased. Dr. Neal Barnard, former head of the Physicians Committee for Responsible Medicine, has stated: "The beef industry has contributed to more deaths than all the wars in this [twentieth] century, all natural disasters, and all automobile accidents combined. If beef is your idea of 'real food for real people', you'd better live real close to a real good hospital."[271]

The seminal work on food, nutrition, and health carried out by such medical researchers as Colin Campbell refers in turn to hundreds of studies conducted by Campbell and his team along with hundreds of other respectable findings carried out by other researchers. The many books authored by Robbins and such health practitioners as John McDougall identify hundreds more kindred research efforts independent of corporate funding or influences. The results are strikingly the same: optimum human health is derived from the enormous physical and mental benefits of consuming plant-based foods, while intake of animal products brings obesity, health challenges, chronic diseases, and death. Attempts to obscure or deny such overwhelming evidence inevitably wind up trapped in a quagmire of phony discourses and claims. Bias against vegetarian or vegan food preferences is hardly a question of simple oversight; it is better understood as a function of special-interest propaganda, as Marion Nestle shows in her aforementioned book *Unsavory Truths*.[272]

As previously noted, the most far-reaching investigation into the linkage of food, nutrition, and health is Campbell's *The China Study*, its conclusions based on exhaustive data from 65 counties, 130 villages, and 6500 adults. Campbell's epic findings, supported by extensive clinical research, systematically demonstrate how high rates of cancer, heart disease, and other chronic diseases are caused by diets heavy in animal proteins and fats. Campbell refers to "diseases of affluence", meaning that as populations move up the food chain, they encounter more health afflictions, usually starting with obesity. The problem is scarcely one of "carbs", as complex types of carbohydrates (including whole grains) are far superior to animal products as well as less healthy *refined* carbohydrates such as sugar. While Campbell's important work has solidified previous evidence regarding the advantages of plant-based diets, the corporate-medical establishment has steadfastly refused to go along.

Campbell's investigation into the nutritional bases of cancer turn out to be especially illuminating – and difficult to refute. He found that animal proteins are basic catalysts behind the three stages of cancer – initiation, promotion, progression. The greater the meat or dairy intake, the higher probability of most types of cancer, and deaths from cancer.[273] This striking evidence does not apply to plant-food consumption, whatever its calorie level. *The China Study* found that "nutrients from animal-based foods increased tumor development while nutrients from plant-based foods decreased tumor development."[274] These findings have been repeated endlessly, both among the Chinese people and across numerous clinical experiments. Although that population was rather homogenous, Campbell and associates made a point of taking into account no fewer than 367 variables.[275]

Campbell compared significant dietary variations from rural China, where people consume (or at the time consumed) little meat and dairy products, with the U.S., where diets are heavily saturated with animal proteins and fats. The differences could not be more revealing. As Campbell notes, American diets are (on average) comprised of 16 percent protein, 80 percent of which comes from animal-based foods – nowadays surely an understatement. In China, out of less than 10 percent protein intake, barely 10 percent of that is derived from meat and dairy foods. Total fat consumption in the U.S. is about 38 percent of daily calories compared to 14.5 percent in China (again, for that period). As for total protein intake, the numbers are 91 grams daily in the U.S. compared to 64 grams in rural China, where blood cholesterol levels amounted to only one-third of the American standard.[276]

The China Study was completed and published in 2006, after many years of nutritional research at a time when China was far less economically developed and urbanized than today – a fact of enormous importance. Chinese development has actually *doubled* since the late 1990s, when Campbell was conducting the bulk of his research. Not only has the country achieved heightened levels of affluence, but also has lethal amounts of air and water pollution. It follows that "diseases of affluence" explored by Campbell have risen dramatically, across the entire society, in the roughly two decades since Campbell finished his work. The fact that China is now catching up to other industrialized countries in rates of cancer, heart disease, and other chronic afflictions merely underscores the study's findings. High levels of economic modernization, accompanied by diets much heavier in meat and dairy products, have given rise to exactly what Campbell would have expected.

At the time of his study, Campbell found enormous differences in animal-foods consumption from countryside to cities, matched by vastly greater incidence of chronic diseases in the latter. In some rural locales such diseases were virtually unknown, though that is no longer true owing to dramatically changing nutritional and environmental conditions. In those days Campbell's conclusions were ironclad: "The people who eat the most animal protein have the most heart disease, cancer, and diabetes."[277] Differences could be readily measured in terms of both obesity levels and cholesterol blood readings. Thus: "As blood cholesterol levels in rural China rise in certain counties, the incidence of 'Western' diseases also increased. What made this so surprising was that Chinese levels were far lower than we had expected. The average level of blood cholesterol was only 127 mg/dL, which is almost 100 points less than the American average ... Some counties had average levels as low as 94 mg/dL."[278]

In the U.S. nowadays, most people (including those in medicine) consider a 30-percent fat diet within the range of a "low-fat diet", while consumption of 40-percent fat is hardly unusual. In China, on the other hand, rural levels of six to ten percent were (in those days) relatively normal owing to nearly vegetarian diets. Campbell writes: "Findings from rural China showed that reducing dietary fat from 24% to 6% was associated with lower breast cancer risk. However, lower dietary fat in rural China meant less consumption not only of fats but, more importantly, of animal-based food."[279] An equally important causal factor in cancer, Campbell emphasizes, is *protein* from meat and especially dairy products. This evidence was replicated in dozens of clinical experiments, before and after *The China Study.*

A country-by-country survey of cancer rates strongly validates the main findings of Campbell's research. At present the data could not be more compelling: those nations where average per capita meat and dairy consumption is highest also suffer the highest incidence of cancer and deaths by cancer. The top eight countries – Denmark, France, Australia, Belgium, Norway, the U.S., Ireland, South Korea – are all industrialized societies where animal-food intake is highest in the world. Countries such as Serbia, Chile, Mongolia, Armenia, Greece, and Japan (far lighter on meat and dairy foods) had the lowest rates of cancer mortality.

Denmark, at the very top, has cancer mortality levels of 338 persons per 100,000 compared to Serbia at 180 per 100,000 – a remarkable difference. The U.S. suffered 318 deaths per 100,000, near the top, as might be expected. According to the National Cancer Institute, however, those numbers were far too conservative: the actual tally for 2018 (1,735,350 deaths) constitutes a huge increase to 530 per 100,000, elevating the U.S. to first place by a wide margin.[280] Given the enormity of the animal-foods economy (and culture) in American society, this should come as no surprise.

The great advantages of a plant-based diet over conventional, meat-based foods across the world have been shown in hundreds of nutritional studies, clinical research, and comparative analysis like that of *The China Study.* Further thousands of anecdotal findings have replicated this evidence. Additional demonstration is supplied by exhaustive historical research into the longevity of particular cultures – the most ambitious being John Robbins' *Healthy at 100,* which explores the conditions of healthy living into peoples' ninetieth year and beyond. The key to extraordinary longevity ought to provide a strong argument for what foods contribute to the best health outcomes.

In fact, Robbins' conclusions in his thoroughly researched volume coincide perfectly with those of Campbell: longevity thrives on a plant-based regimen where obesity and chronic illnesses are extremely rare. Robbins explored the world's healthiest and longest-lived peoples in four widely disparate settings: Abkhasia in the Caucasus, Vikabamba in Ecuador, the Hunza in Pakistan, Okinawa in the Asia-Pacific region. None of those cultures, it should be emphasized, fit the advanced industrial profile, though it is true that Okinawa has been (negatively) impacted by decades of U.S. military presence on the island.

What did Robbins find? Consistent with *The China Study* conclusions, what these four settings had most in common – despite numerous differences – was a low-calorie, low-fat plant-based diet where little if any animal products were consumed. In the case of Okinawa, that Japanese prefecture has been shown to be home of the healthiest and longest-lived people ever studied; they are a culture of "centenarians". These findings were popularized in a bestselling 2001 book titled *The Okinawa Program*.[281] Their diet, on average: seven servings of whole grains a day, two servings of soy products, seven servings of vegetables, fish two or three times a week. Their consumption of animal proteins, fats, and sugar was close to zero. Their diet is precisely what *The China Study* identified as the healthiest regimen. In Okinawa the "diseases of affluence", not to mention obesity, were virtually unknown.[282]

In his analysis of food habits in all four cultures, Robbins writes: "The diets that have enabled the world's longest-lived peoples to live such healthy lives are very high in whole grains and other healthful carbohydrates. In this way they could hardly differ more from the low-carb regimen advocated by Robert Atkins ....".[283] Could longevity of this sort be explained by genetic makeups? Robbins responds by noting that when Okinawans migrate elsewhere and adopt heavier local diets, they get the same diseases at the same rate, and die at the same ages, as people from their new region. The life expectancy for Okinawans who moved to Brazil, for example, dropped by 17 years. Meanwhile, the situation in Okinawa itself has drastically changed in the past few decades owing to the American military presence. Okinawans are now eating more fast foods, meat, and sugar, with the result they "have the highest level of obesity in Japan, the worst cardiovascular risk profile, the highest risk of coronary heart disease, and the highest risk for premature death." Younger Okinawans in particular are nowadays increasingly overweight.[284]

Robbins observes that the downward Okinawa health trajectory has its parallel in modern China. Referring to *The China Study*, he laments that "the nation that has spawned the largest study of diet and health in the history of the world is ignoring its findings. Hundreds of millions of Chinese are abandoning traditional diets rich in fiber and whole grains in favor of diets far higher in sugar and animal fat. The small farms that long supplied open-air markets are being replaced by vast agribusiness conglomerates that feed ever-larger supermarket chains and fast-food restaurants. A traditionally vegetarian culture has been overwhelmed by industrial modernity."[285] Already cancer and heart-disease cases have skyrocketed in China, becoming the leading causes of death among Chinese adults.

In the matter of how food patterns impact health outcomes, it seems clear from the Okinawan and Chinese settings – along with most others – that modernity has not served as a vehicle of human progress; just the opposite, in fact. Here Robbins aptly concludes: "These days, many people fear that the survival of the human race could be threatened by the breakdown of modern society as we know it. I'm beginning to wonder if our survival may be just as threatened by the *continuation* of modern society as we know it."[286] What Robbins says about food and health provides deep insights into the global ecological crisis as a whole.

Meanwhile, denial of such irrefutable factual evidence – namely, the immense superiority of a plant-based diet – remains an article of faith in American society, including among the so-called food, diet, and medical experts. As noted, agribusiness, fast-food interests, the medical apparatus, and corporate advertising all function as outright conduits of the great meat complex, against all logic and experience. Roughly 40 percent of the American population, feasting daily on rich foods, is now overweight to varying degrees. Sickness and disease are the norm, yet the conventional wisdom instructs people to avoid "carbs" and eat more "substantial" food saturated with animal fat and protein. The prevailing mythology is that optimum health depends on large amounts of meat and dairy products. Not surprisingly, the McDonaldized fast-food economy is thriving as never before, its products deeply implicated in the ecological crisis.

The great carb delusion owes much to the shady legacy of Robert Atkins, whose famous diet books have influenced millions, probably tens of millions of people around the world. The idea that "carbs" are inherently bad equates with a similar fiction – that protein (namely animal protein) is the ultimate source of wonderful health. The enormous success of Atkins' chicanery (aside from its perfect congruence with corporate interests) is to appeal to conventional, familiar patterns of behavior; little if any change is demanded. Writes Robbins: "This is the classic profile of a fad diet scam.

Promise people they can eat whatever they want, tell them this is a new and amazing revolution, promise them that it won't take any effort, tell them the results will be nearly instantaneous, and make sure they think that everybody else is doing it."[287]

The fraudulent character of this "diet" is readily apparent, despite its stubborn popularity. As Robbins notes, Atkins' diet program (and many others like it) is based on a mechanism called ketosis, which causes temporary weight loss through a breakdown of fatty acids – an unnatural process that can lead to muscle deterioration, dehydration, kidney problems, even increased risk of heart disease. Atkins and kindred advocates of high-protein, high-fat, low-carbohydrate foods claim that high-glycemic index foods such as bread, potatoes, and pasta create high blood-sugar levels and dangerous insulin response, to be avoided at all costs. This is sheer fiction: no scientific evidence exists to suggest these foods are in any way harmful. On the contrary, it is the high-protein, high-fat products that are most harmful – and these, of course, constitute the standard American diet. No independent studies validate such outlandish claims. Robbins concludes: "The foods on which the Atkins diet is based are the very foods that contribute to our most common causes of disease, disability, and death."[288]

The Atkins legacy and its anti-carb frenzy essentially obscures information regarding precisely what foods provide the best health and longevity. Writes Campbell: "As you will see in this book, there is a mountain of scientific evidence to show that the healthiest diet you can possibly consume is a *high-carbohydrate* diet. It has been shown to reverse heart disease, reverse diabetes, prevent a plethora of chronic diseases, and yes, it has been shown many times to cause significant weight loss."[289]

Campbell's point, developed in *The China Study*, is that the healthiest foods – grains, vegetables, fruits – are primarily carbohydrates. These are *not* the highly processed refined carbohydrates stripped of fiber, vitamins, and minerals and loaded with sugar. That is the stuff of fast foods which combine heavy amounts of *refined* carbohydrates with equal portions of fat and protein. The problem is not carbs as such, but rather the fact that Americans especially consume huge amounts of simple, refined carbohydrates and little in the way of healthy, *complex* carbohydrates. For decades people in the industrialized societies have been targeted by the most harmful food propaganda imaginable, and unfortunately it has worked. In Campbell's words: "Perhaps it is a testament to the power of modern marketing savvy that an obese man with heart disease and high blood pressure became one of the richest snake oil salesmen ever to live ... .".[290]

The Atkins-style diet fads have neatly corresponded to propaganda disseminated by a legion of meat and dairy lobbies dedicated to maximizing corporate profits. Here money and wealth matter above health and environmental concerns. Thus, according to the National Cattlemen's Association, "reported links between diet and cancer have been mostly hypothetical ... No single dietary factor, including far or meat, could possibly account for more than a small fraction of cancer in the U.S."[291] In a similar vein, we have the following statement from Springfield Meats CEO Sam Abramson: "We must be eternally vigilant to guard against those who would undermine confidence in the health benefits of eating meat. If meat-eaters have higher blood pressure, it's from the stress of having to defend the perfectly reasonable desire to chow down on a thick sirloin against the misguided and intrusive efforts of the food police."[292]

According to Marion Nestle, in *Unsavory Truths,* corporate promotion of food sales has become more competitive – and more far-reaching – than at any time in history. This is a well-funded and systematic process, and takes many forms aside from conventional advertising and lobbying. She writes: "We have an onslaught of misleading information and advice that results from food-company manipulation of nutrition research and practice."[293] As in the case of drug corporations, the food system works along many fronts: casting doubt on independent science, funding of biased nutritional research, offering of gifts, use of front groups, the placing of business interests on relevant government or university agencies, committees, publications, and funding sources. Nestle adds: "... the meat and dairy industries are so powerful that U.S. dietary guidelines cannot advise Americans to eat less of their products."[294]

Meanwhile, as Nestle stresses, the nefarious "checkoff" system for both meat and dairy interests means that government-corporate partnership in advertising of these foods is essentially mandated, with the participation of such lobbies as the National Dairy Council working through such entities as the USDA and National Institutes of Health.[295] In these cases the federal government does not serve as guardian of the public interest, as it is supposedly mandated to do. The priorities of the huge food oligopolies are profits, not health or the environment; conflicts of interest are officially proscribed but rarely punished or jettisoned.

As Michele Simon points out along the same lines, the vast power of the American diary lobby has effectively brainwashed the public to think that a wide variety of their products – not only milk but cheese, yogurt, and ice cream – must be essential to any diet, good for athletic performance, mental agility, and overall health. As milk has declined in recent decades, marketing emphasis has focused on cheese, one of the most fat-laden foods available. Some guidelines call for an optimum diet of three servings of dairy products daily.[296] Dairy protein is touted as one of the best of all proteins, yet we know that *The China Study* findings reveal dairy fat and protein to be a major source of cancer.

Sadly, it is the crude marketing agendas of a long list of phony diet gurus – often in the guise of scientific objectivity – that have permeated mass consciousness in the U.S. and a few other advanced industrial countries. More sadly yet, there has been little in the way of counterattacks from the progressive left. At best we are put in a state of confusion: the evidence regarding health and nutrition is said to be ambiguous or incomplete, while the meat complex typically escapes criticism. In *The Omnivore's Dilemma*, for example, Michael Pollan, well-known critical food investigator, ascribes such health issues as obesity mainly to "processed food" and sugar while going light on meat and dairy products, scarcely mentioning the meat complex.[297] A special issue on food and politics in the left-liberal *Nation*, more fully discussed elsewhere in this book, contains only extremely negative references to critics of the meat economy, describing them as violent maniacs in the context of India.[298] Rarely do leftist publications bring their resources to focus on the harm done by animal products, even as the ecological linkage has gained widening awareness.

The aforementioned Marion Nestle offers yet another instance of progressives failing to endorse a vegetarian alternative to standard American food habits. In *Unsavory Truth* Nestle mentions "how food companies skew the science of what we eat" – here again in favor of animal-based products. At the same time, she writes that evidence critical of meat and dairy foods is inconclusive or mixed, while advantages of a plant-based diet are not very clear. Thus: "In the case of vegetarian diets, the preponderance of evidence from all sources supports health benefits. Dietary guidelines promote plant-based diets. The flip side is that diets high in animal products must be less healthful. But which products and how much less? The answers are not simple ... some studies find that vegetarians live longer than non-vegetarians, but others do not." Nestle goes on to say that "we evolved to eat meat, but today meat-eating tracks with other unhealthful dietary and lifestyle practices."[299]

It is odd indeed to see a healthful-food advocate mention that eating habits responsible for massive levels of obesity and millions of deaths from cancer, heart disease, and diabetes *might be* "less healthful" or could lead to better longevity depending on what studies are believed. (There are no references in Nestle's book to the work of Campbell or Robbins.) Given what is known about the debilitating impact of animal products, Nestle's language "preponderance of evidence" likewise appears misplaced, as if the mountains of independent findings remain inconclusive, subject to further research and interpretation. What more is needed? Stranger yet is that such promulgations of ambiguity come from an ardent food activist.

When it comes to food and health, powerful established interests – medical, corporate, agricultural, political – remain closed off to alternatives that might challenge their capacity to dominate the public realm. And those interests, from Tyson to McDonalds, from Pfizer to Wal-Mart and Monsanto, count among the most impregnable fortresses of wealth and power across the global scene. Those interests spend billions on advertising and lobbying, colonize government agencies, shape medical-school curricula, and exert massive influence over medical (and other) research. To mobilize for change against such ubiquitous centers of power – the overriding task ahead – will be a daunting task. Yet those centers of power dominate a food complex (and economic system) that is manifestly destructive, a perpetual attack on human rationality, but entirely *unsustainable* and thus a mortal threat to planetary survival. Overturning those interests is therefore a matter of life and death.

4

The Political Impasse

In this chapter we focus on broad political efforts – or more precisely, the failure of such efforts – to confront and possibly reverse the global crisis. Historical analysis is one thing, social change yet another. Special attention is devoted to American society as the U.S. has for many decades contributed more than any other nation to the ecological predicament humanity now faces. What happens in American society, moreover, will decisively impact worldwide struggles for change. While disaster is no longer a remote prospect, the radical solutions needed to prevail against the downward slide have rarely taken political form. Worse, the political examples visible within advanced capitalism – liberalism, social democracy, Communism, Greens – have mostly proved to be futile. A break with those past failures is crucial for planetary survival.

Bill McKibben, among others, argues that the global crisis has worsened to such an extent that the equivalent of full wartime mobilization, as during World War II, offers the only realistic solution. That means virtually total commitment of human, natural, and technical resources toward a single, all-consuming purpose, in this case a life-and-death struggle to stave off catastrophe. McKibben writes: "The question is not, are we in a world war? The question is, will we fight back?"[300] As late as 2020, unfortunately, the political capacity to "fight back" has fallen drastically short of the ecological imperative.

While new political strategies seem urgent, many old modalities survive as neoliberal globalization takes humanity further along the path of cataclysmic destruction. In the U.S., at least, ecological challenges are met with an ensemble of responses – embrace of market forces, reliance on technological fixes, and a litany of policy reforms. Meanwhile, a confused population seeks retreat or escape in social media, personal transformations, and identity politics – all in some way diversions from the radical politics needed to effectively "fight back". Progressive social movements (including environmentalism) have grown steadily more dispersed, tepid, ineffective. More than at any time in U.S. history, liberal democracy is thoroughly compromised by its alignment with corporate power, statism, bureaucracy, and the war economy; citizen participation has been severely weakened.

An October 2018 IPCC Report had more depressing news on the status of climate change – the crisis was now expected to hit harder, and sooner, than previously expected.[301] In the absence of immediate and sweeping worldwide interventions, all signs of global warming – melting icecaps, rising seas, extreme weather episodes, reduced arable land, etc. – could give rise to the feared tipping-point within two decades, perhaps sooner. The crisis worsens at a time when President Trump has withdrawn the U.S. from the 2015 Paris Accords signed by 195 nations, an agreement commonly viewed as vital to reversing the crisis.

The 728-page IPCC assemblage of findings and predictions calls on major nation states – starting with the U.S., China, India, and the European Union – to take political leadership, yet little has been done to reduce fossil-fuel emissions close to levels recommended. Written by 91 climate-oriented scientists from around the world, the report calls for "rapid, far-reaching, and unprecedented changes in all aspects of society – energy, transport, land use, urban planning." The authors might have included agriculture and food production on this list. In any event, the recommended changes are presently nowhere in sight, meaning the *political crisis* must be regarded as central to any understanding of the sharpening predicament. Abject failure of the U.S. to act, to join even limited world efforts to fight climate change, merely underscores this predicament.

The Great Liberal Mirage

For anyone looking to liberalism – or in common parlance, liberal democracy – for answers to the ecological crisis, disillusionment and despair will be the most likely experiences. Liberal politics, as it has evolved in the

U.S. and other advanced industrial societies, is a recipe for impasse when it comes to pursuit of far-reaching transformations in the realms of economy and government. That is simply a matter of historical evidence.

The historic merger of corporate and state power in advanced capitalism has come to define the "American model" of development, where popular sovereignty, citizenship, and social governance are officially celebrated but increasingly detached from everyday decision making. In the U.S., neither Democrats nor Republicans – twin expressions of the same corporate-state system – seek alternatives to oligarchical rule and the warfare state, hardly surprising given how the power structure has become institutionalized. Chris Hedges argues in *The Death of the Liberal Class* that traditional pillars of liberal politics (unions, academia, Democratic party, community organizations) have eroded during recent decades.[302] Convergence of interests at the summits of power has meant a sharp decline of electoral politics as party competition degenerates into a prolonged media spectacle.

Across the public terrain, in the U.S. and elsewhere, power has grown ever more concentrated within and between dominant sectors: business, finance, government, military, the media. Given this reality, it is hard to see where substantial breaks from the power structure can be achieved, much less sustained. Debates can be intense but are so politically truncated as to diminish focus on such critical challenges as global warming. Questions about who makes decisions, who mobilizes resources, and for what purposes are ritually avoided.

Americans are taught to believe their political system and their Constitution are uniquely democratic, providing abundant space for a free and active citizenry. As part of this enduring narrative people are indoctrinated into the myth that elites represent some variant of the "common good", attached to democratic norms. When it comes to the environmental, however, the historical record demonstrates just the opposite: priorities of wealth and power trump the public interest. To this point C. Wright Mills could write: "To appeal to the powerful on the basis of any knowledge we now have is utopian in the foolish sense of that term. Our relations with them are more likely to be only such relations as they find useful."[303]

As a fully integrated state-capitalism narrows political discourse and erodes citizenship, traditional ideologies (above all conservatism and liberalism) wind up peripheral to actual elite behavior, the ideologies serving mainly to legitimate elite interests. And while giant corporations shape the flow of capital, natural resources, commodities, and information, their scope (ever globalized) inevitably evades the reach of electoral politics.[304] As oligarchical tendencies solidify, we see a political culture rife with illusions, fantasies, and escape mechanisms – that is, signs of a society trapped in a steady downward spiral. The U.S. devours more than 20 percent of world energy resources, yet Washington politicians repeatedly stonewall measures needed to confront the ecological crisis. As of early 2020, Congress had yet to pass any meaningful legislation, leaving the boldest initiatives to a few progressive states. Limits to growth are strongly resisted across the landscape, whether in Congress, the White House, state legislatures, the media, and even mainstream environmental groups. Commenting that "our environment is being dramatically transformed in ways that will soon make it difficult for the human species to survive", Hedges adds: "We stand on the verge of one of the bleakest periods in human history, when the bright lights of civilization will blink out and we will descend for decades, if not centuries, into barbarity."[305]

During early capitalist development, classical liberalism promised a new era of equality, democracy, and prosperity inspired by Enlightenment rationality, but over the past two centuries such expectations were at best partially and unevenly realized. By late twentieth century, liberalism had become associated with a lengthy period of sustained economic growth and globalized power, yet the system would bring sharp inequalities, truncated democracy, affluence for a shrinking minority, perpetual warfare, and ecological ruin. In the U.S. this system would give rise to a war economy and security state requiring vast human and natural resources.

Electoral politics in the U.S. has become increasingly drained of democratic content, detached as it is from the rhythms and flows of everyday social life. There are many examples, one being what was discussed in the primary campaigns in the state of Iowa that inaugurate each presidential election season. In 2016 Iowa would have an outsized role in determining who would enter the White House. Crucial issues would be – or should have been – at the forefront of debates among nearly 20 candidates from each party: agriculture, food, the environment, health care, corporate power. Across many weeks and months of campaigning, however, no candidate took up these issues beyond a few talking points. A Midwestern farming state with three million people, Iowa is home to 21 million hogs, 52 million chickens, 260 animal-food sites, and one of the largest centers of corn and soybean production (mostly for animal feed) in the world. Corn and soybeans cover 23 million of the 24 million acres of cropland in the state. The Iowa food industry is dominated by a networked system involving Tyson Foods, Hormel, Cargill, and JBS.

By 2016, Iowa was overwhelmed by water and soil pollution from nitrogen-based fertilizers, along with waste equivalent to that produced by 45 million people. While federal agricultural subsidies flowed to Iowa farmers, health problems throughout the state soared – nearly 40 percent of inhabitants are obese – along with growth of extreme poverty and related miseries. Highly processed corn syrup, made in Iowa and other Midwestern states, was itself a source of increased obesity and sickness.

How did this presumably celebrated exercise in American politics meet intensifying challenges posed by agriculture, food problems, and environmental crisis? As Richard Manning reported in *Harper's*, the major candidates (including Hillary Clinton and Donald Trump) routinely failed to address any pressing concerns, dwelling instead on such threats as Russia, China, Iran, and Sharia Law. All politicians ritually trumpeted "free markets" and "small government" while overlooking the hovering presence of agribusiness and the meat industry.[306] The Clintons, it should be noted, were big supporters of such corporate giants as Tyson and Wal-Mart. For its part, the media was fully complicit in this scandalous escape from reality. Here as elsewhere, the electoral charade would have no relevance to the ecological crisis.[307]

This impasse was not a matter of terrible Republicans facing off against more enlightened Democrats in Iowa or elsewhere. In fact, both parties were firmly embedded in the power structure – Wall Street, agribusiness, the Pentagon, Big Pharma, the technology sector. When the Clintons launched the "new" Democratic Party in the early 1990s, they set in motion a political force aligned with elite interests, a new class of managers and professionals, the warfare state, the knowledge industry, the media, and higher education, far removed from any vision of a "people's party".[308] The Clintonites would gain ideological legitimacy from a mixture of appeals: technological innovation, an aggressive (neocon) foreign policy, identity politics. Everything – Wall Street banditry, foreign wars, harsh crime regimen, corporate deregulation – would be embellished in high-sounding rhetoric. Beneath all this, as Thomas Frank notes, "... the real Clinton legacy came down to four words: grab what you can." [309]

The Clintonites have been central protagonists of a fast-moving, high-tech, globalized, rapacious capitalism, able to achieve what Republicans generally cannot. Frank writes that they "fueled a steamy climate of market celebrationism" beyond anything seen in American history. [310] Owing to their righteous pretense of "humanitarian intervention" and identity politics, President Clinton and later Hillary Clinton were falsely depicted in the friendly media as "progressive", even as they enthusiastically bowed to every corporate and military design. Frank is on the mark here, commenting: "To judge by what he actually accomplished Bill Clinton was not the lesser of two evils, as people on the left always say about the Democrats at election time; he was the greatest of the two." [311] The same could be said about Hillary's two dismally failed attempts at the White House.

Liberal approaches to the ecological crisis have, on the whole, delivered only modest reforms (emphasis on green technologies, curbs on air and water pollution, market incentives) that, while better than nothing, never counter the existence of a corporate-state-military growth machine. The Clintonites, for their part, fully accept the parameters of existing class and power relations, which inevitably constricts the scope of political action. We have seen the boundaries of modern-day liberalism in Governor Jerry Brown's relatively ambitious moves to fight global warming in California.

One of the more widely celebrated schemes is that of former U.S. Vice President Al Gore, who first took up the motif of global warming in his 1995 best-selling book, *Earth in the Balance*. [312] After leaving office in 2001, Gore devoted the bulk of his time and energy around the threat of global warming, the subject of his documentary *An Inconvenient Truth* (2006), which brought both an Oscar and Nobel Prize. Gore's views are most systematically articulated, embellished with charts and graphs, in his 2009 volume *Our Choice*, dedicated to raising public consciousness about climate change. [313] This would be followed by his 2017 documentary *Truth to Power* accompanied by a book of the same title. [314]

Gore's impressive body of work provides a comprehensive survey of the global challenge – empirically grounded and framed by intellectual passion and keen sense of political urgency. He relies on abundant scientific research, consistent with IPCC findings, to counter the distortions and denials of corporations, their lobbies, and sectors of the media. For Gore, obstacles to political solutions reside in ideological tropes that bolster conservative agendas and reinforce claims that U.S. economic development cannot depart from dependency on fossil fuels. One problem, in Gore's view, is the endless growth and the hyper-consumption of the American model. Indeed the U.S. has witnessed a *tripling* of economic output since the 1950s.

Gore's solution to the crisis begins with education and includes a program of environmental reforms to liberate American society from reliance on oil, gas, and coal. Despite a sense of urgency expressed throughout *Our Choice*, Gore's proposed strategy ultimately hardly departs from standard liberal politics. In the end, his understanding of social change appears rather soft and tentative, well short of the radical vision needed for decisive political intervention. The role of education and technology, of course, is not to be taken lightly. Gore places unwavering faith in the power of new technology to drive alternative energy outputs – a faith surely worth embracing. The same technology that integrates, processes, and transmits vast information flows can facilitate the epic shift to a post-carbon economy.[315]

At the same time, as with *Earth in the Balance*, Gore leans heavily on market-based solutions – despite harsh words about corporate malfeasance. In *Our Choice* a jaundiced view of big business is clear, yet a familiar liberal reformism holds sway based in notions of market efficiency and material incentives. The optimum strategy suggested is to fuse public and private initiatives within a developmental model which accounts for the costs of carbon extraction, processing, use, and pollution. Along with green alternatives like those introduced at Kyoto, Gore favors a carbon tax to supplement cap-and-trade schemes designed to restrict emissions through market-oriented trading arrangements (explored in the next section). The idea is to rationally identify, measure, and assess greenhouse costs while resorting to mechanisms like the U.S. Clean Air Act.[316]

Despite misgivings about capitalism and its destructive tendencies, Gore is unambiguous: "We must develop a sustainable capitalism".[317] Even as energy, agribusiness, food, and military corporations stand to be harmed by genuine reforms, Gore believes that they can be convinced that their self-interest can be compatible with ecological rationality. Thus: "Our market economy can help us solve the climate crisis problem if we send it the right signals."[318] The "right signals" would be adequate carbon-pricing mechanisms combined with green-technological incentives, rising to a new Manhattan Project (or Green New Deal) that, once realized, would bring the U.S. revitalized "moral authority" as world economic and technological leader.[319] Gore's view, here and later, reflects enthusiastic Enlightenment optimism, even messianism: corrupt and dysfunctional as the system might be, it can be steered in the right direction with the proper mixture of creative leadership, good intentions, and green priorities.

This same outlook permeates *Truth to Power* (2017), where Gore's reading of the ecological crisis takes something of a radical turn owing to the decade-long intensification of global warming and new levels of harm to national resources, arable land, forests, oceans, and atmosphere.[320] Here, more than in his previous work, Gore warns of threatened food supplies as crop yields of corn, wheat, and rice (mostly diverted to livestock) enter into decline, along with heightened water shortages and soil depletion. He agrees with a global consensus that carbon emissions should be reduced to zero by 2050, if not sooner. The problem now is that all nations of the world continue to disgorge 110 million tons of greenhouse gases into the planet *daily*. In this context, according to Gore, water and food scarcity will be unavoidable while major urban centers are likely to be unlivable. In other words, the ecological crisis has grown far worse than even the most radical projections a decade earlier.

In *Truth to Power*, Gore joins the 2015 Paris consensus that a post-carbon transition is globally imperative, the sooner the better. The good news is that we are now in the midst of a "sustainability revolution", thanks to the rapid spread of cheaper, more efficient, cleaner renewable energy sources.[321] The greater mood of urgency, however, has not forced any fundamental reassessment of capitalism: "market solutions" remain crucial to the strategy. Despite this myopia – and leaving aside problems associated with wind and solar power – Gore envisions a durable movement toward social change, led by business leaders, investors, elected officials, and (loosely defined) grassroots organizations.[322] His direct message to the corporate elites: "Make your business more sustainable."[323] Gore looks forward to an accelerated greening of capitalism.

Gore is hardly alone in such misplaced liberal optimism. Much of his outlook parallels that of Jerry Brown, discussed earlier. In his best-selling *Hot, Flat, and Crowded,* Thomas L. Friedman makes the case for a "green revolution" that would begin to counter the effects of a dangerously unstable and crisis-ridden planet. He proposes a survival modality built around the same three instruments favored by Gore – alternative energy sources, revitalized markets, and lifestyle changes. The case for drastic measures, no longer simply an option, is made on moral, political, and economic grounds, involving a program of national renewal consistent with wartime mobilization.[324]

Friedman argues that green technology will shape the next major world economic stimulus, while providing abundant, cheap, reliable, and sustainable fuel sources.[325] Given high levels of American industrialization, the lopsided U.S. contribution to global warming, and U.S. economic and military power, Washington is central to pushing the world along a green path, given the political will. Friedman believes it will be possible, with strong enough market incentives, to maintain high levels of economic growth, meaning no reduction in domestic living standards needed.[326] Technological innovation can reshape every sphere of human activity, from manufacturing to agriculture, communications, education, transportation, the military, and cultural life. Rejecting the limits-to-growth approach, Friedman anticipates continued economic development with few limits, as solar, wind, geothermal, and fuel-cell energy sources gradually replace fossil fuels.

Convinced that ecological sustainability and economic growth can coexist, Friedman looks to the greening of personal lifestyles, work, transportation, entertainment, and consumer choices. Sustainable values would be integrated into the rhythms and flows of social life and individual behavior. People would reduce their carbon imprint by driving less, buying more fuel-efficient vehicles, recycling, using alternative energy sources, and joining community projects such as local farms. Assuming that such options are compatible with ideas already espoused by many Democrats and Republicans, Friedman never discusses whether and to what degree powerful vested interests must be confronted or overturned. In fact, the ecological "revolution" he envisions is entirely possible within corporate-state parameters, a system resilient enough to integrate large-scale technological, business, and lifestyle transformations. Now hardly an impediment, capitalism emerges as the catalyst of radical change, Friedman adding: "... the one thing that can stimulate this much innovation in new technologies and the radical improvement of existing ones is the free market."[327]

Thousands of companies, large and small, are to be assimilated into this historic green transformation. While governments impose taxes, regulate businesses, provide subsidies, and enact social policies such as the carbon tax, Friedman embraces the "market" as the main vehicle of innovation and growth, as investment decisions within capitalism prove crucial.[328] The role of state governance is to work in partnership with "thriving markets". The spread of green technology, in Friedman's view, will position the U.S. as world leader in sustainable growth, the basis of a new (ecological) "American model" – later to be understood as a "Green New Deal". While trumpeting the virtues of capitalism, he concedes a dynamic public role for investment, research, pricing, sales, and other supports.

A third important and widely acclaimed liberal strategy is Lester Brown's "Plan B", subtitled "Mobilizing to Save Civilization". Long a key figure in modern environmentalism, Brown offers a more comprehensive "plan" than either Gore or Friedman – one that seeks to push the limits of modern liberalism. His ecological revolution calls for total commitment, including moves toward "climate stabilization", limits to population growth, eradication of world poverty, and rebuilding natural support systems.[329] With the tipping-point menacingly near, change will require new modes of thought and behavior, Brown warns: "In this situation, the failure to act is a de facto decision to stay on the decline-and-collapse path"[330]

In fact, Plan B would be more far-reaching than anything so far undertaken, all the more promising given Brown's strong emphasis on food and agriculture (mentioned only peripherally by Gore and Friedman). He believes carbon emissions can be significantly reduced by 2030, beyond what was proposed at Rio, Kyoto, Copenhagen, and Paris. Radical investment strategies can stimulate green transitions in the U.S., Europe, and across the globe much sooner than previously imagined.[331] Brown's market enthusiasm, along with such measures as a carbon tax, look toward sustainable modes of production and consumption. Clean and efficient systems of public transportation would supplant autos as a major travel option. Green cities would be rationally designed and planned, along with a downsizing and restructuring of global megacities. Cities will have to be rebuilt, planned more deliberately to serve human needs, entailing a shift toward localism, smaller populations, greener environs, more efficient energy sources, and community-based farming.

Extending his gaze well beyond that of Gore and Friedman, Brown views the agricultural predicament as vital to any future ecological politics, as food resources are even now inadequate for a world population at 7.5 billion, much less for possibly ten billion people expected to inhabit the planet by 2050. From this standpoint, agriculture is tightly connected to such issues as resource utilization, climate change, urbanization, and population pressures. Here Brown's Worldwatch Institute has for many years monitored a world of declining resources. He anticipates a steady shift from animal-based to plant-based diets combined with more localized, cost-efficient, greener forms of agriculture. Despite its radical veneer, however, Plan B also relies heavily on market incentives; no overthrow of the corporate-state apparatus is believed necessary.

Gore, Friedman, and Brown surely exemplify the best of liberal environmentalism, testing the limits of what had been previously deemed "practical" or "realistic". Allowing for differences, their outlooks share an action orientation along four overlapping fronts: market initiatives, technological innovations, public sector supports, cultural transformations. All look to something resembling a new Manhattan Project, or Green New Deal, allowing for some ambiguity in terms of political methods. All agree that the planet is nearing an ecological point of no return, and all believe the U.S. is at the epicenter of the crisis owing to its vast wealth, natural resources, global power, and impact on climate change. As liberals, however, they cannot escape ideological boundaries imposed by advanced capitalism, convinced that reforms carried out within institutions will be enough to save the planet. An ecological or "green" reform of capitalism, however, can go only so far. In the end, there is no viable transformative strategy, no embrace of an alternative developmental model, no policies or goals sufficient to overturn business-as-usual.

Gore, Friedman, and Brown share an abiding faith in "the market" – a system that, with enough reforms, can theoretically shed its enormous dysfunctions and allow for sustainable development. At this juncture, a pressing question emerges: can global capitalism (or indeed any *national* capitalism) be reformed in ways that allow for a sustainable economy? The evidence to date – and it is rather abundant – indicates that a deeply entrenched corporate state cannot be reformed sufficiently given its oligarchical character, its logic of profits and growth over public needs, and its combination of structural and ideological barriers to change. Emphasis on markets ("free markets"), moreover, is misplaced in a system where economic exchange is shaped by massive oligopolies, sheer corporate power, the state, and globalization.

To the degree Gore, Friedman, and Brown rely so emphatically on setting market priorities, they wind up trapped in this impasse. While modern capitalism, as in European social democracy, is surely accessible to greening and similar reform initiatives, its very *modus operandi* conflicts with moves toward a fuller ecological rationality. The most far-reaching reforms will not deter world capitalism from its deadly trajectory of profits, growth, and destruction – nor will such measures help empower anti-system forces needed to reverse the crisis. If modern capitalism does so much to fuel the modern crisis, how then could this very system be the mechanism of salvation?

California: The Limits of Greening

As the ecological crisis worsens, the state of California – with the eighth largest economy in the world – finds itself at the epicenter of the modern political challenge, for several reasons: its sheer size and impact, the severity of its potential environmental harm, its vast agricultural economy, its rise to political leadership in the fight against climate change. Its self-appointed vanguard role came when California, and its governor Jerry Brown (having no fewer than four terms in office), looked to forge an ecological model of development at a time when nothing of the sort had been introduced in national politics. President Trump's decision (in early 2017) to withdraw from the Paris Accords simply accelerated this process.

California could face unique devastation from the effects of global warming – a conclusion reached by several environmental reports, including one released in 2018 by the state Office of Environmental Health Hazard Assessment. These findings anticipated a bleak future of hotter and drier weather, droughts leading to shortages of water for commercial, agricultural, and residential use, increasing cycles of wildfires and mud-slides, severe threats to wildlife, and health problems from spreading vec-tors of disease. Water and soil problems are naturally expected to worsen. Meanwhile, as glaciers melt, sea levels along the California coast will begin to rise, upending every aspect of human, animal, and plant life from San Diego to the Bay Area and further north. In general, the report – based on extensive monitoring across the state – tracked no fewer than three dozen results of global warming on weather, natural resources, water, agriculture, plants, and wildlife.[332] Immediate and drastic action is needed to reduce carbon emissions, the authors stress.

Given this harsh scenario, Trump's snub of the Paris agreement and the science underlying it gave California a perfect opening to step forward and take both national and global leadership in the fight against climate change. The challenge was quickly taken up by a governor known for his longstanding dedication to the environment. As late as 2015 the threat of global warming was not placed very high on the list of problems addressed by U.S. politicians, nor was the corporate media especially agitated by a concern that was typically deemed remote, vague, uncertain. Congress had been largely silent on the issue, passing only the most tepid and ineffective legislation. Corporate lobbies had blocked meaningful efforts to confront the crisis, combating initiatives that might call into question the religion of economic growth. Fossil-fuel interests remained more deeply entrenched in the economy and political culture than at any time in American history. So, the great challenge extended far beyond Trump's know-nothing brand of environmental rejectionism.

Into this yawning void stepped governor Brown, looking not only to undercut Trump but to leave his own enduring legacy as heroic fighter against climate change – a priority, moreover, that had strong resonance in California for several decades. In 2016 Brown's crusade finally took off, viewed as something of a quasi-spiritual journey to save the planet. He said that California would do whatever necessary to meet the "existential threat" of climate change; radical change was no longer simply an option, but an imperative. Addressing a legion of deniers and slackers in Washing-ton, Sacramento, and elsewhere, Brown commented: "Climate change is real. It is a threat to organized human existence. Maybe not in my life. I'll be dead." He added: "And you're going to be alive in a horrible situation. You're going to see mass migration, vector diseases, forest fires, southern California burning up. That's real, guys." Those fires, he stressed, "will soon be burning throughout the world.[333]

For Brown, this was to be nothing short of a "global war, fought locally." The main idea was to move rapidly toward 100 percent clean energy; there could be no delays, no compromises. In November 2017 the governor took his campaign to Europe, with the imperative of achieving a post-carbon society, visiting several cities as well as the Vatican. After warning that "human civilization is on the chopping block", Brown proclaimed: "Let's lead the whole world to realize this is not your normal political challenge. This is much bigger. This is life itself. It requires courage and imagination." To face this Promethean challenge, the key is to realize that "ecology is more fundamental than economics."[334] Brown's tour was framed by the media as his "anti-Trump crusade".

In September 2018 Brown organized and hosted an environmental summit aligned with Global Climate Action in San Francisco, attended by 4000 climate-change activists from around the world. Targeting fossil-fuel interests, Brown proclaimed his dedication to a carbon-free world, California in the vanguard, stating: "No more talk. Now is the time for action." Corporate interests were ardently solicited, the idea being to incentivize green markets and bold technological solutions.[335] The technology giants of Silicon Valley would be central to this "landmark summit" and in the larger development of a post-carbon economy. Al Gore, one of the attendees, commented: "It [the shift] has the magnitude of the Industrial Revolution and the speed of the digital revolution". One project to emerge from this gathering was a California satellite that would orbit for the purpose of tracking global emissions. Beyond the "digital revolution", Brown's schema would be aligned with the space age.

Defying the conservative Beltway, Brown vowed to take California into a new age of sustainable energy, mobilizing the forces of government, big corporations, academia, and the high-tech sector to reach "a goal nearly unmatched anywhere in the world." Legislative bill 100, passed in summer 2017, had laid the foundations of a post-carbon economy that other states and indeed other countries might follow. The objective was radical enough: a shift to 60 percent green energy sources (mostly solar and wind) by 2030, followed by a complete phase-out of fossil fuels by 2045, if not sooner.[336] Utilization of oil, gas, and coal sources would become obsolete, soon to be a distant memory. Solar power plants, wind turbines, and other green alternatives would span the California landscape. Surprisingly, such apparently radical aims managed to gain bipartisan support, including from the Chamber of Commerce and dozens of big corporations.

A "renewable California", in Brown's epic vision, would be a land of partnerships involving business, government, academia, and technology. There would be proliferation of electric or hybrid cars, mass transit systems, expanded green space, and eco-friendly buildings supported by a well-funded ecological infrastructure. California would undertake a greening of businesses, banks, universities, public institutions, transportation, and the tourism industry. Meanwhile, the state would follow cap-and-trade programs similar to those in Europe, according to which corporations can purchase and sell "permits" for carbon emissions within generally restricted parameters. Progressive supports would come from the larger environmental community, including the Sierra Club, Climate Justice Alliance, and Environmental Defense Fund. For Brown's California (and for his successor, Gavin Newsom), the future points toward a far-reaching greening of modern capitalism.

Brown and his fellow environmentalists were no doubt correct to insist that "ecology is more fundamental than economics" – that the new crisis "is not your normal political challenge." At first glance what might be called the "California model" seems to call forth the kind of transformative vision needed for a post-carbon rationality. The difficulty lies in the actual economic and political interventions, or lack thereof, that governing elites favor going forward. A refusal to disturb existing power arrangements, for example, means that economic priorities will likely triumph over ecological goals, however ambitious the latter. A frustrating vagueness about political mechanisms only worsens matters.

Laudable as Brown's defiance of Trump might be, he remains just as closely aligned with corporate power as other liberals and conservatives. As in the cases of Gore, Friedman, and Lester Brown, the California governor envisioned no path to change that does not rely on big-business partnership – meaning decisions and policies guaranteed to favor capitalist agendas of profit maximization, technological rationalization, and sustained economic growth. Here again it is worth asking: can "green capitalism" or "climate capitalism" adequately underpin an ecological model of development?

In fact, we have no such model to offer an example of institutional or social force working toward a truly sustainable economy. At his 2018 summit Brown spoke enthusiastically about the role of corporate incentives in a post-carbon transition. Aside from participation in cap-and-trade programs, business would be asked to unveil new "market" approaches; greening would organically unfold within a framework of capitalist profits and growth. Everything would be voluntary, nothing binding, following the pattern of other climate initiatives. Brown could only hope that important sectors – energy, retail, technology, agriculture, etc. – might fall in line to help solve the "existential crisis". There is no distinct ecological strategy. Managers of the "California model" might well depend on the good will of otherwise progressive businesses in Silicon Valley and elsewhere, but just how green capitalism of this sort might reach the ambitious goals set remains uncertain. How far might the chieftains of Fortune 500 companies be prepared to go before re-emphasizing "economics over ecology"? In the end, "climate capitalism" turns out to be riddled with such deep contradictions that even the most far-reaching policies like those embraced by Brown are sure to be crippled or even nullified.

Such accommodation to corporate power, to the illusory magic of "markets" – a hallmark of liberalism – has disastrous consequences. One problem results from the extraordinary leverage of Big Oil in American public life. California is one of the few states where oil and gas are produced (also consumed) at extremely high levels, more so today than at any time in the past. It turns out that Brown, state Democrats, and even environmental groups have done little to curtail the harm done by fossil-fuels – or indeed the economic dominance they continue to exercise. In California oil is still extracted, processed, sold, and used in record amounts, with no sign of reversal. Big Oil itself spends more on lobbying, gaining support of both Democrats and Republicans, than any other corporate interest. Across the state huge sectors of the economy – not only energy, but agriculture, the military, technology, tourism – consume fossil fuels with few restraints. In 2018 California remained among the leading greenhouse polluters in the world, and largest in the U.S.

Brown not only avoided any confrontations with Big Oil – surely an ecological imperative going forward – but actually came to embrace its predatory interests. The biggest refineries in the state (17 all told) were allowed to thrive and expand, exempted as well from cap-and-trade schemes. The Brown administration (which departed Sacramento in January 2019) had awarded 21,000 new oil and gas permits, including 238 for offshore drilling.[337] Since 2009 the number of oil and gas wells in California has *increased* by 23 percent, hardly the sign of "wisdom and commitment" (Brown's words) to a post-carbon transition. The familiar IPCC injunction to "keep it in the ground" seems to be ignored by the ruling interests, including the Democrats. Meanwhile, state oil producers (as elsewhere) have been able to resist efforts to curtail or ban dangerous fracking operations.

While a massive oil infrastructure continues to flourish, the much-lauded cap-and-trade program has been revealed to be sharply limited, a predictable outcome. In 2017 California extended its cap-and-trade legislation to regulate emissions until 2030, meaning corporations can buy extra permits to pollute beyond limits set by the state. This approach allows greater environmental flexibility as it generates large sums of money for state government – an estimated seven billion dollars by the time the permits expire. As revenue is collected from the sale of permits, it is hard to envision how cap-and-trade might lead to zero carbon emissions – a failure already evident where the program has been in force, as in Europe. What Brown stated in 2017 could not be more telling: "Decarbonizing the economy when the economy depends so totally on carbon is not child's play. It's quite daunting."[338]

The great appeal of cap-and-trade revolves around its very elasticity, its compatibility with the corporate *modus operandi*. Since the mid-1990s, when these programs were first adopted, world fossil-fuel consumption has significantly *increased* over 1990 levels, with no sign of radical cutbacks in sight. Starting with the Kyoto Accords, the biggest polluters have been largely exempted from strict controls, with few incentives to drastically alter course. In California, as in Europe, the system has provided a steady stream of inexpensive carbon credits sure to impede any departure from the carbon economy. To date, the results speak loudly in favor of this harsh judgment: state greenhouse emissions rose by nearly 1.5 percent yearly during the Brown era.[339]

Brown's corporate-friendly agenda had especially harmful consequences for the all-important agricultural sector, key to the overall California economy. Brown had long been close to state food interests – the same
interests responsible for lopsided fossil-fuel and water utilization. Agribusiness constitutes the ultimate "private sector" influence that Brown hoped
to integrate into a post-carbon strategy, even as that business demanded
huge concessions and privileges. This is the most lucrative food-production
system in the world, worth more than $50 billion (2018) in revenues yearly,
its lobby presence in Sacramento powerful enough to ensure huge tax, regulation, and other breaks. Commenting on Brown's moderate approach to
the food complex, *Los Angeles Times* columnist George Skelton could write:
"It was a model of how to finesse controversial bills through a legislature.
Willingness to give and take. Both left and right must be happy with the
outcome." He adds: "Preachers can demand purity, but it's a losing cause
for politicians."[340]

Ecological concerns are indeed often a "losing cause" where agricultural lobbies are strong enough to block meaningful change. In 2017
farms and ranches in California produced no less than 13 percent of total
U.S. farming output. Further, state agricultural exports amounted to more
than $20 billion in 2018. More than one-third of American vegetables and
two-thirds of its fruits and nuts are grown in California. Top commodities include dairy productions, nuts, lettuce, tomatoes, and strawberries.
Meanwhile, meat production (including beef and poultry), at nearly four
billion dollars yearly, ranks fourth among state agricultural outputs. Not
surprisingly, this system is a voracious consumer of resources: roughly 80
percent of California water goes to the agricultural sector. Worth noting
is that many of these products are being threatened by climate change, as
temperatures rise and drought intensifies. Most of the state's 77,500 farms
could be severely impacted in coming years.

Years before Governor Brown took office, California was dedicated to
reducing the state carbon footprint, with some impressive results. Legislation AB32 in 2006 proposed to reduced carbon emissions at 1990 levels by
2020, a goal in fact achieved by 2018. A bigger target would be a 40 percent
decrease by 2030. At its peak in 2004 the state had roughly 500 million
metric tons of gas emissions, a total reduced to 429 million metric tons just
12 years later. Since 2007 the California greenhouse impact has lessened

yearly, thanks to new reliance on green technology for electricity along with strong moves away from coal and gas. At the same time, while overall U.S. greenhouse emissions declined slightly (by 0.5 percent in 2018), the global predicament was worsening: totals reached 32.5 gigatons of carbon by 2018, an increase of 1.7 percent over the previous year.

California successes reflect the widening adoption of solar and wind alternatives in electrical power generation, where emissions declined by 18 percent between 2010 and 2016. Meanwhile, other sectors (transport, agriculture, industrial) experienced a *growing* carbon footprint. The environmental impact of cars, trucks, buses, and planes rose by two percent in 2017, partly owing to cheaper gasoline prices. Despite the state having achieved its 2020 goals ahead of schedule, the California economy remained in full growth mode, still overwhelmingly reliant on oil and gas, and still responsible for nearly one percent of total worldwide carbon pollution.

When *per capita* emissions are taken into account, as they should be, a more contextualized picture emerges: for California, as for the U.S. in general, individual footprints dwarf those of others around the globe. For example, carbon emissions per capita total 5.2 metric tons for Russia, 4.9 for India, 2.7 for Brazil, 3.9 for Mexico, 4.2 for Chile, and 5.6 for Sweden, according to 2017 data. At present only the European Union (at 13.3 metric tons) exceeds the greenhouse impact of California, but not that of the U.S. (at 18.3 metric tons).[341]

The California picture ends up more distorted, however, when the massive agricultural sector is considered. Efforts to curb greenhouse emissions in this sector have been far more limited than elsewhere, in part owing to the enormous power of agribusiness and food lobbies in Sacramento. After all, with its 400 crops and thousands of farms, California agriculture has no parallel across the world – and we already know how deeply intertwined food production and the ecological crisis has been during the past few decades. In California, as elsewhere, agriculture both contributes mightily to the crisis and in turn is profoundly shaped and reshaped by that same crisis.

Despite overall reductions in the state carbon footprint, agriculture remains a stubborn problem as Brown's approach to this sector had been essentially business-as-usual. Unfortunately, the crisis will no longer permit continuation of old farming methods, resource utilization, and food priorities. Drastic adaptation is imperative, though nowhere has this been followed in state policies. Here the problem is more complex and variegated than fossil-fuel use alone, extending to such issues as overall economic growth, water use, arable land availability, and the meat complex. As temperatures rise, the atmosphere becomes drier, extreme weather events increase, and water tables shrink. California is destined to plunge deeper into ecological crisis, however successful liberal reforms might be in reducing carbon and other forms of pollution.

California agriculture presently devotes vast resources to meat and dairy production, with no shift on the horizon. The state has nine million acres of farmland to be irrigated, along with nearly six million head of cattle (ranking the state fourth in the nation). Meat and dairy sales are currently the first and fourth most lucrative in California. Not only beef but the poultry sector continues to expand, keeping pace with the steady growth of fast-food restaurants despite a modest shift toward vegetarian diets. Demand for animal foods is expected to rise until at least 2030 – that is, so long as the agricultural system can sustain this dysfunctional regimen.

One outgrowth of global warming is higher temperatures linked to more widespread drought conditions – a potentially devastating turn for agriculture. Within the next two decades California will probably suffer the following: up to 90 percent loss of Sierra snowpack, two inches or more of sea level increase, double the number of heat wave days, extended drought, more wildfires, severe diminution of aquifers – all at a time of rising demand for meat and dairy products, water, land, and energy. This conjuncture of developments is already becoming unsustainable.

Our view of agriculture and ecology is usually limited to the problem of carbon footprint. Dealing with the crisis, however, other factors enter the picture: water resources, arable land, soil deterioration, weather episodes, harm to animals, grains fed to livestock and poultry. We know that just one pound of beef requires a staggering 1700 gallons of water, used directly by animals and indirectly through grains as feed. An equivalent amount of potatoes consumes immeasurably less – nine gallons. The numbers are roughly similar for beans, lettuce, citrus, and most fruits and vegetables. While nearly 80 percent of all water in California goes to agriculture, more than *half* of that total is consumed by the animal-foods industry, and there are no signs of any reduction in meat or dairy consumption in California or indeed the country. As noted previously, Americans presently eat 222 pounds of meat per capita, most in the world – a recipe in itself for ecological catastrophe.

Often forgotten is an underlying dialectic: the same crisis that results from the mechanisms of economic development simultaneously *impacts* that development. Viewed thusly, Brown's ambitious policies were destined to fall short of what might be targeted in fighting climate change. Here little attention has been paid to the disastrous consequences of the animal-foods complex, especially vital to the California economy. Failure to confront this predicament means a dismal future for the entire state food system. Without a drastic alteration of course – most importantly a shift toward plant-based diets – a system producing one-third of vegetables, fruits, nuts, and grains for the entire U.S. will be on the verge of collapse. In fact, the natural habitat of the Central Valley is already in severe decline because of drought and shrinkage of water resources.

According to California environmental statistics, agriculture is responsible for no more than ten percent of global-warming emissions – less than transportation, electrical power, or commercial sources. But this is both understated and misleading: it fails to take into account those areas of transportation and electricity that intersect with agriculture. This calculation also ignores other environmental conditions (above all, water resources) involved in the dynamics of climate change. Brown himself seems to have recognized the general importance of a shift from meat-centered to plant-centered foods. At his 2018 summit the organizers sponsored a "zero food footprint week" for San Francisco, including a regimen of "low impact dining" and offerings of "grass-fed beef patties". The state legislature, with Brown's support, passed SB1138, guaranteeing all state medical patients greater access to plant-based meals. At the same time, discussion of any *systematic* transformation of a wasteful, inefficient, and destructive agricultural system has been deferred.

Meat and dairy intake is expected to remain unsustainably high for the next two or three decades, and no California policies are in place to alter that course. A mounting food crisis seems imminent even before the most disastrous effects of population growth, industrial and urban expansion, and climate change take hold. Unfortunately, meat is still generally regarded as a "personal" or "private" matter left untouched by public intervention; efforts to regulate consumption are often discredited as "food fascism". Further, while earlier decades have witnessed nascent changes in popular attitudes toward animal products, most Americans see no real connection between meat or dairy foods and a broad range of social and ecological problems. And those problems, as we have seen, intersect fully with the advancing global crisis.

Visiting China in 2015, Brown stated: "It's not time for inertia. It's a time for radical change in how to power the modern economy."[342] Successful initiatives in California during the past decade illustrate just how effective far-reaching reforms can be in curbing some of the most harmful effects of climate change. The corporate-state system can be moderated, significantly reducing its ecological imprint – but only to a point. Brown's call for radical action rings true, but policies emanating from Sacramento had not yet moved beyond liberal parameters, in part owing to the influence of huge corporate interests with their effective lobbying and advertising.

In the third decade of the twenty-first century, it seemed California was poised to continue state leadership in the fight against climate change under new (progressive) Governor Gavin Newsome. Despite obstacles imposed by the anti-environmental Trump administration, the state was still just as dedicated to reaching 60 percent renewable energy by 2030, even without any new departure in agriculture. Solar technology was gaining momentum, touted as the wave of the future: sunny California was already covered by fleets of solar farms along with hundreds of thousands of roof-top panels, bringing down prices and generating (from time to time) actual surpluses. Wind farms were likewise expanding across the state. Despite issues of land availability and environmental problems (risk to wildlife) for both solar and wind sources, by 2018 California was getting 34 percent of its electricity from renewables – easily the best record of any state. California, thanks in great measure to Governor Brown's historic initiatives, had taken the role of audacious leadership in the struggle to impede global catastrophe.

Could such leadership survive new challenges and roadblocks? Could Trump's obstructionism derail the march toward sustainable development in California? In fact, Trump had set out in 2017 to reverse even the tepid Obama-era reforms that sought to utilize, among other mechanisms, the Clean Air Act. Trump moved to open space for oil and gas drilling on federal lands, releasing 725,000 acres in California alone – a total that could increase to two million acres in the next decade. There would be as many as 32 new oil and gas wells across the state, projected across two decades. Fracking operations, moreover, would proceed full speed ahead, releasing more carbon into the atmosphere while countering the positive results of solar and wind energy.[343]

The stubborn presence of a fossil-fuel economy in California could not, however, be laid strictly at Trump's doorstep; the economic, if not cultural, dynamics run much deeper. In fact, the state has long been awash in oil – in both production and consumption – with no significant departure in sight. California inhabitants consumed nearly 400,000 barrels of oil daily in 2017 and 2018. The state remains a major global site of oil and gas wells, oil rigs, storage tanks, pipelines, and transport hubs handling vast amounts of fossil fuels. As of 2019, the number of good-paying jobs in the California fossil-fuel sector was 368,000. No fewer than 26 million cars and trucks were still dependent on oil sources, not to mention urban buses, trains, and air traffic. Given this reality, how far along the green-energy path might the state possibly traverse in coming decades, whatever the good intentions of progressive governors?

In fact, Newsome understandably chose a "realistic" or "pragmatic" approach to environmental matters once he assumed office. After all, oil in particular had long been embedded in the California experience, and that pattern was unlikely to be disturbed without enormous social and political explosions, not to mention a severe downturn in economic growth. The state had no fewer than 72,000 oil-producing wells in 2018 – a number that, as mentioned, could quickly expand in coming years. It follows that, while green energy sources (notably in household and commercial electricity) were expected to comprise a larger *percentage* of general state energy sources, the *total* amount of fossil-fuel use will nonetheless increase moving forward, congruent with massive overall economic growth. In this context it was highly unlikely that Newsome, any more than Brown before him, could hope to prevail against the powerful California oil and gas interests. Here again, it is easy to see how even the most zealous environmental reformism winds up blocked by insurmountable (capitalist) barriers.

How Lobbies Impede Change

Even the boldest environmental reforms pushed by American politicians, Brown included, can always be weakened or even nullified by well-funded corporate lobby machines. In California, perhaps more than elsewhere, the oil lobby has been active, its goal to short-circuit public initiatives that might limit the flexibility of its interests. Big oil concerns do not always win, but they remain powerful enough to secure crucial victories. In California, often against Brown's influence, they have been awarded new drilling permits, obtained limits to the carbon tax, managed to loosen state regulations, and resisted a ban on fracking. So long as Big Oil has such extraordinary clout in Sacramento, one result of its millions of dollars in donations to the governor's 2014 campaign, government efforts to roll back carbon emissions will be limited.

Former EPA regional administrator Jared Blumenfeld complained: "California is a world leader when it comes to adopting green legislation. But these measures are only as good as their implementation. Without proper institutional support, funding, and enforcement, environmental laws become paper tigers."[344] While environmental groups do have considerable leverage, fossil-fuel lobbies are better positioned given their deep pockets. Dozens of oil lobbyists in California donate money to election candidates, work nonstop to influence legislation, and carry out skillful media and legal campaigns to bolster some of the most harmful industries. California remains the third largest state oil producer in the U.S., where such corporations as Chevron, ExxonMobil, and Phillips are dominant forces. Their lobbies contribute more or less equally to Democrats and Republicans, having spent $154 million in 2006 to block a proposed state oil tax.

In 2018 corporate interests across California spent a record $360 million on lobbies, with fossil fuels (as might be anticipated) at the top of the list. And the list was mighty impressive: Chevron, ExxonMobil, the utility PG&E, Comcast, AT&T, another utility Southern California Edison.[345] Much of their work, in Sacramento and beyond, sought to influence legislation related to oil and gas regulations. Other efforts involved greater corporate freedoms to drill for oil and gas, employ fracking operations, and conduct trade in fossil fuels. Still other projects were designed to obstruct mobilization to fight climate change, some attacking the work of the IPCC and various environmental groups warning against fossil fuels. As noted in the previous section, money spent on lobbies enjoyed measurable successes.

Fossil-fuel lobbies rely heavily on economic and technological clout in a state where growth and affluence are worshipped by both parties. Those interests, moreover, typically pose as environmentally friendly, fully dedicated to fighting climate change. After all, they furnish jobs, goods, and services, and pay taxes while, they argue, the green organizations are more often the work of the "white middle class". Here the big corporations pretend to ally with labor and minorities against "elitists" far removed from the lives of ordinary people. They depict global warming, moreover, as a nebulous, distant threat being overblown by progressive "elitists". The effectiveness of such tactics has been largely mixed. When it comes to environmental politics, lobbies have expanded and gotten stronger, especially the case for oil and utilities, automobiles, banking, agribusiness, and fast foods. Nationally too such interests have worked to subvert, or at least moderate, public efforts to curb global warming as well as a wide range of ecological harms.

During 2017 and 2018, for example, the National Mining Association (and kindred lobbies) was active on behalf of the coal industry, working to block outdated power plant closings. In response to intense lobbying, the Trump administration ordered the Energy Department to keep coal-fired plants open, arguing (implausibly) that any decline in coal and nuclear electricity poses a national security risk. This directive came at a time when Trump officials were searching to extend the life of money-losing coal and nuclear plants threatened by cheaper natural gas and renewable-energy sources.[346] Under DOE auspices, the federal government invoked national defense to establish a "strategic electric generation reserve" forcing utilities to buy electricity from at-risk plants. On this issue mining interests have battled environmental groups, often getting the upper hand. Federal intervention in the economy, of course, runs counter to Trump's professed faith in "free markets".

Owing to the power of fossil-fuel lobbies in particular, the U.S. Congress has done little to advance green legislation; indeed, such reforms face steep obstacles. One case in point is a proposal by Senators Sheldon Whitehouse and Brian Schatz called the American Opportunity Carbon Free Act, that would establish a price on carbon pollution. The bill immediately encountered fierce opposition from the U.S. Chamber of Commerce, American Petroleum Institute, National Association of Manufacturers, and others. Whitehouse has been one of the few active voices dealing with climate change in mainstream American politics.

In June 2018 Whitehouse wrote an impassioned letter to Pope Francis just as the Pope was preparing to host major oil executives for a conference on global warming. The letter attacked the oil companies for outright duplicity: their professed interest in combating climate change was fraudulent, said Whitehouse. Addressing the Pope, Whitehouse stated: "Many of the oil companies with which you will be meeting are fond of saying, in essence, 'we know climate change is real; we know our product causes it; and we support a price on carbon as a solution.' As the primary author of the U.S. Senate's carbon-pricing legislation, I can assure you of the absence of any support from the large oil companies. If they supported my bill, or one like it, or were even engaged to amend or improve such a bill, I would likely know."[347]

The problem: strong corporate lobbies have resisted "any meaningful climate legislation". Whitehouse continued: "These industry advocacy groups often obscure the sources of their funding, but the likeliest explanation is fossil-fuel industry money buying their hostility to climate action … In this, they join an array of front groups supported by a network of secretive, ultra-rich industrialists, many of whom are massive players in the fossil fuel industry and who have as their primary mission obstructing climate legislation in order to protect their fossil fuel business interests."[348] Whitehouse's reference to "secretive, ultra-rich industrialists" surely includes the Koch brothers, whose long-term obstruction of environmental reforms (including their support of the Heartland Institute) is well known.

While interest-group activity has been a factor in American politics from the outset, long involved with the workings of urban political machines, its stranglehold over crucial decision-making areas is a more recent development, having taken off after World War II. In 1950 total federal lobbying amounted to just a few hundred million dollars (in 2018 value) but reached $2.1 billion by 2012 and $2.6 billion in 2017. According to OpenSecrets data, these lobbies include oil and gas (fifth at $100 million in 2017), electric utilities (sixth at $92 million, and autos (12th at $52 million). Others ranking high included Big Pharma, insurance companies, agribusiness, food sellers, the Pentagon, and health insurance.[349] Many leading corporate interest groups have been implicated in environmentally harmful practices, their influence on both branches of Congress – not to mention state legislatures – decisive on major issues.

Perhaps fearing new attacks from the environmental movement, agribusiness has stepped up its state and federal lobbying, hoping to maintain large subsidies, tax breaks, and political leverage against impactful reforms around water access, animal protection, toxic waste and pollution, and dietary recommendations. In 2018 those efforts were carried out on several fronts, the National Dairy Council, Nestle, Cargill, Hormel, National Chicken Council, National Farmers Union, and Wal-Mart. Targets included the Department of Agriculture, Food and Drug Administration, and Environmental Protection Agency along with most state governments.[350]

As for the all-important EPA itself, its operations have been severely weakened by the work of dozens of aggressive lobbies – from fossil-fuel interests to agribusiness, transportation, utilities, and the military. In 2017 those interests included ExxonMobil, Marathon Petroleum, National Mining Association, American Farm Bureau, Koch Industries, ConocoPhilllips, and First Energy Group.[351] Matters only worsened when Trump entered the White House, at which point EPA administrator Scott Pruitt opened his office to such corporate lobbies as General Motors, Ford, ExxonMobil, and the National Mining Association, none especially friends of the environment. The main goals were to stifle federal regulations on pollution, auto emission standards, animal welfare, and food processing.

The power of oil corporations to subvert ecological politics, through campaign funding and lobbying, has few parallels in American society. The list of usual suspects is long, starting with ExxonMobil, Koch Industries, Chevron, Occidental Petroleum, Royal Dutch Shell, Marathon Petroleum, the American Petroleum Institute, and BP. As noted, fossil-fuel leverage extends to both major parties: like Trump after him, Obama endorsed Alaska drilling operation by ConocoPhillips and others in the wake of sustained lobbying campaigns.[352] Worth mentioning here is the vast power of Saudi oil interests, which spent $5.8 million in 2017 alone to cultivate their notorious oil-for-weapons relationship with Washington – fruits of an alliance going back to World War II.

The expanded role of oil politics in American society has been known for many decades, the dirty relationship between the U.S. and Saudi Arabia having been no secret. We have seen how Juhasz argues persuasively for what she calls the "Bush Agenda": Big Oil shapes the contours of U.S. foreign and military policy, especially in the Middle East. There is abundant force to Juhasz' contention, though American reliance on foreign oil has diminished owing to the rapid development of shale and fracking operations. It seems more likely that distinctly *geopolitical* agendas – driven by the U.S.-Israel alliance – do more to shape geopolitics for the region. Still, as noted, oil corporations have spent billions of dollars to lobby federal, state, and local governments over the past decade, fearful that green technology will begin to replace carbon energy sources. ExxonMobil, Chevron, and Koch Industries have been especially aggressive in their lobbying.[353]

In California, an alliance of oil, food, and agribusiness interests fought tenaciously to limit Governor Brown's climate initiatives. Money from Chevron, Western States Petroleum Association, Tesoro Refining, and the Chamber of Commerce targeted reforms at every turn, hoping even to weaken cap-and-trade legislation. Corporations pursue increasingly sophisticated media campaigns, from state to state, aimed at making sure oil is being extracted, refined, sold, and consumed at the same high levels – and here they have mostly succeeded. While the percentage of sustainable energy sources climbs yearly, that hardly dents the *total* consumption of fossil fuels, especially given the twin effects of economic and population growth.

Commenting on Obama's 2015 agreement to grant ConocoPhillips drilling rights in the Arctic, Alec MacGillis (writing in *Politico*) points out "how ConocoPhillips overcame years of resistance from courts, native Alaskans, environmental groups, and several federal agencies is the story of how Washington really works". He adds: "As environmentalists, energy companies, and politicians brawled over big symbols like the Keystone XL pipeline … the more immediate battles over climate change and fossil fuels were being waged … out of the public eye, away from the cable news showfests and White House dramas."[354] MacGillis concludes: "Industries like Big Oil play Washington as a long game, exhibiting a persistence too often lacking in the people in charge of safeguarding the public good."

In other words, the fossil-fuel lobbies possess a tenacity lacking in most organizations fighting climate change.

In a *Rolling Stone* article exploring the far-reaching activities of state fossil-fuel lobbies, Tim Dickinson reveals how traditional utilities fight to weaken the expansion of green technology.[355] For most energy behemoths, the rise of solar power and other renewables poses an existential threat to their interests– all the more so as those sources become less competitive while alternatives become less costly. Dickinson writes of a "fierce, rear-guard resistance at the state level, pushing rate hikes and punishing fees for homeowners who turn to solar power, funded mainly by the Koch brothers and such front groups as the American Legislative Exchange Council (ALEC)."[356] A nationwide lobby created to obstruct serious environmental reforms, among other issues, ALEC operates in several states but Dickinson's focus here is Florida, "where the utilities powers of obstruction are unrivaled."[357]

In particular, the Florida solar industry has been checked by utility monopolies that reap huge profits from oil, gas, and even coal, their lobbying exploits fully backed by ALEC, which contributes generously to conservative election campaigns and state legislation. Dirty power lobbies dwarf the leverage of environmental and consumer groups. Dickinson quotes Florida state Rep. Dwight Dudley as commenting: "We live in the Stone Age with regard to renewable power. The power companies hold sway here, and the consumers are at their mercy."[358] Fossil-fuel lobbies continue to strongly oppose widespread adoption of home and commercial solar panels, which short-circuit the utilities' monopoly on energy provision. In Florida, as in other states, oil and gas interests counter green alternatives, despite environmental, material, and social costs. As of 2017, Florida remained 61 percent dependent on natural gas, followed by coal at 23 percent; solar comprised a mere one percent in a region saturated with sunshine.[359]

Lobby power explains this irrational discrepancy: from 2004 to 2016, the four largest utilities contributed more than $18 million to Florida politicians and their PACs – mostly to Republicans, who generally control the state legislature. Another $12 million was spent to influence legislators. Governor Rick Scott's narrow 2014 re-election was financed by roughly $1.1 million from these same interests. The extensive Koch donor network, which includes not only ALEC but Americans for Prosperity, is vital to those dark political schemes. ALEC and its spinoffs insist that solar and other alternatives are expensive choices for the privileged, while traditional utilities offer cheaper energy for the most vulnerable sectors.[360] Meanwhile, leading Republicans like Senator Ted Cruz of Texas have called the spread of green technology a "radical attempt to destabilize the nation's energy system."[361]

By the 1990s, American society witnessed the proliferation of think tanks working in tandem with federal and state lobbies, all funded by giant corporations – not only fossil-fuel interests but agribusiness, banks, military contractors, the food industry, and Big Pharma. Such think tanks as the Brookings Institute, American Enterprise Institute, Manhattan Institute, and various Koch operations each receive tens of millions of dollars to carry out friendly research and influence peddling, which typically merge in areas of social and foreign policy. These centers sponsor books, articles, op-ed pieces, conferences, and documentary films that propagandize for economic growth, corporate profits, forceful U.S. global interventions, and of course heavy reliance on oil and gas sources of energy. Brookings, for example, maintains a budget exceeding $100 million yearly, made possible by donations from ExxonMobil, General Electric, and J.P. Morgan. Reports and other media efforts critical of established scientific findings on climate change routinely emanate from the think tanks, most often with conservative biases.

The expanding corporate lobby complex, having increased its leverage over state and federal governments since the 1940s, gains clout through a combination of material resources, institutional power, think-tank activity, and media influence – all with a poorly understood impact on American public life. It dwarfs the capacity of environmental, consumer, and other progressive groups to shape government policy, a goal of corporate oligopolies intent on staving off meaningful reforms. Within this network can be located the great meat and dairy complexes that, as we have seen, now figure centrally in the fate of the planet.

The overriding goal of agribusiness, the food industry, and kindred interests is to ensure high levels of meat and dairy consumption – a goal historically realized with few impediments. As in the case of other lobbies (military contractors, banking, insurance, Big Pharma, etc.), food interests have been able to colonize government and its key agencies. Whether we

are discussing livestock, slaughterhouses, grocery stores, or the McDonaldized sector, animal foods interests have managed to achieve more or less
what they want: massive production and sales of animal foods at reasonable
cost to many tens of millions of American consumers. This achievement,
spurred by ubiquitous media advertising, has given rise to a huge population addicted to meat and dairy products.

Ken Midkiff, in *The Meat You Eat*, writes: "Your doctor might tell you
to eat fewer burgers and steak sandwiches, but thanks to the exceptional
lobbying skills of the American meat industry, the U.S. government probably never will."[362] Those "lobbying skills" influence not only legislation
but media bias, professional advice, medical practice, and everyday decision-making about food choices. Not only corporate propagandists but
think tanks, doctors, clinics, academics, diet experts, and media pundits
help market meat and dairy products, generally based on misinformation,
half-truths, and myths about the special value of animal protein. Best-selling authors emphasize diets rich in protein and fat, light on "carbs" without
reference to valid scientific findings. Lobbyists work tirelessly to ensure
favorable legislation, government subsidies, good branding imagery, and
social habituation. They further help determine various dietary "guidelines"
established and promoted by the U.S. Department of Agriculture, the Food
and Drug Administration, and other federal (and state) agencies.

According to OpenSecrets, an ensemble of agribusiness lobbies spend
far more than $100 million yearly to influence government policy – $28 million on agricultural products, $16 million for food processing, $5.6 million
for dairy interests, $3 billion for livestock.[363] Such groups are especially active
at the USDA, where food information and dietary guidelines are routinely
furnished. The most aggressive lobbies include the National Cattlemen's
Beef Association, National Dairy Council, American Meat Institute, and
National Chicken Council, often allied with such corporations as Hormel,
ConAgra, Tyson Foods, and Nestle. The fast-food industry, led of course by
McDonalds, fields its own well-funded system of operatives. A broad range
of meat interests, in addition, typically donate between $10 and $15 million
to national political campaigns.

Thoroughly colonized by business interests, the USDA serves as faith-
ful instrument of meat and dairy foods, debunking plant-based alternatives. None of the lobbies exhibits much concern, beyond pretenses here

and there, for developmental sustainability, environmental balance, human health, or animal welfare. On the contrary, animal products are promoted as a marker of affluence and progress, a source of marvelous health and strength. Unfortunately, what the USDA and related agencies recommend is passed on routinely to schools, colleges, prisons, hospitals, and other public institutions. Little is ever probed or questioned.

In the U.S., as in other advanced industrial societies, the meat complex is deeply interwoven with the economic and cultural fabric of daily life. At a crucial juncture in 1976 the pathbreaking (Senator George) McGovern Report recommended a diet heavy in plant foods, explicitly linking animal products to a long list of chronic diseases. The backlash was immediate and fierce, led by the usual corporate suspects fearing scientific and governmental challenges to their marketing of harmful foods. The McGovern attempts to inject rationality into American food consumption were subverted by intense lobbying, and the recommendations were jettisoned. Meat and dairy interests held sway, and have done so across succeeding decades, thanks to such groups as the American Meat Institute, National Cattlemen's Association, National Dairy Council, and the National Milk Producers Federation. Agencies like the USDA and the Food and Nutrition Board (FNB) would continue to extoll, against years of scientific evidence, the virtues of high-fat, high-protein, animal-based diets typically in the guise of fighting "carbs".[364]

Backlash against the McGovern Report was fueled by a powerful ensemble of forces: corporations, the media, academia, the medical sector. It turned out that the meat, dairy, and fast-food lobbies were too powerful to fight, their massive contributions triumphant in elections, legislation, nutritional studies, academic journals, the drug industry, and medical schools. Their concerted goal has been to "systematically attempt to conceal, defeat, and destroy viewpoints that oppose the status quo."[365] This exemplifies what Campbell in *The China Study* refers to as the dark side of health research in the U.S., which fosters corporate interests over even minimal definitions of the public good.[366]

For the past several decades, American diets have been overwhelmingly comprised of rich, fatty, and unhealthful animal foods – a regimen that, we have seen, is totally unsustainable. The public has been conditioned to believe that the most harmful foods are in fact the most healthful –

results evident in rising levels of obesity and such chronic afflictions as cancer, heart disease, and diabetes. People have been falsely taught that vast amounts of protein are needed for optimum health, that the best or only source of protein is from animals, that "carbs" (a useless catch-all category) are somehow bad. Flawed research findings are propagated to reinforce this horrendous mythology, and these just happen to coincide with meat-complex interests.[367]

The aforementioned Food and Nutrition Board, historically dominated by meat and dairy interests, recommends a diet saturated in animal protein (up to 35 percent of total intake). Americans now consume on average roughly 30 percent of their food from meat and dairy products, while optimum amounts – as shown by Campbell's exhaustive research – are closer to ten percent protein, that to be derived mainly from plant sources. The FNB guidelines are derided by Campbell as "an unbelievable travesty" considering the weight of scientific evidence.[368] At FNB, as elsewhere in the federal government, challenging voices are indeed scarce; ideological consensus appears rigid and unmovable, ritually endorsed across the media and political landscapes.

From agribusiness to food processing, from the grocery complex to fast foods, corporate lobbies continue to devote vast resources to sustain indefensibly high levels of meat and dairy consumption. Large transnational empires – Tyson, Cargill, McDonalds, Wal-Mart, Nestle – constitute an economic fortress so powerful that counterforces usually seem overmatched. Corporate hegemony is so pervasive that critical awareness of harmful consequences seems mostly invisible. The horrors are shrewdly and effectively hidden from view – a rational outcome for corporate managers, but disastrous for the future of life on the planet.

The Media: Fueling the Crisis

Systemic barriers to reversing the ecological slide cannot be understood without exploring how the corporate media drives material growth, commercial priorities, rampant consumerism, a waste economy. The key here is advertising, which infuses every media outlet: TV, radio, the Internet, print venues, sports branding, and social media. The enormous power of capitalist sales and marketing is ubiquitous, its personal, social, and ecological consequences difficult to overstate. It might be argued that, without the creative mechanisms of advertising, the modern economy would face probable collapse.

Within a widening framework of oligopolistic markets, corporations have both the need and capacity to manipulate beliefs, attitudes, and choices in the service of profits and growth, to create, sustain, legitimate the demand for a steady flow of goods and services. This skillful management of consumption is key to survival of a system riddled with deep contradictions, including overproduction of an endless array of commodities, none more vital than food. At the same time, markets are no longer local but national and, increasingly, global although hardly what is ritually called "free". In the absence of massive sales efforts familiar patterns of consumption (in many cases addiction) related to food choices might be called into question.

Advertising, marketing, sales, packaging, branding – these are indispensable components of corporate dynamism nowadays, accounting for no less than 12 percent of total economic activity in the U.S. As of 2017, overall advertising revenue in the U.S. amounted to roughly $400 billion, feeding a relentless stimulus to mass consumption.[369] Ecological devastation ends up merely another by-product of peak consumerism. Here media culture is a driving force behind modern capitalism, its instruments owned and managed by corporate oligopolies empowered by nonstop advertising, which saturates news, entertainment, sports, information, and political commentary. Consumer preferences, moreover, are shaped by the entire media system, going well beyond advertising. Both food and drugs rank at the top of corporate dollars spent to influence targeted populations.

New generations are accustomed to a capitalist universe saturated with marketing, advertising, and branding – food being near or at the top of the list. Economic development thrives on the power of sales. The line separating social reality and sales imagery becomes increasingly blurred. A huge stratum of marketing experts works endlessly to manipulate human desires, identifying problems and needs for which commodities become "solutions". At a time when fast-food items are being advertised across the landscape, media culture then markets drugs to "treat" virtually everything: high cholesterol, insomnia, anxiety, sleeplessness, sexual dysfunction, depression to name some.[370] In fact, advertising is best viewed as a mode of commercial propaganda, empty in terms of truth content and reliant on misleading imagery. It reinforces prevailing attitudes – for example, trumpeting the aesthetic and health value of meat products – in the process valorizing the most harmful consumerism. Advertising and hyper-consumerism are historically wedded, impossible to separate, feeding waste, destruction, and unsustainability at every turn.

The well-funded universe of advertising in effect serves to counter efforts to combat the ecological crisis. Rampant consumerism drives the growth and profit-maximizing agendas of modern corporations, reinforcing the extreme individualism and materialism that clashes with the logic of environmental sanity.[371] Aggressive marketing of fast foods, central to the McDonaldized society, probably best fits this pattern. Corporate food advertising has created a mass public routinely exposed to counter-ecological images. More than five billion dollars is spent yearly to spread ignorance about food, nutrition, health, and the environment, nearly 90 percent earmarked for TV advertising, mainly in the areas of news, entertainment, and sports. Impressionable youth under 16 are a primary target, McDonalds being especially active here. Meanwhile, per capita meat intake in the U.S. is projected to increase further during the next decade, from roughly 200 pounds in 2014 to nearly 2015 pounds in 2030.

Since 2010 fast-food advertising has steadily expanded, generating super profits for McDonalds and kindred corporations. The McDonaldized sector competes heavily with other leading advertisers – insurance, autos, drugs, electronics, retail outlets – for privileged media exposure. McDonalds ranked fourth in marketing outlays, spending $957,000 in 2014 and more than one billion dollars in 2018, just within the U.S.[372] Advertisers also rely heavily on sexualized imagery along with familiar appeals to taste and affordability. Sales pitches are commonly associated with sports and outdoor activities – that is, entirely wholesome activities which bely the damaging properties of what is being marketed. The American dairy industry served as official endorser of the 2016 summer Olympics in Rio – its slogan "Milk Fuels Team USA on the Road to Rio" the dominant refrain – to be repeated at Tokyo in 2020. Many athletes and other celebrities lend support to dairy and meat products, on TV and the Internet. Corporate sponsorships in the meat, dairy, and fast-food sectors benefit from linkages with the World Cup, National Football League, NASCAR, and major-league baseball. A National Dairy Month touts the wonderful health benefits of milk, cheese, yogurt, and ice cream, its goal to "build lifelong dairy habits" for tens of millions of Americans.

The fast-food sector attempts to appear as more than a sophisticated advertising machine, often functioning as a kind of nutritional counselor, aligned with the USDA and FNB, all promoters of meat and dairy products. Here the federal government works to legitimate some of the most harmful products on the market. We cannot begin to grasp the totality of the ecological crisis – or the worsening obesity problem – without taking into account the vigorous marketing of animal foods across the media landscape. In the U.S., at least, attempts to legislate curbs on such advertising have gained little momentum: commercials remain "protected speech", a legality reaffirmed by the Supreme Court as basic to the First Amendment.

In a word, chieftains of the food oligopoly want nothing more than to have people eat as much of their products as possible, limits be damned. As Marion Nestle points out in *Food Politics*, the advertisers never rest, always on the lookout for new markets. Thus: "They seek new audiences among children, among members of minority groups, or internationally. They expand sales to existing as well as new audiences through advertising but also by developing new products designed to respond to consumer 'demands'. In recent years, they have embraced a new strategy: increasing the sizes of food portions. Advertising, new products, and larger portions all contribute to a food environment that promotes eating more, no less."[373] As in the case of animal products, this too contributes to the rise of obesity and chronic diseases.

Nestle observes that, from an industry standpoint, larger portions make the best marketing sense as the cost of food is low relative to labor and other factors involved in the system. To this end, the food operations have long developed literally thousands of different products embellished with more tens of thousands of packaging options that fill modern supermarkets. She adds: "More than two-thirds of those products are condiments, candy and snacks, baked goods, soft drinks, and dairy products ..." saturated in fat, sugar, and salt.[374]

Beyond such nefarious consequences, the advertising phenomenon needs to be recognized for its indispensable role in perpetuating both national and global capitalism. In reflecting on "ecology and advertising" in his book *Ecosocialism*, Michael Lowy refers to advertising as a form of "mental manipulation" designed to commodify virtually everything and give rise to obsessive consumerism.[375] Thus: "Both capitalism as a whole and advertising as a key mechanism of its rule involve the fetishization of consumption, the reduction of all values to cash, the unlimited accumulation of goods and of capital, and the mercantile culture of a 'consumer society'." In what economic sector of modern society could this dynamic have more debilitating consequences than in food production and consumption?

The Narrowing Terrain

Several decades of political experience show that the liberal tradition cannot establish an ideological or strategic framework for reversing the ecological crisis. The obstacles are simply too numerous, too overwhelming: corporate interests, limits of electoral politics, constraints on reformism, the corrosive force of money, lobbies, and think tanks, the influence of media culture. In the U.S. and across the globe environmental groups and movements – and more rarely parties – have adopted the outlook of ecological radicalism in some form, but so far no viable political *strategy* has constructed any effective counterforce. Liberal reformists can wax eloquently about a "green revolution", a "greening" of capitalism, or a "Green New Deal", but the chosen methods – market incentives, clean technology, altered lifestyles, specific policies – while sometimes efficacious within certain locales remain much too confined to the orbit of corporate-state power.

As the global crisis intensifies and the power structure expands, the bankruptcy of liberal reformism becomes more visible by the day. To be sure, radical politics will have to embrace reforms – big and small – but corrosive limits are reached when liberalism, including that championed by Gore, Friedman, and Brown, winds up as the *only* route. Liberalism inescapably cedes vital terrain to the ruling interests, its *modus operandi* shaped by a normal politics that never disturbs the trajectory of maximum growth, profits, and resource utilization. And those interests are more deeply consolidated today than at any time in both U.S. and world history. To the extent this pattern reproduces itself – while oppositional forces are no closer to a breakthrough – the space for radical politics will be narrowed.

We currently face a predicament in which the power structure remains so detached from the threat of ecological catastrophe that the political system itself does more to block than to empower popular struggles for change.

5

The Crisis Worsens

The long and difficult path toward a radical ecological politics will amount to little unless it leads to effective governance within and across nations. Even with the seemingly rapid spread of environmental consciousness, the challenge is filled with pitfalls and obstacles as the global crisis threatens human survival in a world system unraveling faster than even pessimists anticipated. A worsening crisis is destined to inspire – more likely *force* – new ways of viewing most everything: economic development, mass consumption, work, food, technology, social change.

This new global predicament reveals the extent to which the familiar industrial model (however ideologically framed) has exhausted its potential even as ruling elites scramble to manage and legitimate a modern capitalist order riddled with contradictions and dysfunctions. Joel Kovel writes: "... the current stage of history can be characterized by structural forces that systematically degrade and finally exceed the buffering capacity of nature with respect to human production, thereby setting into motion an unpredictable yet interacting and expanding set of eco-systemic breakdowns."[376] There can be no exit from this crisis without departure from ritual, stultifying patterns of thought and behavior.

Several decades of environmentalism in the U.S. and other advanced capitalist societies have left us well short of the ecological politics needed to make far-reaching changes, despite green reforms and other initiatives here and there. As we have seen, liberal agendas are inadequate on two fronts, offering neither an alternative economic model nor any viable political strategy.[377] Meanwhile, corporate interests reshape the world economy, finance, politics, culture – and the natural habitat. Reforms in many countries have brought change but fall dismally short. As ecological catastrophe lurks, elites use their power and wealth to maintain control while resisting deep change.

That such a powerful and well-defended fortress might be overturned any time soon seems rather improbable given the political impasse. By now we know – or should know – that any future "greening" of world capitalism amounts to a liberal fantasy: sustainable development cannot be achieved in a universe of endless accumulation, growth, resource extraction, and human exploitation. We have seen how well-organized lobbies and think tanks, along with the media, work to block disruptive change, nowhere more so than when it comes to environmental challenges.

A Fortress of Power

The overriding problem facing humanity today is how to confront – and *reverse* – a global crisis unprecedented in scope, intensity, and urgency. The main problem is actually one of *politics*, which requires a counterforce intent on the capture of power made possible by coherent organization, ideology, and strategy. Familiar legacies – liberalism, Marxism, social democracy, anarchism – now appear ill-suited to deal with the multifaceted obstacles ahead. Worth re-emphasizing here is that the task goes well beyond climate change, extending to agriculture, food, and natural resources in general. There are also distinctly *geopolitical* problems associated with declining ecosystems, already visible in many parts of the world.

As the crisis worsens, however, mass counterforces (oppositional groups, movements, parties) are nowhere to be found. Earlier anti-system tendencies have largely disappeared or been destroyed. We are left with movements and parties trapped in cycles of electoralism and reformism, an endemic part of the capitalist landscape. New challenges will impose new social and personal *choices* regarding modes of production and consumption, work, cultural activity, and natural relations in a world that bears little resemblance to earlier decades.

Writing in *Eearth*, Bill McKibben calls attention to what should be obvious: "New planets require new habits ... We simply cannot live on the new earth as if it were the old earth."[378] McKibben goes on to elaborate, stressing that the advanced industrial societies are habituated to economic growth, assuming that "more is better, and that the answer to any problem is another burst of expansion." Elites of all ideological stripes take for granted that endless growth is an obvious public good, however that growth is defined and however it devours resources. That has been central not only to capitalism but to ostensible alternatives in the form of socialism and Communism. McKibben summarizes: "On our new planet growth may be the one big habit we finally must break."[379]

Lester Brown, writing in *Full Planet, Empty Plates,* extends McKibben's thesis, focusing attention on problems of food and agriculture. For Brown, "the world is in transition from an era of food abundance to one of scarcity... Food is the new oil, land is the new gold", adding: "We are entering a new era of rising food prices and spreading hunger. On the demand side of the food equation, population growth, rising affluence, and the conversion of food into fuel for cars are combining to raise consumption by record amounts. On the supply side, extreme soil erosion, growing water shortages, and the earth's rising temperature are making it more difficult to expand production."[380] Brown appropriately raises the question as to whether "food is the weak link in our early twenty-first century civilization ...".[381] No oppositional forces have ever turned to the question of food, much less the more specific problem of meat and dairy foods. The same generalization holds today.

War on the natural habitat proceeds alongside other wars – against workers and local communities, against indigenous peoples, against popular movements, against struggles to achieve a peaceful world order. The U.S., with its unparalleled system of production and consumption along with its warfare state, contributes most to this lethal dynamic. Bruce Gagnon writes: "We [the U.S.] have become an occupied nation. The corporate oligarchy in Washington uses spaced-based technologies to spy on us and to direct all warfare on the planet. . These satellites allow the military to see everything, hear everything, and to target virtually every place on the planet ... The military-industrial complex has become the primary resource-extraction service for corporate capitalism and is preparing future generations for a dead-end street of perpetual war."[382] These looming issues are largely avoided within and outside of present-day environmental movements.

If the long-term goal of ecological sustainability is to be realized, climate change, however imposing, must be seen as simply one part of a broadening matrix of issues and challenges. Even if climate change were not the great threat depicted by the IPCC and "scientific consensus", global catastrophe would remain on the not-too-distant horizon. Far too many environmentalists dwell on atmospheric problems, as if somehow reducing the planetary carbon footprint were enough to reverse the crisis. (It is not.) Sadly, even where we see political commitments to decarbonize the planet – an objective never likely to be reached – important causal factors (population growth, urbanization, resource utilization, meat-based food production, the military impact) are mostly ignored or downplayed. An entire generation of theorists, activists, and politicians has been sidestepping painful truths. Among those truths is the very unsustainability of present-day wasteful and costly levels of human consumption, especially in the industrialized societies. A premise widely held even among progressive and leftists is that the planet is blessed with infinite resources, all waiting to be exploited, marketed, and consumed. That makes a mockery out of any viable ecological agendas, whatever their ideological direction.

Modernity, in the form of capitalism or another social order, has so far failed to meet Enlightenment promises of democracy, freedom, and prosperity – a failure most profoundly felt at the intersection of food, agriculture, and ecology. What only several decades ago appeared as the triumph of modern food production now becomes increasingly problematic. A social order immersed in technological optimism now faces a future of mounting food shortages, the result of shrinking farmlands, declining water availability, soil erosion, droughts, and heavy reliance on animal-based agriculture. Here global warming represents both cause and effect of the food crisis, as the mirage of productivity and abundance comes fully into view. Writing in *The End of Food*, Paul Roberts writes: "On nearly every level, we are reaching the end of what may one day be called the 'golden age of food' ..."[383]

World capitalism has given rise to an expanded, globalized, more aggressive form of corporate power that C. Wright Mills, in *The Power Elite*, first charted for American society in the 1950s. Dominant oligopolies – banking, insurance, food, agribusiness, pharmaceuticals, technology, the military – fit this pattern of modern capitalist power, far removed from the illusion of "free markets". Limits to perpetual growth are fiercely resisted at an historical juncture when rampant development exacerbates the crisis. The newer technology sector is positioned to benefit immensely from its relative economic freedom, able to reshape the vast terrain of communications, knowledge dissemination, and culture. Such corporations as Google, Microsoft, Amazon, Facebook, and Apple have gained unprecedented control over the flow of information, both domestic and national – now bolstered by their affiliation with sectors of intelligence and the warfare state, including the National Security Agency (NSA).

As corporate, state, and military power expands with seemingly few limits, especially in the U.S., the ruling stratum becomes less accessible, barely accountable. The system grows more distant from everyday life, from what remains of democratic processes. The technology giants exemplify oligarchical separation – always, of course, in the name of enhanced knowledge and freedom. This sector has evolved into both structural and ideological matrix of advanced capitalism, its business fortunes linked to government and the military. What Paul Gilding calls the "Great Disruption" is product of a growth mania that has since its outset has been destroying the natural habitat at ever-increasing levels.[384] Despite references to a "Green New Deal" here and there, political leverage to stave off descent into chaos is nowadays missing. Where ecological awareness is on the rise, it is quickly and routinely translated into a tepid environmental reformism locked into technological solutions.

Lester Brown writes: "The notion that our civilization is approaching its demise if we continue with business-as-usual is not an easy concept to grasp or accept. It is difficult to imagine something that we have not previously experienced." He continues: "We are facing issues of near-overwhelming complexity and unprecedented urgency ... Can we move fast enough to avoid economic decline and collapse? Can we change direction before we go over the edge? We are in a race between natural and political tipping points, but we do not know exactly where nature's tipping points are. Nature determines these. Nature is the time-keeper, but we cannot see the clock."[385]

One problem today is that American politics can no longer be considered democratic, if it ever was; it is the kind of oligarchical system Washington elites have always denounced where it exists *elsewhere*. The power structure described by Mills several decades ago has become more integrated over time, more remote from the lives of ordinary people. Both major parties are controlled by corporate interests, Wall Street, wealthy donors, and the warfare state, closely aligned with media culture.

Here we encounter a maze of self-serving illusions and escapist myths that gain credibility across the ideological spectrum. Thanks to the force of media culture, Americans are inclined to believe theirs is a nation of uniquely democratic ideals, a free-enterprise economy, and benevolent foreign policy. A global military apparatus, endless wars, and gun culture are routinely accepted, even celebrated, as natural to the American way of life. Ideological exceptionalism provides special comfort in a universe of evil monsters, hateful oligarchs, menacing terrorists, and rogue states – a *Zeitgeist* hardly compatible with a politics of ecological renewal.

Perhaps the biggest of all the American myths involves deeply embedded patterns of food consumption: heavily marketed meat and dairy products take on a quasi-religious character for the vast majority of people. The media ritually trumpets the great benefits of fatty, high-protein animal foods deemed *necessary* to good health – although precisely the opposite is true. The harm such products bring to personal health, the environment, and processed animals can scarcely be overstated, and the situation is getting worse. As noted, animal-based agriculture is among the most unsustainable of all human practices, whatever the impact on climate change.

Lacking a vibrant democracy, Americans currently face some bitter truths: the most important decisions are made at the summits of power, removed from the harsh vicissitudes of daily life. Corporate-state interests are what matter, and those interests could not be more hostile to the environment. According to a survey of CEOs conducted in 2015 (mainly those on the Fortune 500 list) the issue of global warming did not rank as one of the top 20 concerns; the crisis simply never registered on their radar.[386] What most troubled the executives was the "problem" of business regulation, or "over-regulation". Anything impeding profit maximization is essentially taboo. Referring to both this crisis and the threat of nuclear war, Noam Chomsky writes: "Whatever their individual beliefs, in their institutional roles the CEOs are constrained to adopt policies that are designed to 'pose extraordinary and undeniable threats to the continued existence of humanity', in the words of the Doomsday Clock declaration."[387]

Narrow economic thinking represents yet another delusion as the planet slides toward disaster. In *World on the Edge,* Brown writes: "If we use environmental indicators to evaluate our situation, then the global decline of the economy's natural support systems – the environmental decline that will lead to economic decline and social collapse – is well under way ... Yet economists look at the future through a different lens. Relying heavily on economic data to measure progress, they see the near 10-fold growth of the world economy since 1950 and the associated gains in living standards as the crowning achievement of our modern civilization." In the view of leading economists, "the world has not only an illustrious economic past but also a promising future."[388] Economism of this sort, prevalent across the political spectrum, amounts to one of the great ideological mirages of the contemporary period.

A system ruled by capitalist oligarchy and driven by endless accumulation of wealth and waste of resources cannot be compatible with radical change, reforms or no reforms. The ecological contradictions are too deep, too explosive. Oligarchy coexists with a mass society dominated by a complex ensemble economic, political, technological, and cultural controls – far more imposing than even George Orwell might have imagined. Orwell, it should be remembered, wrote his classic *1984* well before modern instruments of power gained their present level of expansion and integration, no longer only embedded in *state* power.

As the power structure consolidates its hold over industrial society, the political culture grows more fragmented and, in some ways, more depoliticized. Agencies of change are more readily neutralized by myths and illusions like those mentioned above. Some protest movements – for example, the episodic "anti-globalization" uprisings and "occupy" movements – appear on the scene and then rapidly vanish. Others such as once-explosive antiwar mobilizations have not proved durable. Yet others, including some well-known environmental groups, typically morph into different variants of liberal-reformism. In the end, we face a *political* crisis as dangerous as to the ecological crisis.

The Reformist Delusion

A central motif of this book is that deep transformations needed to reverse the global crisis will have to be multiple and far-reaching. Efforts to reform the corporate-state system can make important headway, as they have in many European social democracies, but those gains are sure to reach limits once the power structure imposes its tenacious will. Meanwhile, reformism loses its thrust as the ecological predicament intensifies.

Turning to the question of distinctly American power, it is not only capitalist and global but also imperialist, a system enforced by the largest war machine in history and governed by an aggressive ruling elite – a geopolitical factor usually ignored by environmental theorists and activists. Moreover, the power structure functions the same, whether managed by Republicans or Democrats. In a system that counts its worth in tens of trillions of dollars, with many trillions more invested in fossil fuels, its elites will fight to the end in defense of their unfathomable wealth, power, and geopolitical advantage. Such uncomfortable truths are steadfastly ignored by those hoping for a reformist path out of the crisis.

The idea of a transition from fossil fuels automatically turns toward green technology which, so far in limited capacity, best fits the demands of the residential sector. Other sectors – transportation, agriculture, corporations, the military – rely heavily on fossil fuels, with no great departure from the norm on the near horizon. Fossil fuels retain strong advantages – lower costs, abundance, easy to move from place to place, with complex infrastructures well established. Planes, ships, trucks, and helicopters will continue to depend on fossil fuels well into the future. In the U.S., and more emphatically in countries like China, Russia, and India, use of oil, natural gas, and coal expands so that even with a few exceptions to the dominant pattern (Germany, California) the global impact of carbon emissions will be astronomical. At present there is no indication that the carbon footprint of any major industrial nation will seriously decline, nor that of the many rapidly developing countries that have no intention of shifting to green technologies any time soon.

As for the U.S., its power structure is much too immersed in the fossil-fuel economy for the anticipated shift to sustainable energy sources to have far-reaching consequences. The trillions of dollars in fossil fuels that remain to be extracted are too valuable for those who own and utilize them to be merely set aside, "left in the ground". Moreover, an imperial system dedicated to global economic and military supremacy – and with a labyrinth network of bases and armed-forces deployments around the world – cannot possibly extricate its costly operations from the fossil-fuel regimen. Manuel Garcia, Jr. writes: "The U.S. can only address the existential threat of global climate change by disavowing the imperialistic and self-aggrandizing ambitions of its political and corporate elite."[389]

The main path of American environmentalism has followed a trajectory of liberal reformism, its goal to secure practical improvements in a declining habitat. From the 1960s to the present, creative efforts behind ecological renewal have been inspired by seminal thinkers: Rachel Carson, Murray Bookchin, Barry Commoner, Rudolf Bahro, and others. Their appearance on the scene helped catalyze the new social movements which in turn gave rise to Green tendencies during the late 1970s and 1980s. Many issues came to the fore – air and water pollution, toxic wastes, the nuclear threat, land management, agriculture and food problems, and eventually climate change. These issues have become more salient across the decades.

Since the first Earth Day celebrations in 1970, methods of protest and change have taken many forms: mass demonstrations, local struggles, lifestyle changes, legal tactics, lobbying, social policies, global actions, international treaties, formation of political parties. Alongside such developments came the "back-to-the-country" movement emerging from the counterculture, mostly in Europe and North America. During the 1980s environmentalism took a more distinctly political turn with the arrival of Greens, who sought to provide a framework for a "gathering of the movements" in Germany and across Europe. Within the Greens a new ideology arose – ecosocialism, or "left-green" politics, owing in great measure to the influence of Bookchin, Bahro, and leaders like Petra Kelly.[390]

In the midst of these historic departures, however, American politics would follow in the tracks of environmental reformism that would steadily expand from the 1980s onward consistent with the availability of money and other resources. This naturally worked to the detriment of ecosocialist and other radical approaches, more so in the U.S. than in Europe. Of course, mainstream environmentalism won crucial victories such as formation of Environmental Protection Agency (EPA) and Occupational Safety and Health Administration (OSHA). It might be said that modern environmentalism laid the foundations of a new mode of politics that transcended traditional conservatism associated with such epic thinkers as Thoreau, Emerson, and Muir.

From the outset, reformism imposed severe limits on the transformational potential of environmentalism. Its success depended on the clout of large, well-funded organizations familiar to most Americans: World Wildlife Fund, Environmental Defense Fund, Sierra Club, the Nature Conservancy. What has been called "Big Green" steadily expanded across the years, morphing into something of an institutionalized fixture of the political system. Some groups have become an appendage of the Democratic Party, a by-product of a weak U.S. Greens movement and the failure of the Republicans to take up environmental concerns. In California, thanks mainly to Democrats and the initiatives of governor Jerry Brown, reforms have pushed the energy sector closer to sustainability – though, as we have seen, the state carbon footprint has declined only slightly while many of its sectors (including agriculture) remain largely untouched. Some European countries, with Germany in the lead, have made similar headway on the path to a greener capitalism.

These efforts are destined to run up against strict limits – and indeed have already done so, as the utilization of fossil fuels continues apace. An entrenched power structure has shown no signs of budging in the case of energy priorities. Environmental reformism is more likely to work in *partnership* with these interests than against those interests. In the process many crucial problems wind up overlooked: corporate power, agribusiness, and food, not to mention the warfare state.

What, then, are those restrictive features of environmental reformism? What do these dozens of organizations represent, and how do they operate? The first problem is that they are generally large and bureaucratic, with huge budgets, staffs, and memberships, dependent on aggressive fundraising and recruitment campaigns. Time and energy devoted to these activities usually comes at the cost of political intensity. Funding brings organizational leaders into the orbit of corporate power, its army of lobbyists, and its narrow Beltway priorities. Financing can even depend on fossil-fuel interests, as some of the worst corporate offenders (Wal-Mart, McDonalds, Chevron, Tyson Foods, etc.) furnish largesse. The very *modus operandi* of big environmental groups actually parallels that of the business lobbies – narrow, instrumental, single-issue focused, compromising.

Charting the legacy of Big Green, Mark Dowie (in *Losing Ground*) called attention to the peculiarly insular dimension of liberal-reformism – not only because of its business-friendly model but owing to its limited confines of Washington, D.C. and state capitols.[391] Often at odds with the mass base, leaders seem most comfortable working with elites from the business, legislative, and administrative sectors, far removed from the most pressing issues. Reform organizations express hostility toward radical alternatives that might call into question their tepid environmentalism while probing deeper into the content of economic development and social progress. What Dowie first argued in the late 1980s rings even truer in 2019.

The sad trajectory of Big Green has given rise to a new stratum of liberal operatives – bureaucrats, managers, politicians, lobbyists, think-tank intellectuals, academics, fundraisers, publicists. While their most important reforms (curbing air and water pollution, funding green energy sources, regulating nuclear power, creating new federal agencies, etc.) should not be minimized, attempt to explore the underlying causes of ecological crisis were never forthcoming. The radical influence of Carson, Bookchin, Commoner, and others would never be felt within the Beltway or the state capitols. Indeed, Commoner's run for the presidency in 1980, on the Citizens Party ticket, failed dismally.

In fact, radical perspectives did surface here and there, energized by ideological currents such as Bookchin's social ecology, leftist Green Party factions, Deep Ecology, embryonic forms of ecosocialism, and direct-action groups like Earth First! While none of these ideas and organizations commanded a mass base, some combination of their insurgent visions can be expected to furnish a counterpoint to liberal reformism in coming years. As of 2020, however, such alternatives remained small, isolated, marginalized; moderate environmentalism ruled, and still rules.

The rise of European Green parties in the 1980s brought political articulation, along with electoral success, to environmental priorities, often radicalized in the context of community, peace, and feminist movements. Green popular appeals stoked hopes for anti-system potential, starting in Germany where ecological consciousness was already relatively advanced. The parties, in Germany and elsewhere, incorporated diverse strains of environmentalism in their platforms and added coherence to local movements. But such coherence was usually purchased at a price: taking part in elections brought moderation, just as it had done for Communism and socialism in Europe. Within a decade most European Green parties had become fully social-democratized, at peace with capitalism. By the early 1990s every Green party, having failed to significantly broaden their mass base, ended up as agencies of green capitalism just as ready to embrace corporate growth agendas as was true for mainstream American environmentalism. That would emphatically apply to the rather small U.S. variant of the Greens.

Among the dozens of environmental groups in the advanced capitalist societies, few are prepared to challenge corporate power, few offer a broad anti-system strategy, and even fewer question the scourge of meat-centered agribusiness or the McDonaldized food economy. The general outlook is one that merges "market" incentives with technological innovation to lighten the carbon footprint. Thus the Environmental Defense Fund (EDF) wants to "slow climate pollution" while expanding industrial growth aligned with greater corporate responsibility, empowering "market mechanisms" through partnerships with Wal-Mart, McDonalds, and other business giants.[392] The EDF has a sterling reputation as champion of ecosystem renewal with its expertise in science, economics, law, and market-based solutions to environmental problems. Based in New York, its worldwide presence requires a staff of more than 500, membership of 1.5 million, and yearly operating revenue of nearly $150 million. EDF objectives include drastic reductions in greenhouse emissions, though without altering the hallowed corporate-growth framework.

The aforementioned Sierra Club, oldest and most venerable of U.S. environmental organizations, fits roughly the same pattern. With a reported membership of 3.5 million spread across many local chapters, a staff of 600, and a yearly budget of $110 million, the Club is multifaceted, supporting progressive candidates nationally and locally; advocating policies to reduce carbon emissions, especially coal; publishing books; pushing for better land management; sponsoring a variety of social activities. It is a member of the Blue-Green Alliance, a coalition of environmental groups and labor unions. Its laudable stated mission is "to explore, enjoy, and protect wild places of the earth, to practice and promote the responsible use of the earth's ecosystems and resources . . ".[393] The Sierra Club works to pressure corporations toward more ethical choices.

Sierra Club has done much to raise ecological consciousness in American society since the 1970s, and has helped secure important reforms, though within a market-centered framework. For most of its history the Club has accepted generous financial contributions from big business (including fossil-fuel companies). It generally exemplifies the rigid limits of Big Green environmentalism. Among such limits is leadership refusal to acknowledge the disastrous ecological impact of animal-based agriculture and the meat industry – a criticism leveled by filmmakers of the 2014 documentary *Cowspiracy*. Little has changed even after the Club's failure to confront the ecological crisis had become widely known.

In the film, when asked about the consequences of animal-based agriculture for the environment, Club spokesperson Bruce Hamilton drew an embarrassing blank, as did leaders of other Big Green organizations. It turns out that the Sierra Club had never paid attention to such issues, or to the practice of hunting. The idea that the meat, dairy, and fast-food industries might be harmful to people's health, ecosystems, and animals seems never to have occurred to Club representatives, despite their stated dedication to the natural habitat. They had "Beyond Oil" and "Beyond Coal" programs but no "Beyond Meat" options even in the wake of membership pressures to move in that direction. With the appearance of *Cowspiracy*, Executive Director Michael Brune said the group would move to "draw the connections between animal cruelty and cruelty to the planet as a whole", yet since 2014 it appears little has changed: we still await Sierra Club indictments of meat and dairy interests. Many were fearful that important changes along these lines would rile donors and upset the personal lifestyles of many Club members.

A deeper problem is failure of the Club to address corporate obstacles to change, typical of Big Green. Many organizations – Rainforest Action Network, Friends of the Earth, Carbon War Room, Union of Concerned Scientists, World Resources Institute, the Nature Conservancy – have admirable mission statements about reducing the carbon footprint, but fall dismally short when it comes to political substance and strategy. Most groups favor a comfortable mixture of market incentives and green technology, even where the limits to such initiatives are abundantly clear. Other efforts (climate demonstrations, protests against fracking and oil pipelines, various green projects) help to educate and mobilize, but they too wind up trapped in a certain social immediacy.

For several decades environmental reformism has become accepted by Americans, limiting air and water pollution, reducing greenhouse emissions, moderating the worst consequences of urbanization, fighting nuclear power, expanding the use of green technology, introducing river and lake protectors. These advances should in no way be minimized, yet the ecological crisis seems more or less impervious to such reforms, outpaced by the rapid course of overall economic and population growth.

This predicament is reflected in the evolution of such organizations as the Nature Conservancy, with its million-member base and annual operating revenues of $1.3 billion – a project dedicated to "conserving the land and waters on which all life depends." The Conservancy works to help businesses make better decisions, engage more fully with "nature", and function in a way that protects the land. One recent campaign was the Plant a Billion Trees initiative to restore 2,500,000 acres of land. The Conservancy embraces "pragmatic", non-confrontational tactics, dictated by its many partnerships with large corporations (including Bank of America, Cargill, AT&T, Disney, Dow Chemical, and Goldman Sachs). The rigid limits imposed by such "partnerships" hardly deserve further commentary. Despite its vast size and influence, the Conservancy has nothing to say about the devastating impact of agribusiness or the meat industry.

A mostly youth-based group, the Sunrise movement was launched in 2017 with the general aim of pushing the Democratic Party leftward on climate change – its focus "decarbonization, jobs, and justice". It first target was the 2019 U.S. midterm elections, where activists set out to elect proponents of global-warming legislation, with an eye toward the Green New Deal favored by the "squad" (led by Alexandria Ocasio-Cortez). The Sunrise focus has been overwhelmingly on electoral politics, but the movement as of early 2020 had shown little progress in actually bringing the Democrats closer to any pathbreaking climate-change reforms in Congress, hardly surprising given the extent to which major corporate interests have shaped the party.

Among the most progressive movements is 350.org, founded by Bill McKibben and focused on the threat of climate change – its singular goal being to reduce atmospheric carbon dioxide from the current level of 400 ppm to 350 ppm that is often considered the upper threshold to avoid a global "tipping point". Unlike most Big Green organizations, 350.org defines itself as a grassroots movement, yet it has an international presence. Its thousands of groups have expanded to 188 countries. Its carbon divestment initiatives are at colleges and cities. It has organized efforts to block oil expansion, including the Keystone XL pipeline. Other 350.org pursuits have included teach-ins, marches, tree plantings, and synchronized demonstrations across the U.S. and the world. Just how far 350.org is willing to confront the power of big business – or question the religion of economic growth – is not entirely clear. Similarly, its approach to issues surrounding animal-based agriculture and fast foods remains obscure. Still, liberal reforms of the sort advanced by 350.org will surely be central to any future radical alternative.

A similarly progressive movement, judging from its founding principles, is Friends of the Earth, which goes back to 1971 and now fields a network of groups in 75 countries. As in the case of 350.org, FOE presents itself as a grassroots organization ready to combat the big interests, though its work goes far beyond the issue of global warming. Like 350.org, it pushes hard for carbon reductions and a massive shift toward sustainable energy. Departing from the norm, FOE takes up food challenges: factory farming, genetic engineering, ocean pollution, deforestation, animal welfare. Crucially, it also advocates broadened public spending for elections. Despite this, we find little attention to problems of meat and dairy production, or to its impact on the ecological crisis.

In contrast to 350.org and FOE, both generally viewed as grassroots movements, the Union of Concerned Scientists (UCS) frames its "strategic citizen activism" as a matter of furnishing vital scientific and technical assistance to environmental organizations mainly in the service of greening capitalism. Its overriding goal is to reach one-third renewable energy by 2030, close to targets set in California. With 450,000 members worldwide, UCS is a leading force in opposition to nuclear power, where it has won a few battles thanks to expert opinion. At the same time, UCS rarely ventures onto the crucial terrain of agriculture and food, even less concerning the impact of the meat complex on ecological decline.

Some environmental groups do address food issues, and these might be expected to at least modestly explore the consequences of the consumption of meat and dairy foods for ecological sustainability – but those expectations would be dashed. One exception is the important Worldwatch Institute, which researches issues concerning agribusiness, the meat complex, resource depletion, population pressures, and of course climate change – issues too often ignored by liberal-reform groups. Associated with the prolific work of Lester Brown, Worldwatch has for several decades taken up virtually every facet of the ecological crisis, its reports crucial to many arguments set forth in this book. The Institute sponsors inquiry, online materials, books, and gatherings devoted to understanding (and reversing) the slide toward environmental disaster. Owing to the uncommon breadth of its concerns, Worldwatch remains somewhat unique in the wide pantheon of environmental groups.

According to its mission statement, the Institute's main objectives "are universal access to renewable energy and nutritious food, expansion of environmentally sound jobs and development, transformation of cultures from consumerism to sustainability, and an early end to population growth through healthy and intentional childbearing."[394] In contrast to 350.org and FOE, however, Worldwatch is much closer to a think tank than a movement, its political engagement only peripheral. Further, as noted, the immensely valuable contributions made by Brown and the Institute arrive within a restrictive framework: market incentives and technological innovation are the driving mechanisms of change. In the end, the Institute's goal of "transforming economies, cultures, and societies that meets human needs, promotes prosperity, and is in harmony with nature" must face limits imposed by globalized corporate power.

Other food-directed organizations do not match the breadth of Worldwatch interests, few having any desire to confront the imposing meat and dairy interests. The World Resources Institute, for example, employs nearly 500 scientists, economists, and policy experts to pursue independent research around more "sustainable natural resource management", but the methods of change envisioned are vague and non-confrontational. Independence is compromised by "public-private" collaboration heavily reliant on corporate largesse, ensuring minimalist politics geared to such priorities as food labels, waste, and data-base accumulation. It is hardly clear, moreover, how WRI would effectively support moves toward new energy sources.

One group fully committed to food priorities is the International Food Policy Research Institute (IFPRI), founded in 1972 to advance food and agricultural rationality largely through economic and technological advances. With offices around the world, IFPRI works to reduce hunger and poverty though, as in the case of WRI, the mechanisms of change lack specificity. Nor is there a serious critique of agribusiness or the animal-foods industry. Their prescribed reforms – restructuring global trade, better land-use patterns, fighting disease, more progressive capital investments – all contained in their 2018 *Global Food Policy Report*, will scarcely threaten any ruling interest.[395]

A notable departure from liberal-reformism is Food First, a "people's think tank founded in 1975 by Frances Moore Lappe and Joseph Collins. With its comprehensive and transformative outlook, this organization appears ready to confront the urgent demands of ecological sustainability. Its ambitious work is built on Participatory Action Research, merging intellectual and political engagement in the service of food justice and food sovereignty across the planet. Like Worldwatch Institute, Food First has gained influence through its constant outpouring of books, articles, reports, and gatherings, bringing to American environmentalism a distinctly *radical* voice. Toward this end it boasts a network of dedicated researchers, speakers, and activists.

The Food First call for "food justice" provides several agendas: a break with agribusiness, democratization of agriculture, a turn toward small-scale urban farming, intensified focus on soil and water conservation. Achieving these initiatives would hopefully bring an end to food scarcity, malnutrition, waste, and ecological imbalance – crucial to a world where at least one billion people go hungry. In one report the authors write that "fighting hunger means tackling concentrated political and economic power in order to create new equitable rules. Otherwise hunger will continue no matter how much food we grow."[396] Food First wants to dismantle huge farm oligopolies in favor of "agroecology" – "an evolving practice of growing food within communities that is power-dispersing and power-creating, enhancing the dignity, knowledge, and capacities of all involved."[397]

This agenda would seem to offer something of an updated guidepost to an ecosocialism aligned with grassroots efforts toward sustainable development. Food First places emphasis on the global South and the eradication of poverty, hunger, waste, and disease. Yet its strategic methods remain more or less unspecified, its opposition to "concentrated power" never fully articulated within the framework of an anti-corporate or anti-capitalist politics. Could market mechanisms, for instance, serve those radical ends? In fact, the Food First report argues "the market serves human freedom only on one condition: that people have purchasing power to express their values in the market."[398]

Despite a laudable anti-system outlook and grassroots identity, Food First suffers from a narrowing agenda: there is little, if anything, about the global meat complex, while other key challenges (resource depletion, economic growth, population pressures, etc.) receive at best peripheral notice. Organization literature suggests that endless resource availability is no problem in a crisis-riddled world. It is simply a matter of social inequality and waste – a contention that, even if valid, has little relevance to the short-term future. Global warming appears as something of an afterthought. Even mainstream environmental reports, however, indicate menacing scenarios of more severe climate episodes, waning snowpack, threatened water and food supplies, and vulnerable urban communities – issues that Food First mostly sidesteps.

Food First reveals a certain leftist failure to address the multifaceted character of ecological crisis. As in the case of some Marxist currents, the focus is reductionist, scarcely helpful in an era of widening challenges. Above all, the meat complex is nowhere to be found, even where the primary concern is agriculture and food. Take, for example, a special issue of the *Nation* magazine titled "The Future of Food" (October 30, 2017), edited by Anna Lappe of the Small Planet Institute. Addressing the requirements of a more equitable and sustainable food system, with entries from several well-informed authors, the anthology soon turns into a woeful failure. To be fair, some of these authors do envision alternatives to existing agribusiness nightmares: a shift to smaller-scale farming, more egalitarian access to arable land, an end to next-generation GMOs, increased organic products, technological advances in grain harvesting, a ban on Monsanto's toxic Roundup herbicide. All entirely worthwhile reforms.[399]

Nowhere in the eleven articles of this collection, however, do we find definitions of what is equitable and sustainable, nor is there any critique of the ubiquitous fast-food industry. In "Class-Conflict Cuisine", Sarah Jones debunks the "lazy hillbilly stereotype" of Appalachia and emphasizes the adaptability of poor folks who live in the region, but says little about agricultural sustainability or what might constitute a viable food system. She does argue that "class conflict – warfare, really" shapes the local cuisine, but never specifies what this means. We are informed that "pig products feature heavily, because pigs are relatively easy to raise in the mountains – not far, incidentally, from some of the largest industrial hog centers in the world."[400] Elsewhere, Jones points out that in Appalachia "the introduction of fast, cheap food, ranging from Jiffy cornbread to McDonalds, provided an alternative to labor-intensive farming and cookery", without mentioning how fast foods are anything but healthy, equitable, and sustainable. We hear about supposedly real changes afoot, yet the author notes that in one town she is "surrounded by fast-food restaurants", further observing that "people in Appalachia are still disproportionately more likely to die young."[401] Such comments render more puzzling her conclusion: "There are no trash people, and there is no trash food. There are only trash politics."[402]

Turning to a piece by Amitana Kumar, "Confessions of a Beef Eater", the commentary is even more embarrassing. An instructor at Vassar College, Kumar writes about a trip to India where (in some regions) the ban on cow slaughter and beef eating has reportedly elicited violence against Muslims (mostly meat eaters) by Hindus, who are generally vegetarian. A proudly contented meat-eater herself, Kumar expresses outrage at acts of venomous discrimination and mob violence directed at people who consume a taboo food. Hindus are depicted as inclined toward racist, rightwing extremism, Muslims the victims for "acts of defiance" protesting a fascistic norm. The leftist state government of Kerala is praised for resisting the ban – a source of rationality in a country gone mad. Sadly, this is the only *Nation* article among the eleven that even discusses the issue of meat consumption.

Even if Kumar's accounts of a few acts of vegetarian-inspired mob violence are true, what could this possibly mean? The author leaves the impression that vegetarians are racist fanatics and that, moreover, leftists are enlightened actors in their heroic defense of meat. Kumar writes: "The number of people who eat beef in India – about 80 million – is larger than the population of Britain, France, of Italy" (p. 33) One wonders: just how many of those 80 million are targeted by vegetarian mob violence? If the author set out to mock and discredit vegetarianism while valorizing meat consumption, she has failed the test of logic or common sense. If this "special issue" constitutes the *Nation's* seminal input into a critical discussion of food, agriculture, and the environment, the editors ought to start looking for another vocation.

Liberal reformism is generally shaped by a profound need for recognition, for legitimation, which readily transforms into business-as-usual. Methods can never be too disruptive or combative, as sources of funding, institutional access, and membership support are likely to vanish. If major corporations are the problem here, they obviously become crucial to the solution. If high levels of meat and dairy consumption spell a vast carbon footprint, it is nonetheless more prudent to sidestep the issue so as not to alienate mainstream ways of doing business.

The Big Green debacle is linked to the increasing futility of electoral politics, whose representatives have proven incapable of grasping the severity of the ecological crisis. Leaving aside the noteworthy California exception, efforts so far to reform or "green" capitalism have made relatively little headway toward reversing the crisis. Local struggles sooner or later end up confined to their social immediacy. Broader regional efforts demand more economic and political leverage than is available. The U.S. Congress has failed to act, its members fearful of upsetting corporate sources of largesse. If Republicans oppose action that might in any way interfere with capitalist growth, Democrats are hardly better – their more progressive rhetoric scarcely having produced consequential action or policy.

The Climate Caucus in the U.S. Congress is almost entirely symbolic, having failed to advance any significant environmental legislation for roughly two decades. In March 2018 the Senate summarily rejected a Green New Deal bill that would have begun to seriously address climate change. Even as "greener" images and agendas have become more fashionable, the issue still ranks as a low priority for American voters. In the U.S., at least, candidates are rarely confronted for being lax on environmental concerns, with the partial exception of California.[403]

A program of strictly environmental reforms, as carried out by liberal-mainstream parties and governments around the world – along with some authoritarian states like China – should not be casually dismissed. As Lowy writes, "Not having illusions about 'ecologizing' capitalism does not mean that one cannot join the battle for immediate reforms".[404] Among other things, those reforms could accumulate in such a fashion that radical changes can more easily follow. More advances along the environmental front, moreover, could help to defer some of the worst consequences of climate change and other threats.

What needs to be further emphasized here, however, is that the general *modus operandi* has been to pursue *exclusively* an agenda of reforms, many of which have been implemented in recent years or even decades. Carbon taxes on greenhouse polluters have been adopted in many countries, especially in Europe, helping to lighten the carbon footprint – but only minimally. Such policies as taxation and cap-and-trade, promoted by liberals and social-democrats, have so far managed to place only minimal constraints on corporate behavior while, of course, the major greenhouse culprits continue business-as-usual. In fact, that path toward a "greening" of capitalism has turned out to be a signal failure.

Reformist energies in the advanced industrial societies have taken many forms – all to be supported (even by ecological radicals) as potentially opening space for more expansive future changes. At the top of this list would surely be an ambitious shift from fossil fuels toward renewable sources of energy, embellished through public subsidies and technological innovation. This approach, as we have seen, has gained momentum in California along with a few other states, the European Union, China, Japan, and elsewhere, with significant results. One problem here is that, while the percentage of sustainable energy sources increases, total use of fossil fuels still rises (or remains stable) owing to the effects of economic and population growth. A further problem is that alternatives devour resources too – not only fossil fuels but land and, in some cases, water. To have a transformative impact, sustainable energy forms will have to be incorporated into new modes of production and consumption.

Meanwhile, a multiplicity of individual and social initiatives to further "ecologize" the present developmental trajectory have been embraced, with varying results: moving away from meat-centered to plant-based diets, adoption of faux dairy and meat products, agroecology practices as in the development of local farms, greater reliance on public transportation systems, lifestyle changes involving efforts to recycle, drive electric cars, change diets, and live more simply. Such "greening" departures can feed into broader social and political initiatives, but in themselves do not generate new macro patterns of production and consumption. For that to occur, the entire structure of corporate-state power would have to be overturned.

It might be argued that a labor movement struggling for a combination of economic and environmental reforms across many sectors of public life could lead, sooner or later, toward such transformation. In recent decades, however, no important labor organizations – local structures, councils, unions, or parties – have embraced anything close to anti-system oppositional tendencies. Their struggles, mostly economic, have been waged entirely *within* the capitalist order, within the rules and norms of that system, largely peripheral to environmental challenges. There is no evidence that workers anywhere might spearhead an epic drive toward developmental sustainability, even should they ascend to the summits of power. As Lowy argues: "Workers cannot take possession of the capitalist state apparatus and put it to work at their service. They have to 'break it' and replace it with a radically different, democratic, and non-statist form of political power."[405] This same generalization would apply to any group, movement, or party on the road to state governance.

As we proceed along the present disastrously unsustainable trajectory, the U.S. remains the leading per capita greenhouse polluter among all nations. Failure of radical intervention can only mean further ecological decline. For decades environmental activists have met with politicians, voted for liberals, established lobbies and think tanks, held teach-ins and conferences, produced documentaries, and waged grassroots campaigns – hoping for new leverage and impact. Yet, as worldwide carbon emissions continue to rise and other signs of crisis simultaneously worsen, the global landscape has seen little growth in anti-system opposition. There is no effective counterforce to corporate power or the growth mania, no alternative to agribusiness, the meat complex, no effort (in the U.S.) to dismantle the warfare apparatus that protects and empowers the interests behind possible ecological catastrophe.

A Legacy of Failure

Modernity has bequeathed diverse political traditions across the past two centuries, none however resisting the trajectory toward ecological suicide. Even oppositional forces have fallen short of confronting the logic of capitalist rationalization that fuels not only the crisis but also the general bureaucratization of social and political life. We have already identified the crushing restraints of liberalism, a tradition fully aligned with corporate globalization and the warfare state. At this juncture any prospective greening of capitalism is bound to end as a sad delusion. Liberalism ultimately cedes both institutional and ideological terrain to the ruling interests, a solid recipe for political impasse.

European social democracy amounts to the historical apex of liberal politics, with its strong Keynesian policies to humanize the economy and restrain corporate power – a *social* Keynesianism in contrast to the American variant based on a mixture of social and military-based government intervention. Even as social democracy enlarges the scope of progressive regulations, laws, policies, and treaties, it is not much better positioned to face the ecological threat than conventional American liberalism. The more conservative response – a return to mythical laissez-faire capitalism – merely accelerates further environmental deterioration.

This leaves three identifiable strategic options: some form of Leninist vanguardism or Jacobin revolution from above, anarchist insurgency, or a broadly radical politics that merges local movements and electoral politics along lines of the early German and European Green-Party model. These strategies share two common ends – overturning the corporate-state system in favor of a more ecologically sustainable model of development. Here twentieth-century experience demonstrates that Leninism, where successful, can lead only to a stifling bureaucratic centralism as in the USSR, while anarchism, for its part, has always lacked political-strategic articulation – a capacity to win state power and manage it for transformative goals. Neither of these models seem compatible with either democratic renewal or ecological sustainability, and neither show a way out of the crisis.

Between 1890 and World War I, rival strategic-political views were vigorously debated within Marxism (more accurately, socialism) – views that were subject to political debate through several decades. Eduard Bernstein's evolutionary socialism, theoretical origin of social-democratic reformism in

Europe, resolved the dilemma of class consciousness (proletariat as agency of revolution) by linking politics to immediate social reforms by means of trade union and parliamentary activity. Socialism would be realized gradually and peacefully, a process of continuous democratization. Industrial expansion would give rise to a broadening working class, enabling socialist gains. Akin to liberalism, socialism evolved as an Enlightenment project driven by economic growth: progress would be achieved through the historic development of science, technology, and material abundance. Social-democratic parties flourished within the Second (or Socialist) International across the twentieth century, a vehicle of welfare-state capitalism that ultimately fell short even of Bernstein's modest vision of socialism.

Leninism, for its part, moved to the other end of the continuum: if workers did not spontaneously arrive at revolutionary consciousness, then the best option was a vanguard organization led by professional cadres that could bring such consciousness to a proletariat otherwise immersed in bourgeois ideology. Party leaders would provide ideological cohesion, organizational force, and political strategy directed toward the insurrectionary conquest of state power. Against Bernstein and the reformists, Lenin and the Bolsheviks held that the capitalist system could never be overturned within its own rules and procedures. The idea of a peaceful transition to socialism, moreover, was a dangerous myth as it ignored the extent to which capitalist elites were able to rely on their vast economic, governmental, and military force – the very conditions at work in pre-revolutionary Russia.

For Lenin and later Communists, the main conduit of revolutionary change was a combat party led by a Marxist stratum of full-time cadres. This formula succeeded in Russia in 1917, paving the way for the October Revolution and Third (Communist) International based in the Soviet Union. While in social democracy the masses were at least theoretically anointed as historical agents – their activity mediated by unions and parties – but within a distinctly non-revolutionary matrix. Change would proceed slowly and incrementally, its architects in no great hurry to bring about a new socialist epoch. For Leninism these same masses came under the aegis of a vanguard able to orchestrate political action. Popular forms (unions, councils, co-ops, movements) were eventually reduced to "transmission belts" of party elites, who assumed historical primacy. Once in power, a new ruling stratum moved to destroy the old centers of power (aristocracy, monarchy, capitalism, etc.) that would be mostly left intact by the social democrats. Leninism eventually became the organizational mechanism of twentieth-century revolutions in Yugoslavia, China, Vietnam, and Cuba.

Whatever their Marxist agendas, these revolutions were emphatically nationalist, victorious by means of popular armed insurrections mainly against foreign imperialism, dedicated to the interwoven aims of national independence and economic modernization. These were simultaneously multiclass upheavals based in the working class, pleasantry, and sectors of the middle strata.[406] Despite their Marxist-Leninist outlook, the subsequent party-states typically retreated from emancipatory (democratic, egalitarian, internationalist) objectives, exemplified by the 1930s Soviet "great retreat" under Stalin. With rapid industrialization, moreover, came the very environmental destruction associated with capitalism itself. Ecological concerns did attract some attention from Soviet leadership during the 1920s, but that gave way as industrialization intensified. The Soviet – and other Communist – record of air and water pollution, soil degradation, blighted cities, and high carbon emissions was no better than that of advanced capitalist nations.

Despite their obvious differences, social democracy and Leninism came to share many of the same features, as both were vehicles of Enlightenment rationality and its worship of growth, science, and technology. Leon Trotsky was not the only leftist to observe that both party elites had abandoned socialist ideals at the altar of maximum economic development. The systems depended fully on organizational cohesion, bureaucratic discipline, and social hierarchy – at odds with efforts to break down the social division of labor endemic to capitalist society. These societies, it follows, offered no foundation for a modern ecological politics.

Twentieth-century radicalism – a vigorous tradition, whatever its fate – gave rise to a third strategic path: syndicalism, or council communism. With roots in nineteenth-century anarchism, as well as early Marxism, this approach evolved into a mass-based, democratic alternative to party-centered socialism. Identified with such figures as Georges Sorel, Rosa Luxemburg, the early Antonio Gramsci, and Anton Pannekoek, it turned to spontaneous mass activity as the dynamic essence of social transformation, located mainly in popular and workers' councils that proliferated across Europe from the 1890s to the 1930s. Unfortunately, both Leninism and social democracy represented the ascendancy of a new ruling elite, incompatible with socialist principles.

Council theory held that the masses (notably workers) would gradually be driven toward heightened class consciousness with the sharpening contradictions of capitalism. The council phenomenon thrived before and during the Bolshevik Revolution, in Italy during the turbulent *Biennio Rosso* (1918-20), and in Spain during the 1936-39 Civil War, but it could never sustain political success. Problems of social fragmentation and political isolation were in the end too much to overcome; local forms were impotent against the fortresses of economic and political power.[407] Moreover, the council approach generated no lasting ideas relevant to ecology or sustainable development, perfectly understandable as those concerns were hardly at the forefront in the early twentieth century. Important motifs of this tradition – local organization, self-management, mass spontaneity – would, however, resurface in the 1960s and 1970s with appearance of the new left, counterculture, and new social movements that would include the first stirrings of modern environmentalism.

The emergence of critical or "Western" Marxism after World War I did take up such priorities as popular culture, the media, and family but, with the partial exception of Herbert Marcuse, had little interest in ecology. Such theorists – Luxemburg, Gramsci, Lukacs, Jean-Paul Sartre, Marcuse – worked mostly in a realm far removed from state power thereby freer to create more elaborate theories. But those efforts failed to engage discourses associated with nature, until Marcuse's work in the late 1960s addressed "the environment" or "nature" as one dimension of capitalist dysfunction.

The tortured evolution of Western Marxism reflected a deeper conundrum – recognition that Marxist theory in general had failed to produce a viable revolutionary politics for advanced capitalism. Indeed, much of what motivated these theorists was an effort to understand how the system managed to solidify its power and legitimacy in the face of recurrent economic crises. One task here was to identify debilitating problems of Marxist theory *tout court* – above all, the concept of a revolutionary proletariat as agency of socialist transformation. Worth noting here is that all three strategies mentioned above – Leninism, social democracy, councilism – failed as a matter of historical experience. In one way or another, modern state-capitalism was able to ameliorate crisis-tendencies while neutralizing anti-system forces, including Communist parties.[408]

An enduring legacy, Marxism had for most of the twentieth century never generated any theoretical edifice of ecological politics – that would be left to such non-Marxists as Murray Bookchin, Barry Commoner, Rudolf Bahro, and George Sessions. Their seminal contributions would arrive at a later, more destructive phase of global capitalism. By this time Marxism (notably its organized variant) was already in serious decline. Extended attempts to create an ecological Marxism would not come until the end of the twentieth century, as an underlying productivism cramped efforts to fully theorize natural relations. To be a dynamic force in the modern setting, therefore, Marxism would have to survive myriad issues posed by of globalized capitalism.

From Rio to Paris

As world capitalism expands, engulfing more areas of the planet, problems that humanity faces are ever more global – and so too must prospective solutions be, if any are to be found. Given such reality, meaningful attempts to stave off ecological catastrophe will require a coherent *politics*. Strictly local or national interventions, always vital points of departure, will never be enough; environmental threats recognize no territorial or other boundaries. Politics is indispensable for expanding citizen empowerment within a framework of organization, ideology, and strategy. For oppositional groups, movements, parties, and conceivably states, historical efficacy will depend on dynamic global actions.

Early Marxists were convinced that socialist transformation would unfold as something of a global project, cutting across national borders that perpetuate class divisions. For Marx and Engels, of course, the proletariat was expected to develop class rather than national consciousness, rejecting allegiance to the domestic bourgeoisie and its system of rule. At the time of the Bolshevik Revolution, Leon Trotsky's concept of "permanent revolution" viewed the transition from feudalism to capitalism as (ideally) building toward socialism linked to widening insurgency across Russia, Europe, and beyond. The concept of "socialism in one country", later articulated by

Stalin, was logically implausible, contradictory. Socialist values would be undercut by a resurgent nationalism, which turned out to be the case for the Soviet Union. Conquest of state power in single countries at a time while international capital was retaining its hegemony would lead to isolation and collapse.

Nowadays, as the power of transnational capital dwarfs that of a century earlier, the global imperative advanced within Marxism seems more (not less) persuasive. Further, like capital itself, the ecological crisis respects no national boundaries. From this standpoint, the nation-state as such constitutes a special obstacle to international strategies insofar as it is drawn to national economic competition, resource and trade conflicts, geopolitical struggles, and (for the U.S.) mobilization for war. All anti-system movements, therefore, will require some form of international collaboration as national strategies can be neutralized by the sheer force of nationalism, capital flight, and impotence in the face of transnational corporate power. This dynamic would seem to contribute to the failure, so far, of world summits extending from Rio in 1992 to Paris in 2015.

International partnerships, alliances, and treaties hold obvious advantages when it comes to political efficacy – all the more so given the expansive power of such global capitalist institutions as the World Bank, International Monetary Fund, World Trade Organization, and European Union. While local or national strategies will likely come first, they remain fragile and especially vulnerable to the intrusions of global capital.

The first socialist parties created the Second International in 1891, based mainly in Europe but dedicated to international working-class cooperation and solidarity. This was largely a fiction, however, since social-democratic leaders in Germany and elsewhere held to an uncompromising nationalism revealed at the start of World War I when the parties, with few exceptions, supported their own (bourgeois) national governments in the bloody, protracted conflict. Eventually superseded by the Socialist International (SI) in 1952, which expanded to 54 member parties with some 15 million members by the 1970s, the network bequeathed a legacy of tepid reformism with national parties loosely bound together, their connections weakened by decades of class collaboration and domestic institutionalization. Today the SI parties are more than anything historical agencies of secular liberalism, allied with both capital and particular nation-states.

As for the Communist (Third) International spawned after the Bolshevik conquest of power in 1919, its member parties (typically weak and isolated) were fully subordinate to the Soviet Union until the organization was abandoned in 1943, part of Stalin's move to placate World War II allies. The success of a Leninist revolution in Russia conferred on Moscow the unrivaled "leadership" of world Communism that was codified by the famous 21 Points binding national members and enforced by the Soviet party-state throughout the 1920s and 1930s. Worth noting here is that twentieth-century Communist revolutions gained power largely *independent* of Soviet resources and control.

Sequels to the mostly failed Second, Third, and Socialist Internationals have been numerically few and politically marginalized. A Fourth International founded by a small nucleus of European Trotskyists never escaped its own sectarian isolation. The European Green Party (EGP) was founded in 2004 as a loose federation of 32 parties – theoretically the start of a much larger Green International. The EGP has worked with the European Free Alliance to form a Greens-European Free Alliance group within the European parliament. In the 2004 European Parliament elections the member parties won 35 seats, followed by 48 seats in 2009 and 50 seats in 2014. Within their own national legislatures, Greens have rarely exceeded five percent of the vote – the main exception being the German party, which was also the first. While the EGP continues to embrace founding Green ideals (including sustainable development, social justice, and peace) member parties – after years of electoral participation – have grown rather conservative, nowadays scarcely distinguishable from the rival social democrats.

In 2001 activists from around the globe, inspired by the Seattle protests two years earlier, organized the World Social Forum in Porto Allegre, Brazil, which turned into a yearly gathering of thousands dedicated to an egalitarian, democratic alternative to neoliberal globalization. The Forum established a Charter of Principles geared to non-corporate development, with some environmental priorities, that delegates from dozens of nations endorsed. The second WSF meeting attracted some 12,000 delegates from 123 countries, with 80,000 activists and nearly 700 workshops. By the fourth gathering, held again in Brazil, the attendance swelled to 155,000. Yearly meetings were held at different locales through 2018 – attracting 75,000 participants in 2011 in Dakar, Senegal from 132 countries and nearly the same number from 120 nations in 2018 in Salvador, Brazil. The WSF remains a loosely structured international body engaged in diverse oppositional activities, but without a shared political strategy.

Since 2005 regional forums have been organized in Europe, Asia, Africa, Latin America, and the U.S., all committed to some variant of global radical change – although popular movements have become less visible within the WSF orbit than more conservative NGOs aligned with mainstream parties. While serving as a central axis of international anti-system projects, the forums (as their description implies) have no binding political mission like that of earlier international organizations; there is no WSF party or even strategy, as mentioned, nor has the topic been much discussed. Oriented toward "reinventing democracy", the forums have evolved as mostly intellectual or cultural assemblies – a laudable but nonetheless pre-political enterprise. In contrast to the WSF, the European Greens advance a clear political ideology and strategy, still pursuing some kind of merger of grassroots movements and electoral activity. Yet, while the Greens aspire to worldwide presence, however loosely organized, their influence is overwhelmingly centered in the industrialized North.

The historic pursuit of world environmental organizations, beginning with the 1992 Rio Earth Summit, has reached most nations in the world – but so far without much political direction. The initial U.N. Conference on Environment and Development (UNCED) was attended by 100 heads of state with the objective of global sustainability. Toward that end the Summit established the Commission on Sustainable Development (CSD), forerunner of later international arrangements linking issues of poverty, the environment, and economics – though, as in later such gatherings, no binding decisions would be forthcoming. The first Summit of its kind, UNCED laid out a central principle that "states shall cooperate in a spirit of global partnership to conserve, protect, and restore the health and integrity of the Earth's ecosystem." Dedication to "biological diversity" was affirmed, though the specific challenge of global warming never surfaced in Rio.

Five years later, world leaders gathered at Kyoto, Japan to formulate agreements curbing the effects of global warming – a meeting set in motion by the 1992 U.N. Framework Convention on Climate Change (UNFCCC). The Kyoto Protocol was adopted in December 1997 and entered into force in February 2005, eventually signed by 192 parties. The historic goal was to reduce greenhouse gases to a "level that would prevent dangerous anthropogenic interference with the climate system." The Protocol listed six targeted emissions, including CO_2, methane, and nitrous oxide. The first commitment phase started in 2008 and ended in 2012, followed by a second phase (the Doha Amendment) in which 37 nations accepted binding targets. As of early 2019, 122 states had endorsed the Doha agreement while "entry into force" requires the participation of 144 states. (The U.S. remains a "non-party".) Enormous flexibility mechanisms, including cap-and-trade options, are built into the Kyoto Protocol, allowing for a certain loosening of national emissions targets. Greenhouse reductions were anticipated through combined renewable energy projects, increased efficiency, and "fuel switching."

The most extensive pursuit of international agreement to limit greenhouse-gas emissions to date (early 2020) is the 2015 Paris Accords – an extension of the UNFCCC and Kyoto set to take effect in 2020. As of early 2020, 197 members had signed the agreement, with 190 having become full party to it. The main Paris goal is to curtail global average temperatures below 2 degrees Celsius above pre-industrial levels. To achieve this each country must determine, plan, and report on its specific contribution to greenhouse pollution, although the process set forth is voluntary and flexible, without binding procedures. The Paris Accords have been described as the world's first comprehensive – and effective – climate agreement.

Targets set in Paris are to be achieved through a system of "nationally-determined contributions" (NDCs) where real penalties are levied if countries fail to meet commitments. Central to the Paris framework is a "Sustainable Development Mechanism" (SDM), a flexible approach by which parties can collectively pursue emissions reductions within a framework of variable national criteria. At Paris the most highly industrialized nations agreed to earmark $100 billion yearly to fund sustainable development by 2020, a sum to be invested yearly until 2025 – mostly allocated to developing countries with the idea they will be prepared to restrict emissions. By November 2016 the Paris agreement had obtained enough parties to move forward with the most ambitious national climate agenda ever, but again these are both flexible and voluntary.

A much-celebrated international summit, the Paris Accords raise questions as to how much global warming might be reversed, or even contained, by means of voluntary mechanisms. True enough, member states do include most of the biggest polluters: the U.S., China, India, Russia, Japan, Brazil, Canada among them. These nations generate far more than half of total global carbon emissions. One problem, as mentioned, is that the framework remains essentially open-ended. Climate expert James Hansen criticized the Paris talks for amounting to little more than a series of "promises" based on hopes that member states would move to reduce their carbon footprint without any binding targets set.

In the wake of the Paris gathering, the Obama administration pledged to cut domestic greenhouse emissions by 26 to 28 percent below 2005 levels by 2025, also committing at least three billion dollars to aid poorer countries. China, for its part, vowed to generate about 20 percent of its electricity from carbon-free sources by 2030, to be nearly matched by efforts in Japan and India. In general, the hope is that, on the basis of scientific evidence, peer pressure, and international diplomacy – leaving aside national self-interest – Paris targets could be reached. Yet by early 2020 none of the leading industrialized nations had come close to meeting emission-reduction goals needed to keep rising temperatures below two degrees Celsius. In fact, given existing developmental patterns, very little warming curbs can be anticipated by 2050 – a likely disaster according to many climate scientists and environmentalists. Extensive promises of carbon-mitigation strategies have generally not come to fruition.

The scenario worsens, moreover, when the Trump administration decision to withdraw from the Paris Accords is taken into account. Official notice of U.S withdrawal was given August 2017, although the effective date is two years later. Trump's policies would undermine global cooperation to reverse the crisis, especially as the U.S. was second leading polluter in the world. Under Trump, a rollback process was set in motion, curtailing domestic environmental programs and weakening plans for alternative energy sources, while aid to poorer countries was no longer on the Washington agenda. Trump declared the U.S. would reverse all contributions to the U.N. Green Climate Fund, which the president said was "costing the U.S. a fortune".

International efforts to reach the Paris targets, amidst even more severe IPCC reports on climate change, were addressed at Katowice, Poland in December 2018. The parties agreed on how states should report their greenhouse emissions and steps toward improvement they are taking. Poor countries also gained assurances on getting financial support behind their own struggles to meet targets. At the same time, oil exporting nations (the U.S., Russia, Saudi Arabia, Kuwait) blocked endorsement of the more alarming IPCC findings, which recommended a more drastic shift from fossil-fuels. The parties reaffirmed dedication to a global market in carbon credits but arrived at no specific measures.

In the wake of Trump's planned withdrawal from the Paris Accords, the U.S. in Poland continued its obstructionist strategy: belief in the efficacy of oil and natural gas to fuel economic growth was reaffirmed. Now in possession of even more abundant carbon resources, the U.S. was in a position to supply oil and natural gas to other countries, rejecting the "alarmism" of IPCC scientists. In effect Washington removed itself from leadership in confronting the ecological crisis, and of course this would have a chilling effect on the larger pursuit of worldwide sustainable development.

American rejectionism actually points to a deeper flaw in global mechanisms to address the rising challenge: along with the U.S., few countries are prepared to follow the 2018 IPCC prescription for rapid transition to relatively carbon-free economies. That transition could, for most nations, mean extreme hardship for the immediate future, above all in the realm of agriculture given that sector's intense dependency on fossil fuels. In other words, whatever the reforms currently being implemented or envisioned, the stubborn reality is largely business-as-usual for the leading industrialized countries. Levels of atmospheric carbon, along with other pollutants, will continue to expand throughout the twenty-first century – a formula for catastrophe in the view of IPCC scientists.

An overwhelming problem, therefore, is the epic failure so far to advance new modes of production and consumption broadly aligned with ecological rationality. The obsessive and seemingly exclusive fixation on carbon emissions, moreover, diminishes the importance of *other*, perhaps more urgent, global challenges: the growth mania, population pressures, urbanization, resource shrinkages, military conflict driven by geopolitical rivalries. As we have seen, humanity also faces mounting problems associated with agribusiness, the meat complex, and the McDonaldized economy – challenges addressed at best peripherally in most international reports.

By 2020 there were few signs that the ecological crisis was about to be seriously ameliorated: efforts to face the aforementioned challenges have been tepid, while the growth economies move full-speed ahead, the U.S., China, India, and European Union in the lead. Government, corporate, and military elites in American society, bolstered by a compliant media, have no interest in slowing down or changing course, despite far-reaching greenhouse reforms in California and elsewhere. Referring to the Paris Accords, President Trump called it "simply the latest example of Washington entering into an agreement that disadvantages the U.S. to the exclusive benefit of other countries, leaving American workers and taxpayers to absorb the cost in terms of lost jobs, lower wages, shuttered factories, and vastly-diminished economic production."[409] This outlook, for which Trump has received harsh criticism, turns out to be far more widespread across the world than most observers would like to admit. Meanwhile, the U.S. has emerged as significant net oil exporter owing to an unprecedented boom in domestic oil production. The shale revolution alone has transformed the U.S. into the world's largest petroleum producer, surpassing Russia, Saudi Arabia, and Venezuela, as well as supplier. At the same time, the U.S. consumes no less than 17 million barrels of oil itself daily, with no decline in sight. Prospects that American ruling interests would simply leave these precious resources "in the ground" are virtually zero.

One seemingly insurmountable problem in regulating the global economy turns on just how to guarantee universality of national response to the environmental injunctions of Paris, or indeed any other agreement, especially where (as with Paris) the targets are more or less voluntary. Thus, even should several leading greenhouse emitters reduce their footprint, even substantially, this could easily be offset by others failing to meet consensual objectives. In the present circumstances many rapidly developing countries – Indonesia, Brazil, Mexico, South Korea to name some – balk at being told by wealthier nations to cut back on carbon emissions, to phase out oil, gas, and coal in a modality that was never followed in North America and Europe. Experience so far suggests that greenhouse reductions, not to mention alterations in production and consumption, have not been pursued on any meaningful scale.

What happens, moreover, when advanced industrial nations begin to cut back on their carbon footprint but end up sending huge amounts of fossil fuels abroad as part of trade deals. As of 2018 some Asian countries (China, Japan, South Korea) have been able to reduce greenhouse gases domestically while funding dozens of coal-fired plants abroad, thus negating their own adherence to the Paris accords. Where the new plants flourished, as in Vietnam, Indonesia, Thailand, and South Africa, their contributions to climate change rapidly increased. Such developing nations, dedicated to maximum economic growth, were happy enough to adopt the same fossil fuels that helped drive industrialization in the West.

Paris or no Paris, IPCC or no IPCC, the very expansion of huge transnational corporations, many based in the U.S., starkly conflicts with efforts to reverse the crisis. Above all, the dominant patterns of production and consumption will have to radically change – a strategy that no international organization or national government has so far embraced. Such change would necessarily mean transition from a system of profit-maximization, continuous industrial growth, wasteful agricultural and food systems, resource wars, and militarism. In that case, ruling interests across the planet would have to change their destructive behavior in ways never before shown – or be overthrown.

6

Toward an Ecological Politics

The worsening ecological crisis requires a strategy of urgent change, a new radical politics that supersedes the familiar ideological legacies. Its success would depend on the capacity of organized counterforces to transform the prevailing, dysfunctional modes of production and consumption. The challenge points to the struggle for new relations between human activity and the natural habitat.

A transformative strategy, including the Marxist tradition, Green politics, and some variant of ecosocialism, will have to face a globalized, integrated power structure that will not easily relinquish its hold over power and wealth – over the fate of the planet. As the crisis deepens, the system might eventually implode from its own contradictions, but that moment might not arrive soon enough to reverse the slide downward. That system cannot be allowed to perish from its own unsustainability; radical political intervention is now a moral and ecological imperative.

The natural habitat is now ever more defenseless against the onslaught of corporate predation, industrial growth, urbanization, agribusiness dysfunctions, climate change, and geopolitical conflict. One problem today is that capitalist rationalization creates more obstacles to human agency and, by extension, political opposition. The system perpetuates domination in the sphere of governance, corporate power, the workplace, and the surveillance order, and simply everyday life. Oligarchical and authoritarian rule overwhelms the fragile processes of democratic politics, meaning that pursuit of change through normal politics will surely fail to meet the daunting challenges ahead.

Unfortunately, we seem to have reached a growing political impasse, where counterforces appear weak or nonexistent. Human energies abound, in the form of local protests, lobbies, intellectual work, cultural activities, and technological innovations, but this energy remains scattered and disconnected, far removed from any much-needed *political strategy*. Leading climate activist Bill McKibben, a prolific writer on the ecological crisis, has famously argued that the new era demands full-scale mobilization of economic, technical, and human resources akin to the wartime Manhattan Project -- nothing short of a "wartime mentality" which, in fact, is nowhere in sight in the U.S. or any other country.[410] Elsewhere, McKibben writes in favor of widespread "climate disobedience", a massive outpouring of social protests designed to subvert the stifling limits of normal politics.[411] Both modalities, linked within a broad political framework, will be indispensable for ecological radicalism, yet McKibben (typical for the period) never specifies what that framework might be.

Facing both global crisis and entrenched power structure, the absence of a coherent political strategy can bring only disaggregation, impotence, and defeat. There can be no spontaneous, pre-political exit from corporate-state domination, no simple "alternative" driven by markets or technology. A new transformative politics will have to be broader, more multifaceted, indeed more *radical* than anything before it. To believe otherwise is to indulge in one of the great illusions of the period – that radical change can somehow proceed, magically and seamlessly, as if in a political void.

The Radical Tradition

The decades-old struggle for an ecological politics reflects profound disillusionment with the capacity of earlier traditions – mainly liberalism and socialism – to furnish lasting alternatives to the deepening impasse. What remains of this important struggle – now having been overwhelmed by the spread of environmental reformism -- is dedication to the overthrow of a power structure that assaults the natural habitat at every turn. Ecological radicalism can be seen as an outgrowth of 1960s new-left movements and counterculture, associated with the seminal work of Rachel Carson, Murray

Bookchin, and Barry Commoner, giving rise to the first Earth Day in 1970 and proliferation of environmental groups during the 1970s and beyond.

A new ecological sensibility raised probing questions about the destructive side of industrialism, dangers of a toxic world, and the need to restore balance between society and nature, humans and surrounding ecosystems. Its insurgent, at times utopian, outlook followed a trajectory largely independent of Marxism, aligned with the ideals of local community, ecological renewal, mutual aid, limits to growth, and opposition to any form of concentrated power. It called forth a rich theoretical legacy grounded in nineteenth-century anarchism and utopian socialism, the communitarian ideals of Jean-Jacques Rousseau and Peter Kropotkin, and the work of later critics of industrial modernity like Paul Goodman, Lewis Mumford, Theodore Roszak, and thinkers of the Frankfurt School (notably Herbert Marcuse). The most articulate side of ecological radicalism carried forward an egalitarian, anti-authoritarian, ecocentric view directed against the entire matrix of domination. (Worth noting here is that this tradition evolved, well into the 1990s, before the motif of global warming became part of the political *Zeitgeist*.)

Bookchin's major imprint on this tradition – unfortunately ignored or forgotten within contemporary environmentalism – remains its most developed variant even today. His prolific writings going back to the early 1960s were shaped by a "dialectical naturalism" in which efforts to transform history and nature, society and the environment, unfold simultaneously, a process driven by local struggles against multiple forms of domination: class, bureaucratic, gender, racial, ecological. Bookchin rejected both liberal and socialist politics insofar as they inherited Enlightenment rationality with its pervasive and uncritical embrace of science and technology in the service of industrial growth. His work, from beginning to end, was infused with a sense of urgency, for the most part without reference to climate change. In *The Modern Crisis,* Bookchin wrote: "We may well be approaching a critical juncture in our development that confronts us with a historic choice: whether we will follow an alternative path that yields a humane, rational, and ecological way of life, or a path which will yield the degradation of our species if not its outright extinction."[412] Several decades ago Bookchin was already convinced that humans were facing an "incinerated biosphere" filled with destructive impulses from civic violence to warfare and the ceaseless assault on nature.[413]

For Bookchin, a rational ecological system depends on full realization of "free nature" grounded in local struggles for self-management. All forms of domination would be subject to challenge, humans and the natural world becoming united following centuries of harsh opposition and conflict. To be sure, Bookchin inherited something from the political radicalism of Marx and Engels, above all his embrace of dialectics and popular struggles to overthrow capitalism, yet anarchist sensibilities took him well beyond Marxism in two important ways: a view toward overturning domination in all of its expressions, and the struggle for ecological revitalization that was only vaguely implicit in the Marxist tradition. He further rejected a certain dualism he viewed as endemic to classical Marxism, a "kind of mechanical thinking [that] gives rise to splits between body and mind, reality and thought, object and subject, country and town, and, ultimately, society and the individual."[414]

Bookchin, like many radicals of the sixties and seventies, believed liberal reformism not only subverted ecological politics but, once pursued systematically, would end up serving power- structure legitimacy. It could never be truly oppositional. Liberals, in Bookchin's view, suffered from a refusal to acknowledge the logic of capitalist development: endless growth, profit-maximization, domination of the natural habitat. He argued that "industrially and technologically ... we have placed ecological burdens upon our planet that have no precedent in human history."[415] The problem goes beyond the institutional or material dimensions to the deepest recesses of everyday life. Thus: "The internalization of hierarchy and domination forms the greatest wound in human development and the most deadly engine for steering us toward human immolation."[416] This "internalization" motif aligns with concepts pivotal to Western Marxism – Gramsci's "ideological hegemony", Lukacs' "reification", Wilhelm Reich's "repressive sexuality", Erich Fromm's "escape from freedom", Marcuse's "technological rationality". In each case various ideological or psychological mechanisms functioned to undermine political agency.

Bookchin's keen understanding of ecological crisis was informed by a view of social- psychological tendencies at the core of the modern human predicament. He wrote: "In our discussion of modern ecological and social crisis, we tend to ignore a more underlying mentality of domination that humans have used for centuries to justify the domination of each other and, by extension, nature." Unfortunately, humans seem dedicated to an "image of a demonic and hostile nature [that] goes back to the Greek world and even earlier."[417] This notion of human impulse lies at the very heart of Bookchin's social ecology, which exposes the "all-encompassing image of an intractable nature that must be tamed by a rational humanity [which] has given us a domineering form of reason, science, and technology – a fragmentation of humanity into hierarchies, classes, state institutions, gender and ethnic divisions. It has fostered nationalistic hatreds, imperialistic adventures, and a global philosophy of rule that identifies order with dominance and submission."[418] This approach to power relations, embedded in a deep ecological radicalism, transcends limits of the anarchist, Marxist, and liberal traditions.

From this standpoint, Bookchin looked to a strategy of "libertarian municipalism" designed to subvert the patterns of domination and recover hopes for community, participatory democracy, and ecological renewal. In the U.S., "power is thoroughly bureaucratized, centralized, and concentrated into fewer and fewer hands ... Democracy, far from acquiring a participatory character, becomes purely formal in character ... [and at odds with] a desire to regain citizenship, to end the degradation of politics into statecraft: the need to revive public life."[419] This motif coincides with Bookchin's critique of urbanization discussed in chapter two.

For Bookchin, the solution to widespread alienation and disempowerment lies in a rebirth of local democracy with origins in the 1871 Paris Commune, also inspired by contributions from such theorists as Rousseau and Kropotkin. This meant a return to forms such as soviets, workers' councils, and neighborhood assemblies that surfaced in early twentieth-century Europe and were, in Bookchin's opinion, consistent with an ecological radicalism. Thus: "The need to rescale communities to fit the natural carrying capacity of the regions in which they are located and to create a new balance between town and country – all traditional demands of the great utopian and anarchist thinkers of the last [nineteenth] century – have become ecological imperatives today."[420]

Bookchin's social ecology developed as a challenge to fixed notions of society, nature, and development – counter to the ubiquitous intellectual, social, and cultural fragmentation of the modern epoch. Ecological thought, grounded in dialectical naturalism, is dynamic, holistic, complex, ultimately corrosive of all systems of domination.[421] It conflicts with the myths and rituals that associate "progress" with technology, industrialism, and material abundance. In this setting, Bookchin sees the modern city as a social and ecological monstrosity, an unsustainable, wasteful, undemocratic, alienated mass of humanity. Urban life in the industrialized societies becomes anti-ecological at its very core, at war against the natural habitat as well as every sphere of human life.

Bookchin's approach closely identifies ecology with a broad emancipatory politics, affirming faith in human capacity to re-appropriate "first nature" within a movement toward "second nature" based on struggles for local democracy.[422] Yet Bookchin's radicalism – a bold prescription for reversing the ecological crisis – remains frustratingly vague, above all on matters of political strategy. One problem is his facile rejection of social hierarchy and domination: the question here is not whether humans will continue to "dominate nature", as the capacity and even the necessity to do so is undeniable, but precisely *what form* the human intervention will or should take. The existing corporate-state apparatus is one thing, driven as it is by conquest and exploitation while transforming the natural habitat in reservoirs of wealth and power. But could *any* social order, even the most ecologically sustainable and democratic, avoid some manner of instrumental, controlling approach to nature? In fact, the only alternative would be total depopulation of the planet, so that no water, foodstuffs, metals, woods, and paper, for example, would ever have to be extracted.

The central issue for Bookchin, as for the anarchist/spontaneist tradition in general, turns on the particular *mode* of human domination, including whether a specific developmental model is sustainable, roughly consistent with ecosystem carrying capacity. (This raises additional problems – population, meat-based agriculture, imperialism, etc. – that Bookchin sidesteps or ignores.) Bookchin's refusal *tout court* of all hierarchical forms of organization, including government, ultimately suffers from a disabling utopianism.

The lack of strategic concreteness in social ecology means any transformational process is sure to be poorly defined. Bookchin's libertarian municipalism, connecting hundreds or thousands of local communities across a series of confederal arrangements, is laudable enough, but there is the stubborn matter of exactly how such a vast, dispersed assemblage of groups and movements could be coordinated and translated into political reality – even assuming a consistently high level of ecological consciousness across the landscape. This process would be fraught with obstacles of all sorts. Further, there is the question as to how an assemblage of fragmented social forces could hope to overthrow an integrated power structure. The historical record is hardly encouraging: insurrections and movements aligned with the council legacy have either repeatedly been crushed by superior force, been integrated into the dominant institutional order, or simply been condemned to futility. While social ecology has contributed greatly to ecological awareness in the U.S. and elsewhere, therefore, distinctly *political* value has been marginal.

Still another expression of ecological radicalism – like social ecology, a reaction against both liberalism and Marxism – is deep ecology (DE), its currents strongly felt in the U.S. during the 1970s and later.[423] This variant looks to systemic change across the entire terrain of human-nature relations, an ecocentric "break with modernity" and industrialism earlier referred to as a "back-to-the-country" movement. DE shares with social ecology a repudiation of all forms of domination but, moved by a sense of ecological urgency, takes the realm of natural relations as privileged site of change. It dismisses liberal reformism and the notion of green capitalism in favor of a more all-encompassing "paradigm change" in consciousness, lifestyles, and politics supportive of human-scale community. DE further rejects Enlightenment ideology, urging limits to economic growth, bioregional living arrangements, local and self-sustaining agriculture, and an essentially spiritual worship of natural habitats or "wild nature".

Fundamentalist DE currents call for a return to "unspoiled nature" aligned with principles of local democracy, peaceful social relations, spiritualism, and ecological renewal. A founder of DE, George Sessions, has argued that human self-activity is attainable only through organic unity with surrounding ecosystems – in effect a dismissal of urban society.[424] Some DE theorists insist that all human intervention in the natural world is innately destructive, to be minimized where not totally avoided. The modern crisis, from this rather extreme viewpoint, is surmountable only where the human footprint basically vanishes – an outlook bringing charges from the left of misanthropic or even fascistic tendencies. Most within the dwindling DE orbit, however, retreat from such dogmatic ecocentrism.

DE theory stresses a moral obligation to nature and living systems within it, a presumption of ecological balance at odds with the requisites of modern industrial society. Departing from social ecology, DE looks to transformation of social life and natural relations aligned with the abolition of speciesism, or anthropocentrism. This is no contrived "second nature" but rather progressive adaptation to "first nature", seeking to transcend the age-old dualism of society versus nature, humans versus other species, that is, an outlook more compatible with animal rights.[425] The moral stance here extends to all parts of the natural world, beyond sentient beings to entire natural habitats as part of interconnected ecological systems.

As with social ecology, the blanket DE rejection of human domination over nature sidesteps a crucial problem – that is, mistakenly posing the question of domination in general instead of focusing on the particular *character* of such domination. In practice, however, DE thinkers and fol- lowers have taken a somewhat malleable attitude toward human-nature relations, Arne Naess writing: "My intuition is that the right to live is one and the same for all individuals, whatever the species, but the vital interests of our nearest [i.e., humans] nevertheless have priority."[426] DE literature often defends use of animals as food and other commodities. Naess argues that humans should be allowed to intervene in nature to satisfy vital needs, appearing more like a sympathizer of corporate power in a fast-food culture than principled defender of biospheric equality.[427]

Lacking much in the way of social theory, DE leaves abundant moral and political space for humans to continue their destructive patterns of production and consumption. Such ecological thinking would, in fact, never be so "deep" or "ecological" as to interfere with (exploitative) human practices that contribute toward "satisfying vital needs". Conceivably "wild nature" (itself a problematic concept) would remain untrammeled, but in many locales the environment would be vulnerable to merciless abuse on the part of enterprising human actors.

An even greater difficulty with DE is that its promised "exit" from modernity – including the utopian goal of bioregionalism – turns out to be so far-fetched as to be implausible, a political fantasy. Modernity has so completely and irreversibly transformed every realm of the existing world and has become so embedded in social institutions and practices for so many generations, that any human attempt to "escape" its complex totality would lead to immediate chaos and breakdown. The abolition of any human footprint on the natural world, which no DE theorist has ever concretized beyond individual decisions to relocate closer to the wilderness, becomes a romantic fiction. Further, biocentric equality, itself a fanciful social construct, is far enough removed from any conceivable goal that specific forms of political action are rendered essentially moot. The extension of moral status across the natural landscape seems laudable enough, but, as Tim Luke observes, such sacralization of nature fails to rise above a vague sense of "moral regeneration" detached from politics.[428] Despite its ostensibly radical outlook, therefore, deep ecology offers little guide to tangible change, especially in the midst of unprecedented crisis.

Whether the modern crisis emanates specifically from capitalism or more generally from industrialism (as Communist history suggests), DE provides no viable "exit" from the ecological predicament. It is left to individuals and small groups, living close to the countryside, to resist industrialism and urbanism in their own way, in their personal lives – a process that leaves the power structure intact – an outcome the sixties counterculture amply reflects. In its glorified spontaneism, it privileges local self-activity such that it detaches "nature" from history, society, and politics. As praiseworthy defenders of wilderness and all forms of life, therefore, DE contributes little to organizing movements for change beyond lifestyle preferences. Its break with Enlightenment rationality, along with its departure from liberalism, anarchism, and Marxism, unfortunately carries no relevance to the formation of urgently needed political strategy.

Green Parties – The Alternative?

The great influence of modern environmentalism has passed largely through a wide assemblage of groups, projects, organizations, and movements spanning local communities, institutions, lobbies, and political parties. In contrast to established parties, these smaller formations have given expression to diverse styles, methods, and rhythms – sometimes disruptive, episodically violent, often suspicious of state power. As for movements, they have limited transformative potential, regardless of scope, goals, or levels of militancy. It remains for more well-developed political structures with cohesive organization, ideology, leadership, and strategy to bring historical efficacy to otherwise partial, spontaneous, localized struggles.[429]

If popular movements ultimately require political translation to surpass their social immediacy, their very logic tends to resist such translation given the limits of localism and spontaneity. In the end, however, state institutions offer needed political leverage for change. Given the complexity of advanced capitalism, along with the democratic sensibilities of modern populations, no transformative strategy could hope to "smash" government power Leninist-style – yet none could afford to simply ignore that power. The only viable approach is to democratize and revitalize the system of power. If state governance were imposed on civil society by a vanguard party, hopes for a post-liberal, post-socialist outcome would inevitably turn to dust.

In the American experience, the long and diverse legacy of popular movements has been one of rather mixed results Many grassroots struggles – labor, Civil Rights, feminist, antiwar, environmentalist, community – have reshaped the public landscape enough to sharply impact policies, laws, norms, and everyday life. The outcomes, for the most part, have been liberal-reformist, confined to systemic boundaries – nowhere more so than in the case of environmentalism. The search for leverage within prevailing institutional arrangements typically moderates anti-system impulses, reformist gains usually coming with political costs. New-left insurgencies of the 1960s were generally pre-political, even anti-political: student activism, the counterculture, black insurgency, and antiwar mobilizations were constrained by their well-known worship of spontaneity, cultural radicalism, and hostility to government.

Given its famous anti-authoritarianism, the American new left fetishized democratic localism inherited in part from anarchism, assimilating both its strengths and weaknesses. And weaknesses were abundantly visible as the movements, despite a rebellious fervor, gained little organizational and ideological durability, all too often swept up in the very chaos and spontaneity they celebrated.[430]

By the 1970s, with the emergence of "new social movements" (notably feminism and ecology), the glorification of extra-institutional activity gave way to more developed structures such as the "pre-party" New American Movement. It was mostly these "newer" formations that drove oppositional politics during the 1970s and 1980s, which included the European extra-parliamentary left and, later, the West German Greens. In the U.S., environmental groups that surfaced in the late 1960s never generated a viable political strategy outside the Democratic Party orbit. As we have seen, many opted for interest-group reformism while others grew alienated from politics altogether.[431] Dozens of environmental groups have appeared since, many influenced by deep ecology and other currents aligned with urban revitalization, tree planting, river and bay keepers, protest against toxic wastes, anti-nuclear mobilizations, animal rights, water preservation, climate activism. There has been a proliferation of urban farms within many American cities, promoting community engagement, self-sufficiency, local agriculture, and personal health. Such grassroots activism generally remains outside the formal political system.

Local activity has long pervaded American environmentalism, rooted in community empowerment, urban greening, alternative energy, organic foods, opposition to oil pipelines and fracking, sustainable lifestyles. The Global Justice Ecology Project, based in Vermont, is dedicated to creating bridges across multiple issues and goals, linking grassroots activism with research and education. Other projects fit this description: Institute for Social Ecology (Vermont), Small Planet Institute (Oakland), Environmental Action (Boston), Global Exchange (San Francisco), Center for Progressive Reform (New Mexico) among many others. Similar local projects have proliferated across the world, catalyzed by alarm over global warming.

New social movements of the 1970s helped shape a dispersed "postmodern" landscape, while also detached in many ways from mainstream politics – except where Green parties managed to integrate diverse currents of local activism into broad electoral formations. After the early 1980s, Green parties multiplied across the industrialized world in the form of social blocs that could win local and even national power. Some Green parties eventually won a share of governance, sometimes as part of a "red-green" coalition with social democrats or other leftist parties. In the U.S., however, with its more tightly integrated two-party system, the smaller (also more conservative) Greens were on the fringe of electoral politics except for a scattered presence on city councils and other local bodies. The Greens' dilemma in the U.S. was heightened by a more pervasive corporate colonization of public life. Paradoxically, while the new movements were much stronger in the U.S. than in Europe, their *political* articulation has been relatively weak, in part a reflection of the overpowering influence of identity politics in the U.S. once the oppositional thrust of new movements began to wane in the 1990s.

In Europe, Green electoral gains in 1983 helped legitimate a party that was first to place ecological agendas at the center of political discourse. Energized by the growth of insurgent movements – peace, environmental, feminist, community – the Greens sought a path beyond both social democracy and Soviet-style Communism on the left and corporate agendas on the center-right. This overriding goal was democratization through a merger of popular movements and electoral politics. Winning a series of municipal and federal contests in West Germany while simultaneously forging alliances with the Social Democrats (SPD), by the end of the 1980s the Greens had conquered new governing terrain and managed to raise questions about the nature of power, citizen participation, and ecological renewal, well before the problem of climate change rose to prominence.

In the German context, the Greens won footholds in federal, state, and municipal legislatures, extending their influence to the media, academia, and general political culture. Green leaders (Rudolf Bahro, Daniel Cohn-Bendit, Petra Kelly, et. al.) unfurled a harsh critique of the SPD, which even before the 1980s had degenerated into a catch-all party bereft of socialist identity. What the party shared with most grassroots movements was emphasis on nonviolent direct action, local empowerment, opposition to corporate power, rejection of interest-group reforms, and skepticism of not only liberalism and socialism but nationalism.

Once the Greens, in Germany and elsewhere, reached a position of mass strength, deep internal divisions surfaced. Splits fell along multiple lines – between ecological "Fundis" advocating a holistic politics, ecosocialists favoring a class-based politics, and pragmatic "Realos" calling for a reformist program akin to that of the Social Democrats. There was conflict separating those looking toward parliamentary work and those strongly attuned to popular movements. Further, the Greens' post-liberal, post-Marxist view of multiple and overlapping forms of domination clashed with both interest-group pluralism and the single dialectic of class conflict central to the Marxist tradition. Bahro had argued: "I think it has become very doubtful that the proletariat within bourgeois society will be the bearer of the subject of a new society", adding: "The class struggle is not the solution." [432] On this point all Green factions could agree.

At each governing level in West Germany – federal, state, municipal – the Greens set out to bring representative democracy closer to the grass-roots, broadening debates, sharing material resources, building local decision-making bodies, and creating a more open leadership. Electoral gains (by 1985 reaching some two million supporters, 30,000 party members, and 27 Bundestag deputies) brought the Greens credibility that could be used to empower local citizens' initiatives.[433] Such a broadening of democratic politics was scarcely, if ever, made possible within liberal, social democratic, or Communist politics. The early Green strategy owes more to new-left radicalism and new social movements in the U.S. than to any other ideological current, although the Green synthesis owed more to ecological priorities.

A cornerstone of Green politics, in Germany and elsewhere, was an ecological model of development framed as an alternative to both liberal-capitalism and statist forms of socialism. The global crisis calls for a shift from the corporate-growth economy rooted in finance capital and consumerism to something more geared to human needs and environmental balance. Economic proposals favored progressive socialization of public life, decentralized governance, and expanded public infrastructure, reduced growth levels, and subsidies for green technology –though specific measures were often lacking. That would constitute the original "Green New Deal". The Greens pushed renewable energy sources and a system of "ecological accounting" to replace conventional fiscal methods. The party's influence in this area has been significant: since the 1990s Germany has been a world leader in conversion to a post-carbon economy, shedding nuclear power in the process.

If European Green politics was the fullest expression of integrated oppositional forces, the initial catalyst was huge peace mobilizations that swept the continent during the early 1980s. (No similar protests have taken place since that time.) Mass opposition to NATO's planned nuclear deployments helped galvanize both social movements and the Greens. Public fear surfaced over escalation of the arms race, the nuclear threat, renewed Cold War tensions, and resurgent U.S. militarism under President

Ronald Reagan. At that time the question of military spending and arms production raised the issue of economic conversion – that is, efforts to shift public investments from the military to civilian sectors, from arms to education, health care, housing, and the environment. Green leaders argued, in the early years, that each new cycle of arms production heightened contradictions between economic development and social progress, revealing a systemic linkage of corporate interests, globalization, militarism, and ecological decline. In fact, no other political entity, in Europe or elsewhere, had called attention to this crucial linkage. Liberals, social democrats, Communists – all these had made their peace with the prevailing interests. It was Bahro who predicted that "the peace movement is now at the head of an entire social constellation that is rehearsing the emergence of a new epoch."[434] Bahro, unfortunately, could not foresee the steady decline of antiwar movements, first in Europe and then (following 2003) in the U.S.

The Greens ascent into mainstream politics allowed for new institutional and ideological space for public discourse and decision-making. During the 1980s membership in the German party reached 42,000, the 1987 federal elections bringing three million votes and 7000 office holders at all levels of government. There were multiple red-green coalitions with the SPD, potentially widening the political leverage. Meanwhile, this new oppositional model – gaining momentum from the ecological crisis – quickly spread across Europe, to Sweden, Finland, Holland, Belgium, France, Italy, Austria. Rival leftist parties renewed efforts to integrate environmental concerns into their election platforms, with modest outcomes at best.

By the 1990s, Green electoral and organizational growth brought new political dilemmas – a repeat of what European Socialist and Communist parties had confronted for decades. How could these parties sustain grassroots energies while deeply involved in parliamentarism, which by its very logic demanded compromise and moderation? What strategy would the Greens adopt toward other leftist groups, mainstream parties, trade unions, and labor movement, all with scant interest in ecological agendas? How could any semblance of ecological radicalism be maintained in the face of sharp conflicts over such issues as nonviolence, peace, grassroots democracy, and environmental sustainability? The capacity of Green leaders to handle such challenges would decisively impact the party's trajectory – and the immediate results, especially in Germany, would not be especially hopeful.

The majority Green outlook, in Germany and across Europe, favored some type of red-green alliance so that parties could avoid isolation and impotence, particularly where partnerships were viable and the Greens could enter governing coalitions. The Realo approach was more disposed to compromise, moderation, and casting broad electoral appeals. The Fundi wing, on the other hand, feared collaboration with the SPD would erode Green identity and the capacity to promote ecological politics. Bahro, among others, believed the historic task of the Greens was to *replace* the Social Democrats as the main oppositional force in Germany; partnership would clearly work against that. Further, while the SPD's own corporatism and statism made its leaders fearful of change – of anything offensive to capital – most Greens favored progressive agendas aligned with popular movements.

The Fundis were correct to recognize that long-term Green participation in elections and parliamentary work would sooner or later lead to deradicalization – the very fate of postwar European Socialist and Communist parties. There was little reason to believe European Greens would be more immune to pressures of institutionalization and moderation than were these other (theoretically anti-system) parties. In more than three decades since the Green breakthrough, such deradicalization has in fact been the trajectory of parties in Germany and other countries where the Greens achieved mass appeal, whatever their larger influence on politics and culture. With a steady electoral presence at the municipal, regional, and national levels, the Realo faction established control of party organization between 1998 and 2005. By this time the once-radical Greens had become thoroughly integrated into the political system, locally and nationally, their ambivalence toward the corporate-state apparatus resolved in support of full engagement.

As with earlier leftist parties, the outcome was predictable enough – a more conservative organizational style, ideological moderation, detachment of party leadership from its mass base, professionalization of the top stratum, loss of radical identity. The very originality of Green politics, which spoke the language of "rupture" and "transformation", had by the turn of the new century vanished. The idea of a distinctly post-liberal, post-Marxist ecological radicalism, holding so much promise in the 1980s, had become a distant memory. Not only the domesticating logic of electoral politics, but the steady decline of new social movements, contributed to this atrophy. As we have seen, the Greens in Germany and beyond had turned into replicas of the very social democracy they had initially so despised.

The first European Congress of Greens, held in April 1994, attracted delegates from eight European nations looking for broad organizational and programmatic unity. A European Green Party was formed in 2004, comprised of more than 40 parties. After winning 26 seats to the European Parliament in 1989 and then 38 seats in 1999, the Greens elected 46 deputies in 2009 – their increased popularity owing to the worsening ecological crisis even as movement-based energies had visibly weakened. Here too the parties yielded to the logic of deradicalization: previously opposed to both European integration and NATO, the Greens came around to accepting each. At this point the concept of grassroots democracy, upheld in theory, was largely forgotten in practice.[435]

In the U.S., a Green alternative took shape in 1984 at the gathering of the Greens Committee of Correspondence. There was growing receptivity to the idea of a "new politics" emerging from the new left, social movements, and counterculture – against a backdrop of American traditions of civic participation and community organizing. One problem was that an embryonic Green Party faced a conservative milieu long hostile to leftist or Marxist politics. Adopting the slogan "neither right nor left", the U.S. party embraced different motifs such as new-age spiritualism, shying away from anti-capitalist impulses more common to the European scene. Strong reliance on electoral activity produced local gains beginning in the 1990s: hundreds of Green candidates were voted onto city councils across the country. Close to liberal environmentalism, the U.S. party held a view of ecological sustainability more or less consistent with prevailing institutional arrangements, fearful of being marginalized (its likely fate in any case).

The American Green alternative has in fact never been able to stave off marginal status, its predicament aggravated by strategic differences that came to a head in the mid-1990s. The original formation, Greens/ Green Party USA, favors local organizing and strongly opposes mounting high-profile electoral campaigns like that run by Ralph Nader in 2000 – a presidential contest with no hope of success, yet blamed by many for

George W. Bush's narrow victory that year. Nader's ill-fated campaign was sponsored by Green Party of the United States, which broke from the original Greens in 1996. In 2016 that organization promoted the White House candidacy of Jill Stein, who won barely one percent of the vote but just enough to have denied Hillary Clinton victory in three crucial states. Here again the wrath of establishment politics and media came down hard on the Greens, reflecting nearly insurmountable roadblocks historically faced by third parties in the U.S.

In 2001 the GPUS had become the leading Green organization, an electoral party embracing grassroots democracy, social justice, nonviolence, and environmentalism – its ideology less clearly articulated than that of European counterparts. Greens have won seats to state legislatures in California, Maine, and Arkansas, but their main presence is at the municipal level where (in 2018) a total of nearly 150 serve on city councils and school boards. To date no Greens have been elected to the U.S. Congress, one reason being that they are systematically barred from TV and radio debates reserved for just Democrats and Republicans. At the same time, the GPUS has lacked resources to widely advertise its candidates or otherwise break through ideological barriers to mainstream media exposure. The Greens have never solicited donations from corporations or influential PACs (political-action committees).

European Greens, for their part, continue to promote an "eco-development" strategy: emphasis on alternative technologies, limited growth, social justice, grassroots democracy, peaceful international relations, conversion from military to civilian spending. They remain dedicated to the centrality of social movements that, as mentioned, have been in steady decline since the 1980s. While this sounds emphatically radical, we have seen how most Green parties long ago entered a phase of deradicalization that coincided with (slightly) increased political leverage. Nowadays the Greens are hampered by strategic moderation (becoming a party like any other party) where issues of economic and political power are routinely sidestepped. One result is that the ecological radicalism once championed by Green leaders across Europe has degenerated into another variant of liberal reformism.

In Germany, the Greens' popularity has actually been on something of an upward trajectory, while its political objectives remain more diffuse. In the period 2016 to 2018, the two major parties (SPD and Christian Democrats) have experienced decline, the Greens have moved upward, winning more than 10 percent of the vote in a few state elections and positioning themselves second behind the ruling CDU. The Greens made significant gains in the 2018 state elections held in Hesse and Bavaria. As of early 2019, they boasted seats in 14 or 16 state legislatures, having entered governing coalitions in nine of them. At the same time, observers note that the Greens, once a symbol of radical change and disruption, have come to represent *stability*, although the fact Germany is a world leader is sustainable technology (combined with a shift away from nuclear power) owes much to the historic Greens influence.

Despite everything, the Greens have since the 1980s represented the closest thing the world has seen to a transformative ecological politics. Despite limits and flaws identified above, they remain the only political force dedicated to confronting the ecological crisis – indeed the only party with a coherent strategy, even if that strategy has been compromised. Their electoral gains, in Germany and elsewhere, should be taken seriously, as hopes for later developmental potential. Eventual deeper successes will depend on an historical convergence of ideological tendencies that have surfaced from time to time within the brief Green legacy. One point of optimism is the apparent persistence of eco-socialist currents within and around several European Green parties.

As the deepening ecological crisis sustained Green hopes across Europe, in 2019 the German Greens surged to new heights, rising to near the top of federal politics on the momentum of thriving local movements coinciding with the waning of established parties (Social Democrats, Christian Democrats). In May 2019 the German Greens, calling for "system change not climate change", became the second largest party in the European Parliament, winning 20.5 percent of the vote and sending party leadership into frenzied optimism. [436] Other national Green parties – in France, Finland, Ireland, Holland – experienced a similar boost, owing mainly to the failure of mainstream European parties to confront environmental challenges. As in California, many Green parties were fighting to severely reduce carbon footprint by 2030, beginning with a phasing-out of coal-fired plants. Polling surveys actually placed the German Greens in the lead domestically, with 27 percent support compared to 24 percent for the DC, much less for the SPD. A Greens ascendancy to a leading role in federal governance could mean an historic turning-point for German (indeed European) politics.

Green advances in Europe, where electoral and parliamentary systems are more open and diverse than in the U.S., can bring enough governing power to alter the course of events – all the more likely as the ecological crisis sharpens. The duopoly of Republicans and Democrats in American society presents solid roadblocks in the way of such progress. The system forces politicians to the "center", toward moderation and incrementalism, in order to win a plurality of votes. Institutional and ideological barriers to third-party representation have, if anything, stiffened over the past few decades, especially as the corporate media turns one-dimensional. The legacy of such efforts in the U.S. has been one largely of impotence and futility. Only a crisis of unprecedented intensity will bring to the fore conditions allowing for a Green breakthrough (that is simultaneously anti-capitalist) in American society. That in turn raises a burning question: could the global crisis itself ultimately be that turning point?

The Road to Ecosocialism

No discussion of the global crisis would be complete without engaging Marxist theory – indeed the broader Marxist and socialist tradition – going back to the seminal work of Marx and Engels and to later twentieth-century thinkers, movements, and parties. Anti-system discourses of the Marxist legacy inform the development of ecological radicalism and leftist tendencies within contemporary social movements and Green politics. Some ecological theorists – Rudolf Bahro, John Bellamy Foster, Chris Williams, Victor Wallis among others – rely heavily on some interpretation of Marxism in their analysis of ecological crisis as endemic to world capitalism. Williams argues that the key challenge today is to "unearth the significant contribution of Marx, Engels, and subsequent Marxists have made to ecological thought in the belief that a Marxist framework allows for the most coherent and useful modality for understanding the roots of the ecological crisis and plotting a way out of it."[437] In *Ecology and Socialism*, Williams adds that "ecological devastation is not an accidental outcome of capitalist development but an intrinsic element of the system, just as integral as class exploitation, poverty, racism, and war."[438]

A distinctly socialist outlook brings to ecological politics specifically *critical, dialectical,* and *global* dimensions grounded in systemic analysis of world capitalism: no reversal of the crisis is thinkable within the existing order, ruling out prospects for a "green capitalism". For Marx and Engels, it was in the very logic of capitalism to expand the production apparatus, driven by profits, growth, and power exercised not only over the economy but over government, social life, culture, and indeed nature. Capitalism operates according to the force of commodification, which naturally opposes any efforts to impede that logic. Global crisis is entirely predictable once the deep historical conflict between capitalism and the natural habitat, between private interests and social needs, is fully taken into account.

Marxism and the divergent socialist paths it inspired foresaw intensification of class struggle between workers and capitalists, a prelude to insurrection and overthrow of an order riddled with social contradictions and political instability. At the same time, in its main historical strategies (notably social democracy and Leninism) the Marxist tradition shared with liberal capitalism an attachment to Enlightenment rationality – that is, a belief in human progress through industrial growth rooted in continuous expansion of science, technology, and mastery of the natural environment. For classical Marxism, human alienation could only be abolished by overturning the capitalist division of labor, ultimate stage in the full realization of species-being, or liberation within classless society. Nineteenth-century socialists – not only Marx and Engels but Karl Kautsky, George Plekhanov, and others – inherited a modernizing faith in the blessings of material prosperity historically generated by the forces of production under capitalism itself.

The egalitarian side of Marxism signaled a radical shift in approaches to both class relations and human-nature relations, while the rationalizing, developmental side carried forward strong elements of instrumental rationality and anthropocentrism, or human domination of nature for modernizing purposes. Marxism in all its formulations was resolutely productivist, fixating on economic forces as driving mechanism of history, central to the transition from capitalism to socialism. (fn. 29) Such an outlook meshed with the *Zeitgeist* of the period: Marxism had gained ascendancy during the early modern era, forged between 1850 and 1890 before reaching its zenith in the decades preceding World War I. The theory resonated with powerful intellectual currents at the time and place (Europe), including faith in the liberating potential of science, technology, and industrialism.

It has been argued by Foster and others that Marx (and later Marxists), despite theoretical limitations of time and place, arrived at a conceptual framework universally relevant not only to class struggle and revolution but to ecological renewal.[439] The socialization of production, a shift toward egalitarian class and power relations, breakdown of the separation between urban and rural life, the overcoming of alienated labor – all this is said to point toward a model of sustainable development consistent with increasingly harmonious relations between society and nature.[440] Whether this imputed vision, usually based on very schematic and overly general passages in Marx and Engels, effectively counters a deep productivism of the theory is problematic. But even if we recognize an ecological Marx we are left with his (understandable) silence on the question of developmental sustainability – not to mention issues related to anthropocentrism and non-human life. There is little in Marx (or indeed later Marxists) to indicate serious theoretical reflection on such questions, nor has anyone credibly made such a claim.

As Ted Benton, generally sympathetic to Marx, observes, the overall thrust of the theory is to give humans a much *freer* hand in utilizing the natural habitat for distinctly human purposes, with class struggle in fact a vehicle for the "humanization of nature". [441] Any destructive consequences of this process could be regarded as the inevitable by-product of the transition from capitalism to socialism. Here the much-celebrated humanism of the early Marx can be viewed as replicating a deep-seated ethos of human domination over nature found in most Western religious and philosophical thought, including the Enlightenment. For Marx, following the legacy of Descartes, Kant, and Hegel, humans are innately creative and self-reflective, free to make history, while non-human life remains trapped in a pre-designed biological realm. Thus, instead of an organic connection between humans and the natural world, Marx and Engels effectively stressed dualism and *opposition* between the two – a tendency that would become more pronounced in later, more crudely deterministic, variants of Marxism.

Nowhere in the Marxist tradition do we find a suggestion that in the historical process there will be transformed relations between humans and animals, whatever the depiction of "nature". On the contrary, while non-human life remains rather fixed, trapped, the very self-realization that humans achieve by virtue of their liberation in fact endows humans with augmented power over the natural world, animals included. "Nature" as such is always an external force to be domesticated, regulated, and utilized for human ends. As Benton observes: "… Marx's vision of a 'humanization' of nature is no less anthropocentric than the more characteristically modernist, utilitarian view of the domination of nature."[442] Today it is well understood that this dualism, along with the belief in a fixity of animal life, is no longer tenable; it is simply another reflection of speciesism.

Consistent with Enlightenment ideology, classical Marxism associated prospects for historical change and social progress with an expanded human capacity to master all dimensions of the natural world. This was basically taken for granted. Capitalism had already unleashed new material and technical powers allowing humans to transform and r-eappropriate nature, a development Marx typically greeted as positive. The conquest of nature would be achieved through historical advances in science, technology, and industrialism shared by capitalism and socialism alike. Intensified exploitation of natural resources (including animals) was never regarded as problematic, but instead was treated as "progress", beyond questions of ideology or political choice. From this standpoint, familiar references to "nature" especially in Marx's early work reveal less than has been claimed regarding any progressive ecological outlook. Those references were generally framed in rather abstract terms, as in the somewhat prosaic emphasis on the human/nature conflict.

More crucially, Marx says little about how economic development in a transitional future – before or during socialism -- might follow a path congenial to natural relations. His far-reaching critique of capitalism does not systematically (or *concretely*) encompass its impact on the natural habitat where, as mentioned, he carries forward a dualism consistent with human efforts to domesticate and utilize nature for strictly instrumental purposes. In *Marx's Ecology,* Foster writes: "… Marx, from his earliest years … analyzed the human alienation from nature in a sophisticated and ecologically sensitive form. This tendency was reinforced by his concerns regarding human subsistence and the relationship to the soil, and the whole problem of capitalist agriculture. Central to this thinking was a concern regarding the antagonistic division between town and country."[443] Yet there is nothing in these "concerns" that Marx ever systematically theorizes or sets out to politically situate; we do see passing references here and there, but these are never fully integrated into Marx's larger body of work. The idea that (in Foster's words) "Marx's social thought ... is inextricably bound to an ecological worldview" appears far-fetched, an unsustainable radical leap.[444]

In contrast, there are abundant references in the work of Marx and Engels supporting a far less critical view of Enlightenment rationality. The historic expansion of economic and technological forces in the service of material development, for example, seems more or less uncritically embraced – a clearly progressive advance for humanity in its struggle to overcome exploitation and alienation. In the *Communist Manifesto* Marx and Engels praise the bourgeoisie for having "created more massive and more colossal productive forces than have all preceding generations together." They add: "Subjection of Nature's forces to man, machinery, application of chemistry to industry and agriculture ... what earlier century had even a presentiment that such productive forces slumbered in the lap of social labor?"[445] One looks in vain for even cursory references to an "ecological Marx" in this crucial writing – one of the few where the authors look beyond a critique of capitalism as such.

Writing three decades later, Engels, in *Socialism: Utopian and Scientific*, would lay out Enlightenment premises with even greater clarity. The transition to socialism is presented as the gradual unfolding of human dominion over nature, a continuous extension of capitalist development. With this historical process "for the first time Man, in a certain sense, is finally marked off from the rest of the animal kingdom, and emerges from mere animal conditions of existence into really human ones. The whole sphere of the conditions of life which environ man, and which have hitherto ruled man, now comes under the dominion and control of man, who for the first time becomes the real, conscious *lord of Nature* ..."[446] Human self-actualization is actually dependent on a fully-expressed domination of nature: "In proportion as anarchy in social production vanishes, the political authority of the state dies out, Man, at last the master of his own form of social organization, becomes at the same time the *lord over Nature*, his own master – free."[447] This view is fully consistent with leading strains of nine-teenth-century social thought and indeed with most subsequent Marxist theorizing.

True to its Enlightenment heritage, classical Marxism associated the historical struggle for socialism with expanded human capacity to shape and reshape the natural world. The labor process itself, a crucial site of technological innovation, contained within it vast potential for humans to control the environment as they pursue self-activity, becoming true masters of nature. William Leiss argues that in classical Marxism the unfolding of class conflict itself was seen as broadening human domination over nature that, however, was destined to generate explosive new contradictions within an expanding industrial system.[448] Later Marxists held this view, in one form or another, well into the twentieth century.

A further, equally problematic, set of issues stems from the failure of early Marxism to articulate a political course forward -- to arrive at a theory and strategy of change beyond general references to class struggle, revolution, and transition to socialism. In fact, these were largely schematic notions. There was little if any theoretical framework pointing toward how transition from capitalism to socialism was expected to occur. Among other questions, the issue of class consciousness – more precisely, how it might develop and mature among workers and others – was scarcely posed, in part owing to a crude psychological rationalism that *assumed* formation of an anti-capitalist proletariat within the historical process. How could revolutionary opposition take on a mass character within the matrix of capitalist power, where ruling elites could fully exercise material, institutional, and ideological domination? Neither Marx nor Engels effectively addressed this imperative, apparently convinced that an increasingly exploited and alienated working class would be naturally driven toward opposition and revolution, with no "external element" (vanguard party, intellectuals) fully or even partly theorized.

By the end of the nineteenth century, with growth of a mass socialist party in Germany, it had already become clear that workers, embedded in the daily rhythms of proletarian life, would become trapped in a confining social immediacy without some form of "external element". The epic struggle for socialism would require an elaborate *political* framework built around durable organization, leadership, strategy, and methods for winning power. There would be nothing spontaneous or automatic about this process. In the absence of such a framework, oppositional forces would end up fragmented and depoliticized, whatever their level of militancy and commitment.

It would be the historical task of later Marxists to carve out distinct political strategies derived from an analysis of social conditions and oppositional tendencies at work. Between 1890 and World War I rival strategic views emerged throughout Europe, shaped by intellectual debates that would extend across the twentieth century. Bernstein's evolutionary socialism, theoretical genesis of social-democratic reformism, resolved the dilemma of class consciousness by linking politics to immediate reforms won through elections, labor unions, and parliamentary work. Socialism would arrive through gradual and peaceful transformation, a process of incremental socialization and democratization of liberal capitalism, at a time when industrialization was giving rise of an expanded proletariat. Class consciousness was taken as already established, with the expectation it would lead to a mature socialism on the basis of working-class reforms. Social-democratic parties of the Second International (later Socialist International, or SI) flourished during the twentieth century, agencies of welfare-state capitalism that in fact fell considerably short even of Bernstein's limited vision.

If the social-democratic path could never deliver anti-system objectives, serving instead to legitimate advanced capitalism on new foundations, the two alternatives – Leninism and council communism – likewise fell short, a point more fully discussed in chapter four. Leninism "solved" the dilemma of class consciousness by means of a vanguard party that, where successful, orchestrated twentieth-century Communist revolutions (Russia, China, Yugoslavia, Vietnam) through authoritarian party-states. With economic rationalization came the very domination of nature characteristic of liberal-capitalism and social democracy. Environmental priorities received at best token attention: thus development could only mean worsening habitat destruction, mounting air and water pollution, blighted cities, and severe agricultural dysfunctions. Despite obvious differences, social democracy and Leninism came to share important features – one being fetishism of technological expansion, coinciding with reliance on the very social hierarchy, organizational discipline, and bureaucratic efficiency that defined the bourgeois industrial order.

The third strategic alternative – European council radicalism – faced an imposing challenge of political efficacy owing to its glorification of spontaneous mass insurgency. The local forms were always vulnerable to extreme dispersion and impotence in the face of overwhelming state and corporate power. They were eventually crushed in such countries as Russia and Spain, defeated because of their own fragmentation and localism in Italy, and assimilated into union and party structures in Germany. The council tradition never provided the foundation of durable political organization or governance in any setting.[449] Moreover, while partly inspired by the more ecologically friendly theories of Rousseau, utopian socialists, and such anarchists as Kropotkin, the council alternative never generated useful or lasting ideas pertinent to ecology or sustainable development.

Twentieth-century critical Marxists were scarcely more adequate to this challenge: "Western" Marxists (Luxemburg, Gramsci, Lukacs, Sartre, the Frankfurt School), despite occasional references to "nature", seemed hardly more interested in ecology than nineteenth-century Marxists. At the same time, by the end of the twentieth century it had become obvious that capitalism was able to deflect crisis and integrate potential opposition, owing to the institutionalization of state-corporate power along with systematic capacity for ideological control. With deradicalization of the European Socialist and Communist parties, there would be a pronounced absence of mass-based revolutionary forces across the capitalist world. Influential as the Marxist legacy has been, therefore, the historical search for a broadly radical ecological politics adequate to the later, more destructive phase of capitalism would have to proceed along newer, bolder intellectual and political tracks.

One result of this impasse was that "the environment" would be taken up by theorists (and activists) mostly *outside* the Marxist tradition. For Marxism, notably in the context of organized politics, social transformation was to varying degrees a project for and by humans struggling to conquer nature through expanded science, technology, and production. Nowhere, as mentioned, did issues related to ecological crisis shape political agendas: where addressed, it was assumed such issues would be remedied with the advance of socialism, where capitalist interests were no longer a roadblock.

Communist leaders, for their part, have typically viewed environmental challenges as a bothersome distraction from more urgent (economic) challenges at hand. By the 1960s, as ecology was gaining widespread attention, Marxism (and Communism) was in sharp decline despite its striking resurgence in Western universities.

Intellectual efforts to fuse ecology and Marxism, or socialism, would not be undertaken until later, fueled by the energies of new social movements and Green politics in Europe and North America. Even here the underlying productivism and labor metaphysic of Marxism had imposed limits on critically theorizing natural relations. Further, it had become clear that Marxism, like the "social" and "deep" variants of ecological politics, could not by itself provide the basis of a new radicalism; that would require a more dynamic synthesis. That synthesis would emerge, slowly and unevenly, throughout the sixties, seventies, and eighties, sometimes aligned with leftist tendencies within Green parties. What came to be labeled "ecosocialism" was the product of many influences: the seminal work of Marx and Engels, anarchism, feminism, sixties counterculture, Bookchin's social ecology, the work of such neo-Marxists as Herbert Marcuse and Andre Gorz.[450]

Ecosocialism would signify a radical departure within leftist traditions long dominated by several variants of Marxism. Its ideals were broad and open-ended, revolving around motifs of local community, environmental balance, egalitarian social relations, and opposition to multiple forms of domination. It embraced what would fashionably be called a "red-green" politics based in diverse movements for change.[451] Ecosocialism achieved its first noteworthy presence within the West German Greens during the early 1980s, promoted by such activists as Rainer Trampert and Thomas Ebermann along with Bahro, but this turned out to be rather short-lived.

In Lowy's view, ecosocialism represented a new politics maneuvering past the historical roadblocks set by liberal capitalism, social democracy, and Soviet bureaucratic centralism. Thus: "Ecosocialism is the radical proposition – i.e., one that deals with the roots of the ecological crisis – which distinguishes itself from the productivist varieties of socialism in the twentieth century (either social democracy or the Stalinist brand of 'communism') as well as from the ecological currents that accommodate themselves in one way or another to the capitalist system. This radical proposition aims not only to transform the relations of production, the productive apparatus, and the dominant consumption patterns but to create a new way of life, breaking with the foundations of the modern Western capitalist/industrial civilization." [452] This formulation is closely aligned to the views of the author.

As we enter the third decade of the twenty-first century, world capitalism is overwhelmingly corporate-driven, oligarchical, unsustainable, with few counterforces on the horizon. American power lies at the heart of this system, a locus of unparalleled military force with hundreds of deployments around the globe. This very reality ought to force oppositional tendencies, as presently constituted, toward radical alternatives drawing from multiple traditions. Such alternatives, to be efficacious, will require ideological clarity, organizational cohesion, and strategic direction – properties surely implicit in an ecosocialist model that has barely scratched the surface of the political landscape.

Whatever its theoretical limits and political fate, Marxism remains vital to modern ecological thought, its anti-capitalist legacy and analysis of political economy still indispensable to the success of anti-system movements and parties. Lowy writes: "Ecologists are mistaken if they imagine they can do without the Marxian critique of capitalism. An ecology that does not recognize the relation between 'productivism' and the logic of profit is destined to fail – or worse, to become absorbed by the system."[453] Foster adds that modern socialist hopes "require the abolition of private property in the means of production, a high degree of equality in all things, replacement of the blind forces of the market by planning of the associated producers in accordance with genuine social needs, and the elimination to whatever extent possible of invidious distinctions associated with the division of town and country, mental and manual labor, race relations, gender divisions, etc." Much of this can be found in Marx and Engels, perhaps more in later theorists like Bookchin and Marcuse. Foster adds: "The only way to accomplish this is by altering our human metabolism with nature, along with our human-social relations, transcending both the alienation of nature and of humanity."[454]

More recently, Kohei Saito in his scholarly book *Karl Marx's Ecosocialism*, presented a rather ambitious view of an "ecosocialist Marx", relying heavily on a set of unpublished natural science "notebooks" written during the last 15 years of Marx's life. Saito arrives at a compelling argument:

familiar criticisms of Marx's productivism and his faith in boundless economic development are shown to be off the mark once a more ecologically invested Marx is discovered. Saito goes well beyond any previous claims, insisting on "the immanent systematic character of Marx's ecology" insofar as "the notebooks display just how seriously and laboriously Marx studied the rich field of nineteenth-century ecological theory."[455] Toward the end of his life Marx consciously parted from any form of naïve Prometheanism and came to regard ecological crises as the fundamental contradiction of the capitalist mode of production.

According to Saito, we have inherited not only an "ecological Marx" along lines identified by Foster and others, but a full-blown nineteenth-century ecosocialist whose writings cannot be adequately grasped unless this ecological realm is thoroughly taken into account. Thus: "I maintain that it is not possible to comprehend the full scope of his critique of political economy if one ignores its ecological dimension."[456] More than that: "Modern discussions of ecology owe a great debt to Marx's deep insights into the fundamental nature of a society of generalized commodity production."[457] Saito contends that, based on the notebooks, Marx gradually corrected his optimistic vision of the human mastery of nature …".[458]

Judging from a systematic overview of Marx's general (and published) work, neither an "ecological" nor "ecosocialist" theorist seems particularly visible, so even with the most optimistic reading of the notebooks we are still left with considerable ambiguity. In fact, Saito makes a far stronger case for how capitalism generates debilitating ecological contradictions than Marx himself must have made – hardly surprising given the far less destructive tendencies of nineteenth-century capitalism. How sophisticated in this regard could ecological theory have been at the time of Marx and Engels? Did they ever seek to incorporate Rousseau or Kropotkin into their work? Notions of "metabolic rift" (already emphasized by Foster and others) and nature-human disruption, while possibly useful, scarcely appear as pathbreaking, especially when understood against the general backdrop of Marx's thought.

More crucially yet, as we have seen, Marx's lifetime intellectual partner, Engels, seems mysteriously to have never gotten the word of an ecological Marx – nor of a need to temper any discussion of humans becoming the proud masters of nature. Writing in *Socialism: Utopian and Scientific* (published in English 11 years after Marx's death), Engels refers matter-of-factly and continuously to the "complete development of modern productive forces", the "unlimited extension of production", a complete "freeing" of the "mighty productive forces of today" – all perfectly consistent with humans assuming their rightful place as the "conscious Lord of Nature."[459] Here one of the final elaborations of classical Marxism is entirely devoid of ecological sensibilities. Indeed much the same can be said of influential early Marxists – Kautsky, Plekhanov, Antonio Labriola, Lenin, Trotsky, Luxemburg. Sadly, none of these theorists appears to have been even slightly impacted by the legacy of an "ecological Marx".

In the end, an ecological outlook is at best only vaguely implicit in the writings of Marx, Engels, and later Marxists, who had little concern for ecological priorities at a time (especially before World War II) when the global crisis was far less visible than it is today. As noted above, organized forms of twentieth-century socialism – including above all Communist regimes – did not systematically take up ecological motifs in either theory or practice. During the postwar era, deepening crisis brought structural and ideological disruptions that paved the way toward potentially novel theorizing. Here such theorists as Gorz, Bookchin and Bahro in the 1980s, Commoner in his later work, and, more recently, Foster, Joel Kovel, Michael Lowy, Williams, Saito, and Wallis – all plausibly labeled "ecosocialists" or "red-green" activists – have set forth the need for global transformation based on full-scale alteration of class and power relations resonant with sustainable development.

By the start of the twenty-first century ecosocialist currents appeared, in different form, in areas of the world far removed from Europe where environmentalism had appeared as a vigorous social movement – Brazil, Mexico, China, Russia, Japan, Peru. Ecological networks established in these regions were often tinged with socialist politics, although references to "ecosocialism" as such were not always clearly stated. Peasant movements across Brazil and in southern Mexico were strongly influenced by an environmental radicalism aligned with elements of Marxist theory.

Such development is of course unthinkable within the world system as presently constituted. Williams argues that radical change "must encompass social sustainability, equality, and justice as much as it does ecological concerns", adding: "We can only do this if we collectively and democratically make all decisions based on human need not corporate profits."[460] Foster continues along the same lines: "It is the historic need to combat the absolute destructiveness of the system of capital at this stage – replacing it, as Marx envisioned, with a society of substantive equality and ecological sustainability – which, I am convinced, constitute the essential meaning of revolution in our time." [461]

In *Red-Green Revolution*, Wallis outlines an ecosocialist alternative embedded in a dialectic linking ecology and socialism, where class divisions are abolished and humans can live fully in balance with the natural habitat.[462] For Wallis, ecology and socialism naturally converge insofar as both exhibit properties of holism and sustainable economics, both also rejecting the capitalist imperative of class domination and resource wars. His emphasis on issues of militarism and imperialism (shared here) sets his work apart from that of most other environmentalists, including a majority of ecosocialists. He points out, correctly, that "militarism, expansionism, and environmental plunder are all of a piece", a tendency sure to intensify in a world of depleting resources.[463] Wallis embellishes his ecosocialism with a turn toward the process of economic conversion – an historic shift of human and material resources from military toward peaceful, needs-based, sustainable programs.

Such an outlook is indeed compelling, yet worth noting is that ecosocialism as promoted by Foster, Williams, Saito, and Wallis remains oddly silent on matters of political strategy, including what is to be the agency (or agencies) of anti-system insurgency. What methods of struggle and approaches to corporate-state power are needed to face intensifying challenges when time appears to be very short? Ecosocialism might well pose the ultimate hope for humanity, but its theorists have been strangely vague about strategic options. Given the historic limits of social democracy, Leninism, and the council tradition, fresh strategic thinking would seem to be on the agenda. As for ecosocialism, its most visible expression to date has been on the left fringes of European Green parties, yet to spread beyond those origins.

A good many problematic tenets of Marxism, old and new, have been identified by theorists of social ecology, deep ecology, and Green politics. Central to their critique is a more skeptical view of Enlightenment ideology, the rampant industrialism it bequeathed, the perils of technological rationality, pursuit of material abundance, and failure to extend normative status to much of nonhuman nature. Crucial too is emphasis on sustainable modes of agriculture and food production, a concern addressed only marginally within the Marxist tradition.

The Global Challenge Ahead

With survival of life on the planet at stake – and precious little time to find answers – development of anti-system politics ought to be among the top human priorities. Epic failures of earlier traditions can be a source of pessimism, yet space remains for new opportunities once the old illusions vanish. The new historical juncture requires a strategy that liberalism, social democracy, and Leninism could never furnish, though lessons from history can be useful. As Bookchin has written: "The turning point of radical change is that no general interest of this kind can be achieved by the particular means that marked earlier revolutionary movements."[464]

As the crisis deepens, theoretical perspectives abound while movements and organizations proliferate – yet the *political* dimension remains poorly developed at best. Where is a viable anti-system strategy, in the U.S., Europe, or elsewhere? Where is the counter-hegemonic opposition strong enough to attack the fortresses of power? To date only the European Greens have arrived at a coherent strategy, yet, as we have seen, they soon followed the path of social democracy, with a *modus vivendi* fully adaptable to modern capitalism. And capitalism remains fully immersed in the growth religion, consumerism, technological rationality, and the assault on nature.

After decades of political experience, crucial questions remain. What is the source of radical change in an historical context far removed from earlier traditions? What are the dynamic agencies of change at a time when the industrial proletariat is a declining and mostly conservative force? What indeed can be said nowadays to comprise the central elements of oppositional consciousness? What are the defining elements of ecological radicalism in a situation where human-natural relations demand fundamental change? Beyond the nation-state, how can an effective *global* opposition develop and mature even as resurgent forms of nationalism spread across the landscape? Turning to Gramsci's prescient concept of social bloc, what forces can be mobilized behind such a counterforce, to give it historical substance? Unanswered questions of this sort reveal the ideological inertia prevalent in contemporary progressive circles. Valiant attempts to depict Marx and Engels as ecologists or "ecological materialists" hardly advances matters.

The well-known Marxist faith in technological and industrial progress, credible as nineteenth-century theory, had Enlightenment origins shared with liberal capitalism, including a productivism scarcely consistent with ecological priorities. Paradoxically, the work of Marx and Engels turns out to be much too conservative to provide the basis of any later ecological radicalism: Marxist alignment with pervasive elements of capitalist rationalization could actually be seen as *anti*-ecological. Here Bahro writes: "The technocratic and scientific faith that the progress of industry, science, and technique will solve humanity's social problems virtually automatically is one of the illusions of the present age most hostile to life."[465]

Aside from faith in green technology, views shared by environmentalists, Greens, and even ecosocialists on energy restructuring seem rather lacking in imagination. Where, for instance, do we think about curtailing forms of *military* technology, including the surveillance apparatus? What can be said about innovative modes of public transportation that surpass the venerated electric and hybrid cars? What about liberating workplace technologies? What about sophisticated efforts to coordinate labor patterns and save energy as part of an ambitious global project? What about the need to limit and regulate tyrannical powers exercised by such high-tech corporations as Facebook, Microsoft, Apple, Google, and Twitter? As matters stand, the big technological innovations merely serve to aggravate environmental devastation caused by oligarchical transnational corporations. Where is the pushback?[466]

On these and related questions Marxism has not seemed to be especially helpful, aside from a familiar anti-capitalist analysis of economic power and class relations. This deficiency extends to the sphere of natural relations, including human-animal relations. The dualism in Marx himself has already been noted. Robin Eckersley argues that "an ecocentric perspective cannot be wrested out of Marxism, whether orthodox or humanist, without seriously distorting Marx's own theoretical concepts."[467] Akin to liberalism, the theory approaches animals – like the rest of nature – as resources to be harnessed and exploited, a view upheld by most subsequent oppositional movements and parties. An inevitable speciesism does not resonate with an ecocentrism aligned with animal rights, human health, or integrity of the natural habitat. Only a few Green parties have to date made even modest overtures in this direction.

One problem is that no ecological politics can make headway without adopting an ecocentric outlook, since issues of agricultural sustainability, food security, resource depletion, and environmental decline are so thoroughly interwoven. Writing in *Earth Wars,* Geoff Hiscock comments that as the planet now experiences continuous shrinkage of food, energy, water, land, and other vital resources, few find the world suffering from calamitous "ecological deficit"; the foundations of life are being depleted faster than they can be replaced.[468]   At a time when all focus is directed toward climate change and fossil fuels, global resource shortages are bringing humanity into a perpetual downward spiral. No previous societies could withstand this sustained attack on natural supports needed for a thriving economic and social life. In *World on the Edge,* Brown writes: "We are liquidating the earth's natural resources to fuel our consumption", stressing that ecological collapse is no longer a matter of *whether* but *when.*[469]

More pointedly, according to Brown, we face an era of food shortages unknown across modern history, where "food is the new oil and land is the new gold."[470] Resource shrinkage will be most acutely felt in food production, a challenge largely ignored or downplayed by environmentalists and other progressives. Brown writes: "In addition to some of the most severe soil erosion in human history, we are also facing newer trends such as the depletion of aquifers, the plateauing of grain yields in the more advanced countries, and rising temperatures."[471] Countries where water tables are falling and aquifers are being depleted include the world's three biggest grain producers – the U.S., China, and India. Meanwhile, global consumption of meat and other animal products has multiplied nearly ten times from 1950 to the present, while current trends suggest a continuation of this pattern.

World resource decline, combined with population growth, signifies geopolitical conflict -- a source of civil violence, forced migrations, national tensions, and warfare. In *The Race for What's Left,* Michael Klare observes that we now see a "concerted drive by governments and resource firms to gain control over whatever remains of the world's raw materials base. Government and corporate officials recognize that existing reserves are being depleted at a terrifying pace and will largely be exhausted in the not-too-distant future."[472] He adds: "The race we are on today is the last of its kind that we are likely to undertake."[473] This doomsday-like convergence of geopolitical and ecological disasters, mostly resource driven, seems far too horrific to be overlooked so widely across the ideological spectrum.

Where resource pressures are taken up, the larger problem of economic development – that is, sustained and limitless growth -- cannot be avoided. The planet is increasingly overwhelmed by the enormity of material demands placed on fragile natural-support systems. This was already acknowledged in the early 1970s by the Club of Rome, emphasized in the writings of Bookchin and Deep Ecologists. It is hardly premature to consider Bahro's plea at the birth of the European Greens: "We need to at least consider a great moratorium, a kind of general strike against expansion, the blocking of everything embraced by the word 'development', a pull on the emergency brake."[474] Sadly, during the intervening four decades, nothing of the sort has happened – or been seriously discussed.

As the growth machine continues unchecked, ruling elites look more aggressively to what they consider unlimited natural resources to be extracted and commodified; the myth of boundless resources continues. Modern capitalism and its opulent culture industry have generated a mass addiction to ever-increasing material goods and services, but that addiction (like others) is bound to be self-destructive. Limits imposed by vulnerable ecosystems are already being felt. Beyond the issue of *energy* resources, which are indeed still abundant, the problem more urgently extends to rainforests, oceans, other waterways, arable land, fresh water, crucial metals and minerals, and biodiversity – all threatened by runaway economic growth.

One reason unsustainable growth has not been more seriously addressed is that it raises the sheer difficulty – economically, politically, culturally – of pulling back, of shifting toward more limited and balanced developmental patterns. Adopting a limits-to-growth trajectory would demand restructuring, away from endless wealth accumulation, profits, and material consumption. One of the greatest myths to be dispelled is the convenient notion that perpetual growth is simply built into any viable economy, so little can (or ought) to be done.

In present conditions such arguments can no longer be made in good faith, riddled as they are with self-delusions. At the same time, alternatives to the endless growth are not so difficult to imagine once new sets of priorities – for example, large-scale conversion from military to socially useful investment – are taken into account. As of 2020 world economic growth was moving at roughly three percent, not spectacular but huge in terms of augmented total global output. China, the largest of all economies, was increasing its GDP yearly at an average 6.5 percent rate, with no drastic slowdown on the horizon. The fact is that *any* economic growth rate is nowadays wildly unsustainable, its impact on the natural habitat burdensome in ways that transcend the impact of global warming.

What, then, can be done? How can economic growth be curtailed in ways that are consistent with reversing the crisis? One point of departure might be to sharply reduce expenditures for military systems, global arms deployments, nuclear weaponry, the arms trade, and wars – a savings that could reach two trillion dollars yearly while moderating growth, helping rebuild public infrastructures, and revitalizing social priorities. A second initiative might be toward de-automobilizing societies in favor of greener, more efficient, less costly transportation systems. A third effort would be equally historic – transition from animal-based agriculture, the meat complex, and McDonaldized foods toward plant-based options across the globe. A fourth possibility would involve fundamental revamping of medical systems – from commodified, bureaucratic, costly modalities to more socialized, holistic, local, cost-effective arrangements, thus reducing overall expenses by half or more. No doubt the biggest growth reductions would come from full-scale transition to green energy sources for electricity and transportation. All these combined efforts to curb the growth machine are easily within reach, could reduce world GNP by tens of millions of dollars, and would be relatively painless. In fact, living standards everywhere would be elevated, freer of waste and destruction.

Existing growth patterns are, of course, tightly interwoven with new population pressures: the world could reach ten billion people by 2050, if not soon thereafter – by all accounts far exceeding the planet's carrying capacity. Food production alone would be woefully inadequate to satisfy such a population level. Cities would become teeming centers of congestion, infrastructure failures, malnutrition, disease, and social breakdown.

Brown writes that "One of the leading challenges facing the international community is how to prevent that slide into chaos."[475] Sadly, few progressives seem willing to even recognize this epic challenge.

Much the same can be said about the global (and ecological) consequences of military power, nuclear arms buildups, and continuous warfare. The problem is sure to be exacerbated by the intensifying resource wars over the shrinking material resources needed for economic development. In 2018 Washington spent one trillion dollars to maintain its international military supremacy, the money going to a bloated Pentagon bureaucracy, 800 bases scattered across the planet, a doomsday nuclear arsenal, protracted armed interventions in the Middle East and elsewhere, and preparations for military deployments in space. The American footprint – economic, military, environmental – expands daily. A permanent warfare state, reinforced by a massive security apparatus, has become an institutionalized fixture of American life. As resource conflicts heat up, the rationale for such a behemoth will correspondingly strengthen.

At present no leading state – the U.S., China, India, Russia, Britain – appears ready to dismantle either its growth or military apparatus, and no international organization possesses the power or legitimacy to impose such an outcome. The likely outcome is a world of sharpening conflict, geopolitical rivalries, and extended warfare. As for the U.S., there is nothing in its history, political traditions, or global status to suggest rethinking of its quest for economic and military supremacy. A costly warfare state is now a taken-for-granted feature of American life, its risks and burdens readily absorbed by a mostly willing public. In this universe, global resource wars are bound to aggravate systemic failures, resulting in an even more dangerously militarized world.

While challenges mount, anti-system groups, movements, and parties are difficult to locate across the global terrain. One roadblock is the very character of the world system – an increasingly globalized and rationalized power structure, beyond anything explored by Marx and Engels, Marcuse, or even Mills. Still another problem goes to the very all-encompassing character of modern domination, and the commensurate need for a more complex, multifaceted, and expansive political opposition.

Ecological Suicide?

As the concluding sections of this book are being written (Spring 2020), the specter of global catastrophe looms ever larger – not only from intensifying ecological crisis, but as a failure of politics. While the familiar historical alternatives have clearly exhausted their potential, new models have yet to fill the void. Theoretical visions have been set forth here and there, but the dominant economic and political forces of our time still conduct business as if little has changed. Faith in an ensemble of technological and "free-market" solutions persists across the ideological spectrum, such as it is. It might be argued that we are heading full speed ahead toward ecological suicide. This fearsome prospect is heightened once we consider not only the enormity of the present challenge but the vast difficulty of creating a new way – in the first place, taking on the most powerful ruling stratum in history. However daunting, that stratum is entirely too destructive and unsustainable to survive much longer.

What must be at the center of any future global transformation is a *conversion* process bringing into play multiple spheres of change: economic, cultural, and ecological, as well as political, a breadth and complexity of struggle largely absent from earlier models of change. The closest was no doubt the European Greens, reflected especially in the writings of its leaders and theorists. Here Bahro, writing in *Socialism and Survival,* argued that a growing mood of historical urgency would sooner or later bring to the fore new radical departures: "I believe this conversion is possible, because now humanity feels threatened in its drive for self-preservation." A new vision of what is possible, and how to achieve it "can suddenly take hold of millions – tomorrow or the day after – and expand the horizon of political possibility overnight. Relatively small or medium catastrophes will not fail to remind us how near the hour is." Bahro added: "We must gradually paralyze everything that goes in the old direction: military installations and motorways, nuclear power stations and airports, chemical factories and big hospitals, supermarkets and education works … We must live differently in order to survive!"[476] Time will reveal whether Bahro's optimism was justified, but early returns are hardly promising.

A worsening global crisis today requires the kind of radical political alternative scarcely considered within earlier oppositional movements and parties, when ecological priorities mattered little. Nowadays, when those priorities are more imperative across the industrialized world, distinctly *political* responses are weak if not invisible, again with partial exception of the 1980s European Greens, which have suffered the logic of deradicalization. Political futility is accompanied by an ideological narrowness among what might be broadly labeled green tendencies: failure to address the challenge of shrinking natural resources, growth mania, population pressures, militarism and wars, animal-based agriculture and the meat complex. Given this expansive void, it is worth asking how any far-reaching ecological transformation might presently be achieved.

One noteworthy example of the contemporary impasse can be found in Naomi Klein's widely-praised *This Changes Everything* – a book filled with environmental information and enlightened hopes but largely devoid of an ecological politics.[477] Klein, to her credit, does set forth a radical critique of modern capitalism, which she identifies as the underlying cause of climate change and associated problems. She urges a shift toward a new developmental model aligned with ecologically sustaining priorities and norms. She recognizes some of the massive obstacles blocking such change, including the conservative role played by Big Green – those reformist organizations and lobbies discussed elsewhere.[478] She reveals a healthy opposition to fancy technological schemes, as well as "free-market fundamentalism". Meanwhile, Klein keenly deconstructs familiar efforts at the Heartland Institute and elsewhere to minimize or deny the bulk of global-warming scientific evidence, mostly funded by corporate interests.[479]

The difficulties with Klein's ambitious work, assisted by a team of full-time researchers, are numerous, glaring, and impossible to ignore. Like many environmentalists today, her work is essentially fixated on global warming, here pegged to worst-case scenarios that do not actually mesh with many long-term climate models. Virtually everything else having profound ecological ramifications is either overlooked or mentioned just in passing. When it comes to politics, there is little in Klein's lengthy account that even vaguely points to a way out of the crisis; the motif of radical change is never concretized, never given ideological, organizational, or strategic definition. The closest her writing veers toward politics is a discussion of local protests to block oil pipelines, called "Blockadia". These actions are laudable enough, but in themselves never transcend the confines of spontaneism and localism where small, often isolated struggles will scarcely make a dent in either corporate or governmental power. At best "Blockadia" represents a set of limited tactics that could help energize larger movements from time to time. Tellingly, there is no mention of Greens or indeed any other movement or party experiences.

When the focus turns to economics, Klein does no better: a concrete alternative to the unsustainable capitalist model never emerges from more than 500 pages of dense text. How might a developmental path embedded in ecological principles take shape? What might be a radical, ecological approach to rampant economic growth? Would a new ecological framework follow some variant of historically understood socialist economics, however framed? Could there be some hope for revitalization of the European Green alternative? Or a move in the direction of ecosocialism? Unfortunately, Klein has no answer to such questions. Her facile critique of "free-market fundamentalism" could offer a hint, but this reference is entirely misleading insofar as there is nothing "free-market" driven about globalized corporate-state capitalism today. Klein's discussion lacks historical grounding and therefore fails to advance any sort of ecological agenda.

Problems worsen once we encounter Klein's myopia on the topics of agriculture and food. She does argue for important change, including a shift toward local, family-based, organic farming, including agroecology, that would favor democratic controls.[480] She concedes that the "global food system" accounts for between 19 and 29 percent of greenhouse emissions, but strangely never gets around to mentioning that those figures relate almost exclusively to animal-based agriculture.[481] In fact, Klein ignores that crucial problem altogether; the devastating meat industry never figures in her account. Nor do issues associated with agribusiness and the McDonaldized food regimen. How far can Klein's environmental reforms go without taking into account the impact of food production on the ecological crisis? At this point one is inclined to revisit Howard Lyman's famous injunction: anyone refusing to confront the global meat complex is simply not being serious about saving the environment.

These debilitating voids in Klein's work point to general deficiencies of so much environmental (and progressive) thinking in American society today. Liberal Democrats, for their part, have come to embrace virtually every sector of the establishment: Wall Street, Big Pharma, the Pentagon, deep state, an imperial foreign policy built on military supremacy and regime change. These same Democrats, with all their enlightened rhetoric, offer little beyond a greening of capitalism. Meanwhile, the power structure takes on increasingly oligarchic, authoritarian, and globalized properties that render fundamental change ever more difficult. Electoral politics as such appears to be in serious decline, hardly a source of radical intervention. Congress has been rendered impotent on the most pressing issues, corporate interests dominate the public terrain, the military-industrial complex gains new leverage, and the destructive food industry expands with few impediments. To the extent liberals and progressives wind up trapped in this political morass, radical alternatives are nullified. Klein's book offers no way out of the morass.

In the third decade of the twenty-first century, counterforces face more obstacles than was the case for earlier movements and parties. In the U.S., "resistance" to the Trump presidency after the 2016 elections was nothing more than a partisan charade driven by Democratic party schemers, Clintonites looking for revenge, neocon warmongers, deep-state operatives, and a vengeful corporate media. They waged a campaign, futile as it turns out, that sought to destroy Trump as a Putin agent or "asset". American political culture had sunk so low that this bloc of powerful fanatics could somehow be described as "the left". Their "progressivism" generally went no further than a scolding, smear-mongering form of identity politics.

In reality American society since the 1970s has witnessed little in the way of durable oppositional tendencies. Popular movements – antiwar, "anti-globalization", environmental, immigrant rights, the Occupy protests – have exhibited a pattern of rapid emergence and equally rapid decline, leaving behind in each outpouring a cycle of fading activism. There has been nothing resembling a "social bloc" of anti-system movements that might give substance to a much-needed ecological radicalism, or ecosocialism. That potential has surfaced only at the level of theory.

As throughout history, a dynamic and sustained response to imminent catastrophe lies squarely in the *political* coalescence of insurgent struggles aligned with oppositional tendencies; there are no short-cuts or easy fixes. To be sure, legacies from the recent past can be revisited and utilized – Marxism, new social movements, Green politics, social ecology – but a new synthesis will require levels of organizational and ideological cohesion, not to mention political strategy, so far lacking across the globe. At this juncture the enduring symbols of "red" and "green", representing socialism and ecology, can no longer appear in hostile opposition but as complementary traditions, part of a vibrant radicalism equal to the task of wresting power from perhaps the most dangerous elite stratum in history. There will be no rapid or easy departure, much less "exit", from modern capitalist society or the world system it has built, only the potential to socialize, democratize, and ecologically restructure the global order, and soon.

Conclusion:

Ecosocialism – or Catastrophe

If global catastrophe seems imminent, the sharpening ecological fissures of global capitalism will be decisive – yet a case can be made that the *political* challenge looms just as large. The first imperative is to merge ecology and politics, natural relations and social transformation, at a time when the feared Tipping Point of planetary survival approaches. To speak of "politics" under these worsening conditions calls forth the need for anti-system change: a transformative ideology, dynamic leadership and organization, resources for mass mobilization, cohesive strategy, a goal of winning governmental power. So far, unfortunately, the legacy of oppositional politics in modern society allows little room for optimism: wherever one turns, no anti-system movements or parties are visible. As for the U.S., leading superpower with a huge environmental footprint, the country has the leverage and resources (not to mention *obligation*) to assume world leadership in reversing the crisis. We face a power structure, however, that will struggle mightily to block such a reversal. Meanwhile, time is running perilously short.

One intractable problem is that an oligarchic, globalized system cannot be reformed or fully "greened" from within existing parameters of governance. Meanwhile, political options narrow as threats appear increasingly ominous. As I argued earlier, radical opposition will have to gain momentum if humanity is to survive. Resistance to the corporate-growth regime has so far mainly taken the form of either liberal reformism or localized grassroots struggles. No groups, movements, or parties have yet managed to advance radical-ecological agendas with broad mass support – the one brief and partial exception being the early 1980s European Greens. Matters worsen once we take into account the futility of historical models: social democracy as institutionalized loyal opposition, Leninism as vehicle of authoritarian party-state, anarchism or syndicalism as recipe for political isolation and impotence, liberalism as tepid (and obsolete) reformism. The 1980s Green synthesis did inspire hope for a transformative politics unifying electoral activity and grassroots movements, but that soon followed the social-democratic path of ideological moderation.[482]

One challenge facing humanity is to reinvigorate politics before irreversible catastrophe arrives. At present there are literally thousands of community groups, local movements, environmental organizations, lobbies, and think tanks scattered across the globe, a possible launching point for any future radical change. Youth have become climate activists in large numbers. Yet few of these efforts are prepared to take on the corporate-state fortress. The extent to which widely dispersed oppositional forces become politicized will determine our capacity to stave off ecological decline and, ultimately, collapse. Among many roadblocks is the increasing absorption of most nation-states into the orbit of international capital, a locus of astronomical wealth and resources.

Oppositional activity, to be transformative, will sooner or later have to gravitate toward some variant of ecosocialist politics. While American society has experienced the proliferation of local groups and movements since the 1960s, few of these groups and movements follow anything resembling an anti-system trajectory. In recent decades the concept of ecosocialism has gained intellectual if not political currency – first, within European Green Party debates and then among progressive circles elsewhere. Since the 1980s many theorists have made the case for some type of "red-green" convergence: Rudolf Bahro, Murray Bookchin, Barry Commoner, Joel Kovel, Michael Lowy, John Bellamy Foster, Chris Williams, Harry Magdoff, Victor Wallis among others.

Calling for an "ecosocialist revolution", Magdoff and Williams (in *Creating an Ecological Society*) argue for an egalitarian, democratic, sustainable developmental model – the best and perhaps only hope to avoid planetary catastrophe.[483] In Foster's view, the global crisis can only be reversed through a series of popular uprisings "transgressing the boundaries between humanity and the planet."[484] The vision is a political-strategic merger of oppositional forces similar to what fueled earlier twentieth-century leftist parties and states. In *Ecology and Socialism,* Williams envisions "gigantic systemic change" whereby people "collectively and democratically make all decisions based on human need, not corporate profits."[485]

Victor Wallis, in *Red-Green Revolution,* sees new mobilizing potential in an ecosocialist strategy that, however, is currently lacking a mass base. He writes: "Ecosocialism – the synthesis of ecology and socialism – has enormous potential to inspire a majoritarian political movement [as] ... the ecological and socialist goals could hardly be more compatible in principle."[486] That synthesis could become more explosive as symptoms of the crisis worsen, Wallis adding: "Ecological struggles ... are vital not only for the sake of our collective long-term survival but also, more immediately, as offering a unifying theme around which movements representing various specific oppressed constituencies can come together."[487] Any embrace of ecosocialism leads directly to the question of political strategy: will change be the province of a Leninist vanguard party, social-democratic reformism, anarchist insurrection, a Green "synthesis" – or what? Reliance on the spontaneity of dispersed social movements is destined, as in the past, to bring political formlessness, atomization, and futility. Deep flaws associated with both Leninism and social democracy – neither ultimately supportive of an ecological politics – have been discussed more fully in earlier chapters.

In the early 1980s it was Green party leaders (Bahro, Petra Kelly, Rainer Trampert) who began laying the foundations of an anti-system ecological politics. Despite later problems, those initial articulations of Green radicalism might even today be viewed as something of a template for a transformative political strategy. Joel Kovel was one ecosocialist who even later retained faith in Green party-building, an alternative that hoped to avoid the pitfalls, alternatively, of Leninism, social democracy, liberalism, and anarchism. He writes: "The general model of ecosocialist development is to foster the activity potentials of ensembles [social blocs] in order to draw together those points into even more dynamic bodies [parties]."[488]

The road ahead must encounter the great advantages of wealth, power, and resources that ruling elites possess and will surely defend at all costs. We know that elite power is legitimated through the media, popular culture, advertising, and educational structures across the public landscape. Here Antonio Gramsci wrote that the consensual underpinnings of capitalist power structures were shaped in great measure by capitalist rationalization ("Fordism" or "Americanism"), driven by new types of bureaucratic and technological control.[489] This broadening matrix of power and its legitimation functions to repel or neutralize potential counter-forces is visible probably nowhere more than in postwar American society. Opposition has rarely achieved substantial anti-system leverage: even mass Communist parties, as in Italy and France, long ago ended up thoroughly deradicalized, the result mainly of immersion in electoral politics. Leftist movements and parties have repeatedly absorbed central features of the corporate-state system – economic growth, profit maximization, consumerism, exploitation of nature, and more. As for agribusiness and the fast-food industry, little opposition has come from either the traditional left or mainstream environmental organizations.

Popular resistance to change is nowhere more tenacious than in the realm of food consumption. The destructive impact of agribusiness and the fast-food complex increases yearly, as meat and dairy intake rises parallel to increasing levels of affluence. As emphasized previously, this is entirely unsustainable: the global meat industry accounts for as much as 40 percent of total greenhouse emissions (up to 50 percent, by some estimates). With a projected world population of between 9.2 and ten billion people by 2050, agriculture will be unable to meet projected demand even with moderate reductions in meat and dairy production. Intense pressures on arable land, soil, water resources, oceans, urban infrastructures, and atmospheric supports will easily overwhelm the capacity of natural-support systems to keep pace. The result will be spreading famine, malnutrition, and poverty, along with intensifying resource wars, further climate deterioration, and social breakdown conducive to failed states, civic violence, and warfare.

The meat complex itself continues to expand seemingly without limits, as dietary patterns follow their own insular logic – impervious to ongoing social and ecological harm. Calls to reduce meat intake are met with derision, within and outside mainstream culture. The argument that animal-foods production might contribute to environmental decline is met with blind skepticism, at times hysterical denunciation, in the face of scientific evidence. Never-ending American election campaigns scarcely mention the relevance of agriculture and food to societal and environmental health. Vast advertising and marketing operations, reinforced by well-funded lobbies armed with bogus research, are there to ensure meat and dairy products remain highly profitable. Worldwide meat intake has risen from 50 million tons in 1950 to 310 million tons in 2014 to a projected 350 million tons in 2020 – this on a planet where one-third of all arable land has already been over-used or otherwise impaired.[490]

The need to jettison dysfunctional corporate farming – including factory farms – is beyond urgent. As population increases by 75 to 80 billion people yearly, the planet's most vital resources (land, soil, water, forests) are already in perilous decline, Tim Benton commenting: "Ultimately, we live on a finite planet, with finite resources. It is a fiction to imagine there is a technological solution allowing us to produce as much food as we might ever want, allowing us to overeat and throw food away."[491] To "overeat" mainly refers here to unsustainable meat and dairy foods – not "carbs" or "processed foods", as media fiction would have it.

In what has become something akin to a marriage of Marx and Weber, the economy of food production and its marketing supports has grown more thoroughly commodified and technologically rationalized – in other words, at conflict with healthful, safe, and sustainable outcomes. In their book *Food, Politics, and Society*, Alejandro Colas and colleagues write: "The food system ... moves ever further away from nature and natural ways of living and becomes fully embedded in the social and economic processes that have denaturalized the modern world."[492] Strangely, however, the authors have little to say about the consequences of meat and dairy consumption in a book spanning nearly 400 pages.

The food crisis, as previously indicated, is tightly interwoven with many challenges: rampant economic growth, population pressures, urbanization, resource limits, overburdened public infrastructures, global warming. A revealing 2018 study published in the British journal *Lancet* underscores this point, calling on governments to restructure food systems and alter their marketing operations.[493] Comprised of 43 public health experts from 14 countries, the *Lancet* Commission on Obesity found that linked problems of obesity, malnutrition, and climate change are simultaneously driven by overconsumption, unregulated marketing of harmful foods, and lack of adequate social policy. The role here of meat and dairy consumption, while noted, is again sadly downplayed – no doubt in deference to the enormous clout of the giant meat complex.

Authors of the *Lancet* report see impending global disaster, including severe food shortages, in the absence of an important shift in consumption patterns. As of 2020, roughly two billion people worldwide were seriously overweight. That number was on the rise, especially across industrialized nations, despite well-known health risks explored in previous chapters. To date no modern society has seen any reversal of this trajectory, any serious decline in meat and dairy intake. At the other extreme, chronic malnutrition afflicts nearly a billion people globally, and that figure too is on the increase. The very same food system that perpetuates both extremes also spells disaster for the prospects of ecological balance.

Given this stubborn reality, the *Lancet* study boldly calls for an international treaty, similar to those on climate change, to curb the damage inflicted by giant food corporations – a centerpiece of this book. One recommendation, aside from a list of educational projects, is to remove more than five trillion dollars in government subsidies from animal-food products, then redirect those funds toward green alternatives including plant-based foods. That suggests far-reaching change, however, of the sort the authors seem hesitant to endorse. Even within existing class and power relations, however, a dramatic shift toward healthier, more ecologically friendly foods will make an enormous difference. Obstacles to such change, however, are revealed by the limited attention given the *Lancet* report and its expert advice, which first appeared in 2011. One author lamented that "barely any of these recommendations have been implemented in more than a handful of countries".[494] Efforts to promote higher intake of fruits, vegetables, and nuts while cutting back on meat and dairy consumption have repeatedly failed, as global trends amply reflect. The livestock industry, among others, had fiercely opposed the report findings. Others have referred to the *Lancet* authors and supporters as "nanny-state zealots" and "food fascists".

Congruent with the spiraling ecological crisis, food problems are increasingly visible across the globe, the threat no longer relegated to a distant future. The onset of severe droughts, for example, is now more widely felt than commonly believed. Vast regions of Pakistan have been overcome by extreme dryness, reflecting loss of rain and depleted water tables. Lacking adequate water and arable land, food production declines, posing renewed threats to human and animal survival across a widening terrain. Poverty, hunger, environmental blight, and health problems are reaching a point of humanitarian disaster. In Baluchistan province more than 60 percent of inhabitants no longer have access to safe drinking water, and very little land is being cultivated. Unfortunately, in the midst of such horrors, the Pakistan government appears close to helpless, its resources drastically stretched.[495] And Pakistan, a nation of 180 million people and growing, is hardly alone: similar drought-fueled calamities have befallen large sectors of India, China, and Africa, with no improvement in sight.

Writing in *World on the Edge*, Lester Brown comments: "We are liquidating the earth's natural assets to feed our consumption. Half of us live in countries where water tables are falling and wells are going dry. Soil erosion exceeds soil formation on one-third of the world's cropland ... No previous civilization has survived the ongoing destruction of its natural supports. Nor will ours." Sadly, however, the political and media establishment views the matter differently, Brown adding: "In the eyes of mainstream economists, the world has not only an illustrious economic past but also a promising future."[496]

By 2020 a total of 29 countries, including much of Europe and the Middle East, had experienced their hottest years on record, according to both the National Aeronautical and Space Administration (NASA) and the National Oceanic and Atmospheric Administration (NOAA).[497] Researchers attribute this trend to increased greenhouse gases, along with unsustainable pressures on global resources. NASA climatologist Gavin Schmidt observes that "It's the long-term trends that are having impacts on ice, on the severity of droughts, on heat waves, on sea-level rise, and wildfires."[498] For the U.S., 13 federal agencies found in 2018 that climate change was already bringing severe harm to the national environment, health, and economy. President Trump's response has been to effectively stonewall such warnings.

With each passing year, the crisis raises ever more urgently the question of whether some kind of "Green New Deal" should become central to the political agenda, similar to that proposed by British Labor in 2015. Such far-reaching initiatives would mean assembling material, technological, and human resources at "wartime levels", a Promethean effort to stave off global catastrophe. Such environmental Keynesianism assumes a long-term "greening" of capitalism is in fact possible, theoretically as prelude to a post-carbon society. I have argued in earlier chapters that full-scale reversal of the global crisis can never succeed while corporate-state interests rule the landscape – that is, the very interests responsible for unsustainable modes of production and consumption.

By 2019 environmental priorities had entered American public discourse sufficiently to advance hopes for a Green New Deal that many Democrats embraced as a centerpiece of the anti-Trump "resistance". (see the Postscript.) That stratagem would in fact become rather fashionable in elite circles, championed by the mainstream media following a heralded 2018 proposal by New York Rep. Alexandria Ocasio-Cortez to rebuild the American economy, trillions of dollars to be invested in sustainable forms of energy. The aim was a "greenhouse-gas neutral society" by 2030, though both methods and resources were left somewhat vaguely defined. The "greening" process would surpass incremental reforms to involve sweeping changes in the capitalist economy, no small leap but not quite the "socialism" celebrated (or feared) by many Beltway politicians. Several Democratic presidential candidates, including Bernie Sanders, would later take up the Ocasio-Cortez plan, offering some new details discussed more fully in the Postscript. Conservatives predictably branded the Green New Deal a "job-killing, socialist wish list" destined to bankrupt the American economy; no Republicans joined the campaign.

However framed, some variant of a Green New Deal is bound to enter the political landscape of industrialized societies looking to escape the worst symptoms of the crisis. In the absence of an ecosocialist alternative, ruling elites in the U.S., Europe, and Asia can be expected to adopt greening agendas heavily reliant on technological innovation – in part to help speed capitalist rationalization, in part to avoid systemic collapse. Such costly plans will differ from country to country, yet reforms by their very nature will inevitably be partial, limited, insufficient. In the U.S. any radical model will be fiercely opposed by leading sectors of the power structure including Wall Street, agribusiness, Big Pharma, fossil fuels, technology, and the military. Those interests possess many trillions of dollars in wealth and resources, including endless supplies of oil, gas, and coal with increasingly refined methods (e.g., fracking) to extract them.

As the global neoliberal order expands, ideals associated with classical liberalism – individualism, freedom, rights, democracy – become rather obscured, especially as the dominant corporate system affirms no values beyond growth and profits, their trajectory in conflict with reigning ethical, social, and ecological tenets. There is little resembling "higher values", only crude instrumental rationality, recalling Mills' famous reference to the "higher immorality" of American ruling elites. In his words: "Within the corporate worlds of business, warmaking, and politics, the private conscience is attenuated – and the higher immorality is institutionalized."[499]

The neoliberal behemoth will eventually have to be overturned if ecological catastrophe is to be averted; there is no alternative path, no shortcut. To imagine such a challenge in a political-strategic vacuum is to indulge the unthinkable – yet that is exactly where we stand. As capitalist globalization solidifies its reach, the power elite coexists with vast regions of material poverty, social atomization, and disempowerment – hardly optimum conditions for effective political opposition. In American society, where Enlightenment "progress" is routinely celebrated, the dystopic side of modernity generates social decline and ecological ruin while anti-system politics faces new obstacles. A media culture saturated with advertising, consumerism, and violent escapism – and protracted election spectacles – only heightens the challenge.

It was Mills who, writing in the *Power Elite* several decades ago, depicted an American power structure with nearly unchallenged control over a "mass society" mired in despair and impotence, worsened by the hovering role of a military-industrial complex and security-state. Liberal ideals had been transformed into a series of mostly empty rituals.[500] A few years later, Marcuse, writing in *One-Dimensional Man*, would arrive at much the same conclusion, by a different route: industrialized society, with the spread of technological rationality, had given rise to a system of "total domination" that subverted oppositional tendencies at every turn.[501] For both Mills and Marcuse, that was the (intolerable) price of material and technological expansion under corporate rule. The intervening decades have witnessed the episodic rise and decline of popular struggles, but little in the form of durable anti-system movements or parties. The deeply realistic outlook of Mills and Marcuse, carried forward in the later work of Sheldon Wolin and Chris Hedges, seems more painfully relevant today.[502]

The challenge ahead seems nearly insurmountable at a time when scientific warnings of imminent ecological disaster are more amplified with each new report. In most industrial countries environmental groups and organizations have proliferated, many striving for institutional clout. In *Red-Green Revolution*, as mentioned previously, Wallis argues that ecological struggles, while driven by a goal of long-term survival, simultaneously provide a unifying theme for social movements to come together.[503] This recalls Gramsci's famous "social bloc" concept, which underpinned rise of the European Green parties and their "gathering of social movements". Yet neither the Greens nor other kindred political groups have been able to build a radical opposition in Europe or elsewhere—a task made all the more formidable in the age of postmodern identity politics.

The scenario thickens when *global* dimensions of the ecological crisis are taken into account: no territorial boundaries or national limits pertain to the natural habitat, or indeed to transnational corporate interests at work. Reflecting many years ago on the nascent Green experience, Bahro wrote: "The greatest present problem – i.e., the ecology crisis in which all the contradictions of the prevailing mode of production and way of life, all the dangers of the world situation intersect and coalesce – can by its very nature not be grasped at the level of the national state."[504] Put differently, an ecological politics could never be the mechanism of radical transformation when approached as a strictly *national* project; it would have to be simultaneously global. Unfortunately, many current ideological fashions – multiculturalism, identity politics, populist nationalism – serve to force potential oppositional tendencies in another direction.

Leaving aside such non-binding mechanisms as the Paris Accords, major initiatives will be the province of nation-states well into the future – starting with the most powerful industrialized countries. Yet, while the U.S. exerts the largest carbon footprint among nations, its capacity to reshape the planetary terrain is more limited than generally believed. China will soon have the world's largest economy, as noted, but other nations will experience rapid growth in coming decades, at least until natural-support limits are felt. India, Japan, the EU, Russia, and many developing nations are projected to double or even triple their GDPs in coming decades. With vastly-enlarged footprint, their capacity (and willingness) to fight global warming will be decisive, especially since binding international agreements are currently nowhere in sight.

Global efforts could end up futile if significant contributors to the footprint fail or refuse to maintain high levels of greening through ambitious fossil-fuel reductions. In fact, just two or three major holdouts could interrupt serious multinational efforts to reverse the crisis. We have seen that both China and India are projected to have a combined GDP of nearly $80 trillion by 2030, so their future patterns of resource utilization will be absolutely crucial. Meanwhile, what about such countries as Indonesia, South Korea, Mexico, and Brazil – all rapidly-growing economies? When Brazilian rainforest fires rage by the hundreds, as in summer 2019, the amount of carbon released could nullify the best efforts of more developed nations to decarbonize. Here Wallace-Wells comments: "To the extent the world as a whole needs a stable climate to endure or thrive, its fate will be determined much more by the carbon trajectories of the developing world than by the course of the U.S. and Europe, where emissions have already flattened out ... " [505]

What is required here is an entirely *new form* of globalization, no longer corporate, no longer dominated by a single power, no longer militarized and subject to intense resource wars. "The idea of a 'global order', writes Wallace-Wells, "has always been something of a fiction, or at least an aspiration, and American hegemony inched us toward it over the last century. Very probably, over the next century, climate change will reverse that course."[506] His judgment seems on the mark, though instead of "next century" we should be referring to the "next couple of decades".

Meanwhile, advanced technology – key source of green energy alternatives – runs up against its own set of barriers. Technological change was historically linked to capitalist rationalization, a dynamic fully intact today, now more within the orbit of the Internet and Silicon Valley giants. Twentieth-century theorists (Weber, Gramsci, Marcuse) called attention to the deeply ideological, or hegemonic, properties of modern technology, whether in the realms of production, bureaucracy, the workplace, or everyday life. Systemic development in itself imposes definite limits on prospects for technological solutions. At the same time, a crucial function of modern technology has been surveillance, which has come to threaten personal and social autonomy while narrowing space for political dissent. The U.S. national security-state, built on a confluence of corporate, state, and military power, long ago reached Orwellian levels. An historic assemblage of tech behemoths – Microsoft, Google, Facebook, Amazon, Twitter, Apple, etc. – comprises perhaps the largest economic oligopoly the world has ever seen, its high-tech apparatus a menace to the rise of oppositional movements.

In *No Place to Hide,* Glenn Greenwald writes: "… it is in the realm of privacy where creativity, dissent, and challenges to orthodoxy germinate. A society in which everyone knows they can be watched by the state – where the private realm is effectively eliminated – is one in which those attributes are lost at both the societal and individual levels."[507] Here the most sophisticated forms of digital technology, artificial intelligence, and robotics constitute the most powerful tools for controlling human behavior, Greenwald adding: "The danger posed by the state operating a massive secret surveillance system is far more ominous now than at any point in history."[508] That system includes not only governments, of course, but corporations, banks, universities, medical systems, and the military. Even Marcuse, known for his concept of "one dimensionality" associated with the specter of total domination, never fully anticipated the authoritarian thrust of such an enlarged power structure.

As noted, earlier political traditions could never sustain a durable anti-system radicalism, even as world capitalism generated crisis after crisis. Meanwhile, the institutional, material, and ideological resources available to ruling elites have expanded dramatically since World War II. As the ecological threat sharpens, the need for political-strategic definition will be impossible to sidestep or finesse; radical change never unfolds organically or spontaneously. If direct assault on the fortresses of power is bound to fail under present conditions, the best hope is probably for a continuous process of systemic delegitimation, equivalent to Gramsci's "war of position" – that is, a cultural revolution against dominant belief-systems laying the groundwork for a decisive "war of movement" where oppositional forces can ascend to state power.[509] To defend its great wealth and power, of course, the power structure will mobilize everything at its disposal, including reform palliatives, greenwashing, electoral promises, false science, and, where all else fails, repression. Once ideological supports begin to erode, however, as in Eastern Europe during the late 1980s, radical change can quickly reshape the political landscape.

What always remains to be determined, however, is the all-important political *direction* of anti-system energies; nothing can be taken for granted, as we know abundantly well from history. Systemic crisis offers no automatic guarantee of a progressive, much less ecosocialist, outcome. Yet as widening contradictions open new space for popular insurgency, prospects heighten for a convergence of movements into a social bloc of forces along lines suggested by Wallis and congruent with an ecosocialist politics. Most of all, any social bloc would have to overcome ubiquitous pre-political tendencies – the pull of spontaneism, localism, identity politics – never an easy challenge.

History shows that political outcomes depend on a unique congruence of social forces, material interests, and collective responses, usually at times of great turbulence. In Italy, for example, the rapid transformation of the Communist Party from a tiny, isolated underground nucleus into a thriving mass organization with more than two million members during the War II anti-fascist Resistance – fueled by war and nationalism – followed this logic. This same dynamic spurred wartime Partisan movements in France, Greece, Czechoslovakia, and Yugoslavia, as well as China and Vietnam. The ideological cement of these social blocs was overwhelmingly *nationalism*, embedded in a common (always multi-class) opposition to hated foreign aggressors (in these cases German, Japanese, or French occupiers).

A period of drastically worsening material hardships and shortages could fit this historical matrix – a catastrophic scenario in fact vaguely predicted by some IPCC scientists and environmentalists. The binding ideology, however, cannot any longer be nationalism as that is nowadays more closely associated with economic populism and reactionary politics. Further, in the case of a superpower like the U.S. nationalism has traditionally been aligned with militarism and imperialism; recent social movements have been more likely to *resist* any resurgent American nationalism. Worth re-stating here is that the ecological crisis is a manifestly *global* challenge, in many ways at odds with nationalist sentiment (or solutions). Any new social bloc, it follows, will probably have to depend on a convergence of material and ecological agendas.

A pressing question arises: can the modern crisis ever generate the kind of ideological convergence, or political synthesis, historically provided by nationalism? For this to occur ecological challenges would likely have to sharpen to the level of disrupting everyday life for millions, perhaps tens or hundreds of millions, of people across the planet. Established patterns of thought and behavior would be questioned, giving rise to a more open, potentially transformative milieu – at present a seemingly remote specter. The ideological terrain to be traversed would be expansive, nowhere more than in the realm of agriculture and food, especially as this deeply intersects with the contours of everyday life.

As I have argued earlier, for any ecosocialist future oppositional forces will have to fully engage the sphere of human-natural relations, beyond (while including) the central domain of production and class relations. The origins of such an outlook – framed as a "red-green revolution" – can be located in the seminal work of Bookchin, Bahro, and other leading figures of left-Green politics during the late 1970s and early 1980s, though its origins go back to the 1960s if not earlier. Against the ideological backdrop of social ecology, Bookchin could write several decades ago: "The success of the revolutionary project must now rest on the emergence of a general [global] human interest that cuts across the particularistic interests of class, nationality, ethnicity, and gender."[510] Lifted into the present setting, Bookchin's ecological radicalism seemed to take for granted the eventual politicization (and coordination) of dispersed social movements, the centrality of natural relations, a focus on multiple forms of domination, and transcendence of narrow identity politics – the very essence of early-1980s European Green politics. Though a partisan of multiculturalism, Bookchin (and the Greens) would have recoiled against the anti-political (and narcissistic) drift of contemporary identity politics.

Marcuse, for his part, came to understand the tight linkage of nature and freedom, ecology and revolution as an underlying dialectic of industrialized society that, in the end, transcended modern capitalism as such.[511] Radical change depended on a steady rise in ecological consciousness – now visible in many societies – at a juncture where systemic conflict moves from a strictly class paradigm to more generalized opposition to the entire corporate-state apparatus. Put differently, Marcuse argued that effective anti-system politics would have to embrace the "*totality* of human existence".[512] Could any phenomenon today be more "totalizing" – more ethically and politically imperative – than the global ecological crisis?

Moving beyond flawed twentieth-century political traditions, the entire field of social conflict and historical agency will have to be revisited and redrawn to meet the new juncture of conditions and forces at work. The ecological sphere has gained a certain political as well as theoretical primacy, but it would be mistaken to assume that either an "ecological liberalism" or "ecological Marxism" is adequate as theoretical guide moving forward. We have seen how social ecology and the left-Green outlook – and now ecosocialism – anticipate a unifying strategy that targets a multifaceted system of domination, appropriate to a phase of politics aligned with a extensive rethinking of natural relations, social movements, and political strategy.

In concluding this book, it would be an unpardonable oversight to ignore what might be considered the broad constituent elements of an ecosocialist strategy. We would start with transition from a fossil-fuel to post-carbon economy: widening use of green technologies aided by generous state subsidies along with gradual phasing out of oil, gas, and coal sources (and their subsidies!) by means of taxation, strict regulations, and more binding environmental controls. Major sectors – industry, agriculture, utilities, urban infrastructures – would be steadily decarbonized toward zero (or near-zero) emissions by 2040, if not sooner. A radicalized Green New Deal would bring this transition into every phase of daily life. An indispensable move would be a shift from private automobiles to more efficient, cheaper, safer, greener modes of public transportation, vital to rebuilding urban (and suburban) landscapes and resources.

All nations – beginning with the most industrialized – would adopt a developmental path of reduced-growth economies of the sort never before entertained by any ruling elite. As discussed earlier, rather comfortable living standards could be maintained even with reduced GDP, cutbacks involving the military and security-state, agriculture (a shift toward localized, agroecological, plant-based farming), insurance and advertising industries, health care (dismantling vast layers of bureaucracy and profit-making), and more. It is possible that the GDP of industrialized societies could be reduced by *half* without significant decline in living standards, especially if wealth redistribution is achieved.

A reduced-growth economy requires stewards of national economies to maximize efficiency beyond the familiar claims of those who manage capitalist rationalization. Lester Brown writes: "Beyond energy-saving technologies, vast amounts of energy can be saved by restructuring key sectors of the economy. Designing cities for people, not for cars, is a great place to begin. And if we can move beyond the throwaway society, reusing and recycling almost everything, imagine how much material and energy we can save."[513] He adds: "The opportunities to save energy are everywhere, permeating every corner of the economy, every facet of our lives, and every country. Exploiting this abundance of wasted energy will allow the world to actually increase total energy use over the next decade."[514] We will learn soon enough the extent to which Brown's optimism is well-founded.

An historic transition to a plant-based food system – centerpiece of this book – would accelerate progress toward a post-carbon society while better preserving such resources as land, water, forests, soil, and oceans. The result would be healthier populations, meaning a system far less burdened with medical and drug costs. Not least, it would help resist the dreadful assault on biodiversity across the globe, restore forests and oceans, and re-balance human-natural relations.

Such drastic overhauling of food systems is too often neglected as an ecological priority, partly because of reluctance to insult billions of people habituated to meat and dairy products, partly owing to preoccupation with climate change. We have reached a point where the food challenge, itself deeply interwoven with global warming, can no longer be dismissed. Transforming this sector (actually *many* sectors) cuts across virtually area of human and nonhuman life, including carbon footprint. Writing in *Consortium News*, Ronnie Cummins observes: "If regenerative food, farming, and land use ... are just as essential to our survival as moving beyond fossil fuels, why aren't more people talking about this? Why is it that moving beyond industrial agriculture, factory farms, agro-exports, and highly-processed junk foods to regenerating soils and forests and drawing down enough excess carbon from the atmosphere to re-stabilize our climate is getting so little attention from the media, politicians, and the general public?" [515]

A problem that receives even less attention than agriculture and food is the military, despite its obvious connection to geopolitical conflict and resource wars. At this historical moment an ecosocialist future seems inconceivable without drastic moves toward demilitarization, starting with the U.S. and other major powers. Every nation would reduce its military force to levels appropriate only to national defense; foreign bases would be dismantled as archaic, costly, destructive. Nuclear disarmament would be set in motion, based on principles of universality. In this renovated milieu, nations would have no need for international deployments, imperial expansion, arms races, resource wars, or space militarization. The material, technological, and human resources saved here, in just one year, would be inestimable. Sprawling corporate-military complexes, where the business of war means super profits for big business, would be extensively dismantled. Worldwide armed-forces reductions of this sort would bring an immediate three to four-percent decline in carbon footprint – and, of course, heightened prospects for peace.

Looking toward an ecological politics, the all-consuming issue of technology would need to be addressed. In this book I have been largely critical of the historical role played by technological rationality, a pervasive ideology long integral to the process of capitalist rationalization. It is surely worth asking whether advanced technology in its different modalities might be turned around and utilized in the service of developmental sustainability. There is surely every reason to embellish "technology" as a resource to fight off catastrophe, perhaps as part of some grand technological fix. We know that a variety of green technologies have already done much to reduce carbon emissions, having been adopted more widely across industry, transportation, and everyday life.

Still more ambitious schemes abound – including designs to remove vast amounts of carbon from the atmosphere through geoengineering, although this so far commands relatively little in resources, funding, and indeed practicality. There are projects to cool the Earth by injecting microscopic sulfate aerosols into the stratosphere, others to spray sea salt into the air to make clouds more reflective, yet others to station large mirrors into orbit. Even where possibly viable at some point in the future, such technologies would eliminate just one or two symptoms of the ecological crisis. They would also be time-consuming, would demand a cumbersome decision-making process, and would require complex global decision-making processes (itself both politically and economically intricate). With this in mind, Wallace-Wells comments: "Threaded through the reverie for carbon capture is a fantasy of industrial absolution – that a technology could be almost dreamed into being that could purify the ecological legacy of modernity, even perhaps eliminate its footprint entirely."[516]

Back to earth, other carbon-fighting methods utilizing more feasible modes of technology abound, some widely adopted: reforestation, local farming, solar and wind power, electric cars, and other renewables. Ordinary fossil-fuel reductions – along with carbon absorption – have lessened the carbon footprint in such locales as China, Germany, and California. Widespread use of nuclear energy sources, as in France and Russia, could be an aggressive move toward decarbonizing, but in the wake of Chernobyl and Fukushima that alternative seems rather politically taboo, Germany already having set out to remove all of its reactors.

What usually ends up forgotten is that most technological "solutions" have built-in economic constraints and social harms. Alternatives require their own considerable resources, and these include fossil fuels. They can also cover massive expanses of land, especially for solar and wind farms, which incur new environmental problems and threats to wildlife. Even where workable, however, such carbon-reductive methods have so far made little dent in the overall carbon footprint, which of course expands with economic and population growth even as green technology comprises a larger *percentage* of total emissions. This crucial point was effectively dramatized in the 2020 documentary *Planet of the Humans*, directed by Jeff Gibbs. As of 2019, in fact, the world was burning fully 80 percent more oil, gas, and coal than in the year 2000, and no drastic turnaround is projected. In the end, technological advances alone can achieve only so much in a capitalist setting where the old patterns of production and consumption hold sway.

Most crucially, an ecosocialist strategy will depend on full-scale socialization of modern economies, allowing distinctly public criteria to shape decision making. We know from historical experience that the neoliberal global order, ruled by transnational corporations, will forever reproduce the old patterns: endless growth, profit-maximization, consumerism, meat-centered diets, the commodification of everything. That system will never willingly abandon its enormous reliance on oil, gas, and coal, since that would mean leaving many tens of trillions of dollars in fossil fuels unavailable for profits, wealth, and power.

It follows that any transformative Green New Deal would have to be uncompromisingly anti-capitalist: an ecological agenda is not possible where giant corporations and banks dominate the terrain. A full restructuring of agriculture, industry, urban infrastructures, and transportation will face severe obstacles under transnational capitalism. One problem with the widely heralded Green New Deal proposed by Democrats in the U.S. is that no such rupture with capitalism is anticipated, despite the "socialist" claims of many proponents. A "greening" of corporate-state capitalism might delay but will never reverse the crisis. In Lester Brown's words: "We need an economy for the twenty-first century, one that is in sync with the earth and its natural-support systems, not one that is destroying them."[517]

What, then, about the *politics* of an ecosocialist alternative? My preference, as outlined earlier, follows something akin to the ecological radicalism of the early 1980s European Greens, where electoral politics was aligned with a "gathering of the movements", where ecology would be joined with socialism, where radical ideas could have a direct governing impact. Those parties, as we know, quickly fell under the spell of social-democratization as electoral politics came to subsume everything else. Yet that original model, fragile and short-lived as it was, still retains appeal and perhaps viability. Unfortunately, while Greens nowadays retain a broad presence across Europe, none appears close to the original radicalism, or ecosocialism, operating as they do within the main centers of power. Meanwhile, time is running out as the Tipping Point nears.

While ecosocialism appears naturally aligned with democratic politics, time pressures could render seductive some type of Jacobinism – that is, a Leninist vanguard party – deemed capable of engineering radical change with minimum delay. Arriving at some form of ecosocialism would surely involve a protracted historical process, which means humanity and the natural habitat could eventually be left to disastrous consequences. Where electoral politics is involved, time inevitably becomes something of a peripheral concern. A modern Jacobinism would mean an emphatically "authoritarian solution" at a time when democratic norms may seem too partial, too cumbersome, above all too time-consuming. It was Leninism, of course, that orchestrated the great Communist revolutions of the twentieth century, with all their dictatorial, uneven, and socially (also environmentally) problematic consequences. It is highly questionable whether an even a mass-based Leninist variant could succeed today in any industrialized society – and just as questionable regarding what might happen in the aftermath.

What might ultimately favor this strategy is the very global dimension of the challenge: local or national greening here and there could matter little in the long run, especially if the leading polluters are in charge of their own greening. To wait for an ecological revolution spanning nearly 200 countries means having patience for a future that might never arrive. Again, we know from a series of IPCC warnings that the window for altering the present doomsday trajectory could be more limited than generally believed. With this in mind, Geoff Mann and Joel Wainwright have written *Climate Leviathan*, invoking prospects of a (Thomas) Hobbesian-style sovereign able to resolutely engage the planetary threat.[518] Decisive intervention might bring quick results, negating the role of any messy democratic politics. The question here is whether mass populations – especially those accustomed to some form of electoral participation – might be ready to give up advantages of a democratic political culture in order to "save the planet". If so, that would ultimately vitiate an ideological core (democracy) long considered fundamental to ecological theory and practice.

Though ecologically oriented, Mann and Wainwright appear to have taken a more pessimistic turn – dedicated to locating a political strategy, yet despairing of any conceivable "solution" to the crisis. Their approach makes many assumptions, starting with realization that the Tipping Point has indeed already arrived, that disaster is imminent insofar as no serious carbon-mitigation efforts have been internationally adopted or will likely be adopted in the next few decades. Thus: "The possibility of rapid, global carbon mitigation as a climate-change abatement strategy has passed." The only option today is *adaptation.*[519] In part this is a function of expanded, transnational elite power where those controlling the world economy remain out of touch, insulated from the horrors surrounding them.

A closely related problem is that of democracy. As the deepening ecological crisis raises the specter of a new Dark Age, that would seem to favor an authoritarian political trajectory congruent with either a Hobbesian or Jacobin-type rule. The other side of this dynamic is that, from the viewpoint of Mann and Wainwright, liberal democracy has thoroughly exhausted its potential: "Democracy as we know it ... seems profoundly inadequate to the problems that lie ahead, and to imagine that democracy in another form is going to fix things takes what many might justifiably see as an increasingly ludicrous leap of faith."[520] Put differently, it would be a mistake to believe that mass publics (or large voting blocs) will engage seemingly remote planetary issues like climate change with the requisite sense of radical urgency. This problem is can only be compounded within a turbulent global setting.

To be sure, the historical record of liberal democracy (or liberal reform-ism), as noted, has been rather dismal. The lesson might be, as Mann and Wainwright suggest, that radical politics will emanate from the (enlight-ened) summits of power rather than from an amorphous mass society pacified by the myriad workings of ideological hegemony. We know that popular insurgency can surface from time to time, that social movements can proliferate, that mass mobilization around global issues can take hold – yet we are left with a daunting failure of *political* action. In September 2019, thousands of young students waged a climate strike in many countries across six continents, a prelude to a U.N.-sponsored Youth Climate Sum-mit in New York. The overriding demand was for a worldwide move toward zero-carbon economies – and soon. Argentine activist Bruno Rodriguez said: "Stop the criminal contaminant behavior of big corporations. Enough is enough. We don't want fossil fuels anymore."[521] Such mobilization was a predictable response to spreading climate fear and anxiety. There was much talk of direct action, vegetarianism, entrepreneurial activity, and ecolo-gy-inspired art and poetry.

At the time of the Summit many countries – mostly small and medium sized – pledged to reduce their carbon footprint beyond Paris targets, though these promises were nonetheless rather limited in scope. A few even promised to reach zero-carbon levels within the next decade or so. Unfortunately, none of the major greenhouse contributors followed suit or set forth significant carbon-mitigation plans. In fact several world powers (Japan, Brazil, Australia among them) were absent from the Summit pro-ceedings. Most disturbing, the U.S. under President Trump decided not to participate even as latest reports from the U.N. World Meteorological Organization warned of accelerated consequences from higher levels of carbon emissions. The gathering revealed a wide gulf between protest-ers and world leaders regarding urgency of the crisis. Commented Jake Schmidt of the Natural Resources Defense Council: "World leaders failed to show that they fully understand the crisis and that they stand with young people around the world calling for stronger climate action right now."[522]

Still, it is worth asking: could the gathering youth-driven insurgency mark the beginning of a political breakthrough? Could this kind of psycho-logical awakening on a broad scale wind up translated into more cohesive green movements and parties? As mentioned previously, one powerful obstacle to such change looms in the form of fashionable identity politics, with its fetishization of diversity, pluralism, and localism often coexisting with a deep hostility to politics. Where authoritarian sovereignty (as in China) allows for decisive intervention, mass politics more frequently signifies fragmentation, disunity, and impasse. Taking inspiration from Hobbes or possibly Lenin, the authors reluctantly conclude: "It is a mistake to equate mass politics with radical politics".[523] There is very little in the recent history of liberal democracies to contradict such a contention.

An ideological resistance bred of deeply ingrained behavior – from everyday life to economics and politics – adds to the challenge: habitual patterns of social and cultural life can be extremely difficult to overturn. Promises of repentance and change, even in the midst of crisis, often lead nowhere. One case in point is the great meat addiction: even as alternatives to animal-based food production surface, the vast (and lucrative) McDonalds system has been scarcely disturbed. Democratic candidates for the presidency have begun to champion plant-based diets, yet when campaigning in Iowa joyfully participate in steak and hamburger cook-offs. Another example is plane travel. A moralizing backlash against flying has not been met with any decipherable change in behavior. Long-distance flights can produce up to 100 tons of greenhouse emissions. The general carbon footprint of air travel amounts to between two and five percent of the total, in a context where increased fuel efficiency is more than offset by larger numbers of world air travelers. Enlightened criticism of excessive flying is met with constantly expanding airports and airport space.[524] Old habits do not pass from scene easily.

In the end, any viable oppositional politics will have to be carried out as protracted struggles on multiple fronts, geared to sustainable modes of production, work, consumption, and culture. At the same time, those struggles might unfold at odds with the kind of democratic processes we have come to associate with ecological ideals. Changing established patterns of thought and behavior will involve nothing short of epic personal and social transformations, especially for leading industrial societies where descent into barbarism no longer appears so remote, Wallace-Wells writing: "The threat from climate change is more total than from the bomb. It is also more pervasive." He then adds: "If we allow global warming to proceed, and to punish us with all the ferocity we have fed it, it will be because we have chosen that punishment – collectively walking down a path of suicide. If we avert it, it will be because we have chosen to walk a different path, and endure."[525]

Addendum: The Global Pandemic

In concluding this book, it would be intellectually reckless to ignore the great coronavirus pandemic sweeping the world just as writing (early May 2020) was nearing completion. At a time when the ecological crisis was bringing humanity closer to irreversible disaster, could it be that the pandemic was endowing the crisis with possibly new scope and intensity?

The virus first surfaced in Wuhan, China during December 2019 (possibly earlier), then quickly spread to other parts of Asia, soon after the Middle East, Europe, and North America while some areas of the world were at least temporarily spared. It would carve a wide swath across the globe, exerting untold harm on workers, universities and schools, travel, entertainment and sports, governments, supply chains, and of course both medical and public-health systems. The disease originated either at a wet market where exotic animals were sold or at a virology lab where an experimental virus might have accidentally escaped. Within a few weeks a large region of China was placed on lockdown, with flights into and out of the Wuhan area blocked. Hospital wards filled up as hundreds, then thousands of people were attacked by the virus. Large outbreaks would occur in South Korea, Iran, northern Italy, Spain, and New York state in the U.S. On January 30, the World Health Organization declared a public-health emergency, then six weeks later defined the crisis as a full-blown pandemic.

Not since the Spanish flu epidemic following World War I was the world thrown into such a disease-fueled frenzy, aided by abundant media-driven mass hysteria. From central China to far-flung areas of the world, the virus swept through workplaces, offices, hospitals, public transit, schools, nursing homes, and daily life, leaving behind economic devastation, social chaos, governmental instability, and ultimately massive casualties. Using sophisticated technology, remote work protocols were adopted; lockdowns became the norm, along with a variety of regulatory health practices. Millions of people were sickened, the elderly hit hardest, and children largely spared. Densely populated urban areas (Wuhan, Milan, London, New York City) suffered some of the worst casualties, with hospitals filled to capacity, even beyond, as health-care facilities sometimes ended up as major sources of (nosocomial) disease outbreak.

Facing a citizenry often dazed, suffering, and frightened, governments around the world opened their budgets and doled out large amounts of cash, food, services, and other aid. In the midst of such a crisis austerity concerns routinely vanished. Corporations produced medical supplies, military personnel built hospitals and infrastructure, governments set up ambitious task forces. Many trillions of dollars were spent – and would continue to be spent – hoping somehow to meet an unprecedented set of challenges. Meanwhile, factories closed, offices were left empty, schools were shuttered, sports events were cancelled, many businesses (airlines, hotels, etc.) were decimated. Throughout this ordeal health-care systems in many countries would be overburdened well beyond anything known in recent history.

It was said that, for the U.S. at least, the pandemic rivalled World War II in its sheer degree of civic disruption and public mobilization. Computer modelling had projected virus-related deaths into the millions, though in time such projections were continuously downsized. At the same time, lockdowns meant increasing joblessness and small-business failures, accompanied by expected miseries: poverty, homelessness, addictions, depression, crime, domestic abuse. Especially lengthy stay-at-home policies would obviously exacerbate these miseries. Within a matter of two or three months the pandemic would raise questions about the long-term impact of the disease, public responses to it, and the deepening economic predicament. Could the pandemic turn into something considerably more than a temporary crisis? Could it lead to large-scale transformation of entire societies – for better or worse? Above all, how might this particular crisis intersect with the more general ecological crisis explored in this book?

While it is clearly too soon to proffer generalizations, some preliminary comments seem appropriate, especially where they address topics explored in earlier chapters. As of early May 2020, world casualty rates from the coronavirus totaled nearly three million infected with above 251,000 deaths – figures in fact well short of those from the yearly influenza. Oddly, the most affluent of all nations – the U.S. – was hit by far the hardest: well over one million cases and 75,000 deaths. Particularly striking here is that so many poorer nations – usually those with socialized medicine – fared dramatically better. Thus, as of early May, 2020 we saw the following: Cuba with 1400 cases and 54 deaths, Vietnam with 268 cases and no deaths, Venezuela with 325 cases and 10 deaths, Norway with 7500 cases and 20 deaths, Russia with 87,000 cases and 794 deaths. A more developed country, Japan, had 13,000 cases but just 372 deaths. With only this data, such numbers would seem to be emphatically reflect the quality of medical and public-health services in specific countries – not to mention aggregate national health indicators as measured by the WHO.

For the moment, it is worth calling attention to a motif that pervades this book – the place of animals in modern agriculture, food production, and the global ecology. The most prosperous nations, as we have seen, are generally those with the largest per-capita meat and dairy consumption – the U.S. ranking at or very near the top of this list. The coronavirus, like most other viral infections, is at least an indirect outgrowth of the world meat complex, in this case a sector located in China. In fact, the majority of new diseases impacting humans are "zoonotic", originating in wild (sometimes other) animals before crossing over into humans. The trapping of animals for pets, food, and medicine brings them into close contact with other animals and people. That is precisely what happened in the previous two coronavirus outbreaks – SARS in 2003, MERS in 2012 – where a virus jumped from such creatures as bats, civets, and camels. The HIV virus had also earlier originated in animals. In China, such animal marketing (often under the most horrific conditions) has long been deeply embedded in the economy and culture. It should be added that the animal trade worldwide, including such practices as factory farming and meatpacking, has for many decades contributed to this problem – for example, spread of the Swine flu in 2009.

It is simultaneously true that animal-food consumption severely aggravates virus infections once they develop in humans. The WHO, in its abundant literature has called attention to the importance of co-morbidity factors – obesity, heart disease, diabetes, respiratory problems – in causing severe or fatal reactions. On the whole obese people are six times more likely to succumb to the coronavirus than those with average weight. While the virus registers only mild symptoms (if any) in 80 to 85 percent of all cases, those with chronic diseases are far less likely to escape with minor

problems. The fact that American society has for many decades experienced
very high levels of obesity (currently over 40 percent) makes it especially
vulnerable to high incidences of both virus infection and morbidity. Those
numbers, according to preliminary data, were borne out in the American
data from New York and elsewhere. Obesity, as we know, comes overwhelmingly from diets heavy in animal products.

As of early May 2020, the U.S. alone had lost several trillion dollars in
GDP, was projected to lose 47 million jobs, thousands of small businesses,
and was already enduring widespread social and psychological misery from
government-imposed lockdowns. The virus attack further hastened trends
toward a medicalization of American society, marked by a frenzied search
for new vaccines and drug therapies to treat coronavirus that was destined
to enhance the already-swollen power of Big Pharma. As of early May
2020, many governments in cooperation with large pharmaceutical companies were working feverishly to develop and disseminate some form of
coronavirus vaccine. Microsoft founder Bill Gates and his foundation, a
major funder of these efforts around the world, believes those eventually
receiving vaccinations be issued a "digital certificate" proving evidence of
immunity. Dr. Anthony Fauci, a leading virologist and part of President
Trump's taskforce, has argued the Americans carry proof of vaccination.
Others have suggested a scheme that forces everyone – in the U.S. and
around the world – to download a phone app that will track personal movements, yet another step toward a full-blown surveillance society. Many politicians have gone so far as to insist on total social lockdown until a vaccine
is developed, a process that could take several years. It is often forgotten,
moreover, that flu vaccines that have been around many years are typically
effective for less than 60 percent of all people.

Even with gradual opening of economies – fiercely resisted by many
"experts" and politicians – harsh long-term consequences were to be
expected, including higher levels of unemployment and poverty. Whether
this historic pandemic will force transformative changes in the economy,
social life, the medical system, lifestyle patterns, or politics – in the U.S. or
elsewhere – is rather uncertain, but any future virus outbreaks would almost
surely give rise to new conditions, from global relations to the environment
to daily life. In any event, great health crises of the future are sure to figure
strongly in how the ecological crisis ultimately plays out.

Postscript: a Green New Deal?

The idea of a Green New Deal, recently proposed in the United States by a group of Democrats led by New York representative Alexandria Ocasio-Cortez, is hardly novel on the world scene, though potentially a breakthrough for American politics. European Green parties, for example, introduced far-reaching policies in support of an ecological (sustainable) model of development as early as 1980. A few other European leftist parties later followed with their own "greening" initiatives in the broader struggle to reverse the effects of climate disruption. Even the authoritarian Chinese government has introduced its own ambitious policies to curb greenhouse emissions while theoretically shifting away from a fossil-fuel economy. The general outlook in these cases, more or less consistent with the 2015 Paris objectives, was a zero-carbon footprint to be achieved within two decades or so while keeping global average temperatures from rising more than another two degree Celsius.

The American proposals could end up bringing significant change, but that assumes federal legislative consensus is within reach – currently a utopian prospect. The Ocasio-Cortez plan was co-sponsored by Senator Ed Markey (D-Mass) and joined by 60 House members and nine Senators, winning support from such environmentalists as Ken Kimmel, president of the Union of Concerned Scientists. The main goal was 100 percent carbon-free economic development by 2050, to be achieved by gradually substituting green energy sources (solar, wind, thermal) for oil, gas, and coal, a target that could mean full-scale transformation of American society. Vast public funding would begin to subsidize ecologically relevant research. Huge areas of natural habitat would be restored through endless creative interventions, from tree-planting to river protections, water renovation, and massive recycling campaigns. More than anything, a vigorous Green New Deal – said to demand wartime-level resource and labor mobilization – would require a broadened and revitalized public infrastructure. While initially costing many trillions of dollars (estimates vary widely), the cost would be justified as a giant leap forward to "save life on the planet". The program would presumably generate new sources of economic growth, jobs, community life, and of course environmental renewal.

Green New Deal sponsors have promoted their scheme as both a moral and political imperative – a radical departure from business-as-usual, however generally sketched. After all, as we have seen, IPCC reports suggest that time to reverse the global crisis is narrowing rapidly, with perhaps just a decade or so avoid the infamous Tipping Point. While the U.S. Congress was nowhere close to passing such legislation, strong green initiatives were being taken up by nearly a dozen states and many cities, large and small, across the country. For their part, many elites seemed anxious to join the widening ecological *Zeitgeist*, hoping to be seen as champions of environmental sanity. New York state unveiled its Green New Deal in summer 2019, calling for rapid proliferation of solar panels, building retrofits, wind turbines, and electric cars, its goal at least 70 percent electricity from renewable sources by 2030. According to the state Climate Action Council, the program would "fully transform the way New Yorkers work, live, and play" in coming decades, all congruent with the nationwide Green program embraced by Democrats and others.

The goal of reducing carbon footprint was increasingly viewed by many Democratic mayors and liberal city councils as essentially a double benefit – both catalyst of economic development and vehicle of political revitalization geared to building mass support. In July 2019 Los Angeles mayor Eric Garcetti announced a more extensive Green New Deal, replete with solar panels on every building, new water recycling systems, electrified public transport, and expanded public infrastructure. The plan would eliminate all carbon energy sources by 2045 – more optimistic even than objectives set at Paris. "Greening", at least for Garcetti and his backers, would simultaneously attack poverty, homelessness, urban pollution, and public-health problems. At the time of this writing (Summer 2020) no fewer than 88 American cities had set forth some variant of a Green New

Deal, usually underpinned by expensive "climate action plans" merging a range of urban, economic, social, and environmental priorities.

Anticipating the watershed 2020 presidential election, most Democratic candidates (at one point more than 20) paid some homage to a Green New Deal, wanting to be counted among those working to stave off imminent catastrophe that President Trump had so contemptuously dismissed. The three most progressive candidates – Bernie Sanders, Elizabeth Warren, Tulsi Gabbard – argued for an immediate, systemic greening process aimed at zero carbon emissions for the American economy within two or three decades. Some defined the problem as something of an "existential crisis", a challenge without historical precedent, urging efforts to reshape American capitalism. One (ultimately-failed) Democratic candidate, Beto O'Rourke, exemplified the sense of crisis, declaring: "By far the greatest threat we face, which will test our country, our communities, and every single one of us, is climate change."[526]

As of early 2020, it appeared that Sanders' greening scenario was the most robust – and most costly, projected at no less than $16 trillion over ten years. His more radical goal was 70-percent fossil-free emissions by 2030, made possible by significant rebuilding of the American economy starting with the energy sector, Sanders commenting: "It is expensive but the cost of doing nothing is far more expensive."[527] He would enlist participation of the labor movement, including the all-important AFL-CIO with its millions of workers involved directly or indirectly in the fossil-fuel industry.

One problem here is that the American labor movement never mustered real enthusiasm for a Green New Deal, authored by Sanders or anyone else. There is always the fear of enormous job loss as certain sectors are reduced or shut down entirely: mining operations, utilities, oil and gas production among others. What dramatic impact might a post-carbon society have on millions of relatively good-paying jobs? Would alternative energy systems furnish enough new employment to compensate for massive losses? Those were questions at the heart of modern labor movements everywhere – one source of their ambivalence if not outright hostility to any "greening" reforms. These very concerns were advanced by AFL-CIO head Richard Trumka in 2019, who also feared the possibility corporations would ship major operations abroad to avoid stricter environmental regulations.

A Green New Deal for the U.S., should it gain political momentum, would presumably follow the example of Franklin Roosevelt's New Deal programs of the 1930s that brought the U.S. into the orbit of European social democracy. Contemporary Democrats foresee an expansive "greening" of the American economy, on the path to a system both more efficient and sustainable than what exists. Proposals differ widely according to how much the system is expected to be transformed. None, however, seem ready to challenge the basic firmaments of corporate power, agribusiness, or Wall Street – not to mention the military-security apparatus, which has long been off-limits for public debate. The ultimate question, therefore, is just how far architects of a Green New Deal are willing go in "overhauling" capitalist modes of production and consumption.

To be sure, any genuine reform of the corporate-state system would be a much-welcomed step beyond familiar "carbon offset" plans such as cap-and-trade, direct carbon taxation, or tepid public regulations. Yet a reform scenario as such could never begin to reverse the present environmentally disastrous course. As formulated by American Democrats, a Green New Deal – while no doubt improving the overall carbon footprint – would (as in the California experience) leave basic capitalist priorities more or less intact: the same growth agenda, same agribusiness complex, same meat and dairy interests, same warfare state, same ecological imbalance between urban and rural life. While the transnational corporate order remains undisturbed, it is hard to imagine how the pervasive fossil-fuel empire might end up dismantled, given the many trillions of dollars it has invested across virtually all economic sectors. In reality global fossil-fuel extraction is proceeding at record levels.

The problem runs deeper yet: proponents of a Green New Deal, with few exceptions, have looked to a Democratic Party that simply cannot serve as a mechanism of far-reaching change. The limits are both institutional and ideological. Today more than ever, the Democrats are wedded to corporate and military power, so that any reforms will be constrained by what is tolerable at the summits of power. Even more than Republicans, Democrats have pursued confrontational strategies abroad, especially targeting geopolitical rival Russia regardless of the global risks and consequences. As the Democrats have essentially morphed into a bigger "war party", their neocon foreign policy establishment has morphed into a bigger "war party".

Its neocon foreign policy needs a universe of mortal threats – a major driving force behind the Russiagate hoax perpetrated by an unholy alliance of Democratic elites, Pentagon, the intelligence apparatus, and corporate media. So long as these forces dominate American public life, a radical Green New Deal has little if any chance of far-reaching success.

By 2020 the U.S. had reached a point of sharpening conflict with much of the world: not only Russia and China, but many targets in the Middle East, North Africa, Asia, and Latin America were on its hated-enemies list, from Iran to Venezuela, Yemen, Somalia, and North Korea. Washington routinely carries out some mode of warfare through an ensemble of covert operations, global surveillance, sponsored coups, economic sanctions, and proxy combat not to mention outright military threats or attacks. The Democrats, going back to the Bill Clinton presidency of the early 1990s, had begun framing a neocon strategy within a matrix of identity politics and progressive gestures that could deflect attention from problematic foreign adventures.

As the global crisis worsens, Green New Deal architects could emerge as facilitators of what might be called a green Keynesianism. For American politics, we have already witnessed two distinct forms of Keynesian economics (social and military), suggesting that these – along with the green variant – will be jostling for prevalence in coming decades. Should Democrats manage to put forward a Green New Deal with some measure of success, that would indicate what Keynesianism has always indicated: a Herculean effort to stabilize capitalism on new economic (also political) foundations. Such a project cannot be dismissed, even if hardly compatible with a more ecologically friendly road forward. Such "greening" would rely on a program of distinctly liberal reforms – public regulations, carbon offsets, technological restructuring, revitalized social infrastructure, and so forth. While probably within reach, these reforms would leave intact the power of Wall Street, the technology giants, warfare/security state, and corporate-media system –in other words, a fortress of power and wealth at odds with requirements for an ecological society. The capitalist growth machine would be left more or less undisturbed.

Consistent with a program of capitalist greening, a Green New Deal would incentivize global corporations to combine their familiar pursuit of profits with norms of developmental sustainability, mainly through technological renewal dependent on billions of dollars for solar and wind power. By 2020 such tech corporations as Amazon, Alphabet Inc's Google, Facebook, and Microsoft had ostensibly taken the lead in green investments, itself a great source of profits. According to Tom Murray, working for such groups as the Environmental Defense Fund: "We've moved past this concept that business versus the environment is a tradeoff, adding: "The business benefits were always there, but more and more companies are going after them."[528]

As pressures for some type of Green New Deal intensify, many large corporations have begun lining up behind carbon-free targets, wagering that sustainability will follow increased efficiency and savings. Not only tech oligopolies but such fossil-fuel behemoths as ExxonMobil have signed on to new greening incentives.[529] United Airlines has arrived at a series of bold initiatives – making planes lighter, using more efficient fuels – that could result in billions of dollars in savings. Other corporate giants (Walmart, McDonalds) have enthusiastically signed on to what they envision as a form of capitalist greening.

Naomi's Klein's 2019 book, *On Fire,* lays out an especially urgent case for a Green New Deal in the tracks of FDR's original New Deal. Drawing on the emergent power of a revitalized "youth climate movement", Klein identifies a broad green strategy as the last viable alternative to "climate barbarism" that threatens planetary life.[530] A "people's emergency" reflected in a Green New Deal would ideally bring historical achievement to the recent cycle of sit-ins, blockades, protests, and demonstrations that have sparked the activism of millions of people around the world. As with the Paris accords, the objective would be for the U.S. (and other advanced industrial nations) to reach net-zero carbon emissions within a decade, or at least by 2040.

For Klein, inspired by a widening bloc of green-oriented politicians, the idea would be to elect a new generation of Democrats to take over the White House and Congress, roll out a comprehensive plan for "rapid decarbonization", then rapidly implement those reforms as a model for worldwide ecological renewal. Referring to AOC and her cohorts, Klein writes: "If the IPCC report (of October 2018) was the clanging fire alarm that grabbed the attention of the world, the Green New Deal is the beginning of a fire safety and prevention plan."[531] For this schema to work, both technology and "markets" would be crucial, though precisely in what ways remains to be clarified. Klein urges adoption of "forceful policy mechanisms", but these too lack clear articulation. She insists on departure from "free-market fundamentalism" and "market euphoria", but just how such delusional thinking exists in the realm of actually existing corporate-state power is a mystery.

In the pages of *On Fire* Klein appears to believe Green New Deal proposals now circulating among political and media elites are both novel and radical, although neither is true. As noted, more ambitious versions of a Green New Deal have been around the public sphere for years, indeed decades, first surfacing within European Green parties of the early 1980s. Those programs usually embraced a visible ecosocialist outlook, a term avoided by Klein. More recently, Jill Stein laid out the constituent elements of a far more radical Green New Deal during her 2016 presidential candidacy. Stein's version argued for a full break with "corporate domination of the economy and society", an imperative scarcely evident in the more widely advertised schemes of Klein and the Dems. Why Klein chose to ignore this hardly secret Green experience is rather puzzling.

While for Klein (as for the Dems) a Green New Deal signifies a "sweeping industrial and infrastructure overhaul", in reality there is no stated break with the neoliberal corporate system. We have instead a variant of green Keynesianism fully compatible with existing forms of production and consumption endemic to the capitalist growth machine – in other words, a renovated social democracy. There is some notion that the fossil-fuel giants will have to be "confronted", but precisely how remains elusive. Indeed, once placed in the nervous hands of Democratic Party elites tied to Wall Street, agribusiness, and the warfare state, any genuinely transformative potential of a Green New Deal is sure to quickly fade from view.

The early European Greens had enough ideological diversity to permit vigorous debates over political strategy – a rare phenomenon in American political culture, where opposition to corporate power is generally off limits, more or less taboo. References to ecosocialism, for example, seem like utopian exercises even among progressives. An early program of the German Greens states the following: "Political ecology is not merely an addition to traditional politics; it does not merely add a new element. Rather, it is based on a radical critique of unfettered industrialism and its history." The program adds: "The classic reformist path involves giving up on any kind of fundamental change in the ecological and social system that would oppose the logic of capital."[532]

Such futility is inescapable to the extent a Green New Deal winds up making peace with the ruling interests. It is worth asking whether the Democratic Party as we know it could be a vehicle of radical change when, in fact, any dedication to ecological politics has surfaced only recently on the fringes of party organization. One major obstacle to such politics – the widely overlooked military-industrial behemoth – is now responsible for roughly five percent of the global carbon footprint, a problem at best only peripherally addressed by Klein and the Dems. In *On Fire* we find calls for a modest 25-percent reduction in worldwide military spending, but that appears to exhaust discussion of the matter. Compare that to Stein's Green New Deal, which calls for initial 50-percent military cutbacks leading to a general dismantling of the *American* warfare state, including its sprawling empire of bases, ongoing wars, and nuclear buildup (never mentioned by Klein).

While the U.S. military alone contributes as much as five percent of global carbon emissions – a staggering total for one sector – that is hardly the end of the story. The Pentagon has long served as protector of transnational corporate interests, none perhaps more crucial (to American interests) than the fossil-fuel industry. Future resource wars, surely involving U.S. armed forces, will likely revolve around reserves of oil and natural gas – already the case in Iraq. This vast mobilization of material, technological, and human resources could better be utilized to *restore* instead of *destroy* global ecosystems. That destruction, it is often forgotten, comes from not only global military deployments but the especially savage legacy of warfare visible in the form of bombs, missiles, vehicles, toxic wastes, and pollution across the habitat.

Just as telling, the AOC-Klein-Dems vision of a Green New Deal entirely skirts the pressing issue of *resources* – that is, the extent to which the planet faces a specter of sharply declining natural resources (notably water, land, soil, forests) endemic to an ever-expanding growth apparatus. Obsession with climate change to the exclusion of resource pressures – and imminent resource *wars* – leads inexorably to a profoundly myopic (and losing) strategy of change. Economic projections show that leading industrialized nations (U.S., China, India, the EU, Russia, Japan) could easily *double* their GDP output within the next two or three decades. Unfortunately, ecological support systems cannot endure such overburdening "development", whatever the optimistic (indeed utopian) fantasies harbored by global corporate elites and other true-believers. Exactly why a Green New Deal entertained by Klein and the Dems essentially sidesteps this question is difficult to fathom.

Global resource competition, with its implicit legitimation of perpetual growth, could in fact be the dynamic that most hastens planetary disaster. Limitless material expansion drives not only competition for markets, resources, and cheap labor but exacerbates national rivalries, geopolitical conflict, and international warfare. Klein largely avoids this issue, commenting: "As the world warms, the reigning ideology that tells us it's everyone for themselves, that victims deserve their fate, that we can master nature, will take us to a very dark place indeed."[533] That darkest of all journeys will be fueled, above all, by fierce economic and geopolitical rivalries over increasingly scarce resources.

Resource wars could most acutely take shape in the realm of agriculture and food – a topic Klein systematically evades in both *On Fire* and *This Changes Everything*. It is now well known among environmentalists across the political spectrum that the immensely destructive and unsustainable global meat complex is responsible for massive greenhouse emissions (credible estimates range up to 45 percent of the total) given its extensive reliance on fossil fuels and its planetary toxic legacy. It is likewise well known that meat and dairy production on average devours more than ten times the amount of land, water, and fossil fuels than plant-based foods – a figure that goes much higher when the McDonaldized fast-food sector is taken into account. No single phenomenon contributes more to climate change, its worsening impact ensured by worldwide association of meat and dairy products with elevated "affluence" and "modernity".

Klein's Green New Deal somehow manages to ignore what is central to understanding (also *reversing*) the global ecological crisis. There can be no far-reaching "greening" of modern societies – however widespread the use of sustainable technologies – in the absence of a far-reaching break with the destructive, not to mention cruel, world meat complex. To believe otherwise is to indulge in yet another form of denialism, in this case rooted in harmful everyday practices. As mentioned in the introduction to this book, there can be no excuses for such narrow provincialism and willful ignorance. Dietary preferences? Lifestyle choices? That would rationalize the saddest forms of both escapism and denialism. Interviewed in the documentary *Cowspiracy*, environmentalist Howard Liman puts the question bluntly: "You can't be an environmentalist and eat animal products, period. Kid yourself if you want. If you want to feed your [meat] addiction, so be it. But don't call yourself an environmentalist."

A truly effective Green New Deal would require what Klein and the Democrats have somehow overlooked – a thorough reconstitution of the entire agricultural and food system. That means a dramatic shift from agribusiness operations, the meat complex, and McDonaldized fast-food empire toward more sustainable forms of production and consumption: agroecology with a focus on local, organic farming, emphasis on plant-based foods, termination of pesticides, fertilizers, and other carbon-based materials, end of public subsidies for meat and dairy interests, dismantling of barbaric factory farms and slaughterhouses.

More generally, as both social and military forms of Keynesianism have historically functioned to stabilize a crisis-ridden capitalism, worth asking is whether a distinctly green variant of Keynesianism might work the same magic in the future. This is surely the expectation of many forward-thinking corporate and Democratic Party elites in the U.S., a motif also increasingly championed throughout the mainstream media. One might be justified in such a comforting view, yet any sort of capitalist greening is destined to face logical constraints, where short-term results cannot be expected to deliver long-term success. One problem is that the Green New Deal, as formulated, is in the end perfectly compatible with a harshly unsustainable system. Another problem is that such a plan cannot be limited to particular nation-states or even regions, as any political strategy will have to be emphatically *global* in its ecological and political reach. Architects of a specifically American green Keynesianism have yet to embrace such a perspective.

This raises further questions: could, for example, rival nationalisms (at a time of mounting resources wars) finally be rendered obsolete? Could the U.S. and China (or the U.S. and Russia) agree to much of anything in the realm of global affairs? Referring to this dilemma in *Climate Leviathan*,

Geoff Mann and Joel Wainwright argue: "A transnational Keynesianism can only be predicated on the consolidation of a transnational variation of the sovereign subject without which Keynesianism is inconceivable."[534] As of summer 2020 the world still awaits even the vision of such a sovereign.

Some have argued that the Paris Accords (and kindred international agreements) might establish conditions for a worldwide green Keynesianism, but it should be remembered those climate targets are in fact voluntary, limited, and partial, which allows little space for optimism. In fall 2019 representatives from more than 60 nations met in New York, under U.N. auspices, looking to energize (and further concretize) international commitments to a more sustainable path forward. The consensus, however, was that most nations (including those with the largest carbon footprints) are moving far too slowly at a time when general promises – not concrete plans – shape the elite outlook. Sadly, as of 2020, few heavy violators had significantly reduced their carbon footprint, while developing countries naturally resent being cajoled by major powers into adopting a green path at a time when fossil capitalism is generally moving full-speed ahead. Several modernizing countries (South Korea, India, Indonesia, South Africa among them) continue to widen their use of coal-fired electricity generation, at odds with officially stated goals. As leading per-capita source of greenhouse emissions, the U.S. under President Trump has chosen to withdraw summarily from the Paris Accords. We should hardly be astonished, therefore, to see an increase in worldwide carbon emissions just as other problems (water shortages, shrinking arable land, deforestation, pollution etc.) steadily escalate, with few if any effective counter-forces visible. That point was dramatically brought forward by the 2020 documentary, *Planet of the Humans*, the work of Jeff Gibbs, Ozzie Zellner, and Michael Moore. Meanwhile, no international Green New Deal appears on the horizon.

Endnotes

1   Barry Commoner, *The Poverty of Power* (New York: Bantam Books, 1977), pp. 1-4.

2   Helen Caldicott, ed., *Sleepwalking to Armageddon* (New York: the New Press, 2017).

3   C. Wright Mills, *The Power Elite* (New York: Oxford University Press, 1956).

4   Peter Phillips, *Giants: the Global Power Elite* (New York: Seven Stories, 2018), p. 29.

5   Ibid., p. 30.

6   Tess Riley, "Just 100 Companies Responsible for Global Emissions", *Guardian* (July 10, 2017).

7   Phillips, *Giants*, p. 59.

8   See David Wallace-Wells, *The Uninhabitable Earth* (New York: Tim Duggan Books, 2019), p. 6.

9   Ibid., p. 13.

10   Ibid., p. 15.

11   Ian Angus, *Facing the Anthropocene* (New York: Monthly Review Press, 2016), p. 138.

12   For a fuller discussion of the Green New Deal, see the postscript.

13   See Max Horkheimer and Theodor Adorno, *Dialectic of Enlightenment* (New York: Continuum, 1995), p. 20.

14   Andreas Malm, *Fossil Capital* (London: Verso, 2016), p. 115.

15   For a list of top-10 projected economies for 2050, see www.businessinsider.com/ranked-pwc-predicts.

16   For a list of top-10 military spenders by 2030, see www.nextbigfuture.com/2018/02/Infographics.

17   The mounting threat of nuclear war, once a central motif of American politics, seems to have been largely forgotten in recent years. One noteworthy exception here is Daniel Ellsberg's *The Doomsday Machine* (New York: Bloomsbury, 2017). See especially pages 12-18 of the introduction. Another excellent source is Stephen F. Cohen, *War with Russia?* (New York: Skyhorse, 2019). Cohen's book was written in the midst of the seemingly never-ending Russiagate propaganda that started even before Donald Trump's 2016 election victory.

18   Mills, *The Power Elite*, ch. 9.

19   Victor Wallis, *The Red-Green Revolution* (Toronto: Political Animal Press, 2018), p. 2.

20 Noam Chomsky, *Who Rules the World?* (New York: Henry Holt and Co., 2016), p. 261.

21 Oliver Boyd-Barrett, "Russiagate as Organized Distraction", *Consortium News* (August 2, 2019).

22 Wallace-Wells, *Uninhabitable Earth*, p. 30.

23 Ibid., p. 35.

24 One noteworthy exception here is Richard A. Oppenlander's *Comfortably Unaware* (New York: Beaufort Books, 2012). This book has been followed by several excellent documentaries linking food and agriculture with the ecological crisis: *Cowspiracy, Forks over Knives, What the Health* among others.

25 See George Ritzer's classic *The McDonaldization of Society* (Thousand Oaks: Pine Forge Press, 2000), especially chapters 2 and 3.

26 Karl Marx, "Manifesto of the Communist Party", in Robert C. Tucker, ed., *The Marx-Engels Reader* (New York: W.W. Norton, 1972), p. 477.

27 Paul Gilding, *The Great Disruption* (New York: Bloomsbury, 2011), p. 5.

28 On the theme technology as ideology, see Herbert Marcuse, *One-Dimensional Man* (Boston: Beacon Press, 1964), pp. 158-59.

29 See Ritzer, *McDonaldization*, ch. 2.

30 For an extensive, and critical, historical account of the American meat complex, see Christopher Leonard, *The Meat Racket* (New York: Simon and Schuster, 2014).

31 Estimates of the global impact of meat production and consumption on the natural habitat vary immensely. One reliable – at the same time extremely liberal – assessment is that of Jeff Anhang and Paul Goodland, in "Livestock and Climate Change", Worldwatch Institute report (November-December 2009). Their estimate (51 percent of total emissions) has been roughly embraced since 2009 by many Worldwatch researchers, though at somewhat less than the 51 percent level. A figure of 40 percent has been rather frequent.

32 Angus, *Anthropocene*, p. 222.

33 Michael Lowy, *Ecosocialism* (Chicago: Haymarket Books, 2015), p. 17.

34 Malm, *Fossil Capital*, p. 9.

35 See Edward O. Wilson, *Half-Earth: Our Planet's Fight for Life* (New York: W.W Norton, 2016), p. 48

36 Murray Bookchin, *The Modern Crisis* (Philadelphia: New Society Publishers, 1986, p. 99.

37 www.ers.usda/2018.

38 Report of the United Nations Food and Agriculture Organization (FAO), 2018. See www.fao.org/2018.

39 Lester R. Brown, *Full Planet, Empty Plates* (New York: W.W. Norton, 2012), p. 3.

40   Eric Holt-Gimenez, *A Foodie's Guide to Capitalism* (New York: Monthly
     Review, 2017), p. 126.

41   Christopher Leonard, *The Meat Racket* (New York: Simon and Schuster,
     2014), ch. 10.

42   Ibid., p. 213.

43   www.en.wikipedia.org/wiki/Tyson Foods.

44   Leonard, *Meat Racket*, p.235.

45   www.corpresearch.org/Cargill/2017.

46   See Eric Schlosser, *Fast Food Nation* (Boston: Houghton-Mifflin, 2001), p.
     154.

47   See Anahad O'Connor, "How the Government Supports Your Junk Food
     Habit", *New York Times* (July 19, 2016).

48   Leonard, *Meat Racket*, p. 291.

49   www.opensecrets.org/news/2018.

50   Ibid.

51   www.allgov/March 25, 2014.

52   Leonard, *Meat Racket*, p. 301.

53   Ibid., pp. 268-69.

54   Ibid., p. 263.

55   For the IPCC report, see www.coolearth.org/2018/10/ipcc-report-2.

56   www.ucsusa.org/global-warming/science. (August 16, 2017)

57   www.nasa.gov/pressrelease/2018.

58   See Richard A. Oppenlander, *Comfortably Unaware* (New York: Beaufort
     Books, 2012), p. 5.

59   On carbon footprint by country, see www.ucsusa.org/ ... /each-country's-
     share-of-co2.html.

60   See Hannah Devlin, "Rising Global Meat Consumption will Devastate
     Environment", *The Guardian* (July 19, 2018). Also the Worldwatch report "Is
     Meat Sustainable?" (number 549) www.worldwatch.org/node/549.

61   www.merid.org/sector/climate change (2008)

62   See Laura Reynolds and Danielle Nierenberg, "A World of Shrinking
     Resources". Worldwatch report 188 (2012) www.worldwatch.org/node/188.

63   Oppenlander, *Comfortably Unaware*, p. 12.

64   David Lobell, et. al., "Climate Trends ad Global Crop Production Since
     1980", *Science* (May 5, 2011).

65   See Lester R. Brown, *Plan B 4.0: Mobilizing to Save Civilization* (New York:
     W.W. Norton, 2009), p. 71.

66   Much of this research is set forth in Brown, *Full Planet*, p. 14.

67 Ibid., p. 87.

68 David Wallace-Wells, *Uninhabitable Earth* (New York: Tim Duggan Books, 2019), p. 119.

69 www.nas.gov/pressrelease/2018.

70 Brown, *World on the Edge*, pp. 60-61.

71 While the Tipping Point could reportedly be reached with a warming of two degrees Celsius, we know that even a rapid cessation of carbon (and related emissions) could exceed that level before the end of the twenty-first century. See the Wallace-Wells discussion on this point, in *Uninhabitable Earth*, pp. 11-13. It might be worth adding here that such rapid cessation is very unlikely given the present social and political reality.

72 See Wallace-Wells, *Uninhabitable Earth*, pp. 55-56.

73 Rachel Warren, *Science*.

74 Steffen Bohm, in www.theconversation.com-68202. (November 4, 2018).

75 See "Livestock's Long Shadow". www.fao.org/2006.

76 www.veg4planet.bbgspot.com/2009/02/dr-james-hansen.

77 Robert Goodland and Jeff Anhang, "Livestock and Climate Change". Worldwatch. (November-December, 2009). See www.worldwatch.org/2009.

78 Ibid.

79 Ibid., p. 14.

80 Brown, *Full Planet, Empty Plates*, p. 116.

81 Wallace-Wells, *Uninhabitable Earth*, p. 55.

82 See www.worldhunger.org/world-hunger-and-poverty/2018.

83 www.goveg.com/environ-wastedresources-food-asp.

84 Jeffrey Moussaieff Mason, *When Elephants Weep* (New York: Delacorte Press, 1995), p. 226.

85 Jane Goodall, *Through a Window* (Boston: Houghton-Mifflin, 1990), pp. 12-23.

86 Peter Singer, *Animal Liberation* (New York: Avon Books, 1975), p. xii.

87 Ibid., p. xv.

88 Ibid., p. 220.

89 Ibid., p. 235.

90 Tom Regan, *The Case for Animal Rights* (Berkeley: University of California Press, 2004), p. 351.

91 Mason, *When Elephants Weep*, p. 232.

92 Peter Wohlleben, *The Inner Life of Animals* (New York: Penguin, 2017), pp. 43-44.

93 See John Sanbonmatsu, "Introduction" to Sanbonmatsu, ed., *Critical Theory and Animal Liberation* (Lanham, Md.: Rowman and Littlefield, 2011), pp. 20-21.

94 Ibid., p. 21.

95 Theodor Adorno and Max Horkheimer, *Dialectic of Enlightenment* (New York: Continuum, 1995), pp. 253-54.

96 Ibid., p. 24.

97 Ibid., p. 20.

98 See Colin Campbell, *The China Study* (Ithaca, N.Y.: Cornell University Press, 2006).

99 John Robbins, *The Food Revolution* (Berkeley: Conari Press, 2001).

100 Sanbonmatsu, op.cit., p. 13.

101 One notable example here is Joel Kovel, *The Enemy of Nature* (London: Zed Books, 2002), p. 210.

102 Sanbonmatsu, op.cit., p. 17.

103 Ibid.

104 Ted Benton, *Natural Relations* (London: Verso, 1993), pp. 32-45.

105 Ted Benton, "Humanism – Speciesism?: Marx on Humans and Animals", in Sanbonmatsu, ed., *Critical Theory*, p. 111.

106 Ibid., p. 119.

107 Andreas Malm, *Fossil Capital* (London: Verso, 2016).

108 Lester Brown, *Full Planet, Empty Plates* (New York: W.W. Norton, 2012), p. 23.

109 www.fao.org/docrep/005.

110 Ibid.

111 Ibid.

112 Brown, *Full Planet*, p. 31.

113 Ibid., p. 70.

114 Ibid., p. 71.

115 For an extensive comparison of water usage in food production, see John Robbins, *The Food Revolution* (Berkeley: Conari Press, 2001), p. 236. According to some estimates, the amount of water required to produce one pound of beef is over 5000 gallons, compared to 23 gallons for one pound of lettuce, 25 gallons for one pound of wheat, 24 gallons for one pound of potatoes, and so on. This huge discrepancy is rarely discussed in even the most progressive analyses of resource utilization and climate change. There is no indication that the evidence furnished by Robbins at the start of the twenty-first century has significantly changed.

116 That stark comparison can be gleaned from the extensive data assembled by Robbins, starting with meat and plant-based utilization of water resources on page 236 of *The Food Revolution*.

117 Michael T. Klare, *The Race for What's Left* (New York: Henry Holt and Co., 2012), p. 228.

118 Brown, *Full Planet*, p. 37.

119 Lester Brown, *World on the Edge* (New York: W.W. Norton, 2011), pp. 60-63.

120 Brown, *Full Planet*, pp. 46-51.

121 See Christina Nunez, "Climate 101" Deforestation", *National Geographic* (February 7, 2019).

122 *Guardian Weekly* (October 6-12, 2017).

123 John Vidal, "We are Destroying Rainforests so Quickly They May be Gone in 100 Years", *Guardian* (January 23, 2017.)

124 www.ran.org/mission.

125 See Robert Hunziker, "The Sick Oceans", *CounterPunch* (September 18, 2016).

126 Richard A. Oppenlander, *Comfortably Unaware* (New York: Beaufort Books, 2012), p. 54.

127 Ibid, p. 58.

128 See Hunziker, in *CounterPunch*.

129 Lester Brown, *Who Will Feed China?* (New York: W.W. Norton, 1995), p. 24.

130 www.fao.Agri/outlook/2014.

131 Murray Bookchin, *The Rise of Urbanization and the Decline of Citizenship* (San Francisco: Sierra Club Books, 1987), p. ix.

132 Ibid., p. x.

133 Ibid., pp. x-xi.

134 Ibid., p. 4.

135 Ibid., p. 12.

136 For the top ten cities in the world, see www.worldatlas.com/articles/the-10-largest.

137 Brown, *World on Edge*, p. 32.

138 On this development, see Mike Davis, *Planet of Slums* (London: Verso, 2006).

139 Brown, *Full Planet*, p. 5.

140 Ibid., p. 25.

141 Ibid., p. 115.

142 Gary Gardner, "World Cities at a Glance", in Gardner, et. al., eds, *Can a City be Sustainable?* (New York: Island Press, 2016), pp. 22-23.

143 *Los Angeles Times* (April 28, 2019).

144 Bookchin, *Urbanization*, p. 12.

145 Ibid., p. 221.

146 Lester Brown, *Beyond Malthus* (New York: W.W. Norton, 1999), p. 22.

147 Chris Hedges, *The World as it Is* ( ), p. 271.

148 See Brown, *Full Planet*, p. 23.

149 Paul R. Ehrlich and Anne H. Ehrlich, *The Population Explosion* (New York: Simon and Schuster, 1990), p. 44.

150 Chris Williams, *Ecology and Socialism* (Chicago: Haymarket Books, 2010), pp. 76-78.

151 Ibid., p. 49.

152 See Paul Ehrlich and Anne Ehrlich, "The Population Explosion", www. jayhanson.us/page 27 html (p. 1).

153 Ibid., p. 2.

154 Ibid., pp. 2-3.

155 Williams, *Ecology and Socialism*, p. 42.

156 Bill McKibben, *Eaarth* (New York: Henry Holt and Co., 2010), p. 44.

157 Sandra Postel, "Water: Adapting to a New Normal", in Richard Heinberg and Daniel Lerch, eds., *The Post Carbon Reader* (Healdsburg, Ca.: Watershed Media, 2010), p. 80.

158 See Lester Brown, *Plan B 4.0* (New York: W.W. Norton and Co., 2009), p. 234.

159 David and Marcia Pimentel, "World Population, Food, Natural Resources, and Survival", in Ervin Laszlo and Peter Seidel, eds., *Global Survival* (New York: SelectBooks, 2006), p. 45.

160 Brown, *World on the Edge*, p. 71.

161 Michael T. Klare, *Resource Wars* (Henry Holt and Co., 2001), pp. 213-14.

162 Ibid., p. 221.

163 Ibid., p. 7.

164 Ibid., p. 15.

165 Ibid., p. 20.

166 See Antonia Juhasz, *The Bush Agenda* (New York: HarperCollins, 2006).

167 Ibid., p. 4.

168 Ibid., pp. 42-43.

169 Ibid., pp. 145-46.

170 Holt-Gimenez, *Foodie;s Guide*, p. 51.

171 Ibid., pp. 52-53.

172 Ibid., p. 54.

173 Ibid.

174 Klare, *Resource Wars*, pp. 139-40.

175 Ibid., p. 140.

176 Ibid., p. 14.

177 Ibid., p. 147.

178 Michael Klare, "The Hunger Wars of our Future". www.historynewsnetwork. org. August 17, 2012.

179 Klare, *The Race for What's Left*, p. 229.

180 Brown, *World on the Edge*, p. 88.

181 *Los Angeles Times* (August 4, 2019).

182 Geoff Hiscock, *Earth Wars* (Singapore: John Wiley and Sons, 2012), pp. 15-16.

183 On the role of the military-industrial complex in the American global presence, see Carl Boggs, *Origins of the Warfare State* (New York: Routledge, 2017), ch. 3.

184 On the Pentagon carbon footprint, see Murtaza Hassain, "War on the World", *The Intercept* (September 15, 2019). In fact the U.S. military turns out to be the largest single emitter of carbon dioxide in the world, leaving aside entire nations.

185 Bruce Gagnon, "Addicted to Weapons", in Helen Caldicott, ed., *Sleepwalking to Armageddon* (New York: The New Press, 2017), pp. 35-37.

186 Istvan Meszaros, *Socialism or Barbarism* (New York: Monthly Review Press, 2001), p. 37.

187 See Paul Roberts, *The End of Food* (Boston: Mariner Books, 2009), p. xii.

188 For an overview of American meat consumption, see Richard Waite, "2018 Will See a High Consumption of Meat in the U.S." *World Resources Institute* (January 24, 2018). Meat intake in the U.S. reached 200 pounds yearly per capita by 1995 and was expected to total at least 220 pounds per capita in 2018. These levels exceed those of any other country in the world.

189 Paul Gilding, *The Great Disruption* (New York: Bloomsbury, 2011), p. 5.

190 Eric Holt-Gimenez, *A Foodie;s Guide to Capitalism* (New York: Monthly Review, 2017), p. 57.

191 Ibid., p. 58.

192 Ibid., p. 59.

193 Marion Nestle, *Food Politics* (Berkeley: University of California Press, 2007), p. 11.

194 Ibid., p. 4.

195 Jonathan Safran Foer, *Eating Animals* Boston: Back Bay, 2010), p. 33.

196 Jeremy Rifkin, *Beyond Beef* (New York: Penguin, 1992), pp. 89-107.

197 Ibid., pp. 107-08.

198 Ibid., pp. 118-21.

199 Rifkin, *Beyond Beef,* p. 159.

200 Roberts, *End of Food,* p. 317.

201 www.en.wikipedia.org/wiki/Nestle.

202 www.en.wikipedia.org/wiki/Cargill.

203 www.en.wikipedia.org/JBS.

204 www.en.wikipedia.org/Walmart.

205 See Eric Schlosser, *Fast Food Nation* (Boston: Houghton-Mifflin, 2001), pp 152-57.

206 Ibid., pp. 40-57.

207 George Ritzer, *The McDonaldization of Society* (Thousand Oaks: Pine Forge Press, 2000), pp. 22-23.

208 Ibid., p. 170.

209 Ibid., p. 171.

210 Ibid., p. 183.

211 Ibid., p. 183.

212 Ibid., p. 123.

213 Ibid., p. 110.

214 Ibid., p. 137.

215 Ibid., p. 137.

216 Schlosser, *Fast Food Nation,* p. 154.

217 Ritzer, *McDonaldization,* p. 121.

218 Ibid., p. 2.

219 Ibid., p. 25.

220 See Gary Null, *Death by Medicine* (Mt. Jackson, Va.: Praktikos Books, 2011), introduction

221 Herbert Marcuse, *One-Dimensional Man* (Boston: Beacon Press,1964), p. xvi.

222 Ibid., p. 158.

223 Ibid., p. xii.

224 Ibid., p. 3.

225 Ibid., p. 14.

226 On the growing concentration of power in American society, at the summits, see Sheldon Wolin, *Democracy, Inc.* (Princeton, N.J.: Princeton University Press, 2008), and Carl Boggs, *Fascism Old and New* (New York: Routledge, 2018).

227 Franklin Foer, *World Without Mind* (New York: Penguin, 2017), p. 33.

228 Cited in Foer, p. 48.

229 See Glenn Greenwald, *No Place to Hide* (New York: Henry Holt and Co., 2014), ch. 3.

230 Foer, *World Without Mind*, p. 76.

231 Ibid., p. 14.

232 Shoshana Zuboff, *The Age of Surveillance Capitalism* (London: Profile, 2018).

233 John Robbins, *The Food Revolution* (Berkeley: Conari Press, 2001), p. 16.

234 See Ralph W. Moss, *The Cancer Industry* (New York: Equinox Press, 1996, chs. 17, 18.

235 Devra Davis, *The Secret History of the War on Cancer* (New York: Basic Books, 2007.

236 On the many deep flaws of establishment cancer research, see Campbell, *The China Study*, chs. 3, 14.

237 See Davis, *Secret History*, p. 4.

238 For an excellent critique of Sloan Kettering, see Moss, *Cancer Industry*, pp. 441-50.

239 Campbell, *China Study*, ch. 3.

240 Ibid., pp. 163-64.

241 Robbins, *Food Revolution*, pp. 37-38.

242 Campbell, *China Study*, ch. 7.

243 Ibid., p. 258.

244 Ibid., pp. 261-64.

245 Ibid., p. 265.

246 Ibid., p. 312.

247 Ibid., p. 318.

248 On this crucial point, see Harriet A. Washington, *Deadly Monopolies: The Shocking Corporate Takeover of Life Itself* (New York: Doubleday, 2011), introduction. See also Ivan Illich, *Medical Nemesis* (New York: Pantheon, 1976).

249 On the problem of addiction and the medicalization of American society, see Stanton Peele, *The Diseasing of America* (Lexington, MA.: Lexington Books, 1989), chs. 3 and 5.

250 See Joel Fuhrman, *Fast Food Genocide* (New York: HarperOne, 2017), p. 15.

251 Rifkin, *Beyond Beef*, p. 171.

252 Campbell, *China Study*, pp. 99-101.

253 Ibid., p. 110.

254 Sidney Wolfe, et. al. *Worst Pills, Best Pills* (New York: Pocket Books, 2005), p. 434.

255 Ibid., p. 431.

256 Ibid., p. 430.

257 See John Abramson, *Overdosed America* (New York: HarperCollins, 2004), pp. 235-37.

258 Popkin, *The World is Fat*, p. 162.

259 On the mainstream bias regarding drugs and obesity, see Gina Kolata, *Rethinking the New Science of Weight Loss* (New York: Farrar, Strauss, and Giroux, 2007).

260 On the faulty "low-carb" approach to weight loss, see *Robert Atkins' New Diet Revolution* (New York: Avon Books, 2002), and John Mansfield, *The Six Secrets of Successful Weight Loss* (London: Hammersmith Heath Books, 2012).

261 Campbell, *China Study*, p. 95.

262 For an extensive critique of the Atkins and related programs, see ibid., pp. 95-102.

263 Robbins, *Food Revolution*, p.61.

264 Ibid., pp. 62-63.

265 Campbell, *China Study*, pp. 97-98.

266 Null, et. al., *Death by Medicine*, p. 59.

267 According to National Center for Health Statistics, anti-depressant pre-scriptions rose steadily in the U.S. between 1988 and 2008 before levelling off in the midst of a growing national opioid epidemic. See Peter Wehrwein, "Astounding Increase in Antidepressant Use by Americans", *Harvard Health Publication* (October 20, 2011).

268 Drug overdoes killed a total of 72,000 Americans in 2017, 49,000 from opioids. See www.theguardian.com/US/news/2018.

269 Ivan Illich, et. al., *Disabling Professions* (New York: Marion Boyars, 1987), pp. 14-17.

270 Robbins, *Food Revolution*, p. 31.

271 Quoted in Robbins, p. 51.

272 Marion Nestle, *Unsavory Truth* (New York: Basic Books, 2018).

273 Campbell, *China Study*, ch. 3.

274 Ibid., p. 66.

275 Ibid., p. 73.

276 Ibid, p. 78.

277 Ibid., p. 102.

278 Ibid., pp. 78-79.

279 Ibid., p. 87.

280 www.en.wikipedia.orgwiki/Listofcountriesbycancerrate/2019.

281 Bradley J. Wilcox, et. al., *The Okinawa Program* (New York: Penguin, 2002).

282 John Robbins, *Healthy at 100* (New York: Random House, 2006), pp. 89-90.

283 Ibid., p. 93.

284 Ibid., pp. 107-08.

285 Ibid., pp. 132-33.

286 Ibid., p. 292.

287 Ibid., p. 61.

288 Ibid., p. 64.

289 Campbell, *China Study*, p. 98.

290 Ibid, p. 97.

291 Cited in Robbins, *Food Revolution*, p. 47.

292 Ibid., p. 30.

293 See Nestle, *Unsavory Truth*, p. 12.

294 Ibid., p. 62.

295 Ibid., p. 68.

296 See Michele Simon, *Whitewashed: How Industry and Government Promote Dairy Junk Foods.* EatDrinkPolitics.com. (June 2014.

297 Michael Pollan, *The Omnivore's Dilemma* (New York: Penguin, 2006).

298 Special issue "The Future of Food", *The Nation* (October 30, 2017).

299 Nestle, *Unsavory Truth*, pp. 61-62.

300 Bill McKibben, "A World at War", *New Republic* (September, 2016).

301 Intergovernmental Panel on Climate Change (IPCC) Report, October 2018. www.coolearth.org/2018/10/ipcc.report-2.

302 Chris Hedges, *Death of the Liberal Class* (New York: Nation Books, 2010), p. 196.

303 C. Wright Mills, *The Power Elite* (New York: Oxford University Press, 1956), p. 193.

304 See Zygmunt Bauman, *In Search of Politics* (Stanford, Ca.: Stanford University Press, 1999), pp. 120-22.

305 Hedges, *Liberal Class*, pp. 194-95.

306 Richard Manning, "The Trouble with Iowa", *Harpers* (February, 2016).

307 Ibid., p. 30.

308 This is the central motif of Thomas Frank's *Listen, Liberal* (New York: Henry Holt and Co., 2016), especially ch. 1.

309 Ibid., p. 115.

310 Ibid., p. 120.

311 Ibid., p. 122.

312 Al Gore, *Earth In the Balance* (New York: Houghton-Mifflin, 1992).

313 Al Gore, *Our Choice: A Plan to Solve the Climate Crisis* (New York: Melcher Media, 2009).

314 Al Gore, *Truth to Power* (New York: Rodale Books, 2017).

315 Gore, *Our Choice*, p. 388.

316 Ibid., pp. 342-43.

317 Ibid., p. 346.

318 Ibid., p. 320.

319 Ibid., pp. 399-401.

320 Gore, *Truth to Power*, p. 17.

321 Ibid., pp. 24-27.

322 Ibid., pp. 10-11.

323 Ibid., p. 246.

324 Thomas L. Friedman, *Hot, Flat, and Crowded* (New York: Farrar, Straus, and Giroux, 2009), pp. 458-59.

325 Ibid., pp. 212-13.

326 Ibid., pp. 226-27.

327 Ibid., p. 291.

328 Ibid., p. 298.

329 Lester R. Brown, *Plan B 4.0: Mobilizing to Save Civilization* (New York: W.W. Norton and Co., 2009), ch. 10.

330 Ibid., pp. 264-65.

331 Ibid., p. 71.

332 For the California Report on Global Warming, see www.weather.com/science/environment/news/2018-05-10.

333 *Los Angeles Times* (July 14, 2017).

334 *Los Angeles Times* (November 9, 2017).

335 *Los Angeles Times* (September 12, 2018).

336 *Los Angeles Times* (August 31, 2017).

337 On the crucial issue of oil drilling, see www.consumerwatchdog.org/taxonomy/term.

338 *Los Angeles Times* (September 11, 2017).

339 *Los Angeles Times* (July 14, 2017).

340 *Los Angeles Times* (July 24, 2017).

341 See www.cotap.org/per-capita-carbon-emissions-by-country/2017.

342 *Los Angeles Times* (September 22, 2015).

343 *Los Angeles Times*, (April 26, 2019).

344 See "Big Oil's Grip on California". Center for Public Integrity, pp. 12-13. www.publicintegrity.org/2017.

345 *Los Angeles Times* (June 25, 2019).

346 *Los Angeles Times* (October 28, 2018).

347 See www.whitehouse.senate.gov/news/release/2018.

348 Ibid.

349 www.opensecrets.org/lobby/top/php?/2018..

350 www.opensecrets.org/lobby/agency/un.php?/2017.

351 www.opensecrets.olrg/lobby/top/php?/2018.

352 See www.politico.commagazine/story/2015/12.

353 Antonia Juhasz, *The Bush Agenda* (New York: HarperCollins, 2006).

354 See Alec Macgillis, "How Obama Let Big Oil Drill in the Pristine Alaska Wilderness", *Politico* (December 21, 2015).

355 Tim Dickinson, "The Koch Brothers Dirty War on Solar Power", *Rolling Stone* (February 11, 2016).

356 Ibid., pp. 46-47.

357 Ibid., p. 47.

358 Ibid., p. 49.

359 Ibid., p. 50.

360 Ibid. pp. 50-51.

361 Ibid., p. 51.

362 Ken Midkiff, *The Meat You Eat* (New York: St. Martin's, 2005), p. 11.

363 www.opensecrets.org/lobby/php?/2018.

364 See Colin Campbell, *The China Study* (Ithaca, NY: Cornell University Press, 2006), pp. 252-59.

365 Ibid., p. 266.

366 Ibid., pp. 271-73.

367 Ibid., pp. 278-79.

368 Ibid., p. 308.

369 Overall spending on advertising in the U.S. was projected at $221 billion. See www.emarketer.com/content/us-ad-spending/2018.

370 Robert McChesney, *The Problem of the Media* (New York: Monthly Review Press, 2004), p. 138.

371 Charles Derber, *The Sociopathic Society* (Boulder: Paradigm, 2013.

372 www.cheshnotes.com/mcdonalds-advertising-expenses-2018.

373 See Marion Nestle, *Food Politics* (Berkeley: University of California Press, 2007), p. 21.

374 Ibid., p. 25.

375 Michael Lowy, *Ecosocialism* (Chicago: Haymarket Books, 2015.

376 See Joel Kovel, *The End of Nature* (London: Zed Books, 2002), p. 21.

377 Chris Hedges, *Death of the Liberal Class* (New York: Nation Books, 2010).

378 Bill McKibben, *earth* (New York: Henry Holt and Co., 2010), p. 47.

379 Ibid., p. 48.

380 Lester R. Brown, *Full Planet, Empty Plates* (New York: W.W. Norton, 2012), p. 3.

381 Ibid., p. 4.

382 See Bruce Gagnon, "Addicted to Weapons", in Helen Caldicott, ed., *Sleepwalking to Armageddon* (New York: New Press, 2017), p. 37.

383 Paul Roberts, *The End of Food* (Boston: Houghton-Mifflin, 2008), p. xii.

384 Paul Gilding, *The Great Disruption* (New York: Bloomsbury, 2011).

385 Lester R. Brown, *World on the Edge* (New York: W.W. Norton, 2011), pp. 15-16.

386 Noam Chomsky, "National Politics versus National Security", in *Caldicott*, op. cit., pp. 90-91.

387 Ibid.

388 Brown, *World on the Edge*, p. 7.

389 Manuel Garcia, Jr., "Climate Change Activism would Kill Imperialism", *CounterPunch* (November 21, 2018).

390 On early Green Party evolution, see Rudolf Bahro, *From Red to Green* (London: Verso, 1984), ch. 8.

391 Mark Dowie, *Losing Ground* (Cambridge, Mal.: MIT Press, 1995).

392 www.edf.org/climate?

393 www.en.wikipedia.org/wiki/Sierra Club.

394 www.en.wikipedia.rg/wiki/Worldwatch Institute

395 See www.ifpri.org/publication/2018-global-food.

396 www.foodfrst.org/publication/world-hunger-ten-myths/

397 Ibid.

398 Ibid.

399 Anna Lappe, ed., "The Future of Food", *The Nation* (October 30, 2017).

400 Ibid., p. 29.

401 Ibid., p. 30.

402 Ibid., p. 31.

403 *Los Angeles Times* (October 25, 2018).

404 Michael Lowy, *Ecosocialism* (Chicago: Haymarket Books, 2015), p. 11.

405 Ibid., p. 22.

406 On Communist revolutions of the twentieth century, see Eric Wolf, *Peasant Wars of the Twentieth Century* (New York: Harper and Row, 1969).

407 For an extensive discussion and critique of the council tradition, see Carl Boggs, *The Two Revolutions: Gramsci and the Dilemmas of Western Marxism* (Boston: South End Press, 1984), pp. 69-118.

408 On the theorization of ideological hegemony in Western Marxism, see Boggs, *The Two Revolutions*, pp.153-98.

409 www.westernjournal.com.

410 Bill McKibben, "The World at War", *New Republic* (September, 2016).

411 *Los Angeles Times* (September 10, 2018).

412 Bookchin, *The Modern Crisis* (Philadelphia: New Society Publishers, 1986), p. 99.

413 Ibid., pp. 99-100.

414 Bookchin, *The Philosophy of Social Ecology* (Montreal: Black Rose Books, 1990), p. 103.

415 Bookchin, *The Modern Crisis*, p. 106.

416 Ibid., p. 121.

417 Ibid., p. 50.

418 Ibid., pp. 52-53.

419 Ibid., p. 182.

420 Ibid., pp. 184-85.

421 Bookchin, *Philosophy of Social Ecology*, introduction.

422 Bookchin, *Re-enchanting Humanity* (London: Cassell, 1995), p. 236.

423 For an excellent overview of Deep Ecology, see George Sessions, ed., *Deep Ecology for the 21st Century* (Boston: Shambala, 1995).

424 Sessions, "Ecocentrism and the Anthropocentric Detour", in *Deep Ecology*, pp. 169-77.

425 See, for example, Jack Turner, "In Wilderness is the Preservation of the World", in *Deep Ecology*, pp. 331-38.

426 Arne Naess, "Equality, Sameness, and Rights", in *Deep Ecology*, p. 222.

427 Naess, "The Deep Ecology Movement", in *Deep Ecology*, p. 68.

428 Timothy W. Luke, *Ecocritique* (Minneapolis: University of Minnesota Press, 1997), p., 23.

429 On the relationship between social movements and political strategy, see Carl Boggs, *Social Movements and Political Power* (Philadelphia: Temple University Press, 1986), ch. 6.

430 On the spontaneist character of the American new left, see Judith Clavir Albert and Steward Albert, eds., *The Sixties Papers* (Westport, Ct.: Praeger, 1984), pp. 10-63.

431 On the limits of liberal reformism, see Chris Hedges, *Death of the Liberal Class* (New York: Nation Books, 2010), pp. 184-95.

432 Rudolf Bahro, *From Red to Green* (London: Verso, 1984), p. 219.

433 For an excellent overview of the German Greens, see Horst Mewes, "A Brief History of the German Green Party", in *The German Greens.*

434 Rudolf Bahro,"The SPD and the Peace Movement", *New Left Review* (January-February, 1982), p. 46.

435 Jon Burchell, *The Evolution of Green Politics* (London: Earthscan, 2002).

436 *Los Angeles Times* (June 6, 2019).

437 Chris Williams, *Ecology and Socialism* (Chicago: Haymarket Books, 2010), p. 13.

438 Ibid., p. 230.

439 John Bellamy Foster, "Ecology and the Transition from Capitalism to Socialism", *Monthly Review* (November, 2008).

440 See, for example, "Ecology, Capitalism, and the Socialization of Nature", an interview with *Monthly Review* editor Jon Bellamy Foster, in *Monthly Review* (November 2004), especially pp. 1-2.

441 Ted Benton, *Natural Relations* (London: Verso, 1998), pp. 23-31.

442 Ibid., p. 32.

443 John Bellamy Foster, *Marx's Ecology* (New York: Monthly Review Press, 2000), p. 20.

444 Ibid.

445 Marx and Engels, "Manifesto", in *Marx-Engels Reader,* p. 477.

446 Engels, "Socialism: Utopian and Scientific", in *Marx-Engels Reader,* p. 715. (Italics added)

447 Ibid., p. 717. (Italics added)

448 William Leiss, *The Domination of Nature* (New York: George Braziller, 1972), p. ix.

449 For a critical discussion of the council tradition, see Carl Boggs, *The Two Revolutions* (Boston: South End Press, 1984), pp. 69-118.

450 On Andre Gorz' outlook, see his *Ecology and Politics* (Boston: South End Press, 1980).

451 On the emergence of a red-green tendency in Europe, see Bahro, *From Red to Green*, ch. 8.

452 Michael Lowy, *Ecosocialism* (Chicago: Haymarket Books, 2015), p. xi.

453 Ibid., p. 5

454 Foster, "Ecology and the Transition from Capitalism to Socialism", *Monthly Review,* p.8.

455 Kohei Saito, *Karl Marx's Ecosocialism* (New York: Monthly Review Press, 2017), pp. 12-13.

456 Ibid., p. 14.

457 Ibid., p. 257.

458 Ibid., p. 259.

459 Engels, "Socialism: Utopian and Scientific", *Marx-Engels Reader*, pp. 712-17.

460 Williams, *Ecology and Socialism*, pp. 233, 235.

461 Foster, *Marx's Ecology*, p. 14.

462 Wallis, *Red-Green Revolution*, p. 21.

463 Ibid., p. 194.

464 Bookchin, *Remaking Society*, p 172.

465 Bahro, *Socialism and Survival*, p. 28.

466 Wallis, *Red-Green Revolution*, pp. 188-89.

467 Robyn Eckersley, *Environmentalism and Political Theory* (Albany, NY: SUNY Press, 1992), p. 94.

468 Geoff Hiskock, *Earth Wars* (Singapore: John Wiley and Sons, 2012), p. 16.

469 Lester Brown, *World on the Edge* (New York: W.W. Norton, 2011), p. 6.

470 Lester Brown, *Full Planet, Empty Plates* (New York: W.W. Norton, 2012), p. 3.

471 Ibid., p. 6.

472 Michael T. Klare, *The Race for What's Left* (New York, 2012), p. 12.

473 Ibid., p. 18.

474 See Bahro, *Socialism and Survival*, p. 150.

475 Brown, *World on the Edge*, p. 161.

476 Bahro, *Socialism and Survival*, p. 142.

477 Naomi Klein, *This Changes Everything* (New York: Simon and Schuster, 2014).

478 Ibid., pp. 83-88.

479 Ibid., pp. 38-45.

480 Ibid., pp. 133-36.

481 Ibid., p. 78.

482 For an account of Green-Party deradicalization, see Carl Boggs, *Social Movements and Political Power* (Philadelphia: Temple University Press, 1985), ch. 5. See also Lilian Klotzsch, et. al., "What Has Happened to Green Principles in Electoral and Parliamentary Politics?", in Margit Mayer and John Ely, eds., *The German Greens* (Philadelphia: Temple University Press, 1998).

483 Fred Magdoff and Chris Williams, *Creating and Ecological Society* (New York: Monthly Review Press, 2017).

484 John Bellamy Foster, "The Ecology of Marxian Political Economy", *Monthly Review* (September 2011), p. 14.

485 Chris Williams, *Ecology and Socialism* (Chicago: Haymarket Books, 2010), p. 233.

486 Wallis, *Red-Green Revolution,* p. 3.

487 Ibid., p. 193.

488 Joel Kovel, *The Enemy of Nature* (London: Zed Books, 2002), p. 226.

489 See Antonio Gramsci, "Americanism and Fordism", in *Selections from the Prison Notebooks,* (New York: International Publishers, 1971).

490 For trends in global meat production, see reports by the U.N. Food and Agriculture Organization (FAO). Recent evidence presented here and elsewhere shows a production level of 335 million tons in 2018, slightly more than the 330 million tons in 2017. The long-term trajectory reveals a four-fold increase since 1950, from 84 million tons to the present numbers. See www.globalagriculture.org/2018.

491 *Guardian* (October 18, 2018).

492 Alejandro Colas, et. al., *Food, Politics, and Society* (Berkeley: University of California Press, 2018), p. 77.

493 See www.lancetcountdown.org/the-report/2018.

494 *Los Angeles Times* (January 11, 2019).

495 *Los Angeles Times* (December 28, 2018).

496 Brown, *World on the Edge,* pp. 6-7.

497 www.noaa.gov/news/2018.

498 *Los Angeles Times* (February 7, 2019).

499 Mills, *Power Elite,* p. 343.

500 Ibid., pp. 343-61.

501 Marcuse, *One-Dimensional Man,* pp. 85-120.

502 See Sheldon Wolin, *Democracy, Inc.* (Princeton: Princeton University Press, 2007), and Chris Hedges, *The Death of Liberalism* (New York: Nation Books, 2010).

503 Wallis, *Red-Green Revolution,* p. 193.

504 Rudolf Bahro, *Socialism and Survival* (London: Heretic Books, 1982), p. 13.

505 Wallace-Wells, *Uninhabitable Earth,* p. 194.

506 Ibid., p. 196.

507 Glenn Greenwald, *No Place to Hide* (New York: Henry Holt and Co., 2014), p. 174.

508 Ibid., p. 208.

509 On Gramsci's famous "war of position", see his "State and Civil Society", in *SPN,* pp. 229-35.

510 Bookchin, *Remaking Society* (Montreal: Black Rose Books, 1989), p. 169.

511 Herbert Marcuse, *Counterrevolution and Revolt* (Boston: Beacon Press, 1972), p. 61.

512 Ibid., p. 74.

513 Brown, *World on the Edge*, p. 99.

514 Ibid., p. 115.

515 Ronnie Cummins, "Industrial Food and Climate Change", *Consortium News* (August 13, 2019).

516 Wallace-Wells, *Uninhabitable Earth*, p. 181.

517 Brown, *World on the Edge*, p. 184.

518 See Geoff Mann and Joel Wainwright, *Climate Leviathan* (London: Verso, 2019).

519 Ibid., p. 28.

520 Ibid., p. 182.

521 *Los Angeles Times* (September 22, 2019).

522 *Los Angeles Times* (September 24, 2019).

523 Ibid.

524 *Los Angeles Times* (September 16, 2019).

525 Wallace-Wells, *Uninhabitable Earth*, pp. 226, 220.

526 *Los Angeles Times* (April 30, 2019).

527 *Los Angeles Times* (August 23, 2019).

528 *Los Angeles, Times* (September 21, 2019).

529 Ibid.

530 Naomi Klein, *On Fire: The (Burning) Case for a Green New Deal* (New York: Simon and Schuster, 2019), pp. 49-53.

531 Ibid., p. 31.

532 See Margit Mayer and John Ely, eds., *The German Greens* (Philadelphia: Temple University Press, 1998), p. 241.

533 Klein, *On Fire*, p. 97.

534 See Geoff Mann and Joel Wainwright, *Climate Leviathan* (London: Verso, 2019), p. 126.

OTHER BOOKS BY CARL BOGGS

Gramsci's Marxism

The Politics of Eurocommunism.

The Impasse of European Communism

The Two Revolutions: Antonio Gramsci and
the Dilemma of Western Marxism

Social Movements and Political Power

Intellectuals and the Crisis of Modernity

The Socialist Tradition: from Crisis to Decline

The End of Politics: Corporate Power and Decline of the Public Sphere

A World in Chaos: Social Crisis and the Rise
of Postmodern Cinema (coauthored)

Masters of War

Imperial Delusions: American Militarism and Endless War

The Hollywood War Machine: U.S. Militarism
and Popular Culture (coauthored)

The Crimes of Empire

Empire versus Democracy

Phantom Democracy: Corporate Interests and Political Power

Ecology and Revolution

Drugs, Power, and Politics

Origins of the Warfare State

Fascism Old and New